STATUTES

Family Law

Second Edition (revised and updated by D G Cracknell
LLB, of the Middle Temple, Barrister

SERIES EDITOR: D G CRACKNELL
EDITOR: MALCOLM DODDS
BA, LLM, Barrister
Deputy Clerk to the Justices, North Kent Magistrates' Court

OLD BAILEY PRESS

OLD BAILEY PRESS
200 Greyhound Road, London W14 9RY

First published 1994
Second edition 1997

ISBN 1 85836 066 8

British Library Cataloguing-in-Publication.

A CIP Catalogue record for this book is available from the
British Library.

Printed and bound in Great Britain.

CONTENTS

Contents

PREFACE

THE most significant aspect of this edition is that Part I (principles of Parts II and III), s22 (funding for support services), Part III (legal aid for mediation in family matters) and Schedule 8, Part II (amendments connected with Part III) of the Family Law Act 1996 came into force on 21 March 1997 and that it has been assumed that Part IV (family homes and domestic violence) will come into force on 1 October 1997. Accordingly, Parts I and IV, and connected amendments and repeals, are covered within the main body of the text.

With the important exception mentioned above and with the exception of the Deregulation (Validity of Civil Preliminaries to Marriage) Order 1997 (which comes into force on 1 October 1997), the text takes account of legislation in force on 1 July 1997. The remaining provision of the Child Support Act 1995 came into force on 13 January 1997 and its amendments and additions are duly covered.

The source of any changes is noted at the end of each particular Act.

It is not expected that Part II (divorce and separation) of the Family Law Act 1996 will come into force before 1999. However, the principal provisions of that part are included in an Appendix.

ALPHABETICAL TABLE OF STATUTES

MARRIED WOMEN'S PROPERTY ACT 1882

(45 & 46 Vict c 75)

17   Questions between husband and wife as to property to be decided in a summary way

In any question between husband and wife as to the title to or possession of property, either party may apply by summons or otherwise in a summary way to the High Court or such county court as may be prescribed and the court may, on such application (which may be heard in private), make such order with respect to the property as it thinks fit.

In this section 'prescribed' means prescribed by rules of court and rules made for the purpose of this section may confer jurisdiction on county courts whatever the situation or value of the property in dispute.

As amended by the Statute Law (Repeals) Act 1969; Matrimonial and Family Proceedings Act 1984, s43.

CHILDREN AND YOUNG PERSONS ACT 1933

(23 & 24 Geo 5 c 12)

1 Cruelty to person under sixteen

(1) If any person who has attained the age of sixteen years and has responsibility for any child or young person under that age, wilfully assaults, ill-treats, neglects, abandons, or exposes him, or causes or procures him to be assaulted, ill-treated, neglected, abandoned, or exposed, in a manner likely to cause him unnecessary suffering or injury to health (including injury to or loss of sight, or hearing, or limb, or organ of body, and any mental derangement), that person shall be guilty of a misdemeanour, and shall be liable –

(a) on conviction on indictment, to a fine, or alternatively, or in addition thereto, to imprisonment for any term not exceeding ten years;

(b) on summary conviction, to a fine not exceeding the statutory maximum, or alternatively, or in addition thereto, to imprisonment for any term not exceeding six months.

(2) For the purpose of this section –

(a) a parent or other person legally liable to maintain a child or young person, or the legal guardian of a child or young person, shall be deemed to have neglected him in a manner likely to cause injury to his health if he has failed to provide adequate food, clothing, medical aid or lodging for him, or if, having been unable otherwise to provide such food, clothing, medical aid or lodging, he has failed to take steps to procure it to be provided under the enactments applicable in that behalf;

(b) where it is proved that the death of an infant under three years of age was caused by suffocation (not being suffocation caused by disease or the presence of any foreign body in the throat or air passages of the infant) while the infant was in bed with some other person who has attained the age of sixteen years, that other person shall, if he was, when he went to bed, under the influence of drink, be deemed to have neglected the infant in a manner likely to cause injury to health.

(3) A person may be convicted of an offence under this section –

(a) notwithstanding that actual suffering or injury to health, or the likelihood of actual suffering or injury to health, was obviated by the action of another person;

(b) notwithstanding the death of the child or young person in question.

(7) Nothing in this section shall be construed as affecting the right of any parent, teacher, or other person having lawful control or charge of a child or young person to administer punishment to him.

18   Restrictions on the employment of children

(1) Subject to the provisions of this section and of any byelaws made thereunder no child shall be employed –

(a) so long as he is under the age of 13 years; or

(b) before the close of school hours on any day on which he is required to attend school; or

(c) before seven o'clock in the morning or after seven o'clock in the evening on any day; or

(d) for more than two hours on any day on which he is required to attend school; or

(e) for more than two hours on any Sunday.

(2) A local authority may make byelaws with respect to the employment of children, and any such byelaws may distinguish between children of different ages and sexes and between different localities, trades, occupations and circumstances, and may contain provisions –

(a) authorising –

(i) the employment of children under the age of thirteen years (notwithstanding anything in paragraph (a) of the last foregoing subsection) by their parents or guardians in light agricultural or horticultural work;

(ii) the employment of children (notwithstanding anything in paragraph (b) of the last foregoing subsection) for not more than one hour before the commencement of school hours on any day on which they are required to attend school;

(b) prohibiting absolutely the employment of children in any specified occupation;

(c) prescribing –

(i) the age below which children are not to be employed;

(ii) the number of hours in each day, or in each week, for which, and the times of day at which, they may be employed;

(iii) the intervals to be allowed to them for meals and rest;

(iv) the holidays or half-holidays to be allowed to them;

(v) any other conditions to be observed in relation to their employment;

so, however, that no such byelaws shall modify the restrictions contained in the last foregoing subsection save in so far as is expressly permitted by paragraph (a) of that subsection, and any restrictions contained in any such byelaws shall have effect in addition to the said restrictions.

(3) Nothing in this section, or in any byelaw made under this section, shall prevent a child from taking part in a performance –

(a) under the authority of a licence granted under this Part of the Act; or

(b) in a case where by virtue of s37(3) of the Children and Young Persons Act 1963 no licence under that section is required for him to take part in the performance.

20   Street trading

(1) Subject to subsection (2) of this section, no child shall be engaged or employed in street trading.

(2) A local authority may make byelaws authorising children who have attained the age of fourteen years to be employed by their parents in street trading to such extent as may be specified in the byelaws, and for regulating street trading under the byelaws by persons who are so authorised to be employed in such trading; and byelaws so made may distinguish between persons of different ages and sexes and between different localities and may contain provisions –

(a) forbidding any such person to engage or be employed in street trading unless he holds a licence granted by the authority, and regulating the conditions on which such licences may be granted, suspended and revoked;

(b) determining the days and hours during which, and the places at which, such persons may engage or be employed in street trading;

(c) requiring such persons so engaged or employed to wear badges;

(d) regulating in any other respect the conduct of such persons while so engaged or employed.

30   Interpretation

(1) For the purposes of this Part of this Act and of any byelaws made thereunder, the expression 'child' means –

(a) in relation to England and Wales, a person who is not for the purposes of the Education Act 1944 over compulsory school age.

55   Power to order parent or guardian to pay fine

(1) Where –

(a) a child or young person is convicted or found guilty of any offence for the commission of which a fine or costs may be imposed or a compensation order may be made under s35 of the Powers of Criminal Courts Act 1973; and

(b) the court is of opinion that the case would best be met by the imposition of a fine or costs or the making of such an order, whether with or without any further punishment,

it shall be the duty of the court to order that the fine, compensation or costs awarded be paid by the parent or guardian of the child or young person instead of by the child or young person himself, unless the court is satisfied –

(i) that the parent or guardian cannot be found; or

(ii) that it would be unreasonable to make an order for payment, having regard to all the circumstances of the case.

(1A) Where but for this subsection –

(a) a court would order a child or young person to pay a fine under section 15(2A) of the Children and Young Persons Act 1969 (failure to comply with requirement included in a supervision order); or

(b) a court would impose a fine on a young person under section 16(3) of the Powers of Criminal Courts Act 1973 (breach of requirements of community service order),

it shall be the duty of the court to order that the fine be paid by the parent or guardian of the child or young person instead of by the child or young person himself, unless the court is satisfied –

(i) that the parent or guardian cannot be found; or

(ii) that it would be unreasonable to make an order for payment, having regard to the circumstances of the case.

(1B) In the case of a young person who has attained the age of sixteen years, subsections (1) and (1A) above shall have effect as if, instead of imposing a duty, they conferred a power to make such an order as is mentioned in those subsections.

(2) An order under this section may be made against a parent or guardian who, having been required to attend, has failed to do so, but, save as aforesaid, no such order shall be made without giving the parent or guardian an opportunity of being heard.

(3) A parent or guardian may appeal to the Crown Court against an order under this section made by a magistrates' court.

(4) A parent or guardian may appeal to the Court of Appeal against an order made under this section by the Crown Court, as if he had been convicted on indictment and the order were a sentence passed on his conviction.

(5) In relation to a child or young person for whom a local authority have parental responsibility and who –

(a) is in their care; or

(b) is provided with accommodation by them in exercise of any functions (in particular those under the Children Act 1989) which stand referred to their social services committee under the Local Authority Social Services Act 1970,

references in this section to his parent or guardian shall be construed as references to that authority.

In this subsection 'local authority' and 'parental responsibility' have the same meanings as in the Children Act 1989.

107 Interpretation

(1) In this Act, unless the context otherwise requires, the following expressions have the meanings respectively assigned to them, that is to say – ...

'child' means a person under the age of fourteen years;

'guardian', in relation to a child or young person, includes any person who, in the opinion of the court having cognisance of any case in relation to the child or young person or in which the child or young person is concerned, has for the time being the care of the child or young person; ...

'legal guardian', in relation to a child or young person, means a guardian of a child as defined in the Children Act 1989; ...

'young person' means a person who attained the age of fourteen years and is under the age of eighteen years.

As amended by the National Assistance (Adaptation of Enactments) Regulations 1950; Children and Young Persons Act 1963, ss34, 35(3), 64(1), (3), Schedule 3, paras 1, 4, Schedule 5; Children Act 1972, s1(2); Children Act 1975, s108(1)(b), Schedule 4, Pt III; Criminal Justice Act 1982, s26; Criminal Justice Act 1988, ss45, 127, 170(2), Schedule 16; Children Act 1989, s108(4), (5), Schedule 13, paras 2, 7; Employment Act 1989, s10(2), Schedule 3, Pt III, paras 2(a), (b), (c), 8; Criminal Justice Act 1991, ss57(1), (2), 68, Schedule 8, para 1(3); Manual Handling Operations Regulations 1992, reg 8(1), Schedule 2, Pt I; Sunday Trading Act 1994, ss4, 9(2), Schedule 2, Pt I.

EDUCATION ACT 1944
(7 & 8 Geo 6 c 31)

35   Compulsory school age

In this Act the expression 'compulsory school age' means any age between five years and sixteen years, and accordingly a person shall be deemed to be of compulsory school age if he has attained the age of five years and has not attained the age of sixteen years and a person shall be deemed to be over compulsory school age as soon as he has attained the age of sixteen years.

As amended by the Raising of the School Leaving Age Order 1972, art 2.

MARRIAGE ACT 1949
(12, 13 & 14 Geo 6 c 76)

PART I

RESTRICTIONS ON MARRIAGE

1   Marriages within prohibited degrees

(1) A marriage solemnised between between a man and any of the persons mentioned in the first column of Part 1 of the First Schedule to the Act, or between a woman and any of the persons mentioned in the second column of the said Part 1, shall be void.

(2) Subject to subsection (3) of this section, a marriage solemnised between a man and any of the persons mentioned in the first column of Part II of the First Schedule to this Act, or between a woman and any of the persons mentioned in the second column of the said Part II, shall be void.

(3) Any such marriage as is mentioned in subsection (2) of this section shall not be void by reason only of affinity if both the parties to the marriage have attained the age of twenty-one at the time of the marriage and the younger party has not at any time before attaining the age of eighteen been a child of the family in relation to the other party.

(4) Subject to subsection (5) of this section, a marriage solemnised between a man and any of the persons mentioned in the first column of Part III of the First Schedule to this Act or between a woman and any of the persons mentioned in the second column of the said Part III shall be void.

(5) Any such marriage as is mentioned in subsection (4) of this section shall not be void by reason only of affinity if both the parties to the marriage have attained the age of twenty-one at the time of the marriage and the marriage is solemnised –

(a) in the case of a marriage between a man and the mother of a former wife of his, after the death of both the former wife and the father of the former wife;

(b) in the case of a marriage between a man and the former wife of his son, after the death of both his son and the mother of his son;

(c) in the case of a marriage between a woman and the father of a former husband of hers, after the death of both the former husband and the mother of the former husband;

(d) in the case of a marriage between a woman and a former husband of her daughter, after the death of both her daughter and the father of her daughter.

2 Marriages of persons under sixteen

A marriage solemnised between persons either of whom is under the age of sixteen shall be void.

3 Marriages of persons under twenty-one

(1) Where the marriage of a child, not being a widower or widow, is intended to be solemnised on the authority of a certificate issued by a superintendent registrar under Part III of this Act, whether by licence or without licence, the consent of the person or persons specified in subsection (1A) of this section shall be required:

Provided that –

(a) if the superintendent registrar is satisfied that the consent of any person whose consent is so required cannot be obtained by reason of absence or inaccessibility or by reason of his being under any disability, the necessity for the consent of that person shall be dispensed with, if there is any other person whose consent is also required; and if the consent of no other person is required, the Registrar General may dispense with the necessity of obtaining any consent, or the court may, on application being made, consent to the marriage, and the consent of the court so given shall have the same effect as if it had been given by the person whose consent cannot be so obtained;

(b) if any person whose consent is required refuses his consent, the court may, on application being made, consent to the marriage, and the consent of the court so given shall have the same effect as if it had been given by the person whose consent is refused.

(1A) The consents are –

(a) subject to paragraphs (b) to (d) of this subsection, the consent of –
(i) each parent (if any) of the child who has parental responsibility for him; and
(ii) each guardian (if any) of the child;

(b) where a residence order is in force with respect to the child, the consent of the person or persons with whom he lives, or is to live, as a result of the order (in substitution for the consents mentioned in paragraph (a) of the subsection);

(c) where a care order is in force with respect to the child, the consent of the local authority designated in the order (in addition to the consents mentioned in paragraph (a) of this subsection);

(d) where neither paragraph (b) nor (c) of this subsection applies but a residence order was in force with respect to the child immediately before he reached the age of sixteen, the consent of the person or persons with whom he lived, or was to live, as a result of the order (in substitution for the consents mentioned in paragraph (a) of this subsection).

(1B) In this section 'guardian of a child', 'parental responsibility', 'residence order' and 'care order' have the same meaning as in the Children Act 1989.

(2) The last foregoing subsection shall apply to marriages intended to be solemnised on the authority of a common licence, with the substitution of references to the ecclesiastical authority by whom the licence was granted for references to the superintendent registrar, and with the substitution of a reference to the Master of the Faculties for the reference to the Registrar General.

(3) Where the marriage of a child, not being a widower or widow, is intended to be solemnised after the publication of banns of matrimony then, if any person whose consent to the marriage would have been required under this section in the case of a marriage intended to be solemnised otherwise than after the publication of the banns, openly and publicly declares or causes to be declared, in the church or chapel in which the banns are published, at the time of the publication, his dissent from the intended marriage, the publication of banns shall be void.

(4) A clergyman shall not be liable to ecclesiastical censure for solemnising the marriage of a child after the publication of banns without the consent of the parents or guardians of the child unless he had notice of the dissent of any person who is entitled to give notice of dissent under the last foregoing subsection.

(5) For the purposes of this section, 'the court' means the High Court, the county court of the district in which any applicant or respondent resides or a court of summary jurisdiction appointed for the commission area (within the meaning of the Justices of the Peace Act 1997) in which any applicant or respondent resides and rules of court may be made for enabling applications under this section –

(a) if made to the High Court, to be heard in chambers;

(b) if made to the county court, to be heard and determined by the registrar subject to appeal to the judge;

(c) if made to a court of summary jurisdiction, to be heard and determined otherwise than in open court,

and shall provide that, where an application is made in consequence of a refusal to give consent, notice of the application shall be served on the person who has refused consent.

(6) Nothing in this section shall dispense with the necessity of obtaining the consent of the High Court to the marriage of a ward of court.

4   Hours for solemnisation of marriages

A marriage may be solemnised at any time between the hours of eight in the forenoon and six in the afternoon.

PART II

MARRIAGE ACCORDING TO RITES OF THE CHURCH OF ENGLAND

5   Methods of authorising marriages

A marriage according to the rites of the Church of England may be solemnised –

(a) after the publication of banns of matrimony;

(b) on the authority of a special licence of marriage granted by the Archbishop of Canterbury or any other person by virtue of the Ecclesiastical Licences Act 1533 (in this Act referred to as a 'special licence');

(c) on the authority of a licence of marriage (other than a special licence) granted by an ecclesiastical authority having power to grant such a licence (in this Act referred to as a 'common licence'); or

(d) on the authority of a certificate issued by a superintendent registrar under Part III of this Act;

except that paragraph (a) of this section shall not apply in relation to the solemnisation of any marriage mentioned in subsection (2) of section 1 of this Act.

5A Marriages between certain persons related by affinity

No clergyman shall be obliged –

(a) to solemnise a marriage which, apart from the Marriage (Prohibited Degrees of Relationship) Act 1986, would have been void by reason of the relationship of the persons to be married; or

(b) to permit such a marriage to be solemnised in the church or chapel of which he is the minister.

6   Place of publication of banns

(1) Subject to the provisions of this Act, where a marriage is intended to be solemnised after the publication of banns of matrimony, the banns shall be published –

(a) if the persons to be married reside in the same parish, in the parish church of that parish;

(b) if the persons to be married do not reside in the same parish, in the parish church of each parish in which one of them resides:

Provided that if either of the persons to be married resides in a chapelry or in a district specified in a licence granted under section twenty of this Act, the banns may be published in an authorised chapel of that chapelry or district instead of in the parish church of the parish in which that person resides.

(2) In relation to a person who resides in an extra-parochial place, the last foregoing subsection shall have effect as if for references to a parish there were substituted references to that extra-parochial place, and as if for references to a parish church there were substituted references to an authorised chapel of that place.

(3) For the purposes of this section, any parish in which there is no parish church or chapel belonging thereto or no church or chapel in which divine service is usually solemnised every Sunday, and any extra-parochial place which has no authorised chapel, shall be deemed to belong to any adjoining parish or chapelry.

(4) Banns of matrimony may be published in any parish church or authorised chapel which is the usual place of worship of the persons to be married or of one of them although neither of those persons resides in the parish or chapelry to which the church or chapel belongs:

Provided that the publication of banns by virtue of this subsection shall be in addition to and not in substitution for the publication of banns required by subsection (1) of this section.

7 Time and manner of publication of banns

(1) Subject to the provisions of section nine of this Act, banns of matrimony shall be published on three Sundays preceding the solemnisation of the marriage during morning service or, if there is no morning service on a Sunday on which the banns are to be published, during evening service.

(2) Banns of matrimony shall be published in an audible manner and in accordance with the form of words prescribed by the rubric prefixed to the office of matrimony in the Book of Common Prayer, and all the other rules prescribed by the said rubric concerning the publication of banns and the solemnisation of matrimony shall, so far as they are consistent with the provisions of the Part of this Act, be duly observed.

(3) The parochial church council of a parish shall provide for every church and chapel in the parish in which marriages may be solemnised, a register book of banns made of durable materials and marked in the manner directed by section fifty-four of this Act for the register book of marriages, and all banns shall be published from the said register book of banns by the officiating clergyman, and not from loose papers, and after each publication the entry in the register book shall be signed by the officiating clergyman, or by some person under his direction.

(4) Any reference in the last foregoing subsection to a parochial church council shall, in relation to an authorised chapel in an extra-parochial place, be construed as a reference to the chapel warden or other officer exercising analogous duties in the chapel or, if there is no such officer, such person as may be appointed in that behalf by the bishop of the diocese.

8 Notice to clergyman before publication of banns

No clergyman shall be obliged to publish banns of matrimony unless the persons to be married, at least seven days before the date on which they wish the banns to be published for the first time, deliver or cause to be delivered to him a notice in writing, dated on the day on which it is so delivered, stating the christian name and surname and the place of residence of each of them, and the period during which each of them has resided at his or her place of residence.

9 Persons by whom banns may be published

(1) Subject to the provisions of this section and of section fourteen of this Act, it shall not be lawful for any person other than a clergyman to publish banns of matrimony.

(2) Where on any Sunday in any church or other building in which banns of matrimony may be published a clergyman does not officiate at the service at which it is usual in that church or building to publish banns, the banns may be published –

(a) by a clergyman at some other service at which banns of matrimony may be published; or

(b) by a layman during the course of a public reading authorised by the bishop of the diocese of a portion or portions of the service of morning or evening prayer, the public reading being at the hour when the service at which it is usual to publish banns is commonly held or as such other hour as the bishop may authorise:

Provided that banns shall not be published by a layman unless the incumbent or minister in charge of the said church or building, or some other clergyman nominated in that behalf by the bishop, has authorised to be made the requisite entry in the register book of banns of the said church or building.

(3) Where a layman publishes banns of matrimony by virtue of this section the layman shall sign the register book of banns provided under section seven of this Act and for that purpose shall be deemed to be the officiating clergyman within the meaning of that section.

10   Publication of banns commenced in one church and completed in another

(1) Where the publication of banns of matrimony has been duly commenced in any church, the publication may be completed in the same church or in any other church which, by virtue of the Union of Benefices Measure 1923 or the New Parishes Measure 1943, has at the time of the completion taken the place of the first-mentioned church for the purpose of publication of banns of matrimony either generally or in relation to the parties to the intended marriage.

(2) Where the publication of banns of matrimony has been duly commenced in any building which by virtue of a reorganisation scheme under the Reorganisation Areas Measure 1944 ceases to be a parish church or, as the case may be, ceases to be licensed for marriages, the publication may be completed in such other building, being either a parish church or a building licensed for marriages, as may be directed by the bishop of the diocese to take the place of the first-mentioned building for the purposes of the publication of banns.

11   Certificates of publication of banns

(1) Where a marriage is intended to be solemnised after the publication of banns of matrimony and the persons to be married do not reside in the same parish or other ecclesiastical district, a clergyman shall not solemnise the marriage in the parish or district in which one of those persons resides unless there is produced to him a certificate that the banns have been published in accordance with the provisions of this Part of this Act in the parish or other ecclesiastical district in which the other person resides.

(2) Where a marriage is intended to be solemnised in a church or chapel of a parish or other ecclesiastical district in which neither of the persons to be married resides, after the publication of banns therein by virtue of subsection (4) of section six of this Act, a clergyman shall not solemnise the marriage unless there is produced to him –

(a) if the persons to be married reside in the same parish or other ecclesiastical district, a certificate that the banns have been published in accordance with the provisions of the Part of this Act in that parish or district; or

(b) if the persons to be married do not reside in the same parish or other ecclesiastical district, certificates that the banns have been published as aforesaid in each parish or district in which one of them resides.

(3) Where banns are published by virtue of subsection (3) of section six of this Act in a parish or chapelry adjoining the parish or extra-parochial place in which the banns would otherwise be required to be published, a certificate that the banns have been published in that parish or chapelry shall have the like force and effect as a certificate that banns have been published in a parish in which one of the persons to be married resides.

(4) Any certificate required under this section shall be signed by the incumbent or minister in charge of the building in which the banns were published or by a clergyman nominated in that behalf by the bishop of the diocese.

12   Solemnisation of marriage after publication of banns

(1) Subject to the provisions of this Part of this Act, where banns of matrimony have been published, the marriage shall be solemnised in the church or chapel or, as the case may be, one of the churches or chapels in which the banns have been published.

(2) Where a marriage is not solemnised within three months after the completion of the publication of the banns, that publication shall be void and no clergyman shall solemnise the marriage on the authority thereof.

15 Places in which marriages may be solemnised by common licence

(1) Subject to the provisions of this Part of this Act, a common licence shall not be granted for the solemnisation of a marriage in any church or chapel other than –

(a) the parish church of the parish, or an authorised chapel of the ecclesiastical district, in which one of the persons to be married has had his or her usual place of residence for fifteen days immediately before the grant of the licence; or

(b) a parish church or authorised chapel which is the usual place of worship of the persons to be married or of one of them.

(2) For the purposes of this section, any parish in which there is no parish church or chapel belonging thereto or no church or chapel in which divine service is usually solemnised every Sunday, and any extra-parochial place which has no authorised chapel, shall be deemed to belong to any adjoining parish or chapelry.

16 Provisions as to common licences

(1) A common licence shall not be granted unless one of the persons to be married has sworn before a person having authority to grant such a licence –

(a) that he or she believes that there is no impediment of kindred or alliance or any other lawful cause, nor any suit commenced in any court, to bar or hinder the solemnisation of the marriage in accordance with the licence;

(b) that one of the persons to be married has had his or her usual place of residence in the parish or other ecclesiastical district in which the marriage is to be solemnised for fifteen days immediately before the grant of the licence or that the parish church or authorised chapel in which the marriage is to be solemnised is the usual place of worship of those persons or of one of them;

(c) where one of the persons to be married is a child and is not a widower or widow, that the consent of the person or persons whose consent to the marriage is required under section three of this Act has been obtained, that the necessity of obtaining any such consent has been dispensed with under that section, that the court has consented to the marriage under that section, or that there is no person whose consent to the marriage is so required.

(1A) A common licence shall not be granted for the solemnisation of a marriage mentioned in subsection (2) of section 1 of this Act unless –

(a) the persons having authority to grant the licence is satisfied by the production of evidence that both the persons to be married have attained the age of twenty-one; and

(b) he has received a declaration in writing made by each of those persons specifying their affinal relationship and declaring that the younger of those persons has not at any time before attaining the age of eighteen been a child of the family in relation to the other.

(1B) In the case of a marriage mentioned in subsection (4) of section 1 of this Act which by virtue of subsection (5) of that section is valid only if at the time of the marriage both the parties to the marriage have attained the age of twenty-one and the death has taken place of two other persons related to those parties in the manner mentioned in the said subsection (5), a common licence shall not be granted for the solemnisation of the marriage unless the person having authority to grant the licence is satisfied by the production of evidence –

(a) that both the parties to the marriage have attained the age of twenty-one; and

(b) that both those other persons are dead.

(2) Subject to subsection (2A) of this section if any caveat is entered against the grant of a common licence, the caveat having been duly signed by or on behalf of the person by whom it is entered and stating his place of residence and the ground of objection on which the caveat is founded, no licence shall be granted until the caveat or a copy thereof is transmitted to the ecclesiastical judge out of whose office the licence is to issue, and the judge has certified to the registrar of the diocese that he has examined into the matter of the caveat and is satisfied that it ought not to obstruct the grant of the licence, or until the caveat is withdrawn by the person who entered it.

(2A) Where in the case of a marriage mentioned in subsection (2) of section 1 of this Act a caveat is entered under subsection (2) of this section on the ground that the persons to be married have not both attained the age of twenty-one or that one of those persons has at any time before attaining the age of eighteen been a child of the family in relation to the other, then, notwithstanding that the caveat is withdrawn by the person who entered it, no licence shall be issued unless the judge has certified that he has examined into that ground of objection and is satisfied that that ground ought not to obstruct the grant of the licence.

(2B) In the case of a marriage mentioned in subsection (2) of section 1 of this Act, one of the persons to be married may apply to the ecclesiastical judge out of whose office the licence is to issue for a declaration that, both those persons having attained the age of twenty-one and the younger of those persons not having at any time before attaining the age of eighteen been a child of the family in relation to the other, there is no impediment of affinity to the solemnisation of the marriage; and where any such declaration is obtained the common licence may be granted notwithstanding that no declaration has been made under the said subsection (1A).

(3) Where a marriage is not solemnised within three months after the grant of a common licence, the licence shall be void and no clergyman shall solemnise the marriage on the authority thereof.

(4) No surrogate deputed by an ecclesiastical judge who has power to grant common licences shall grant any such licence until he has taken an oath before that judge, or a commissioner appointed under the seal of that judge, faithfully to execute his office according to law, to the best of his knowledge.

17 Marriage under superintendent registrar's certificate

A marriage according to the rites of the Church of England may be solemnised on the authority of a certificate of a superintendent registrar in force under Part III of this Act in any church or chapel in which banns of matrimony may be published or in the case of a marriage in pursuance of section 26(1) (dd) of this Act the place specified in the notice of marriage and certificate as the place where the marriage is to be solemnised:

Provided that a marriage shall not be solemnised as aforesaid in any such church or chapel without the consent of the minister thereof or (wherever the marriage is solemnised) by any person other than a clergyman.

22 Witnesses

All marriages solemnised according to the rites of the Church of England shall be solemnised in the presence of two or more witnesses in addition to the clergyman by whom the marriage is solemnised.

24 Proof of residence not necessary to validity of banns or marriage by common licence

(1) Where any marriage has been solemnised after the publication of banns of matrimony, it shall not be necessary in support of the marriage to give any proof of the residence of the parties or either of them in any parish or other ecclesiastical district in which the banns were published, and no evidence shall be given to prove the contrary in any proceedings touching the validity of the marriage.

(2) Where any marriage has been solemnised on the authority of a common licence, it shall not be necessary in support of the marriage to give any

proof that the usual place of residence of one of the parties was for fifteen days immediately before the grant of the licence in the parish or other ecclesiastical district in which the marriage was solemnised, and no evidence shall be given to prove the contrary in any proceedings touching the validity of the marriage.

25   Void marriages

If any persons knowingly and wilfully intermarry according to the rites of the Church of England (otherwise than by special licence) –

(a) except in the case of a marriage in pursuance of section 26(1)(dd) of this Act, in any place other than a church or other building in which banns may be published;

(b) without banns having been duly published, a common licence having been obtained, or a certificate having been duly issued under Part III of this Act by a superintendent registrar to whom due notice of marriage has been given; or

(c) on the authority of a publication of banns which is void by virtue of subsection (3) of section three or subsection (2) of section twelve of this Act, on the authority of a common licence which is void by the virtue of subsection (3) of section sixteen of this Act, or on the authority of a certificate of a superintendent registrar which is void by virtue of subsection (2) of section thirty-three of this Act;

(d) in the case of a marriage on the authority of a certificate of a superintendent registrar, in any place other than the church building or other place specified in the notice of marriage and certificate as the place where the marriage is to be solemnised,

or if they knowingly and wilfully consent to or acquiesce in the solemnisation of the marriage by any person who is not in Holy Orders, the marriage shall be void.

PART III

MARRIAGE UNDER SUPERINTENDENT REGISTRAR'S CERTIFICATE

26   Marriages which may be solemnised on authority of superintendent registrar's certificate

(1) Subject to the provisions of this Part of this Act, the following marriages may be solemnised on the authority of a certificate of a superintendent registrar –

(a) a marriage in a registered building according to such form and ceremony as the persons to be married see fit to adopt;

(b) a marriage in the office of a superintendent registrar;

(bb) a marriage on approved premises;

(c) a marriage according to the usages of the Society of Friends (commonly called Quakers);

(d) a marriage between two persons professing the Jewish religion according the usages of the Jews;

(dd) the marriage (other than a marriage in pursuance of paragraph (c) or (d) above) of a person who is house-bound or is a detained person at the place where he or she usually resides;

(e) a marriage according to the rites of the Church of England in any church or chapel in which banns of matrimony may be published.

(2) A marriage on the authority of a certificate of a superintendent registrar may be either by a licence issued by the superintendent registrar or without a licence:

Provided that a superintendent registrar shall not issue a licence for a marriage intended to be solemnised at a person's residence in pursuance of subsection (1)(dd) of this section or for a marriage in any church or chapel in which marriages may be solemnised according to the rites of the Church of England, or in any church or chapel belonging to the Church of England or licensed for the celebration of divine worship according to the rites and ceremonies of the Church of England.

27   Notice of marriage

(1) Where a marriage is intended to be solemnised on the authority of a certificate of a superintendent registrar without licence, notice of marriage in the prescribed form shall be given –

(a) if the persons to be married have resided in the same registration district for the period of seven days immediately before the giving of the notice, by either of those persons to the superintendent registrar of that district;

(b) if the persons to be married have not resided in the same registration district for the said period of seven days as aforesaid, by either of those persons to the superintendent registrar of each registration district in which one of them has resided for that period.

(2) Where a marriage is intended to be solemnised as aforesaid by licence, then, whether the persons to be married reside in the same or in different registration districts, notice of marriage in the prescribed form shall be

given by either of those persons to the superintendent registrar of the registration district in which one of them has resided for the period of fifteen days immediately before the giving of the notice, and it shall not be required that notice of marriage shall be given to more than one superintendent registrar.

(3) A notice of marriage shall state the name and surname, marital status, occupation and place of residence of each of the persons to be married and in the case of a marriage intended to be solemnised at a person's residence in pursuance of section 26(1)(dd) of this Act, which residence is to be the place of solemnisation of the marriage and, in any other case, the church or other building or premises in or on which the marriage is to be solemnised and –

(a) in the case of a marriage intended to be solemnised without licence, shall state the period, not being less than seven days, during which each of the persons to be married has resided in his or her place of residence;

(b) in the case of a marriage intended to be solemnised by licence, shall state the period, not being less than fifteen days, during which one of the persons to be married has resided in the district in which notice of marriage is given:

Provided that if either of the persons to be married has resided in the place stated in the notice for more than one month, the notice may state that he or she has resided there for more than one month.

(4) The superintendent registrar shall file all notices of marriage and keep them with the records of his office, and shall subject to section 27A of this Act also forthwith enter the particulars given in every such notice, together with the date of the notice and the name of the person by whom the notice was given, in a book (in this Act referred to as 'the marriage notice book') furnished to him for that purpose by the Registrar General, and the marriage notice book shall be open for inspection free of charge at all reasonable hours.

(5) If the persons to be married wish to be married in the presence of a registrar in a registered building for which an authorised person has been appointed they shall, at the time when notice of marriage is given to the superintendent registrar under this section, give notice to him that they require a registrar to be present at the marriage.

(6) The superintendent registrar shall be entitled to a fee of £19.00 for every entry made in the marriage notice book under this section.

(7) The superintendent registrar shall be entitled to receive from any person intending to be married in pursuance of section 26(1)(dd) of this Act upon

whom he attends at a place other than his office in order to be given notice of marriage under this section the sum of £37.00.

27A Additional information required in certain cases

(1) This section applies in relation to any marriage intended to be solemnised at a person's residence in pursuance of section 26(1)(dd) of this Act, and in the following provisions of this section that person is referred to as 'the relevant person'.

(2) Where the relevant person is not a detained person, the notice of marriage by section 27 of this Act shall be accompanied by a medical statement relating to that person made not more than fourteen days before the date on which the notice is given.

(3) Where the relevant person is a detained person, the notice of marriage required by section 27 of this Act shall be accompanied by a statement made in the prescribed form by the responsible authority not more than twenty-one days before the date on which notice of the marriage is given under section 27 –

   (a) identifying the establishment where the person is detained; and

   (b) stating that the responsible authority has no objection to that establishment being specified in the notice of marriage as the place where that marriage is to be solemnised.

(4) The person who gives notice of the marriage to the superintendent registrar in accordance with section 27 of this Act shall give the superintendent registrar the prescribed particulars, in the prescribed form, of the person by or before whom the marriage is intended to be solemnised.

(5) The superintendent registrar shall not enter the particulars given in the marriage notice book until he has received the statement and the particulars required by subsections (2) or (3) and (4) of this section.

(6) The fact that a superintendent registrar has received a statement under subsection (2) or (as the case may be) (3) of this section shall be entered in the marriage notice book together with the particulars given in the notice of marriage and any such statement together with the form received under subsection (4) of this section shall be filed and kept with the records of the office of the superintendent registrar or, where notice of marriage is required to be given to two superintendent registrars, of either of them.

(7) In this section–

'medical statement', in relation to any person, means a statement made in the prescribed form by a registered medical practitioner that in his opinion at the time the statement is made –

(a) by reason of illness or disability, he or she ought not to move or be moved from the place where he or she is at that time, and

(b) it is likely that it will be the case for at least the following three months that by reason of the illness or disability he or she ought not to move or be moved from that place; and

'registered medical practitioner' has the meaning given by Schedule 1 to the Interpretation Act 1978; and

'responsible authority' means–

(a) if the person is detained in a hospital (within the meaning of Part II of the Mental Health Act 1983), the managers of that hospital (within the meaning of section 145(1) of that Act); or

(b) if the person is detained in a prison or other place to which the Prison Act 1952 applies, the governor or other officer for the time being in charge of that prison or other place.

27B Provisions relating to section 1(3) marriages

(1) This section applies in relation to any marriage mentioned in subsection (2) of section 1 of this Act which is intended to be solemnised on the authority of a certificate of a superintendent registrar.

(2) The superintendent registrar shall not enter notice of the marriage in the marriage notice book unless –

(a) he is satisfied by the production of evidence that both the persons to be married have attained the age of twenty-one; and

(b) he has received a declaration made in the prescribed form by each of those persons, each declaration having been signed and attested in the prescribed manner, specifying their affinal relationship and declaring that the younger of those persons has not at any time before attaining the age of eighteen been a child of the family in relation to the other.

(3) The fact that a superintendent registrar has received a declaration under subsection (2) of this section shall be entered in the marriage notice book together with the particulars given in the notice of marriage and any such declaration shall be filed and kept with the records of the office of the superintendent registrar or, where notice of marriage is required to be given to two superintendent registrars, of each of them.

(4) Where the superintendent registrar receives from some person other

than the persons to be married a written statement signed by that person which alleges that the declaration made under subsection (2) of this section is false in a material particular, the superintendent registrar shall not issue a certificate or licence unless a declaration is obtained from the High Court under subsection (5) of this section.

(5) Either of the persons to be married may, whether or not any statement has been received by the superintendent registrar under subsection (4) of this section, apply to the High Court for a declaration that, both those persons having attained the age of twenty-one and the younger of those persons not having at any time before attaining the age of eighteen been a child of the family in relation to the other, there is no impediment of affinity to the solemnisation of the marriage; and where such a declaration is obtained the superintendent registrar may enter notice of the marriage in the marriage notice book and may issue a certificate, or certificate and licence, whether or not any declaration has been made under subsection (2) of this section.

(6) Section 29 of this Act shall not apply in relation to a marriage to which this section applies, except so far as a caveat against the issue of a certificate or licence for the marriage is entered under that section on a ground other than the relationship of the persons to be married.

27C Provisions relating to section 1(5) marriages

In the case of a marriage mentioned in subsection (4) of section 1 of this Act which by virtue of subsection (5) of that section is valid only if at the time of the marriage both the parties to the marriage have attained the age of twenty-one and the death has taken place of two other persons related to those parties in the manner mentioned in the said subsection (5), the superintendent registrar shall not enter notice of the marriage in the marriage notice book unless satisfied by the production of evidence –

(a) that both parties to the marriage have attained the age of twenty-one, and

(b) that both those other persons are dead.

28   Declaration to accompany notice of marriage

(1) No certificate or licence for marriage shall be issued by a superintendent registrar unless the notice of marriage is accompanied by a solemn declaration in writing, in the body or at the foot of the notice, made and signed at the time of the giving of the notice by the person by whom the notice is given and attested as mentioned in subsection (2) of this section –

(a) that he or she believes that there is no impediment of kindred or alliance or other lawful hindrance to the marriage;

(b) in the case of a marriage intended to be solemnised without licence, that the persons to be married have for the period of seven days immediately before the giving of the notice had their usual places of residence within the registration district or registration districts in which notice is given, or, in the case of a marriage intended to be solemnised by licence, that one of the persons to be married has for the period of fifteen days immediately before the giving of the notice had his or her usual place of residence within the registration district in which notice is given;

(c) where one of the persons to be married is a child and is not a widower or widow, that the consent of the person or persons whose consent to the marriage is required under section three of this Act has been obtained, that the necessity of obtaining any such consent has been dispensed with under that section, that the court has consented to the marriage under that section, or that there is no person whose consent to the marriage is so required.

(2) Any such declaration as aforesaid shall be signed by the person giving the notice of marriage in the presence of the superintendent registrar to whom the notice is given or his deputy, or in the presence of a registrar of births and deaths or of marriages for the registration district in which the person giving the notice resides or his deputy, and that superintendent registrar, deputy superintendent registrar, registrar or deputy registrar, as the case may be, shall attest the declaration by adding thereto his name, description and place of residence.

29   Caveat against issue of certificate or licence

(1) Any person may enter a caveat with the superintendent registrar against the issue of a certificate or licence for the marriage of any person named therin.

(2) If any caveat is entered as aforesaid, the caveat having been signed by or on behalf or the person by whom it was entered and stating his place of residence and the ground of objection on which the caveat is founded, no certificate or licence shall be issued until the superintendent registrar has examined into the matter of the caveat and is satisfied that it ought not obstruct the issue of the certificate or licence, or until the caveat has been withdrawn by the person who entered it; and if the superintendent registrar is doubtful whether to issue a certificate or licence he may refer the matter of the caveat to the Registrar General.

(3) Where a superintendent registrar refuses, by reason of any such caveat as aforesaid, to issue a certificate or licence, the person applying therefor may appeal to the Registrar General who shall either confirm the refusal or direct that a certificate or licence shall be issued.

(4) Any person who enters a caveat against the issue of a certificate or licence on grounds which the Registrar General declares to be frivolous and to be such that they ought not to obstruct the issue of the certificate or licence, shall be liable for the costs of the proceedings before the Registrar General and for damages recoverable by the person against whose marriage the caveat was entered.

(5) For the purpose of enabling any person to recover any such costs and damages as aforesaid, a copy of the declaration of the Registrar General purporting to be sealed with the seal of the General Registrar Office shall be evidence that the Registrar General has declared the caveat to have been entered on grounds which are frivolous and such that they ought not to obstruct the issue of the certificate or licence.

30   Forbidding of issue of certificate

Any person whose consent to a marriage intended to be solemnised on the authority of a certificate of a superintendent registrar is required under section three of this Act may forbid the issue of such a certificate by writing, at any time before the issue of the certificate, the word 'forbidden' opposite to the entry of the notice of marriage in the marriage notice book, and by subscribing thereto his name and place of residence and the capacity, in relation to either of the persons to be married, in which he forbids the issue of the certificate; and where the issue of a certificate has been so forbidden, the notice of marriage and all proceedings thereon shall be void:

Provided that where, by virtue of paragraph (b) of the proviso to subsection (1) of the said section three, the court has consented to a marriage and the consent of the court has the same effect as if it had been given by a person whose consent has been refused, that person shall not be entitled to forbid the issue of a certificate for that marriage under this section, and the notice of marriage and the proceedings thereon shall not be void by virtue of this section.

31   Marriage under certificate without licence

(1) Where a marriage is intended to be solemnised on the authority of a certificate of a superintendent registrar without licence, the superintendent registrar to whom notice of marriage has been given shall suspend or affix in some conspicuous place in his office, for twenty-one successive days next

after the day on which the notice was entered in the marriage book, the notice of marriage, or an exact copy signed by him of the particulars thereof as entered in the marriage notice book.

(2) At the expiration of the said period of twenty-one days the superintendent registrar, on the request of the person by whom the notice of marriage was given, shall issue a certificate in the prescribed form unless –

(a) any lawful impediment to the issue of the certificate has been shown to the satisfaction of the superintendent registrar; or

(b) the issue of the certificate has been forbidden under the last foregoing section by any person authorised in that behalf.

(3) Every such certificate shall set out the particulars contained in the notice of marriage and the day on which the notice was entered in the marriage notice book and shall contain a statement that the issue of the certificate has not been forbidden as aforesaid.

(4) No marriage shall be solemnised on the production of a certificate of a superintendent registrar without licence until after the expiration of the said period of twenty-one days.

(5) Where a marriage is to be solemnised in a registered building for which an authorised person has been appointed and no notice requiring a registrar to be present at the marriage has been given to the superintendent registrar under subsection (5) of section twenty-seven of this Act, the superintendent registrar shall, when issuing a certificate under this section, give to one of the persons to be married printed instructions in the prescribed form for the due solemnisation of the marriage.

32 Marriage under certificate by licence

(1) Where a marriage is intended to be solemnised on the authority of a certificate of a superintendent registrar by licence, the person by whom notice of marriage is given shall state in the notice that the marriage is intended to be solemnised by licence, and the notice shall not be suspended in the office of the superintendent registrar.

(2) Where a notice of marriage containing such a statement as aforesaid has been received by a superintendent registrar, then, after the expiration of one whole day next after the day on which the notice was entered in the marriage notice book, the superintendent registrar, on the request of the person by whom the notice was given, shall issue a certificate and a licence in the prescribed form unless –

(a) any lawful impediment to the issue of the certificate has been shown to the satisfaction of the superintendent registrar; or

(b) the issue of the certificate has been forbidden under section thirty of this Act by any person authorised in that behalf.

(3) Every such certificate shall set out the particulars contained in the notice of marriage and the day on which the notice was entered in the marriage notice book, and shall contain a statement that the issue of the certificate has not been forbidden as aforesaid.

(4) Where a marriage is to be solemnised in a registered building for which an authorised person has been appointed and no notice requiring a registrar to be present at the marriage has been given to the superintendent registrar under subsection (5) of section twenty-seven of this Act, the superintendent registrar shall, when issuing a certificate and licence under this section, give to one of the persons to be married printed instructions in the prescribed form for the due solemnisation of the marriage.

(5) A superintendent registrar shall be entitled to receive for every licence so issued the sum of £45.00 over and above the amount paid for the stamps necessary on the issue of the licence.

33   Period of validity of certificate and licence

(1) A marriage may be solemnised on the authority of a certificate of a superintendent registrar, whether by licence or without licence, at any time within the period which is the applicable period in relation to that marriage.

(2) If the marriage is not solemnised within the applicable period, the notice of marriage and the certificate, and any licence which may have been granted thereon, shall be void, and no person shall solemnise the marriage on the authority thereof.

(3) For the purposes of this section, the applicable period, in relation to a marriage, is the period beginning with the day on which the notice of marriage was entered in the marriage notice book and ending –

(a) in the case of a marriage which is to be solemnized in pursuance of any of the following provisions of this Act, namely –

(i) section 26(1)(dd),
(ii) section 37, and
(iii) section 38,

on the expiry of three months; and

(b) in the case of any other marriage, on the expiry of twelve months.

34 Marriages normally to be solemnised in registration district in which one of parties resides

Subject to the provisions of the next following section, a superintendent registrar shall not issue a certificate for the solemnisation of a marriage elsewhere than within a registration district in which one of the persons to be married has resided, in the case of a marriage without licence, for the period of seven days immediately before the giving of the notice of marriage or, in the case of a marriage by licence, for the period of fifteen days immediately before the giving of that notice.

35 Marriages in registration district in which neither party resides

(1) A superintendent registrar may issue a certificate, or if the marriage is to be by licence, a certificate and a licence, for the solemnisation of a marriage in registered building which is not within a registration district in which either of the persons to be married resides, where the person giving the notice of marriage declares by endorsement thereon in the prescribed form –

(a) that the persons to be married desire the marriage to be solemnised according to a specified form, rite or ceremony, being a form, rite or ceremony of a body or denomination of christians or other persons meeting for religious worship to which one of them professes to belong;

(b) that, to the best of his or her belief, there is not within the registration district in which one of them resides any registered building in which marriage is solemnised according to that form, rite or ceremony;

(c) the registration district nearest to the residence of that person in which there is a registered building in which marriage may be so solemnised; and

(d) the registered building in that district in which the marriage is intended to be solemnised;

and where any such certificate or certificate and licence is issued, the marriage may be solemnised in the registered building stated in the notice.

(2) A superintendent registrar may issue a certificate or, if the marriage is to be by licence, a certificate and a licence, for the solemnisation of a marriage in a registered building which is the usual place of worship of the persons to be married, or of one of them, notwithstanding that the building is not within a registration district in which either of those persons resides.

(2A) A superintendent registrar may issue a certificate or, if the marriage is to be by licence, a certificate and licence, for the solemnisation of a marriage in the office of another superintendent registrar, notwithstanding that the office is not within a registration district in which either of the persons to be married resides.

(2B) A superintendent registrar may issue a certificate or, if the marriage is to be by licence, a certificate and licence, for the solemnisation of a marriage on approved premises, notwithstanding that the premises are not within a registration district in which either of the persons to be married resides.

(3) A superintendent registrar may issue a certificate for the solemnisation of a marriage in any parish church or authorised chapel which is the usual place of worship of the persons to be married, or of one of them, notwithstanding that the church or chapel is not within a registration district in which either of those persons resides.

(4) A superintendent registrar may issue a certificate or, if the marriage is to be by licence, a certificate and a licence, for the solemnisation of a marriage according to the usages of the Society of Friends or in accordance with the usages of persons professing the Jewish religion, notwithstanding that the building or place in which the marriage is to be solemnised is not within a registered district in which either of the persons to be married resides.

(5) Where a marriage is intended to be solemnised on the authority of a certificate of a superintendent registrar issued under subsection (2) or subsection (3) of this section, the notice of marriage given to the superintendent registrar and the certificate issued by the superintendent registrar shall state, in addition to the description of the registered building or, as the case may be, the parish church or authorised chapel, in which the marriage is to be solemnised, that it is the usual place of worship of the persons to be married or of one of them and, in the latter case, shall state the name of the person whose usual place of worship it is.

36 Superintendent registrar not normally to issue licences for marriages in registered buildings outside his district

Subject to section 35 of this Act, a superintendent registrar shall not issue a licence for the solemnisation of a marriage in a registered building which is not within his registration district.

40 Forms of certificate to be furnished by Registrar General

(1) The Registrar General shall furnish to every superintendent registrar a sufficient number of forms of certificates for marriage.

(2) In order to distinguish the certificates to be issued for marriages by licence from the certificates to be issued for marriages without licence, a water-mark in the form of the word 'licence', in Roman letters, shall be laid and manufactured in the substance of the paper on which the certificates to be issued for marriage by licence are written or printed, and every certificate to be issued for marriage by licence shall be printed with red ink and every certificate to be issued for marriage without licence shall be printed with black ink, and such other distinctive marks between the two kinds of certificates as the Registrar General may from time to time think fit shall be used.

41   Registration of buildings

(1) Any proprietor or trustee of a building which has been certified as required by law as a place of religious worship may apply to the superintendent registrar of the registration district in which the building is situated for the building to be registered for the solemnisation of marriages therein.

(2) Any person making such an application as aforesaid shall deliver to the superintendent registrar a certificate, signed in duplicate by at least twenty householders and dated not earlier than one month before the making of the application, stating that the building is being used by them as their usual place of public religious worship and that they desire that the building should be registered as aforesaid, and both certificates shall be countersigned by the proprietor or trustee by whom they are delivered.

(3) The superintendent registrar shall send both certificates delivered to him under the last foregoing subsection to the Registrar General who shall register the building in a book to be kept for that purpose in the General Register Office.

(4) The Registrar General shall endorse on both certificates sent to him as aforesaid the date of the registration, and shall keep one certificate with the records of the General Register Office and shall return the other certificate to the superintendent registrar who shall keep it with the records of his office.

(5) On the return of the certificate under the last foregoing subsection, the superintendent registrar shall –

(a) enter the date of the registration of the building in a book to be provided for that purpose by the Registrar General;

(b) give a certificate of the registration signed by him, on durable materials, to the proprietor or trustee by whom the certificates delivered to him under subsection (2) of this section were countersigned; and

(c) give public notice of the registration of the building by advertisement in some newspaper circulating in the county in which the building is situated and in the London Gazette.

(6) For every entry, certificate and notice made or given under the last foregoing subsection the superintendent registrar shall be entitled to receive, at the time of the delivery of the certificates under subsection (2) of this section, the sum of £93.00.

(7) A building may be registered for the solemnisation of marriages under this section whether it is a separate building or forms part of another building.

42 Cancellation of registration and substitution of another building

(1) Where, on an application made by or through the superintendent registrar of the registration district in which the building is situated, it is shown to the satisfaction of the Registrar General that a registered building is no longer used for the purpose of public religious worship by the congregation on whose behalf it was registered, he shall cause the registration to be cancelled.

(3) Where the Registrar General cancels the registration of any building under this section, he shall inform the superintendent registrar who shall enter that fact and the date thereof in the book provided for the registration of buildings, and shall certify and publish the cancellation in the manner provided by subsection (5) of the last foregoing section in the case of the registration of a building.

(5) Where the registration of any building has been cancelled under this section, it shall not be lawful to solemnise any marriage in the disused building, unless the building has been registered again in accordance with the provisions of the Part of this Act.

43 Appointment of authorised persons

(1) For the purpose of enabling marriages to be solemnised in a registered building without the presence of a registrar, the trustees or governing body of that building may authorise a person to be present at the solemnisation of marriages in that building and, where a person is so authorised in respect of any registered building, the trustees or governing body of that building shall, within the prescribed manner, certify the name and address of the person so authorised to the Registrar General and to the superintendent registrar of the registration district in which the building is situated:

Provided that in relation to a building which becomes registered after the thirty-first day of December, nineteen hundred and fifty-eight, the power conferred by this subsection to authorise a person to be present as aforesaid shall not be exercisable before the expiration of one year from the date of registration of the building or, where the congregation on whose behalf the building is registered previously used for the purpose of public religious worship another building of which the registration has been cancelled not earlier than one month before the date of registration aforesaid, one year from the date of registration of that other building.

(2) Any person whose name and address have been certified as aforesaid is in this Act referred to as an 'authorised person'.

(3) Nothing in this section shall be taken to relate or have any reference to marriages solemnised according to the usages of the Society of Friends or of persons professing the Jewish religion.

44 Solemnisation of marriage in registered building

(1) Subject to the provisions of this section, where a notice of marriage and certificate issued by a superintendent registrar state that a marriage between the persons named therein is intended to be solemnised in a registered building, the marriage may be solemnised in that building according to such form and ceremony as those persons may see fit to adopt:

Provided that no marriage shall be solemnised in any registered building without the consent of the minister or of one of the trustees, owners, deacons or managers thereof, or in the case of a registered building of the Roman Catholic Church, without the consent of the officiating minister thereof.

(2) Subject to the provisions of this section, a marriage solemnised in a registered building shall be solemnised with open doors in the presence of two or more witnesses and in the presence of either –

(a) a registrar of the registration district in which the registered building is situated, or

(b) an authorised person whose name and address have been certified in accordance with the last foregoing section by the trustees or governing body of that registered building or of some other registered building in the same registration district.

(3) Where a marriage is solemnised in a registered building each of the persons contracting the marriage shall, in some part of the ceremony and in the presence of the witnesses and the registrar or authorised person, make the following declaration:

'I do solemnly declare that I know not of any lawful impediment why I, *AB*, may not be joined in matrimony to *CD*'

and each of them shall say to the other:

'I call upon these persons here present to witness that I, *AB*, do take thee, *CD*, to be my lawful wedded wife [or husband]'.

(3A) As an alternative to the declaration set out in subsection (3) of this section the persons contracting the marriage may make the requisite declaration either–

> (a) by saying 'I declare that I know of no legal reason why I [*name*] may not be joined in marriage to [*name*]'; or
>
> (b) by replying 'I am' to the question put to them successively 'Are you [*name*] free lawfully to marry [*name*]?';

and as an alternative to the words of contract set out in that subsection the persons to be married may say to each other 'I [*name*] take you [or thee] [*name*] to be my wedded wife [*or* husband]'.

(4) A marriage shall not be solemnised in a registered building without the presence of a registrar until duplicate marriage register books have been supplied by the Registrar General under Part IV of this Act to the authorised person or to the trustees or governing body of the building.

(5) If the Registrar General is not satisfied with respect to any building registered or proposed to be registered for the solemnisation of marriages therein that sufficient security exists for the due registration of marriages by an authorised person under Part IV of this Act and for the safe custody of marriage register books, he may in his discretion attach to the continuance of the registration, or to the registration, of the building a condition that no marriage may be solemnised therein without the presence of a registrar.

45 Solemnisation of marriage in register office

(1) Where a marriage is intended to be solemnised on the authority of a certificate of a superintendent registrar, the persons to be married may state in the notice of marriage that they wish to be married in the office of the superintendent registrar or one of the superintendent registrars, as the case may be, to whom notice of marriage is given, and where any such notice has been given and the certificate or certificate and licence, as the case may be, has or have been issued accordingly, the marriage may be solemnised in the said office, with open doors, in the presence of the superintendent registrar and a registrar of the registration district of that superintendent registrar and in the presence of two witnesses, and the

persons to be married shall make the declarations and the use the form of words set out in subsection (3) or (3A) of the last foregoing section in the case of marriages in registered buildings.

(2) No religious service shall be used at any marriage solemnised in the office of a superintendent registrar.

45A Solemnisation of certain marriages

(1) This section applies to marriages solemnised, otherwise than according to the rites of the Church of England, in the pursuance of section 26(1)(dd) of this Act at the place where a person usually resides.

(2) The marriage may be solemnised according to a relevant form, rite or ceremony in the presence of a registrar of the registration district in which the place where the marriage is solemnised is situated and of two witnesses and each of the persons contracting the marriage shall make the declaration and use the form of words set out in subsection (3) or (3A) of section 44 of this Act in the case of marriages in registered buildings.

(3) Where the marriage is not solemnised in pursuance of subsection (2) of this section it shall be solemnised in the presence of the superintendent registrar and a registrar of the registration district in which the place where the marriage is solemnised is situated and in the presence of two witnesses, and the persons to be married shall make the declarations and use the form of words set out in subsection (3) or (3A) of section 44 of this Act in the case of marriages in registered buildings.

(4) No religious service shall be used at any marriage solemnised in the presence of a superintendent registrar.

(5) In subsection (2) of this section a 'relevant form, rite or ceremony' means a form, rite or ceremony of a body of persons who meet for religious worship in any registered building being a form, rite or ceremony in accordance with which members of that body are married in any such registered building.

46 Register office marriage followed by religious ceremony

(1) If the parties to a marriage solemnised in the presence of a superintendent registrar desire to add the religious ceremony ordained or used by the church or persuasion of which they are members, they may present themselves, after giving notice of their intention so to do, to the clergyman or minister of the church or persuasion of which they are members, and the clergyman or minister, upon the production of a

certificate of their marriage before the superintendent registrar and upon the payment of the customary fees (if any), may, if he sees fit, read or celebrate in the church or chapel of which he is the regular minister the marriage service of the church or persuasion to which he belongs or nominate some other minister to do so.

(2) Nothing in the reading or celebration of a marriage service under this section shall supersede or invalidate any marriage previously solemnised in the presence of a superintendent registrar, and the reading or celebration shall not be entered as a marriage in any marriage register book kept under Part IV of this Act.

(3) No person who is not entitled to solemnise marriages according to the rites of the Church of England shall by virtue of this section be entitled to read or celebrate the marriage service in any church or chapel of the Church of England.

46A Approval of premises

(1) The Chancellor of the Exchequer may by regulations make provision for and in connection with the approval by local authorities of premises for the solemnisation of marriages in pursuance of section 26(1)(bb) of this Act. ...

46B Solemnisation of marriage on approved premises

(1) Any marriage on approved premises in pursuance of section 26(1)(bb) of this Act shall be solemnised in the presence of –

(a) two witnesses, and

(b) the superintendent registrar and a registrar of the registration district in which the premises are situated.

(2) Without prejudice to the width of section 46A(2)(e) of this Act, the Chancellor of the Exchequer shall exercise his power to provide for the imposition of conditions as there mentioned so as to secure that members of the public are permitted to attend any marriage solemnised on approved premises in pursuance of section 26(1)(bb) of this Act.

(3) Each of the persons contracting such a marriage shall make the declaration and use the form of words set out in section 44(3) or (3A) of this Act in the case of marriages in registered buildings.

(4) No religious service shall be used at a marriage on approved premises in pursuance of section 26(1)(bb) of this Act.

47 Marriages according to usages of Society of Friends

(1) No person who is not a member of the Society of Friends shall be married according to the usages of that Society unless he or she is authorised to be so married under or in pursuance of a general rule of the said Society in England.

(2) A marriage solemnised according to the said usages shall not be valid unless either –

(a) the person giving notice of marriage declares, either verbally or, if so required, in writing, that each of the parties to the marriage is either a member of the Society of Friends or is in profession with or of the persuasion of that Society; or

(b) there is produced to the superintendent registrar, at the time when notice of marriage is given, a certificate purporting to be signed by a registering officer of the Society of Friends in England to the effect that any party to the marriage who is not a member of the Society of Friends or in profession with or of the persuasion of that Society, is authorised to be married according to the said usages under or in pursuance of a general rule of the said Society in England.

(3) Any such certificate as aforesaid shall be for all purposes conclusive evidence that any person to whom it relates is authorised to be married according to the usages of the said Society, and the entry of the marriage in a marriage register book under Part IV of this Act, or a certified copy thereof made under the said Part IV, shall be conclusive evidence of the production of such a certificate.

(4) A copy of any general rule of the Society of Friends purporting to be signed by the recording clerk for the time being of the said Society in London shall be admitted as evidence of the general rule in all proceedings touching the validity of any marriage solemnised according to the usages of the said Society.

48 Proof of certain matters not necessary to validity of marriages

(1) Where any marriage has been solemnised under the provisions of this Part of this Act, it shall not be necessary in support of the marriage to give any proof –

(a) that before the marriage either of the parties thereto resided, or resided for any period, in the registration district stated in the notice of marriage to be that of his or her place of residence;

(b) that any person whose consent to the marriage was required by section three of this Act had given his consent;

(c) that the registered building in which the marriage was solemnised had been certified as required by law as a place of religious worship;

(d) that the building was the usual place of worship for either of the parties to the marriage; or

(e) that the facts stated in a declaration made under subsection (1) of section thirty-five of this Act were correct;

nor shall any evidence be given to prove the contrary in any proceedings touching the validity of the marriage.

(2) A marriage solemnised in accordance with the provisions of this Part of this Act in a registered building which has not been certified as required by law as a place of religious worship shall be as valid as if the building had been so certified.

49   Void marriages

If any persons knowingly and wilfully intermarry under the provisions of the Part of this Act –

(a) without having given due notice of marriage to the superintendent registrar;

(b) without a certificate for marriage having been duly issued by the superintendent registrar to whom notice of marriage was given;

(c) without a licence having been so issued, in a case in which a licence is necessary;

(d) on the authority of a certificate which is void by virtue of subsection (2) of section thirty-three of this Act;

(e) in any place other than the church, chapel, registered building, office or other place specified in the notice of marriage and certificate of the superintendent registrar;

(ee) in the case of a marriage purporting to be in pursuance of section 26(1)(bb) of this Act, on any premises that at the time the marriage is solemnised are not approved premises;

(f) in the case of a marriage in a registered building (not being a marriage in the presence of an authorised person), in the absence of a registrar of the registration district in which the registered building is situated;

(g) in the case of a marriage in the office of a superintendent registrar, in the absence of the superintendent registrar or of a registrar of the registration district of that superintendent registrar;

(gg) in the case of a marriage on approved premises, in the absence of the superintendent registrar of the registration district in which the premises are situated or in the absence of a registrar of that district; or

(h) in the case of a marriage to which section 45A of this Act applies, in the absence of any superintendent registrar or registrar whose presence at that marriage is required by that section;

the marriage shall be void.

50   Person to whom certificate to be delivered

(1) Where a marriage is intended to be solemnised on the authority of a certificate of a superintendent registrar, the certificate or, if notice of marriage has been given to more than one superintendent registrar, the certificates shall be delivered to the following person, that is to say –

(a) if the marriage is to be solemnised in a registered building or at a person's residence in the presence of a registrar, that registrar;

(b) if the marriage is to be solemnised in a registered building without the presence of a registrar, the authorised person in whose presence the marriage is to be solemnised;

(c) if the marriage is to be solemnised in the office of a superintendent registrar, the registrar in whose presence the marriage is to be solemnised;

(cc) if the marriage is to be solemnised on approved premises, the registrar in whose presence the marriage is to be solemnised;

(d) if the marriage is to be solemnised according to the usages of the Society of Friends, the registering officer of that Society for the place where the marriage is to be solemnised;

(e) if the marriage is to be solemnised according to the usages of persons professing the Jewish religion, the officer of a synagogue by whom the marriage is required to be registered under Part IV of this Act;

(f) if the marriage is to be solemnised according to the rites of the Church of England, the officiating clergyman.

(2) In the application of the last foregoing subsection to a marriage solemnised otherwise than according to the rites of the Church of England, the reference therein to a certificate shall, if the marriage is by licence, be construed as a reference to the certificate and licence.

(3) Where a marriage is solemnised in a registered building without the presence of a registrar, the certificate or certificate and licence, as the case may be, shall be kept in the prescribed custody and shall be produced with the marriage register books kept by the authorised person under Part IV of this Act as and when required by the Registrar General.

75 Offences relating to solemnisation of marriages

(1) Any person who knowingly and wilfully –

(a) solemnises a marriage at any other time than between the hours of eight in the forenoon and six in the afternoon (not being a marriage by special licence, a marriage according to the usages of the Society of Friends or a marriage between two persons professing the Jewish religion according to the usages of the Jews);

(b) solemnises a marriage according to the rites of the Church of England without banns of matrimony having been duly published (not being a marriage solemnised on the authority of a special licence, a common licence, or a certificate of a superintendent registrar);

(c) solemnises a marriage according to the said rites (not being a marriage by special licence or a marriage in pursuance of section 26(1)(dd) of this Act) in any place other than a church or other building in which banns may be published;

(d) solemnises a marriage according to the said rites falsely pretending to be in Holy Orders;

shall be guilty of felony and shall be liable to imprisonment for a term not exceeding fourteen years.

(2) Any person who knowingly and wilfully –

(a) solemnises a marriage (not being a marriage by special licence, a marriage according to the usages of the Society of Friends or a marriage between two persons professing the Jewish religion according to the usages of the Jews) in any place other than –

(i) a church or other building in which marriages may be solemnised according to the rites of the Church of England, or

(ii) the registered building, office, approved premises or person's residence specified as the place where the marriage was to be solemnised in the notice of marriage and certificate required under Part III of this Act;

(aa) solemnises a marriage purporting to be in pursuance of section 26(1)(bb) of this Act on premises that are not approved premises;

(b) solemnises a marriage in any such registered building as aforesaid (not being a marriage in the presence of an authorised person) in the absence of a registrar of the district in which the registered building is situated;

(bb) solemnises a marriage in pursuance of section 26(1)(dd) of this Act, otherwise than according to the rites of the Church of England, in the absence of a registrar of the registration district in which the place where the marriage is solemnised is situated;

(c) solemnises a marriage in the office of a superintendent registrar in the absence of a registrar of the district in which the office is situated;

(cc) solemnises a marriage on approved premises in pursuance of section 26(1)(bb) of this Act in the absence of a registrar of the district in which the premises are situated;

(d) solemnises a marriage on the authority of a certificate of a superintendent registrar (not being a marriage by licence) within twenty-one days after the day on which the notice of marriage was entered in the marriage notice book; or

(e) solemnises a marriage on the authority of a certificate of a superintendent registrar after the expiration of the period which is, in relation to that marriage, the applicable period for the purposes of section 33 of this Act;

shall be guilty of felony and shall be liable to imprisonment for a term not exceeding five years.

(3) A superintendent registrar who knowingly and wilfully-

(a) issues any certificate for marriage (not being a marriage by licence) before the expiration of twenty-one days from the day on which the notice of marriage was entered in the marriage notice book, or issues a certificate for marriage by licence before the expiration of one whole day from the said day on which the notice was entered as aforesaid;

(b) issues any certificate or licence for marriage after the expiration of the period which is, in relation to that marriage, the applicable period for the purposes of section 33 of this Act;

(c) issues any certificate the issue of which has been forbidden under section thirty of this Act by any person entitled to forbid the issue of such a certificate; or

(d) solemnises or permits to be solemnised in his office or, in the case of a marriage in pursuance of section 26(1)(bb) or (dd) of this Act, in any other place any marriage which is void by virtue of any of the provisions of Part III of this Act;

shall be guilty of felony and shall be liable to imprisonment for a term not exceeding five years.

(4) No prosecution under this section shall be commenced after the expiration of three years from the commission of the offence.

(5) Any reference in subsection (2) of this section to a registered building

shall be construed as including a reference to any chapel registered under section seventy of this Act.

77   Offences by authorised persons

Any authorised person who refuses or fails to comply with the provisions of this Act or of any regulations made under section seventy-four thereof shall be guilty of an offence against this Act, and, unless the offence is one for which a specific penalty is provided under the foregoing provisions of this Part of this Act, shall be liable, on summary conviction, to a fine not exceeding the prescribed sum or, on conviction on indictment, to imprisonment for a term not exceeding two years or to a fine and shall upon conviction cease to be authorised person.

78   Interpretation

(1) In this Act, except where the context otherwise requires, the following expressions have the meanings hereby respectively assigned to them, that is to say –

'approved premises' means approved in accordance with regulations under section 46A of this Act as premises on which marriages may be solemnised in pursuance of section 26(1)(bb) of this Act.

'authorised chapel' means –

(a) in relation to a chapelry, a chapel of the chapelry in which banns of matrimony could lawfully be published immediately before the passing of the Marriage Act 1823, or in which banns may be published and marriages may be solemnised by virtue of section two of the Marriages Confirmation Act 1825, or of an authorisation given under section three of the Marriage Act 1823;

(b) in relation to an extra-parochial place, a church or chapel of that place in which banns may be published and marriages may be solemnised by virtue of section two of the Marriages Confirmation Act 1825, or of an authorisation given under section three of the Marriage Act 1823, or section twenty-one of this Act;

(c) in relation to a district specified in a licence granted under section twenty of this Act, the chapel in which banns may be published and marriages may be solemnised by virtue of that licence;

'authorised person' has the meaning assigned to it by section forty-three of this Act;

'brother' includes a brother of the half blood;

'child' means a person under the age of eighteen;

'child of the family', in relation to any person, means a child who has lived in the same household as that person and been treated by that person as a child of his family;

'clergyman' means a clerk in Holy Orders of the Church of England;

'common licence' has the meaning assigned to it by section five of this Act;

'ecclesiastical district', in relation to a district other than a parish, means a district specified in a licence granted under section twenty of this Act, a chapelry or an extra-parochial place;

'marriage notice book' has the meaning assigned to it by section twenty-seven of this Act;

'parish' means an ecclesiastical parish and includes a district constituted under the Church Building Acts 1818 to 1884 notwithstanding that the district has not become a new parish by virtue of section fourteen of the New Parishes Act 1856, or section five of the New Parishes Measure 1943, being a district to which Acts of Parliament relating to the publication of banns of matrimony and the solemnisation of marriages were applied by the said Church Building Acts as if the district had been an ancient parish, and the expression 'parish church' shall be construed accordingly;

'prescribed' means prescribed by regulations made under section seventy-four of this Act;

'registered building' means a building registered under Part III of this Act;

'registrar' means a registrar of marriages;

'Registrar General' means the Registrar General of Births, Deaths and Marriages in England;

'registration district' means the district of a superintendent registrar;

'sister' includes a sister of the half blood;

'special licence' has the meaning assigned to it by section five of this Act;

'superintendent registrar' means a superintendent registrar of births, deaths and marriages;

'trustees or governing body', in relation to Roman Catholic registered buildings, includes a bishop or vicar general of the diocese.

(2) Any reference in this Act to the Church of England shall, unless the context otherwise requires, be construed as including a reference to the Church in Wales.

(3) For the purposes of this Act a person is house-bound if –

(a) the notice of his or her marriage given in accordance with section 27 of this Act is accompanied by a medical statement (within the meaning of section 27A(7) of this Act) made, not more than fourteen days before the date on which that notice was given, in relation to that person; and

(b) he or she is not a detained person.

(4) For the purpose of this Act a person is a detained person if he or she is for the time being detained –

(a) otherwise than by virtue of section 2, 4, 5, 35, 36 or 136 of the Mental Health Act 1983 (short term detentions), as a patient in a hospital; or

(b) in a prison or other place to which the Prison Act 1952 applies,

and in paragraph (a) above 'patient' and 'hospital' have the same meanings as in Part II of the Mental Health Act 1983.

(5) For the purposes of this Act a person who is house-bound or is a detained person shall be taken, if he or she would not otherwise be, to be resident and usually resident at the place where he or she is for the time being.

FIRST SCHEDULE

KINDRED AND AFFINITY

PART I

Prohibited degrees of relationship

Mother	Father
Adoptive mother or former adoptive mother	Adoptive father or former adoptive father
Daughter	Son
Adoptive daughter or former adoptive daughter	Adoptive son or former adoptive son
Father's mother	Father's father
Mother's mother	Mother's father

Son's daughter	Son's son
Daughter's daughter	Daughter's son
Sister	Brother
Father's sister	Father's brother
Mother's sister	Mother's brother
Brother's daughter	Brother's son
Sister's daughter	Sister's son

PART II

Degrees of affinity referred to in section 1(2) and (3) of this Act

Daughter of former wife	Son of former husband
Former wife of father	Former husband of mother
Former wife of father's father	Former husband of father's mother
Former wife of mother's father	Former husband of mother's mother
Daughter of son of former wife	Son of son of former husband
Daughter of daughter of former wife	Son of daughter of former husband

PART III

Degrees of affinity referred to in section 1(4) and (5) of this Act

Mother of former wife	Father of former husband
Former wife of son	Former husband of daughter

As amended by the Marriage Act 1949 (Amendment) Act 1954, ss1, 2; Marriage Acts Amendment Act 1958, s1(1), (2); Registration of Births, Deaths and Marriages (Fees) Order 1968, art 4(1), (2); Family Law Reform Act 1969, s2(2); Children Act 1975, s108(1)(a), Schedule 3, para 8; Statute Law (Repeals) Act 1975; Criminal Law Act 1977, s32(1); Domestic Proceedings and Magistrates' Courts Act 1978, s89(2)(a), Schedule 2, para 9; Justices of the Peace Act 1979, s71, Schedule 2, para 5; Magistrates' Courts Act 1980, s32(2); Marriage Act 1983, s1(3), (7), Schedule 1, paras 2, 3, 4, 5, 6, 7, 11, 12, 13, 14, 20, 21; Marriage (Prohibited Degrees of Relationship) Act 1986, ss1(4), (6), 3, Schedule 1, paras 2, 3, 4, 5, 7, 8; Family

Law Reform Act 1987, s33(1), Schedule 2, paras 9, 10(a); Children Act 1989, s108(4), (7), Schedule 12, para 5, Schedule 15; Marriage (Registration of Buildings) Act 1990, s1(1); Marriage Act 1994, ss1(1)–(3), 2(1), (2), Schedule, paras 1–4, 7, 8; Registration of Births, Deaths and Marriages (Fees) Order 1995; Transfer of Functions (Registration and Statistics) Order 1996, art 5(1), Schedule 2, para 10; Marriage Ceremony (Prescribed Words) Act 1996, s1; Justices of the Peace Act 1997, s73(2), Schedule 5, para 6; Deregulation (Validity of Civil Preliminaries to Marriage) Order 1997, art 2.

MARRIAGE (ENABLING) ACT 1960
(8 & 9 Eliz c 29)

1 Certain marriages not to be void

(1) No marriage hereafter contracted (whether in or out of Great Britain) between a man or a woman who is the sister, aunt or niece of a former wife of his (whether living or not), or was formerly the wife of his brother, uncle or nephew (whether living or not), shall by reason of that relationship be void or voidable under any enactment or rule of law applying in Great Britain as a marriage between persons within the prohibited degrees of affinity.

(2) In the foregoing subsection words of kinship apply equally to kin of the whole and of the half blood.

(3) This section does not validate a marriage, if either party to it is at the time of the marriage domiciled in a country outside Great Britain, and under the law of that country there cannot be a valid marriage between the parties.

MARRIED WOMEN'S PROPERTY ACT 1964
(1964 c 19)

1   Money and property derived from housekeeping allowance

If any question arises as to the right of a husband or wife to money derived from any allowance made by the husband for the expenses of the matrimonial home or for similar purposes, or to any property acquired out of such money, the money or property shall, in the absence of any agreement between them to the contrary, be treated as belonging to the husband and the wife in equal shares.

CIVIL EVIDENCE ACT 1968
(1968 c 64)

12 Findings of adultery and paternity as evidence in civil proceedings

(1) In any civil proceedings –

(a) the fact that a person has been found guilty of adultery in any matrimonial proceedings; and

(b) the fact that a person has been found to be the father of a child in relevant proceedings before any court in England and Wales or Northern Ireland or has been adjudged to be the father of a child in affiliation proceedings before any court in the United Kingdom;

shall (subject to subsection (3) below) be admissible in evidence for the purpose of proving, where to do so is relevant to any issue in those civil proceedings, that he committed the adultery to which the finding relates or, as the case may be, is (or was) the father of that child, whether or not he offered any defence to the allegation of adultery or paternity and whether or not he is a party to the civil proceedings; but no finding or adjudication other than a subsisting one shall be admissible in evidence by virtue of this section.

(2) In any civil proceedings in which by virtue of this section a person is proved to have been found guilty of adultery as mentioned in subsection (1)(a) above or to have been found or adjudged to be the father of a child as mentioned in subsection (1)(b) above –

(a) he shall be taken to have committed the adultery to which the finding relates or, as the case may be, to be (or have been) the father of that child, unless the contrary is proved; and

(b) without prejudice to the reception of any other admissible evidence for the purpose of identifying the facts on which the finding or adjudication was based, the contents of any document which was before the court, or which contains any pronouncement of the court, in the other proceedings in question shall be admissible in evidence for that purpose.

(3) Nothing in this section shall prejudice the operation of any enactment whereby a finding of fact in any matrimonial or affiliation proceedings is for the purpose of any other proceedings made conclusive evidence of any fact.

(4) Subsection (4) of section 11 of this Act shall apply for the purposes of this section as if the reference to subsection (2) were a reference to subsection (2) of this section.

(5) In this section –

'matrimonial proceedings' means any matrimonial cause in the High Court or a county court in England and Wales ... or any appeal arising out of any such cause or action;

'relevant proceedings' means –

(a) proceedings on a complaint under section 42 of the National Assistance Act 1948 or section 26 of the Social Security Act 1986;

(b) proceedings under the Children Act 1989;

(c) proceedings which would have been relevant proceedings for the purposes of this section in the form in which it was in force before the passing of the Children Act 1989;

(d) section 27 of the Child Support Act 1991;

(e) proceedings which are relevant proceedings as defined in section 8(5) of the Civil Evidence Act (Northern Ireland) 1971.

14   Privilege against incrimination of self or spouse

(1) The right of a person in any legal proceedings other than criminal proceedings to refuse to answer any question or produce any document or thing if to do so would tend to expose that person to proceedings for an offence or for the recovery of a penalty –

(a) shall apply only as regards criminal offences under the law of any part of the United Kingdom and penalties provided for by such law; and

(b) shall include a like right to refuse to answer any question or produce any document or thing if to do so would tend to expose the husband or wife of that person to proceedings for any such criminal offence or for the recovery of any such penalty.

(2) In so far as any existing enactment conferring (in whatever words) powers of inspection or investigation confers on a person (in whatever words) any right otherwise than in criminal proceedings to refuse to answer any question or give any evidence tending to incriminate that person,

subsection (1) above shall apply to that right as it applies to the right described in that subsection; and every such existing enactment shall be construed accordingly.

(3) In so far as any existing enactment provides (in whatever words) that in any proceedings other than criminal proceedings a person shall not be excused from answering any question or giving any evidence on the ground that to do so may incriminate that person, that enactment shall be construed as providing also that in such proceedings a person shall not be excused from answering any question or giving any evidence on the ground that to do so may incriminate the husband or wife of that person.

(4) Where any existing enactment (however worded) that –

    (a) confers powers of inspection or investigation; or

    (b) provides as mentioned in subsection (3) above,

further provides (in whatever words) that any answer or evidence given by a person shall not be admissible in evidence against that person in any proceedings or class of proceedings (however described, and whether criminal or not), that enactment shall be construed as providing also that any answer or evidence given by that person shall not be admissible in evidence against the husband or wife of that person in the proceedings or class of proceedings in question.

(5) In this section 'existing enactment' means any enactment passed before this Act; and the references to giving evidence are references to giving evidence in any manner, whether by furnishing information, making discovery, producing documents or otherwise.

As amended by the Family Law Reform Act 1987, s29(1)-(3); Courts and Legal Services Act 1990, s116, Schedule 16, para 2(1); Child Support Act 1991, s27(5); Children (Northern Ireland Consequential Amendments) Order 1995, art 6.

FAMILY LAW REFORM ACT 1969
(1969 c 46)

1   Reduction of age of majority from 21 to 18

(1) As from the date on which this section comes into force a person shall attain full age on attaining the age of eighteen instead of on attaining the age of twenty-one; and a person shall attain full age on that date if he has then already attained the age of eighteen but not the age of twenty-one.

8   Consent by persons over 16 to surgical, medical and dental treatment

(1) The consent of a minor who has attained the age of sixteen years to any surgical, medical or dental treatment which, in the absence of consent, would constitute a trespass to his person, shall be as effective as it would be if he were of full age; and where a minor has by virtue of this section given an effective consent to any treatment it shall not be necessary to obtain any consent for it from his parent or guardian.

(2) In this section 'surgical, medical or dental treatment' includes any procedure undertaken for the purposes of diagnosis, and this section applies to any procedure (including, in particular, the administration of an anaesthetic) which is ancillary to any treatment as it applies to that treatment.

(3) Nothing in this section shall be construed as making ineffective any consent which would have been effective if this section had not been enacted.

12   Persons under full age may be described as minors instead of infants

A person who is not of full age may be described as a minor instead of as an infant, and accordingly in this Act 'minor' means such a person as aforesaid.

PART III

PROVISIONS FOR USE OF BLOOD TESTS IN
DETERMINING PATERNITY

20 Power of court to require use of blood tests

(1) In any civil proceedings in which the paternity of any person falls to be determined by the court hearing the proceedings, the court may, on an application by any party to the proceedings, give a direction for the use of blood tests to ascertain whether such tests show that a party to the proceedings is or is not thereby excluded from being the father of that person and for the taking, within a period to be specified in the direction, of blood samples from that person, the mother of that person and any party alleged to be the father of that person or from any, or any two, of those persons.

A court may at any time revoke or vary a direction previously given by it under this section.

(1A) An application for a direction under this section shall specify who is to carry out the tests.

(1B) A direction under this section shall –

(a) specify, as the person who is to carry out the tests, the person specified in the application; or

(b) where the court considers that it would be inappropriate to specify that person (whether because to specify him would be incompatible with any provision made by or under regulations made under section 22 of this Act or for any other reason), decline to give the direction applied for.

(2) The person responsible for carrying out blood tests taken for the purpose of giving effect to a direction under this section shall make to the court by which the direction was given a report in which he shall state –

(a) the results of the tests;

(b) whether the party to whom the report relates is or is not excluded by the results from being the father of the person whose paternity is to be determined; and

(c) if that party is not so excluded, the value, if any, of the results in determining whether that party is that person's father;

and the report shall be received by the court as evidence in the proceedings of the matters stated therein.

(3) A report under subsection (2) of this section shall be in the form prescribed by regulations made under section 22 of this Act.

(4) Where a report has been made to a court under subsection (2) of this section, any party may, with the leave of the court, or shall, if the court so directs, obtain from the person who made the report a written statement explaining or amplifying any statement made in the report, and that statement shall be deemed for the purposes of this section (except subsection (3) thereof) to form part of the report made to the court.

(5) Where a direction is given under this section in any proceedings, a party to the proceedings, unless the court otherwise directs, shall not be entitled to call as a witness the person responsible for carrying out the tests taken for the purpose of giving effect to the direction, or any person to whom any thing necessary for the purpose of enabling those tests to be carried out was done, unless within fourteen days after receiving a copy of the report he serves notice on the other parties to the proceedings, or on such of them as the court may direct, of his intention to call that person; and where any such person is called as a witness the party who called him shall be entitled to cross-examine him.

(6) Where a direction is given under this section the party on whose applicant the direction is given shall pay the cost of taking and testing blood samples for the purpose of giving effect to the direction (including any expenses reasonably incurred by any person in taking any steps required of him for the purpose), and of making a report to the court under this section, but the amount paid shall be treated as costs incurred by him in the proceedings.

21 Consents, etc required for taking of blood samples

(1) Subject to the provisions of subsections (3) and (4) of this section, a blood sample which is required to be taken from any person for the purpose of giving effect to a direction under section 20 of this Act shall not be taken from that person except with his consent.

(2) The consent of a minor who has attained the age of sixteen years to the taking from himself of a blood sample shall be as effective as it would be if he were of full age; and where a minor has by virtue of this subsection given an effective consent to the taking of a blood sample it shall not be necessary to obtain consent for it from any other person.

(3) A blood sample may be taken from a person under the age of sixteen years, not being such a person as is referred to in subsection (4) of this section, if the person who has the care and control of him consents.

(4) A blood sample may be taken from a person who is suffering from mental disorder within the meaning of the Mental Health Act 1983 and is incapable of understanding the nature and purpose of blood tests if the person who has the care and control of him consents and the medical practitioner in whose care he is has certified that the taking of a blood sample from him will not be prejudicial to his proper care and treatment.

(5) The foregoing provisions of this section are without prejudice to the provisions of section 23 of this Act.

23 Failure to comply with direction for taking blood tests

(1) Where a court gives a direction under section 20 of this Act and any person fails to take any step required of him for the purpose of giving effect to the direction, the court may draw such inferences, if any, from that fact as appear proper in the circumstances.

(2) Where in any proceedings in which the paternity of any person falls to be determined by the court hearing the proceedings there is a presumption of law that that person is legitimate, then if –

(a) a direction is given under section 20 of this Act in those proceedings, and

(b) any party who is claiming any relief in the proceedings and who for the purpose of obtaining that relief is entitled to rely on the presumption fails to take any step required of him for the purpose of giving effect to the direction,

the court may adjourn the hearing for such period as it thinks fit to enable that party to take that step, and if at the end of that period he has failed without reasonable cause to take it the court may, without prejudice to subsection (1) of this section, dismiss his claim for relief notwithstanding the absence of evidence to rebut the presumption.

(3) Where any person named in a direction under section 20 of this Act fails to consent to the taking of a blood sample from himself or from any person named in the direction of whom he has the care and control, he shall be deemed for the purpose of this section to have failed to take a step required of him for the purpose of giving effect to the direction.

24 Penalty for personating another, etc for purpose of providing blood sample

If for the purpose of providing a blood sample for a test required to give effect to a direction under section 20 of this Act any person personates another, or proffers a child knowing that it is not the child named in the direction, he shall be liable –

(a) on conviction on indictment, to imprisonment for a term not exceeding two years, or

(b) on summary conviction, to a fine not exceeding the prescribed sum.

25 Interpretation of Part III

In this Part of this Act the following expressions have the meanings hereby respectively assigned to them, that is to say –

'blood samples' means blood taken for the purpose of blood tests;

'blood tests' means blood tests carried out under this Part of this Act and includes any test made with the object of ascertaining the inheritable characteristics of blood;

'excluded' means excluded subject to the occurrence of mutation to section 27 of the Family Law Reform Act 1987 and to sections 27 to 29 of the Human Fertilisation and Embryology Act 1990.

PART IV

MISCELLANEOUS AND GENERAL

26 Rebuttal of presumption as to legitimacy and illegitimacy

Any presumption of law as to the legitimacy or illegitimacy of any person may in any civil proceedings be rebutted by evidence which shows that it is more probable than not that that person is illegitimate or legitimate, as the case may be, and it shall not be necessary to prove that fact beyond reasonable doubt in order to rebut the presumption.

As amended by the Magistrates' Court Act 1980, s32(2); Mental Health Act 1983, s148, Schedule 4, para 25; Children Act 1989, s89; Human Fertilisation and Embryology Act 1990, s49(5), Schedule 4, para 1; Courts and Legal Services Act 1990, s116, Schedule 16, Pt I, para 3.

LAW REFORM (MISCELLANEOUS PROVISIONS) ACT 1970
(1970 c 33)

1 Engagements to marry not enforceable at law

(1) An agreement between two persons to marry one another shall not under the law of England and Wales have effect as a contract giving rise to legal rights and no action shall lie in England and Wales for breach of such an agreement, whatever the law applicable to the agreement.

(2) This section shall have effect in relation to agreements entered into before it comes into force, except that it shall not affect any action commenced before it comes into force.

2 Property of engaged couples

(1) Where an agreement to marry is terminated, any rule of law relating to the rights of husbands and wives in relation to property in which either or both has or have a beneficial interest, including any such rule as explained by section 37 of the Matrimonial Proceedings and Property Act 1970, shall apply, in relation to any property in which either or both of the parties to the agreement had a beneficial interest while the agreement was in force, as it applies in relation to property in which a husband or wife has a beneficial interest.

(2) Where an agreement to marry is terminated, section 17 of the Married Women's Property Act 1882 and section 7 of the Matrimonial Causes (Property and Maintenance) Act 1958 (which sections confer power on a judge of the High Court or a county court to settle disputes between husband and wife about property) shall apply, as if the parties were married, to any dispute between, or claim by, one of them in relation to property in which either or both had a beneficial interest while the agreement was in force; but an application made by virtue of this section to the judge under the said section 17, as originally enacted or as extended by the said section 7, shall be made within three years of the termination of the agreement.

3   Gifts between engaged couples

(1) A party to an agreement to marry who makes a gift of property to the other party to the agreement on the condition (express or implied) that it shall be returned if the agreement is terminated shall not be prevented from recovering the property by reason only of his having terminated the agreement.

(2) The gift of an engagement ring shall be presumed to be an absolute gift; this presumption may be rebutted by proving that the ring was given on the condition, express or implied, that it should be returned if the marriage did not take place for any reason.

5   Abolition of actions for enticement, seduction and harbouring of spouse or child

No person shall be liable in tort under the law of England and Wales –

(a) to any other person on the ground only of his having induced the wife or husband of that other person to leave or remain apart from the other spouse;

(b) to a parent (or person standing in the place of a parent) on the ground only of his having deprived the parent (or other person) of the services of his or her child by raping, seducing or enticing that child; or

(c) to any other person for harbouring the wife or child of that other person,

except in the case of action accruing before this Act comes into force if an action in respect thereof has begun before this Act comes into force.

MARRIAGE (REGISTRAR GENERAL'S LICENCE) ACT 1970

(1970 c 34)

1 Marriages which may be solemnised by Registrar General's licence

(1) Subject to the provisions of subsection (2) below, any marriage which may be solemnised on the authority of a certificate of a superintendent registrar may be solemnised on the authority of the Registrar General's licence elsewhere than at a registered building, the office of a superintendent registrar or approved premises:

Provided that any such marriage shall not be solemnised according to the rites of the Church of England or the Church in Wales.

(2) The Registrar General shall not issue any licence for the solemnisation of a marriage as is mentioned in subsection (1) above unless he is satisfied that one of the persons to be married is seriously ill and is not expected to recover and cannot be moved to a place at which under the provisions of the Marriage Act 1949 (hereinafter called the 'principal Act') the marriage could be solemnised (disregarding for this purpose the provisions of that Act relating to marriages in pursuance of section 26(1)(dd) of that Act).

2 Notice of marriage

(1) Where a marriage is intended to be solemnised on the authority of the Registrar General's licence, notice shall be given in the prescribed form by either of the persons to be married to the superintendent registrar of the registration district in which it is intended that the marriage shall be solemnised, and the notice shall state by or before whom it is intended that the marriage shall be solemnised.

(2) The provisions of section 27(4) of the principal Act (which relate to entries in the marriage notice book) shall apply to notices of marriage on the authority of the Registrar General's licence.

(3) The provisions of section 28 of the principal Act (declaration to

accompany notice of marriage) shall apply to the giving of notice under this Act with the exception of paragraph (b) of subsection (1) of that section and with the modification that in section 28(2) references to the registrar of births and deaths or of marriages and deputy registrar shall be omitted.

3 Evidence of capacity, consent, etc to be produced

The person giving notice to the superintendent registrar under the provisions of the foregoing section shall produce to the superintendent registrar such evidence as the Registrar General may require to satisfy him –

(a) that there is no lawful impediment to the marriage;

(b) that the consent of any person whose consent to the marriage is required under section 3 of the principal Act has been duly given; and

(c) that there is sufficient reason why a licence should be granted;

(d) that the conditions contained in section 1(2) of this Act are satisfied and that the person in respect of whom such conditions are satisfied is able to and does understand the nature and purport of the marriage ceremony:

Provided that the certificate of a registered medical practitioner shall be sufficient evidence of any or all of the matters in subsection (1)(d) of this section referred to.

4 Application to be reported to Registrar General

Upon receipt of any notice and evidence as mentioned in sections 2 and 3 above respectively the superintendent registrar shall inform the Registrar General and shall comply with any directions he may give for verifying the evidence given.

5 Caveat against issue of Registrar General's licence

The provisions of section 29 of the principal Act (caveat against issue of certificate or licence) shall apply to the issue of a licence by the Registrar General with the modification that a caveat may be entered with either the superintendent registrar or the Registrar General and either case it shall be for the Registrar General to examine into the matter of the caveat and to decide whether or not the licence should be granted and his decision shall be final, and with a further modification that the references to the superintendent registrar in that section shall refer to the superintendent registrar of the registration district in which the marriage is intended to be solemnised.

6   Marriage of person under eighteen

The provisions of section 3 of the principal Act (marriage of persons under 18) shall apply for the purposes of this Act to a marriage intended to be solemnised by Registrar General's licence as they apply to a marriage intended to be solemnised on the authority of a certificate of a superintendent registrar under Part III of the principal Act with the modification that if the consent of any person whose consent is required under that Act cannot be obtained by reason of absence or inaccessibility or by reason of his being under any disability, the superintendent registrar shall not be required to dispense with the necessity for the consent of that person and the Registrar General may dispense with the necessity of obtaining the consent of that person, whether or not there is any other person whose consent is also required.

7   Issue of licence by Registrar General

Where the marriage is intended to be solemnised on the authority of the Registrar General and he is satisfied that sufficient grounds exist why a licence should be granted he shall issue a licence in the prescribed form unless –

(a) any lawful impediment to the issue of the licence has been shown to his satisfaction to exist; or

(b) the issue of the licence has been forbidden under section 30 of the principal Act.

8   Period of validity of licence

(1) A marriage may be solemnised on the authority of the Registrar General's licence at any time within one month from the day on which the notice of marriage was entered in the marriage notice book.

(2) If the marriage is not solemnised within the said period of one month, the notice of marriage and the licence shall be void, and no person shall solemnise the marriage on the authority thereof.

9   Place of solemnisation

A marriage on the authority of the Registrar General's licence shall be solemnised in the place stated in the notice of marriage.

10 Manner of solemnisation

(1) Any marriage to be solemnised on the authority of the Registrar General's licence shall be solemnised at the wish of the persons to be married either –

(a) according to such form or ceremony, not being the rites or ceremonies of the Church of England or the Church in Wales, as the persons to be married shall see fit to adopt, or

(b) by civil ceremony.

(2) Except where the marriage is solemnised according to the usages of the Society of Friends or is a marriage between two persons professing the Jewish religion according to the usages of the Jews, it shall be solemnised in the presence of a registrar:

Provided that where the marriage is to be by civil ceremony it shall be solemnised in the presence of the superintendent registrar as well as the registrar.

(3) Except where the marriage is solemnised according to the usages of the Society of Friends or is a marriage between two persons professing the Jewish religion according to the usages of the Jews, the persons to be married shall in some part of the ceremony in the presence of two or more witnesses and the registrar and, where appropriate, the superintendent registrar, make the declaration and say to one another the words prescribed by section 44(3) or (3A) of the principal Act.

(4) No person who is a clergyman within the meaning of section 78 of the principal Act shall solemnise any marriage which is solemnised on the authority of the Registrar General.

11 Civil marriage followed by religious ceremony

(1) If the parties to a marriage solemnised on the authority of the Registrar General's licence before a superintendent registrar desire to add the religious ceremony ordained or used by the church or persuasion of which they are members and have given notice of their desire so to do a clergyman or minister of that church or persuasion upon the production of a certificate of their marriage before the superintendent registrar and upon the payment of the customary fees (if any), may, if he sees fit, read or celebrate in the presence of the parties to the marriage the marriage service of the church or persuasion to which he belongs or nominate some other minister to do so.

(2) The provisions of section 46(2) and (3) of the principal Act shall apply to such a reading or celebration as they apply to the reading or celebration of

a marriage service following a marriage solemnised in the office of a superintendent registrar.

12 Proof of certain matters not necessary to validity of marriages

The provisions of section 48 of the principal Act (proof of certain matters not necessary to validity of marriages) shall apply with the appropriate modifications to a marriage solemnised under the authority of the Registrar General's licence as they apply to a marriage solemnised under the authority of a certificate of a superintendent registrar.

14 Documentary authority for marriage

Where a marriage is to be solemnised on the authority of the Registrar General's licence a document issued by the superintendent registrar stating that the Registrar General's licence has been granted and that authority for the marriage to be solemnised has been given shall be delivered before the marriage to the following person, that is to say –

(a) if the marriage is to be solemnised according to the usages of the Society of Friends, the registering officer of that Society for the place where the marriage is to be solemnised;

(b) if the marriage is to be solemnised according to the usages of persons professing the Jewish religion, the officer of the synagogue by whom the marriage is required to be registered under Part IV of the principal Act;

(c) in any other case, the registrar in whose presence the marriage is to be solemnised.

15 Registration of marriages

A marriage solemnised on the authority of the Registrar General's licence shall be registered in accordance with the provisions of the principal Act which apply to the registration of marriages solemnised in the presence of a registrar or according to the usages of the Society of Friends or of persons professing the Jewish religion.

16 Offences

(1) It shall be an offence knowingly and wilfully –

(a) to solemnise a marriage by Registrar General's licence in any place other than the place specified in the licence;

(b) to solemnise a marriage by Registrar General's licence without the presence of a registrar except in the case of a marriage according to the usages of the Society of Friends or a marriage between two persons professing the Jewish religion according to the usages of the Jews;

(c) to solemnise a marriage by Registrar General's licence after the expiration of one month from the date of entry of the notice of marriage in the marriage notice book;

(d) to give false information by way of evidence as required by section 3 of this Act;

(e) to give a false certificate as provided for in section 3(1)(d) of this Act;

and any person found guilty of any of the above-mentioned offences shall be liable on summary conviction to a fine not exceeding the prescribed sum or on indictment to a fine or to imprisonment not exceeding three years or to both such fine and such imprisonment.

(2) A superintendent registrar who knowingly and wilfully solemnises or permits to be solemnised in his presence, or a registrar who knowingly and wilfully registers, a marriage by Registrar General's which is void by virtue of Part III of the principal Act as amended by this Act shall be guilty of an offence and shall be liable on summary conviction to a fine not exceeding the prescribed sum or on indictment to a fine or to imprisonment not exceeding three years or to both such fine and such imprisonment.

(3) No prosecution under this section shall be commenced after the expiration of three years from the commission of the offence.

(4) The provisions of sections 75(1)(a) and 75(2)(a) of the principal Act shall not apply to a marriage solemnised on the authority of the Registrar General's licence.

As amended by the Criminal Law Act 1977, s32(1); Magistrates' Courts Act 1980, s32(2); Marriage Act 1983, s2(3); Children Act 1989, s108(7), Schedule 15; Marriage Act 1994, s1(3), Schedule, para 9; Marriage Ceremony (Prescribed Words) Act 1996, s1(2)(b).

MATRIMONIAL PROCEEDINGS AND PROPERTY ACT 1970

(1970 c 45)

37 Contributions by spouse in money or money's worth to the improvement of property

It is hereby declared that where a husband or wife contributes in money or money's worth to the improvement of real or personal property in which or in the proceeds of sale of which either or both of them has or have a beneficial interest, the husband or wife so contributing shall, if the contribution is of a substantial nature and subject to any agreement between them to the contrary express or implied, be treated as having then acquired by virtue of his or her contribution a share or an enlarged share, as the case may be, in that beneficial interest of such an extent as may have been then agreed or, in default of such agreement, as may seem in all the circumstances just to any court before which the question of the existence or extent of the beneficial interest of the husband or wife arises (whether in proceedings between them or in any other proceedings).

39 Extension of s17 of Married Women's Property Act 1882

An application may be made to the High Court or a county court under section 17 of the Married Women's Property Act 1882 (powers of the court in disputes between husband and wife about property) (including that section as extended by section 7 of the Matrimonial Causes (Property and Maintenance) Act 1958) by either of the parties to a marriage notwithstanding that their marriage has been dissolved or annulled so long as the application is made within the period of three years beginning with the date on which the marriage was dissolved or annulled; and references in the said section 17 and the said section 7 to a husband or a wife shall be construed accordingly.

MATRIMONIAL CAUSES ACT 1973
(1973 c 18)

PART I

DIVORCE, NULLITY AND OTHER MATRIMONIAL SUITS

1 Divorce on breakdown of marriage

(1) Subject to section 3 below, a petition for divorce may be presented to the court by either party to a marriage on the ground that the marriage has broken down irretrievably.

(2) The court hearing a petition for divorce shall not hold the marriage to have broken down irretrievably unless the petitioner satisfies the court of one or more of the following facts, that is to say –

    (a) that the respondent has committed adultery and the petitioner finds it intolerable to live with the respondent;

    (b) that the respondent has behaved in such a way that the petitioner cannot reasonably be expected to live with the respondent;

    (c) that the respondent has deserted the petitioner for a continuous period of at least two years immediately preceding the presentation of the petition;

    (d) that the parties to the marriage have lived apart for a continuous period of at least two years immediately preceding the presentation of the petition (hereafter in this Act referred to as 'two years' separation') and the respondent consents to a decree being granted;

    (e) that the parties to the marriage have lived apart for a continuous period of at least five years immediately preceding the presentation of the petition (hereafter in this Act referred to as 'five years' separation').

(3) On a petition for divorce it shall be the duty of the court to inquire, so far as it reasonably can, into the facts alleged by the petitioner and into any facts alleged by the respondent.

(4) If the court is satisfied on the evidence of any such fact as is mentioned in subsection (2) above, then, unless it is satisfied on all the evidence that

the marriage has not broken down irretrievably, it shall, subject to section 5 below, grant a decree of divorce.

(5) Every decree of divorce shall in the first instance be a decree nisi and shall not be made absolute before the expiration of six months from its grant unless the High Court by general order from time to time fixes a shorter period, or unless in any particular case the court in which the proceedings are for the time being pending from time to time by special order fixes a shorter period than the period otherwise applicable for the time being by virtue of this subsection.

2   Supplemental provisions as to facts raising presumption of breakdown

(1) One party to a marriage shall not be entitled to rely for the purposes of section 1(2)(a) above on adultery committed by the other if, after it became known to him that the other had committed that adultery, the parties have lived with each other for a period exceeding, or periods together exceeding, six months.

(2) Where the parties to a marriage have lived with each other after it became known to one party that the other had committed adultery, but subsection (1) above does not apply, in any proceedings for divorce in which the petitioner relies on that adultery the fact that the parties have lived with each other after that time shall be disregarded in determining for the purposes of section 1(2)(a) above whether the petitioner finds it intolerable to live with the respondent.

(3) Where in any proceedings for divorce the petitioner alleges that the respondent has behaved in such a way that the petitioner cannot reasonably be expected to live with him, but the parties to the marriage have lived with each other for a period or periods after the date of the occurrence of the final incident relied on by the petitioner and held by the court to support his allegation, that fact shall be disregarded in determining for the purposes of section 1(2)(b) above whether the petitioner cannot reasonably be expected to live with the respondent if the length of that period or of those periods together was six months or less.

(4) For the purposes of section 1(2)(c) above the court may treat a period of desertion as having continued at a time when the deserting party was incapable of continuing the necessary intention if the evidence before the court is such that, had that party not been so incapable, the court would have inferred that his desertion continued at that time.

(5) In considering for the purposes of section 1(2) above whether the period for which the respondent has deserted the petitioner or the period for which

the parties to a marriage have lived apart has been continuous, no account shall be taken of any one period (not exceeding six months) or of any two or more periods (not exceeding six months in all) during which the parties resumed living with each other, but no period during which the parties lived with each other shall count as part of the period of desertion, or of the period for which the parties to the marriage lived apart, as the case may be.

(6) For the purposes of section 1(2)(d) and (e) above and this section a husband and wife shall be treated as living apart unless they are living with each other in the same household, and references in this section to the parties to a marriage living with each other shall be construed as references to their living with each other in the same household.

(7) Provision shall be made by rules of court for the purpose of ensuring that where in pursuance of section 1(2)(d) above the petitioner alleges that the respondent consents to a decree being granted the respondent has been given such information as will enable him to understand the consequences to him of his consenting to a decree being granted and the steps which he must take to indicate that he consents to the grant of a decree.

3   Bar on petitions for divorce within one year of marriage

(1) No petition for divorce shall be presented to the court before the expiration of the period of one year from the date of the marriage.

(2) Nothing in this section shall prohibit the presentation of a petition based on matters which occurred before the expiration of that period.

4   Divorce not precluded by previous judicial separation

(1) A person shall not be prevented from presenting a petition for divorce, or the court from granting a decree of divorce, by reason only that the petitioner or respondent has at any time, on the same facts or substantially the same facts as those proved in support of the petition, been granted a decree of judicial separation or an order under, or having effect as if made under, the Matrimonial Proceedings (Magistrates' Courts) Act 1960 or Part I of the Domestic Proceedings and Magistrates' Courts Act 1978 or any corresponding enactments in force in Northern Ireland, the Isle of Man or any of the Channel Islands.

(2) On a petition for divorce in such a case as is mentioned in subsection (1) above, the court may treat the decree or order as sufficient proof of any adultery, desertion or other fact by reference to which it was granted, but

shall not grant a decree of divorce without receiving evidence from the petitioner.

(3) Where a petition for divorce in such a case follows a decree of judicial separation (subject to subsection (5) below) or an order containing a provision exempting one party to the marriage from the obligation to cohabit with the other, for the purposes of that petition a period of desertion immediately preceding the institution of the proceedings for the decree or order shall, if the parties have not resumed cohabitation and the decree or order has been continuously in force since it was granted, be deemed immediately to precede the presentation of the petition.

(4) For the purposes of section 1(2)(c) above the court may treat as a period during which the respondent has deserted the petitioner any of the following periods, that is to say –

(a) any period during which there is in force an injunction granted by the High Court or a county court which excludes the respondent from the matrimonial home;

(b) any period during which there is in force an order made by the High Court or a county court under section 1 or 9 of the Matrimonial Homes Act 1983 which prohibits the exercise by the respondent of the right to occupy a dwelling-house in which the applicant and the respondent have or at any time have had a matrimonial home;

(c) any period during which there is in force an order made by a magistrates' court under section 16(3) of the Domestic Proceedings and Magistrates' Courts Act 1978 which requires the respondent to leave the matrimonial home or prohibits the respondent from entering the matrimonial home.

(5) Where –

(a) a petition for divorce is presented after the date on which Part I of the Domestic Proceedings and Magistrates' Court Act 1978 comes into force, and

(b) an order made under the Matrimonial Proceedings (Magistrates' Courts) Act 1960 containing a provision exempting the petitioner from the obligation to cohabit with the respondent is in force on that date,

then, for the purposes of section 1(2)(c) above, the court may treat a period during which such a provision was included in that order (whether before or after that date) as a period during which the respondent has deserted the petitioner.

5 Refusal of decree in five-year separation cases on grounds of grave hardship to respondent

(1) The respondent to a petition for divorce in which the petitioner alleges five years' separation may oppose the grant of a decree on the ground that the dissolution of the marriage will result in grave financial or other hardship to him and that it would in all the circumstances be wrong to dissolve the marriage.

(2) Where the grant of a decree is opposed by virtue of this section, then –

(a) if the court finds that the petitioner is entitled to rely in support of his petition on the fact of five years' separation and makes no such finding as to any other fact mentioned in section 1(2) above, and

(b) if apart from this section the court would grant a decree on the petition,

the court shall consider all the circumstances, including the conduct of the parties to the marriage and the interests of those parties and of any children or other persons concerned, and if of opinion that the dissolution of the marriage will result in grave financial or other hardship to the respondent and that it would in all the circumstances be wrong to dissolve the marriage it shall dismiss the petition.

(3) For the purposes of this section hardship shall include the loss of the chance of acquiring any benefit which the respondent might acquire if the marriage were not dissolved.

6 Attempts at reconciliation of parties to marriage

(1) Provision shall be made by rules of court for requiring the solicitor acting for a petitioner for divorce to certify whether he has discussed with the petitioner the possibility of a reconciliation and given him the names and addresses of persons qualified to help effect a reconciliation between parties to a marriage who have become estranged.

(2) If at any stage of proceedings for divorce it appears to the court that there is a reasonable possibility of a reconciliation between the parties to the marriage, the court may adjourn the proceedings for such period as it thinks fit to enable attempts to be made to effect such a reconciliation.

The power conferred by the foregoing provision is additional to any other power of the court to adjourn proceedings.

7 Consideration by the court of certain agreements or arrangements

Provision may be made by rules of court for enabling the parties to a marriage, or either of them, on application made either before or after the presentation of a petition for divorce, to refer to the court any agreement or arrangement made or proposed to be made between them, being an agreement or arrangement which relates to, arises out of, or is connected with, the proceedings for divorce which are contemplated or, as the case may be, have begun, and for enabling the court to express an opinion, should it think it desirable to do so, as to the reasonableness of the agreement or arrangement and to give such directions, if any, in the matter as it thinks fit.

8 Intervention of Queen's Proctor

(1) In the case of a petition for divorce –

(a) the court may, if it thinks fit, direct all necessary papers in the matter to be sent to the Queen's Proctor, who shall under the directions of the Attorney-General instruct counsel to argue before the court any question in relation to the matter which the court considers it necessary or expedient to have fully argued;

(b) any person may at any time during the progress of the proceedings or before the decree nisi is made absolute give information to the Queen's Proctor on any matter material to the due decision of the case, and the Queen's Proctor may thereupon take such steps as the Attorney General considers necessary or expedient.

(2) Where the Queen's Proctor intervenes or shows cause against a decree nisi in any proceedings for divorce, the court may make such order as may be just as to the payment by other parties to the proceedings of the costs incurred by him in so doing or as to the payment by him of any costs incurred by any of those parties by reason of his so doing.

(3) The Queen's Proctor shall be entitled to charge as part of the expenses of his office –

(a) the costs of any proceedings under subsection (1)(a) above;

(b) where his reasonable costs of intervening or showing cause as mentioned in subsection (2) above are not fully satisfied by any order under that subsection, the amount of the difference;

(c) if the Treasury so directs, any cost which he pays to any parties under an order made under subsection (2).

9 Proceedings after decree nisi: general powers of court

(1) Where a decree of divorce has been granted but not made absolute, then, without prejudice to section 8 above, any person (excluding a party to the proceedings other than the Queen's Proctor) may show cause why the decree should not be made absolute by reason of material facts not having been brought before the court; and in such a case the court may –

(a) notwithstanding anything in section 1(5) above (but subject to sections 10(2) to (4) and 41 below) make the decree absolute; or

(b) rescind the decree; or

(c) require further inquiry; or

(d) otherwise deal with the case as it thinks fit.

(2) Where a decree of divorce has been granted and no application for it to be made absolute has been made by the party to whom it was granted, then, at any time after the expiration of three months from the earliest date on which that party could have made such an application, the party against whom it was granted may make an application to the court, and on that application the court may exercise any of the powers mentioned in paragraphs (a) to (d) of subsection (1) above.

10 Proceedings after decree nisi: special protection for respondent in separation cases

(1) Where in any case the court has granted a decree of divorce on the basis of a finding that the petitioner was entitled to rely in support of his petition on the fact of two years' separation coupled with the respondent's consent to a decree being granted and has made no such finding as to any other fact mentioned in section 1(2) above, the court may, on an application made by the respondent at any time before the decree is made absolute, rescind the decree if it is satisfied that the petitioner misled the respondent (whether intentionally or unintentionally) about any matter which the respondent took into account in deciding to give his consent.

(2) The following provisions of this section apply where –

(a) the respondent to a petition for divorce in which the petitioner alleged two years' or five years' separation coupled, in the former case, with the respondent's consent to a decree being granted, has applied to the court for consideration under subsection (3) below of his financial position after the divorce; and

(b) the court has granted a decree on the petition on the basis of a finding that the petitioner was entitled to rely in support of his petition on the fact of two years' or five years' separation (as the case may be) and has made no such finding as to any other fact mentioned in section 1(2) above.

(3) The court hearing an application by the respondent under subsection (2) above shall consider all the circumstances including the age, health, conduct, earning capacity, financial resources and financial obligations of each of the parties, and the financial position of the respondent as, having regard to the divorce, it is likely to be after the death of the petitioner should the petitioner die first; and, subject to subsection (4) below, the court shall not make the decree absolute unless it is satisfied –

(a) that the petitioner should not be required to make any financial provision for the respondent, or

(b) that the financial provision made by the petitioner for the respondent is reasonable and fair or the best that can be made in the circumstances.

(4) The court may if it thinks fit make the decree absolute notwithstanding the requirements of subsection (3) above if –

(a) it appears that there are circumstances making it desirable that the decree should be made absolute without delay, and

(b) the court has obtained a satisfactory undertaking from the petitioner that he will make such financial provision for the respondent as the court may approve.

11 Grounds on which a marriage is void

A marriage celebrated after 31 July 1971 shall be void on the following grounds only, that is to say –

(a) that it is not a valid marriage under the provisions of the Marriages Acts 1949 to 1986 (that is to say where –

(i) the parties are within the prohibited degrees of relationship;

(ii) either party is under the age of sixteen; or

(iii) the parties have intermarried in disregard of certain requirements as to the formation of marriage);

(b) that at the time of the marriage either party was already lawfully married;

(c) that the parties are not respectively male and female;

(d) in the case of a polygamous marriage entered into outside England and Wales, that either party was at the time of the marriage domiciled in England and Wales.

For the purposes of paragraph (d) of this subsection a marriage is not polygamous if at its inception neither party has any spouse additional to the other.

12 Grounds on which a marriage is voidable

A marriage celebrated after 31 July 1971 shall be voidable on the following grounds only, that is to say –

(a) that the marriage has not been consummated owing to the incapacity of either party to consummate it;

(b) that the marriage has not been consummated owing to the wilful refusal of the respondent to consummate it;

(c) that either party to the marriage did not validly consent to it, whether in consequence of duress, mistake, unsoundness of mind or otherwise;

(d) that at the time of the marriage either party, though capable of giving a valid consent, was suffering (whether continuously or intermittently) from mental disorder within the meaning of the Mental Health Act 1983 of such kind or to such an extent as to be unfitted for marriage;

(e) that at the time of the marriage the respondent was suffering from venereal disease in a communicable form;

(f) that at the time of the marriage the respondent was pregnant by some person other than the petitioner.

13 Bars to relief where marriage is voidable

(1) The court shall not, in proceedings instituted after 31 July 1971, grant a decree of nullity on the ground that a marriage is voidable if the respondent satisfies the court –

(a) that the petitioner, with knowledge that it was open to him to have the marriage avoided, so conducted himself in relation to the respondent as to lead the respondent reasonably to believe that he would not seek to do so; and

(b) that it would be unjust to the respondent to grant the decree.

(2) Without prejudice to subsection (1) above, the court shall not grant a decree of nullity by virtue of section 12 above on the grounds mentioned in paragraph (c), (d), (e) or (f) of that section unless –

(a) it is satisfied that proceedings were instituted within the period of three years from the date of the marriage, or

(b) leave for the institution of proceedings after the expiration of that period has been granted under subsection (4) below.

(3) Without prejudice to subsections (1) and (2) above, the court shall not grant a decree of nullity by virtue of section 12 above on the grounds mentioned in paragraph (e) or (f) of that section unless it is satisfied that the petitioner was at the time of the marriage ignorant of the facts alleged.

(4) In the case of proceedings for the grant of a decree of nullity by virtue of section 12 above on the grounds mentioned in paragraph (c), (d), (e) or (f) of that section, a judge of the court may, on an application made to him, grant leave for the institution of proceedings after the expiration of the period of three years from the date of the marriage if –

(a) he is satisfied that the petitioner has at some time during that period suffered from mental disorder within the meaning of the Mental Health Act 1983, and

(b) he considers that in all the circumstances of the case it would be just to grant leave for the institution of proceedings.

(5) An application for leave under subsection (4) above may be made after the expiration of the period of three years from the date of the marriage.

14 Marriages governed by foreign law or celebrated abroad under English law

(1) Where, apart from this Act, any matters affecting the validity of a marriage would fall to be determined (in accordance with the rules of private international law) by reference to the law of a country outside England and Wales, nothing in section 11, 12 or 13(1) above shall –

(a) preclude the determination of that matter as aforesaid; or

(b) require the application to the marriage of the grounds or bar there mentioned except so far as applicable in accordance with those rules.

(2) In the case of a marriage which purports to have been celebrated under the Foreign Marriage Acts 1892 to 1947 or has taken place outside England and Wales and purports to be a marriage under common law, section 11 above is without prejudice to any ground on which the marriage may be void under those Acts or, as the case may be, by virtue of the rules governing the celebration of marriages outside England and Wales under common law.

15 Application of ss1(5), 8 and 9 to nullity proceedings

Sections 1(5), 8 and 9 as above shall apply in relation to proceedings for nullity of marriage as if for any reference in those provisions to divorce there were substituted a reference to nullity of marriage.

16 Effect of decree of nullity in case of voidable marriage

A decree of nullity granted after 31 July 1971 in respect of a voidable marriage shall operate to annul the marriage only as respects any time after the decree has been made absolute, and the marriage shall, notwithstanding the decree, be treated as if it had existed up to that time.

17 Judicial separation

(1) A petition for judicial separation may be presented to the court by either party to a marriage on the ground that any such fact as is mentioned in section 1(2) above exists, and the provisions of section 2 above shall apply accordingly for the purposes of a petition for judicial separation alleging any such fact, as they apply in relation to a petition for divorce alleging that fact.

(2) On a petition for judicial separation it shall be the duty of the court to inquire, so far as it reasonably can, into the facts alleged by the petitioner and into any facts alleged by the respondent, but the court shall not be concerned to consider whether the marriage has broken down irretrievably, and if it is satisfied on the evidence of any such fact as is mentioned in section 1(2) above it shall, subject to section 41 below, grant a decree of judicial separation.

(3) Sections 6 and 7 above shall apply for the purpose of encouraging the reconciliation of parties to proceedings for judicial separation and of enabling the parties to a marriage to refer to the court for its opinion an agreement or arrangement relevant to actual or contemplated proceedings for judicial separation, as they apply in relation to proceedings for divorce.

18 Effects of judicial separation

(1) Where the court grants a decree of judicial separation it shall no longer be obligatory for the petitioner to cohabit with the respondent.

(2) If while a decree of judicial separation is in force and the separation is continuing either of the parties to the marriage dies intestate as respects all or any of his or her real or personal property, the property as respects which he or she died intestate shall devolve as if the other party to the marriage had then been dead.

(3) Notwithstanding anything in section 2(1)(a) of the Matrimonial Proceedings (Magistrates' Court) Act 1960, a provision in force under an

order made, or having effect as if made, under that section exempting one party to a marriage from the obligation to cohabit with the other shall not have effect as a decree of judicial separation for the purposes of subsection (2) above.

19 Presumption of death and dissolution of marriage

(1) Any married person who alleges that reasonable grounds exist for supposing that the other party to the marriage is dead may present a petition to the court to have it presumed that the other party is dead and to have the marriage dissolved, and the court may, if satisfied that such reasonable grounds exist, grant a decree of presumption of death and dissolution of the marriage.

(3) In any proceedings under this section the fact that for a period of seven years or more the other party to the marriage has been continually absent from the petitioner and the petitioner has no reason to believe that the other party has been living within that time shall be evidence that the other party is dead until the contrary is proved.

(4) Sections 1(5), 8 and 9 above shall apply to a petition and a decree under this section as they apply to a petition for divorce and a decree of divorce respectively.

(6) It is hereby declared that neither collusion nor any other conduct on the part of the petitioner which has at any time been a bar to relief in matrimonial proceedings constitutes a bar to the grant of a decree under this section.

20 Relief for respondent in divorce proceedings

If in any proceedings for divorce the respondent alleges and proves any such fact as is mentioned in subsection (2) of section 1 above (treating the respondent as the petitioner and the petitioner as the respondent for the purposes of that subsection) the court may give to the respondent the relief to which he would have been entitled if he had presented a petition seeking that relief.

21 Financial provision and property adjustment orders

(1) The financial provision orders for the purpose of the Act are the orders for periodical or lump sum provision available (subject to the provisions of this Act) under section 23 below for the purpose of adjusting the financial position of the parties to a marriage and any children of the family in connection with

proceedings for divorce, nullity of marriage or judicial separation and under section 27(6) below on proof of neglect by one party to a marriage to provide, or to make a proper contribution towards, reasonable maintenance for the other or a child of the family, that is to say –

(a) any order for periodical payments in favour of a party to a marriage under section 23(1)(a) or 27(6)(a) or in favour of a child of the family under section 23(1)(d), (2) or (4) or 27(6)(d);

(b) any order for secured periodical payments in favour of a party to a marriage under section 23(1)(b) or 27(6)(b) or in favour of a child of the family under section 23(1)(e), (2) or (4) or 27(6)(e); and

(c) any order for lump sum provision in favour of a party to a marriage under section 23(1)(c) or 27(6)(c) or in favour of a child of the family under section 23(1)(f), (2) or (4) or 27(6)(f);

and references in this Act (except in paragraphs 17(1) and 23 of Schedule 1 below) to periodical payments orders, secured periodical payments orders and orders for the payment of a lump sum are references to all or some of the financial provision orders requiring the sort of financial provision in question according as the context of each reference may require.

(2) The property adjustment orders for the purposes of this Act are the orders dealing with property rights available (subject to the provisions of this Act) under section 24 below for the purpose of adjusting the financial position of the parties to a marriage and any children of the family on or after the grant of a decree of divorce, nullity of marriage or judicial separation, that is to say –

(a) any order under subsection (1)(a) of that section for a transfer of property;

(b) any order under subsection (1)(b) of that section for a settlement of property; and

(c) any order under subsection (1)(c) or (d) of that section for a variation of settlement.

22 Maintenance pending suit

On a petition for divorce, nullity of marriage or judicial separation, the court may make an order for maintenance pending suit, that is to say, an order requiring either party to the marriage to make to the other such periodical payments for his or her maintenance and for such term, being a term beginning not earlier than the date of the presentation of the petition and ending with the date of the determination of the suit, as the court thinks reasonable.

23 Financial provision orders in connection with divorce proceedings, etc

(1) On granting a decree of divorce, a decree of nullity of marriage or a decree of judicial separation or at any time thereafter (whether, in the case of a decree of divorce or of nullity of marriage, before or after the decree is made absolute), the court may make any one or more of the following orders, that is to say –

(a) an order that either party to the marriage shall make to the other such periodical payments, for such term, as may be specified in the order;

(b) an order that either party to the marriage shall secure to the other to the satisfaction of the court such periodical payments, for such term, as may be so specified;

(c) an order that either party to the marriage shall pay to the other such lump sum or sums as may be so specified;

(d) an order that a party to the marriage shall make to such person as may be specified in the order for the benefit of a child of the family, or to such a child, such periodical payments, for such term, as may be so specified;

(e) an order that a party to the marriage shall secure to such person as may be so specified for the benefit of such a child, or to such a child, to the satisfaction of the court, such periodical payments, for such term, as may be so specified;

(f) an order that a party to the marriage shall pay to such person as may be so specified for the benefit of such a child, or to such a child, such lump sum as may be so specified;

subject however, in the case of an order under under paragraph (d), (e) or (f) above, to the restrictions imposed by section 29(1) and (3) below on the making of financial provision orders in favour of children who have attained the age of eighteen.

(2) The court may also, subject to those restrictions, make any one or more of the orders mentioned in subsection (1)(d), (e) and (f) above-

(a) in any proceedings for divorce, nullity of marriage or judicial separation, before granting a decree; and

(b) where any such proceedings are dismissed after the beginning of the trial, either forthwith or within a reasonable period after the dismissal.

(3) Without prejudice to the generality of subsection (1)(c) or (f) above –

(a) an order under this section that a party to a marriage shall pay a lump sum to the other party may be made for the purpose of enabling that other party to meet any liabilities or expenses reasonably incurred by him or her in maintaining himself or herself or any child of the family before making an application for an order under this section in his or her favour;

(b) an order under this section for the payment of a lump sum to or for the benefit of a child of the family may be made for the purpose of enabling any liabilities or expenses reasonably incurred by or for the benefit of that child before the making of an application for an order under this section in his favour to be met; and

(c) an order under this section for the payment of a lump sum may provide for the payment of that sum by instalments of such amount as may be specified in the order and may require the payment of the instalments to be secured to the satisfaction of the court.

(4) The power of the court under subsection (1) or (2)(a) above to make an order in favour of a child of the family shall be exercisable from time to time; and where the court makes an order in favour of a child under subsection (2)(b) above, it may from time to time, subject to the restrictions mentioned in subsection (1) above, make a further order in his favour of any of the kinds mentioned in subsection (1)(d), (e) or (f) above.

(5) Without prejudice to the power to give a direction under section 30 below for the settlement of an instrument by conveyancing counsel, where an order is made under subsection (1)(a), (b) or (c) above on or after granting a decree of divorce or nullity of marriage, neither the order nor any settlement made in pursuance of the order shall take effect unless the decree has been made absolute.

(6) Where the court –

(a) makes an order under this section for the payment of a lump sum; and

(b) directs –

(i) that payment of that sum or any part of it shall be deferred; or

(ii) that that sum or any part of it shall be paid by instalments,

the court may order that the amount deferred or the instalments shall carry interest at such rate as may be specified by the order from such date, not earlier than the date of the order, as may be so specified, until the date when payment of it is due.

24 Property adjustment orders in connection with divorce proceedings, etc

(1) On granting a decree of divorce, a decree of nullity of marriage or a decree of judicial separation or at any time thereafter (whether, in the case of a decree of divorce, or of nullity of marriage, before or after the decree is made absolute), the court may make any one or more of the following orders, that is to say –

(a) an order that a party to the marriage shall transfer to the other party, to any child of the family or to such person as may be specified in the order for the benefit of such a child such property as may be so specified, being property to which the first-mentioned party is entitled, either in possession or reversion;

(b) an order that a settlement of such property as may be so specified, being property to which a party to the marriage is so entitled, be made to the satisfaction of the court for the benefit of the other party to the marriage and of the children of the family or either or any of them;

(c) an order varying for the benefit of the parties to the marriage and of the children of the family or either or any of them any ante-nuptial or post-nuptial settlement (including such a settlement made by will or codicil) made on the parties to the marriage;

(d) an order extinguishing or reducing the interest of either of the parties to the marriage under any such settlement;

subject, however, in the case of an order under paragraph (a) above, to the restrictions imposed by section 29(1) and (3) below on the making of orders for a transfer of property in favour of children who have attained the age of eighteen.

(2) The court may make an order under subsection (1)(c) above notwithstanding that there are no children of the family.

(3) Without prejudice to the power to give a direction under section 30 below for the settlement of an instrument by conveyancing counsel, where an order is made under this section on or after granting a decree of divorce or nullity of marriage, neither the order nor any settlement made in pursuance of the order shall take effect unless the decree has been made absolute.

24A Orders for sale of property

(1) Where the court makes under section 23 or 24 of this Act a secured periodical payments order, an order for the payment of a lump sum or a property adjustment order, then, on making that order or at any time thereafter, the court may make a further order for the sale of such property

as may be specified in the order, being property in which or in the proceeds of sale of which either or both of the parties to the marriage has or have a beneficial interest, either in possession or reversion.

(2) Any order made under subsection (1) above may contain such consequential or supplementary provisions as the court thinks fit and, without prejudice to the generality of the foregoing provision, may include –

(a) provision requiring the making of a payment out of the proceeds of sale of the property to which the order relates, and

(b) provision requiring any such property to be offered for sale to a person, or class of persons, specified in the order.

(3) Where an order is made under subsection (1) above on or after the grant of a decree of divorce or nullity of marriage, the order shall not take effect unless the decree has been made absolute.

(4) Where an order is made under subsection (1) above, the court may direct that the order, or such provision thereof as the court may specify, shall not take effect until the occurrence of an event specified by the court or the expiration of a period so specified.

(5) Where an order under subsection (1) above contains a provision requiring the proceeds of sale of the property to which the order relates to be used to secure periodical payments to a party to the marriage, the order shall cease to have effect on the death or re-marriage of that person.

(6) Where a party to a marriage has a beneficial interest in any property, or in the proceeds of sale thereof, and some other person who is not a party to the marriage also has a beneficial interest in that property or in the proceeds of sale thereof, then, before deciding whether to make an order under this section in relation to that property, it shall be the duty of the court to give that other person an opportunity to make representations with respect to the order; and any representations made by that other person shall be included among the circumstances to which the court is required to have regard under section 25(1) below.

25 Matters to which court is to have regard in deciding how to exercise its powers under sections 23, 24 and 24A

(1) It shall be the duty of the court in deciding whether to exercise its powers under section 23, 24 or 24A above and, if so, in what manner, to have regard to all the circumstances of the case, first consideration being given to the welfare while a minor of any child of the family who has not attained the age of eighteen.

(2) As regards the exercise of the powers of the court under section 23(1)(a), (b) or (c), 24 or 24A above in relation to a party to the marriage, the court shall in particular have regard to the following matters –

(a) the income, earning capacity, property and other financial resources which each of the parties to the marriage has or is likely to have in the foreseeable future, including in the case of earning capacity any increase in that capacity which it would in the opinion of the court be reasonable to expect a party to the marriage to take steps to acquire;

(b) the financial needs, obligations and responsibilities which each of the parties to the marriage has or is likely to have in the foreseeable future;

(c) the standard of living enjoyed by the family before the breakdown of the marriage;

(d) the age of each party to the marriage and the duration of the marriage;

(e) any physical or mental disability of either of the parties to the marriage;

(f) the contributions which each of the parties has made or is likely in the foreseeable future to make to the welfare of the family, including any contribution by looking after the home or caring for the family;

(g) the conduct of each of the parties, if that conduct is such that it would in the opinion of the court be inequitable to disregard it;

(h) in the case of proceedings for divorce or nullity of marriage, the value to each of the parties to the marriage of any benefit which, by reason of the dissolution or annulment of the marriage, that party will lose the chance of acquiring.

(3) As regards the exercise of the powers of the court under section 23(1)(d), (e) or (f), (2) or (4), 24 or 24A above in relation to a child of the family, the court shall in particular have regard to the following matters –

(a) the financial needs of the child;

(b) the income, earning capacity (if any), property and other financial resources of the child;

(c) any physical or mental disability of the child;

(d) the manner in which he was being and in which the parties to the marriage expected him to be educated or trained;

(e) the considerations mentioned in relation to the parties to the marriage in paragraphs (a), (b), (c) and (e) of subsection (2) above.

(4) As regards the exercise of the powers of the court under section 23(1)(d), (e) or (f), (2) or (4), 24 or 24A above against a party to a marriage in favour of a child of the family who is not the child of that party, the court shall also have regard –

(a) to whether that party assumed any responsibility for the child's maintenance, and, if so, to the extent to which, and the basis upon which, that party assumed such responsibility and to the length of time for which that party discharged such responsibility;

(b) to whether in assuming and discharging such responsibility that party did so knowing that the child was not his or her own;

(c) to the liability of any other person to maintain the child.

25A Exercise of court's power in favour of party to marriage on decree of divorce or nullity of marriage

(1) Where on or after the grant of a decree of divorce or nullity of marriage the court decides to exercise its powers under section 23(1)(a), (b) or (c), 24 or 24A above in favour of a party to the marriage, it shall be the duty of the court to consider whether it would be appropriate so to exercise those powers that the financial obligations of each party towards the other will be terminated as soon after the grant of the decree as the court considers just and reasonable.

(2) Where the court decides in such a case to make a periodical payments or secured periodical payments order in favour of a party to the marriage, the court shall in particular consider whether it would be appropriate to require those payments to be made or secured only for such term as would in the opinion of the court be sufficient to enable the party in whose favour the order is made to adjust without undue hardship to the termination of his or her financial dependence on the other party.

(3) Where on or after the grant of a decree of divorce or nullity of marriage an application is made by a party to the marriage for a periodical payments order in his or her favour, then, if the court considers that no continuing obligation should be imposed on either party to make or secure periodical payments in favour of the other, the court may dismiss the application with a direction that the applicant shall not be entitled to make any further application in relation to that marriage for an order under section 23(1)(a) or (b) above.

25B Pensions

(1) The matters to which the court is to have regard under section 25(2) above include –

(a) in the case of paragraph (a), any benefits under a pension scheme which a party to the marriage has or is likely to have, and

(b) in the case of paragraph (h), any benefits under a pension scheme which, by reason of the dissolution or annulment of the marriage, a party to the marriage will lose the chance of acquiring,

and, accordingly, in relation to benefits under a pension scheme, section 25(2)(a) above shall have effect as if 'in the foreseeable future' were omitted.

(2) In any proceedings for a financial provision order under section 23 above in a case where a party to the marriage has, or is likely to have, any benefit under a pension scheme, the court shall, in addition to considering any other matter which it is required to consider apart from this subsection, consider –

(a) whether, having regard to any matter to which it is required to have regard in the proceedings by virtue of subsection (1) above, such an order (whether deferred or not) should be made, and

(b) where the court determines to make such an order, how the terms of the order should be affected, having regard to any such matter.

(3) The following provisions apply where, having regard to any benefits under a pension scheme, the court determines to make an order under section 23 above.

(4) To the extent to which the order is made having regard to any benefits under a pension scheme, the order may require the trustee or managers of the pension scheme in question, if at any time any payment in respect of any benefits under the scheme becomes due to the party with pension rights, to make a payment for the benefit of the other party.

(5) The amount of any payment which, by virtue of subsection (4) above, the trustee or managers are required to make under the order at any time shall not exceed the amount of the payment which is due at that time to the party with pension rights.

(6) Any such payment by the trustees or managers –

(a) shall discharge so much of the trustee or managers liability to the party with pension rights as corresponds to the amount of the payment, and

(b) shall be treated for all purposes as a payment made by the party with pension rights in or towards the discharge of his liability under the order.

(7) Where the party with pension rights may require any benefits which he has or is likely to have under the scheme to be commuted, the order may require him to commute the whole or part of those benefits; and this section applies to the payment of any amounted commuted in pursuance of the order as it applies to other payments in respect of benefits under the scheme.

25C Pensions: lump sums

(1) The power of the court under section 23 above to order a party to a marriage to pay a lump sum to the other party includes, where the benefits which the party with pension rights has or is likely to have under a pension scheme include any lump sum payable in respect of his death, power to make any of the following provisions by the order.

(2) The court may –

(a) if the trustees or managers of the pension scheme in question have power to determine the person to whom the sum, or any part of it, is to be paid, require them to pay the whole or part of that sum, when it becomes due, to the other party,

(b) if the party with pension rights has power to nominate the person to whom the sum, or any part of it, is to be paid, require the party with pension rights to nominate the other party in respect of the whole or part of that sum,

(c) in any other case, require the trustees or managers of the pension scheme in question to pay the whole or part of that sum, when it becomes due, for the benefit of the other party instead of to the person to whom, apart from the order, it would be paid.

(3) Any payment by the trustees or managers under an order made under section 23 above by virtue of this section shall discharge so much of the trustees, or managers, liability in respect of the party with pension rights as corresponds to the amount of the payment.

25D Pensions: supplementary

(1) Where –

(a) an order made under section 23 above by virtue of sections 25B or 25C above imposes any requirement on the trustees or managers of a pension scheme ('the first scheme') and the party with pension rights acquires transfer credits under another pension scheme ('the new scheme') which are derived (directly or indirectly) from a transfer from the first scheme of all his accrued rights under that scheme (including transfer credits allowed by that scheme), and

(b) the trustees or managers of the new scheme have been given notice in accordance with regulations,

the order shall have effect as if it has been made instead in respect of the trustees or managers of the new scheme; and in this subsection 'transfer credits' has the same meaning as in the Pension Schemes Act 1993.

(2) Regulations may –

(a) in relation to any provision of sections 25B or 25C above which authorises the court making an order under section 23 above to require the trustees or managers of a pension scheme to make a payment for the benefit of the other party, make provision as to the person to whom, and the terms on which, the payment is to be made,

(b) require notices to be given in respect of changes of circumstances relevant to such orders which include provision made by virtue of sections 25B and 25C above,

(c) make provision for the trustees or managers of any pension scheme to provide, for the purposes of orders under section 23 above, information as to the value of any benefits under the scheme,

(d) make provision for the recovery of the administrative expenses of –

(i) complying with such orders, so far as they include provision made by virtue of sections 25B and 25C above, and

(ii) providing such information,

from the party with pension rights or the other party,

(e) make provision for the value of any benefits under a pension scheme to be calculated and verified, for the purposes of orders under section 23 above, in a prescribed manner,

and regulations made by virtue of paragraph (e) above may provide for that value to be calculated and verified in accordance with guidance which is prepared and from time to time revised by a prescribed person and approved by the Secretary of State.

(3) In this section and sections 25B and 25C above –

(a) references to a pension scheme include –

(i) a retirement annuity contract, or

(ii) an annuity, or insurance policy, purchased or transferred for the purpose of giving effect to rights under a pension scheme,

(b) in relation to such a contract or annuity, references to the trustees or managers shall be read as references to the provider of the annuity,

(c) in relation to such a policy, references to the trustees or managers shall be read as references to the insurer,

and in section 25B(1) and (2) above, references to benefits under a pension scheme include any benefits by way of pension, whether under a pension scheme or not.

(4) In this section and sections 25B and 25C above –

'the party with pension rights' means the party to the marriage who has or is likely to have benefits under a pension scheme and 'the other party' means the other party to the marriage,

'pension scheme' means an occupational pension scheme or a personal pension scheme (applying the definitions in section 1 of the Pension Schemes Act 1993, but as if the reference to employed earners in the definition of 'personal pension scheme' were to any earners),

'prescribed' means prescribed by regulations, and

'regulations' means regulations made by the Lord Chancellor;

and the power to make regulations under this section shall be exercisable by statutory instrument, which shall be subject to annulment in pursuance of a resolution of either House of Parliament.

26   Commencement of proceedings for ancillary relief, etc

(1) Where a petition for divorce, nullity of marriage or judicial separation has been presented, then, subject to subsection (2) below, proceedings for maintenance pending suit under section 22 above, for a financial provision order under section 23 above, or for a property adjustment order may be begun, subject to and in accordance with rules of court, at any time after the presentation of the petition.

(2) Rules of court may provide, in such cases as may be prescribed by the rules –

(a) that applications for any such relief as is mentioned in subsection (1) above shall be made in the petition or answer; and

(b) that applications for any such relief which are not so made, or are not made until after the expiration of such period following the presentation of the petition or filing of the answer as may be so prescribed, shall be made only with the leave of the court.

27   Financial provision orders, etc in case of neglect by party to marriage to maintain other party or child of the family

(1) Either party to a marriage may apply to the court for an order under this section on the ground that the other party to the marriage (in this section referred to as the respondent) –

(a) has failed to provide reasonable maintenance for the applicant, or

(b) has failed to provide, or to make proper contribution towards, reasonable maintenance for any child of the family.

(2) The court shall not entertain an application under this section unless –

(a) the applicant or the respondent is domiciled in England and Wales on the date of the application; or

(b) the applicant has been habitually resident there throughout the period of one year ending with that date; or

(c) the respondent is resident there on that date.

(3) Where an application under this section is made on the ground mentioned in subsection (1)(a) above, then, in deciding –

(a) whether the respondent has failed to provide reasonable maintenance for the applicant, and

(b) what order, if any, to make under this section in favour of the applicant,

the court shall have regard to all the circumstances of the case including the matters mentioned in section 25(2) above, and where an application is also made under this section in respect of a child of the family who has not attained the age of eighteen, first consideration shall be given to the welfare of the child while a minor.

(3A) Where an application under this section is made on the ground mentioned in subsection (1)(b) above then, in deciding –

(a) whether the respondent has failed to provide, or to make a proper contribution towards, reasonable maintenance for the child of the family to whom the application relates, and

(b) what order, if any, to make under this section in favour of the child,

the court shall have regard to all the circumstances of the case including the matters mentioned in section 25(3)(a) to (e) above, and where the child of the family to whom the application relates is not the child of the respondent, including also the matters mentioned in section 25(4) above.

(3B) In relation to an application under this section on the ground mentioned in subsection (1)(a) above, section 25(2)(c) above shall have effect as if for the reference therein to the breakdown of the marriage there were substituted a reference to the failure to provide reasonable maintenance for the applicant, and in relation to an application under this section on the ground mentioned in subsection (1)(b) above, section 25(2)(c) above (as it applies by virtue of section 25(3)(e) above) shall have effect as if for the reference therein to the breakdown of the marriage there were substituted a reference to the failure to provide, or to make a proper contribution towards, reasonable maintenance for the child of the family to whom the application relates.

(5) Where on an application under this section it appears to the court that the applicant or any child of the family to whom the application relates is in immediate need of financial assistance, but it is not yet possible to determine what order, if any, should be made on the application, the court may make an interim order for maintenance, that is to say, an order requiring the respondent to make to the applicant until the determination of the application such periodical payments as the court thinks reasonable.

(6) Where on an application under this section the applicant satisfies the court of any ground mentioned in subsection (1) above, the court may make any one or more of the following orders, that is to say –

(a) an order that the respondent shall make to the applicant such periodical payments, for such term, as may be specified in the order;

(b) an order that the respondent shall secure to the applicant, to the satisfaction of the court, such periodical payments, for such term, as may be so specified;

(c) an order that the respondent shall pay to the applicant such lump sum as may be so specified;

(d) an order that the respondent shall make to such person as may be specified in the order for the benefit of the child to whom the application relates, or to that child, such periodical payments, for such term, as may be so specified;

(e) an order that the respondent shall secure to such person as may be so specified for the benefit of that child, or to that child, to the satisfaction of the court, such periodical payments, for such term, as may be so specified;

(f) an order that the respondent shall pay to such person as may be so specified for the benefit of that child, or to that child, such lump sum as may be so specified;

subject, however, in the case of an order under paragraph (d), (e) or (f) above, to the restrictions imposed by section 29(1) and (3) below on the making of financial provision orders in favour of children who have attained the age of eighteen.

(6A) An application for the variation under section 31 of this Act of a periodical payments order or secured periodical payments order made under this section in favour of a child may, if the child has attained the age of sixteen, be made by the child himself.

(6B) Where a periodical payments order made in favour of a child under this section ceases to have effect on the date on which the child attains the age of sixteen or at any time after that date but before or on the date on which he attains the age of eighteen, then if, on an application made to the court for an order under this subsection, it appears to the court that –

(a) the child is, will be or (if an order were made under this subsection) would be receiving instruction at an educational establishment or undergoing training for a trade, profession or vocation, whether or not he also is, will be or would be in gainful employment; or

(b) there are special circumstances which justify the making of an order under this subsection,

the court shall have power by order to revive the first mentioned order from such date as the court may specify, not being earlier then the date of the making of the application, and to exercise its power under section 31 of the Act in relation to any order so revived.

(7) Without prejudice to the generality of subsection (6)(c) or (f) above, an order under this section for the payment of a lump sum –

(a) may be made for the purpose of enabling any liabilities or expenses reasonably incurred in maintaining the applicant or any child of the family to whom the application relates before the making of the application to be met;

(b) may provide for the payment of that sum by instalments of such amount as may be specified in the order and may require the payment of the instalments to be secured to the satisfaction of the court.

28 Duration of continuing financial provision orders in favour of party to marriage, and effect of remarriage

(1) Subject in the case of an order made on or after the grant of a decree of divorce or nullity of marriage to the provisions of section 25A(2) above and 31(7) below, the term to be specified in a periodical payments or secured periodical payments order in favour of a party to a marriage shall be such term as the court thinks fit, except that the term shall not begin before or extend beyond the following limits, that is to say –

(a) in the case of a periodical payments order, the term shall begin not earlier than the date of the making of an application for the order, and shall be so defined as not to extend beyond the death of either of the parties to the marriage or, where the order is made on or after the grant of a decree of divorce or nullity of marriage, the remarriage of the party in whose favour the order is made; and

(b) in the case of a secured periodical payments order, the term shall begin not earlier than the date of the making of an application for the order, and shall be so defined as not to extend beyond the death or, where the order is made on or after the grant of such a decree, the remarriage of the party in whose favour the order is made.

(1A) Where a periodical payments or secured periodical payments order in favour of a party to a marriage is made on or after the grant of a decree of divorce or nullity of marriage, the court may direct that that party shall not be entitled to apply under section 31 below for the extension of the term specified in the order.

(2) Where a periodical payments or secured periodical payments order in favour of a party to a marriage is made otherwise than on or after a grant of a decree of divorce or nullity of marriage, and the marriage in question is subsequently dissolved or annulled but the order continues in force, the order shall, notwithstanding anything in it, cease to have effect on the remarriage of that party, except in relation to any arrears due under or on the date of the remarriage.

(3) If after the grant of a decree dissolving or annulling a marriage either party to that marriage remarries whether at any time before or after the commencement of this Act, that party shall not be entitled to apply, by reference to the grant of that decree, for a financial provision order in his or her favour, or for a property adjustment order, against the other party to that marriage.

29 Duration of continuing financial provision orders in favour of children, and age limit on making certain orders in their favour

(1) Subject to subsection (3) below, no financial provision order and no order for a transfer of property under section 24(1)(a) above shall be made in favour of a child who has attained the age of eighteen.

(2) The term to be specified in a periodical payments or secured periodical payments order in favour of a child may begin with the date of the making of an application for the order in question or any later date or a date ascertained in accordance with subsection (5) or (6) below but –

(a) shall not in the first instance extend beyond the date of the birthday of the child next following his attaining the upper limit of the compulsory school age (that is to say, the age that is for the time being that limit by virtue of section 35 of the Education Act 1944 together with any Order in Council made under that section) unless the court considers that in the circumstances of the case the welfare of the child requires that it should extend to a later date; and

(b) shall not in any event, subject to subsection (3) below, extend beyond the date of the child's eighteenth birthday.

(3) Subsection (1) above, and paragraph (b) of subsection (2), shall not apply in the case of a child, if it appears to the court that –

(a) the child is, or will be, or if an order were made without complying with either or both of those provisions would be, receiving instruction at an educational establishment or undergoing training for a trade, profession or vocation, whether or not he is also, or will also be, in gainful employment; or

(b) there are special circumstances which justify the making of an order without complying with either or both of those provisions.

(4) Any periodical payments order in favour of a child shall, notwithstanding anything in the order, cease to have effect on the death of the person liable to make payments under the order, except in relation to any arrears due under the order on the date of the death.

(5) Where –

(a) a maintenance assessment ('the current assessment') is in force with respect to a child; and

(b) an application is made under Part II of this Act for a periodical payments or secured periodical payments order in favour of that child –

(i) in accordance with section 8 of the Child Support Act 1991, and

(ii) before the end of the period of 6 months beginning with the making of the current assessment

the term to be specified in any such order made on that application may be expressed to begin on, or at any time after, the earliest permitted date.

(6) For the purposes of subsection (5) above, 'the earliest permitted date' is whichever is the later of –

(a) the date 6 months before the application is made; or

(b) the date on which the current assessment took effect or, where successive maintenance assessments have been continuously in force with respect to a child, on which the first of those assessments took effect,

(7) Where –

(a) a maintenance assessment ceases to have effect or is cancelled by or under any provision of the Child Support Act 1991; and

(b) an application is made, before the end of the period of 6 months beginning with the relevant date, for a periodical payments or secured periodical payments order in favour of a child with respect to whom that maintenance assessment was in force immediately before it ceased to have effect or was cancelled,

the term to be specified in any such order made on that application may begin with the date on which the maintenance assessment ceased to have effect or, as the case may be, the date with effect from which it was cancelled, or any later date.

(8) In subsection (7)(b) above –

(a) where the maintenance assessment ceased to have effect, the relevant date is the date on which it so ceased; and

(b) where the maintenance assessment was cancelled, the relevant date is the later of –

(i) the date on which the person who cancelled it did so, and

(ii) the date from which the cancellation first had effect.

31   Variation, discharge, etc of certain orders for financial relief

(1) Where the court has made an order to which this section applies, then, subject to the provisions of this section and of section 28(1A) above, the court shall have power to vary or discharge the order or to suspend any provision thereof temporarily and to revive the operation of any provision so suspended.

(2) This section applies to the following orders, that is to say –

(a) any order for maintenance pending suit and any interim order for maintenance;

(b) any periodical payments order;

(c) any secured periodical payments order;

(d) any order made by virtue of section 23(3)(c) or 27(7)(b) above (provision for payment of a lump sum by instalments);

(dd) any deferred order made by virtue of section 23(1)(c) (lump sums) which includes provision made by virtue of –

(i) section 25B(4), or

(ii) section 25C,

(provision in respect of pension rights);

(e) any order for a settlement of property under section 24(1)(b) or for a variation of settlement under section 24(1)(c) or (d) above, being an order made on or after the grant of a decree of judicial separation;

(f) any order made under section 24A(1) above for the sale of property.

(2A) Where the court has made an order referred to in subsection (2)(a), (b) or (c) above, then, subject to the provisions of this section, the court shall have power to remit the payment of any arrears due under the order or of any part thereof.

(2B) Where the court has made an order referred to in subsection (2)(dd)(ii) above, this section shall cease to apply to the order on the death of either of the parties to the marriage.

(3) The powers exercisable by the court under this section in relation to an order shall be exercisable also in relation to any instrument executed in pursuance of the order.

(4) The court shall not exercise the powers conferred by this section in relation to an order for a settlement under section 24(1)(b) or for a variation of settlement under section 24(1)(c) or (d) above except on an application made in proceedings –

(a) for the rescission of the decree of judicial separation by reference to which the order was made, or

(b) for the dissolution of the marriage in question.

(5) No property adjustment order shall be made on an application for the variation of a periodical payments or secured periodical payments order made (whether in favour of a party to a marriage or in favour of a child of the family) under section 23 above, and no order for the payment of a lump sum shall be made on an application for the variation of a periodical payments or secured periodical payments order in favour of a party to a marriage (whether made under section 23 or under section 27 above).

(6) Where the person liable to make payments under a secured periodical payments order has died, an application under this section relating to that order (and to any order made under section 24A(1) above which requires the proceeds of sale of property to be used for securing those payments) may be made by the person entitled to payments under the periodical payments order, or by the personal representatives of the deceased person, but no such application shall, except with the permission of the court, be made after the end of the period of six months from the date on which representation in regard to the estate of that person is first taken out.

(7) In exercising the powers conferred by this section the court shall have regard to all the circumstances of the case, first consideration being given to the welfare while a minor of any child of the family who has not attained the age of eighteen, and the circumstances of the case shall include any change in any of the matters to which the court was required to have regard when making the order to which the application relates, and –

(a) in the case of a periodical payments or secured periodical payments order made on or after the grant of a decree of divorce or nullity of marriage, the court shall consider whether in all the circumstances and after having regard to any such change it would be appropriate to vary the order so that payments under the order are required to be made or secured only for such further period as will in the opinion of the court be sufficient to enable the party in whose favour the order was made to adjust without undue hardship to the termination of those payments;

(b) in a case where the party against whom the order was made has died, the circumstances of the case shall also include the changed circumstances resulting from his or her death.

(8) The personal representatives of a deceased person against whom a secured periodical payments order was made shall not be liable for having distributed any part of the estate of the deceased after the expiration of the period of six months referred to in subsection (6) above on the ground that they ought to have taken into account the possibility that the court might permit an application under this section to be made after that period by the person entitled to payments under the order; but this subsection shall not prejudice any power to recover any part of the estate so distributed arising by virtue of the making of an order in pursuance of this section.

(9) In considering for the purposes of subsection (6) above the question when representation was first taken out, a grant limited to settled land or to trust property shall be left out of account and a grant limited to real estate or to personal estate shall be left out of account unless a grant limited to the remainder of the estate has previously been made or is made at the same time.

(10) Where the court, in exercise of its powers under this section, decides to vary or discharge a periodical payments or secured periodical payments order, then, subject to section 28(1) and (2) above, the court shall have power to direct that the variation or discharge shall not take effect until the expiration of such period as may be specified in the order.

(11) Where –

(a) a periodical payments or secured periodical payments order in favour of more than one child ('the order') is in force;

(b) the order requires payments specified in it to be made to or for the benefit of more than one child without apportioning those payments between them;

(c) a maintenance assessment ('the assessment') is made with respect to one or more, but not all, of the children with respect to whom those payments are to be made; and

(d) an application is made, before the end of the period of 6 months beginning with the date on which the assessment was made, for the variation or discharge of the order,

the court may, in exercise of its powers under this section to vary or discharge the order, direct that the variation or discharge shall take effect from the date on which the assessment took effect or any later date.

(12) Where –

(a) an order ('the child order') of a kind prescribed for the purposes of section 10(1) of the Child Support Act 1991 is affected by a maintenance assessment;

(b) on the date on which the child order became so affected there was in force a periodical payments or secured periodical payments order ('the spousal order') in favour of a party to a marriage having the care of the child in whose favour the child order was made; and

(c) an application is made, before the end of the period of 6 months beginning with the date on which the maintenance assessment was made, for the spousal order to be varied or discharged,

the court may, in exercise of its powers under this section to vary or discharge the spousal order, direct that the variation or discharge shall take effect from the date on which the child order became so affected or any later date.

(13) For the purposes of subsection (12) above, an order is affected if it ceases to have effect or is modified by or under section 10 of the Child Support Act 1991.

(14) Subsections (11) and (12) above are without prejudice to any other power of the court to direct that the variation or discharge of an order under this section shall take effect from a date earlier than that on which the order for variation or discharge was made.

33A Consent orders for financial provision or property adjustment

(1) Notwithstanding anything in the preceding provisions of this Part of this Act, on an application for a consent order for financial relief the court may,

unless it has reason to think that there are other circumstances into which it ought to inquire, make an order in the terms agreed on the basis only of the prescribed information furnished with the application.

(2) Subsection (1) above applies to an application for a consent order varying or discharging an order for financial relief as it applies to an application for an order for financial relief.

(3) In this section –

'consent order', in relation to an application for an order, means an order in the terms applied for to which the respondent agrees;

'order for financial relief' means an order under any of sections 23, 24, 24A or 27 above; and

'prescribed' means prescribed by rules of court.

34   Validity of maintenance agreements

(1) If a maintenance agreement includes a provision purporting to restrict any right to apply to a court for an order containing financial arrangements, then –

(a) that provision shall be void; but

(b) any other financial arrangements contained in the agreement shall not thereby be rendered void or unenforceable and shall, unless they are void or unenforceable for any other reason (and subject to sections 35 and 36 below), be binding on the parties to the agreement.

(2) In this section and in section 35 below –

'maintenance agreement' means any agreement in writing made, whether before or after the commencement of this Act, between the parties to a marriage, being –

(a) an agreement containing financial arrangements, whether made during the continuance or after the dissolution or annulment of the marriage; or

(b) a separation agreement which contains no financial arrangements in a case where no other agreement in writing between the same parties contains such arrangements;

'financial arrangements' means provisions governing the rights and liabilities towards one another when living separately of the parties to a marriage (including a marriage which has been dissolved or annulled) in respect of the making or securing of payments or the disposition or use of any property, including such rights and liabilities with respect to the maintenance or education of any child, whether or not a child of the family.

35 Alteration of agreements by court during lives of parties

(1) Where a maintenance agreement is for the time being subsisting and each of the parties to the agreement is for the time being either domiciled or resident in England and Wales, then, subject to subsection (3) below, either party may apply to the court or to a magistrates' court for an order under this section.

(2) If the court to which the application is made is satisfied either –

(a) that by reason of a change in the circumstances in the light of which any financial arrangements contained in the agreement were made or, as the case may be, financial arrangements were omitted from it (including a change foreseen by the parties when making the agreement), the agreement should be altered so as to make different, or, as the case may be, so as to contain, financial arrangements, or

(b) that the agreement does not contain proper financial arrangements with respect to any child of the family,

then subject to subsections (3), (4) and (5) below, that court may by order make such alterations in the agreement –

(i) by varying or revoking any financial arrangements contained in it, or

(ii) by inserting in it financial arrangements for the benefit of one of the parties to the agreement or of a child of the family,

as may appear to that court to be just having regard to all the circumstances, including, if relevant, the matters mentioned in section 25(4) above; and the agreement shall have effect thereafter as if any alteration made by the order had been made by agreement between the parties and for valuable consideration.

(3) A magistrates' court shall not entertain an application under subsection (1) above unless both the parties to the agreement are resident in England and Wales and at least one of the parties is resident within the commission area (within the meaning of the Justices of the Peace Act 1997) for which the court is appointed, and shall not have power to make any order on such an application except –

(a) in a case where the agreement includes no provision for periodical payments by either of the parties, an order inserting provision for the making by one of the parties of periodical payments for the maintenance of the other party or for the maintenance of any child of the family;

(b) in a case where the agreement includes provision for the making by one of the parties of periodical payments, an order increasing or reducing the rate of, or terminating, any of those payments.

(4) Where a court decides to alter, by order under this section, an agreement by inserting provision for the making or securing by one of the parties to the agreement of periodical payments for the maintenance of the other party or by increasing the rate of the periodical payments which the agreement provides shall be made by one of the parties for the maintenance of the other, the term for which the payments or, as the case may be, the additional payments attributable to the increase are to be made under the agreement as altered by the order shall be such term as the court may specify, subject to the following limits, that is to say –

(a) where the payments will not be secured, the term shall be so defined as not to extend beyond the death of either of the parties to the agreement or the remarriage of the party to whom the payments are to be made;

(b) where the payments will be secured, the term shall be so defined as not to extend beyond the death or remarriage of that party.

(5) Where a court decides to alter, by order under this section, an agreement by inserting provision for the making or securing by one of the parties to the agreement of periodical payments for the maintenance of a child of the family or by increasing the rate of the periodical payments which the agreement provides shall be made or secured by one of the parties for the maintenance of such a child, then, in deciding the term for which under the agreement as altered by the order the payments, or as the case may be, the additional payments attributable to the increase are to be made or secured for the benefit of the child, the court shall apply the provisions of section 29(2) and (3) above as to age limits as if the order in question were a periodical payments or secured periodical payments order in favour of the child.

(6) For the avoidance of doubt it is hereby declared that nothing in this section or in section 34 above affects any power of a court before which any proceedings between the parties to a maintenance agreement are brought under any other enactment (including a provision of this Act) to make an order containing financial arrangements or any right of either party to apply for such an order in such proceedings.

36 Alteration of agreements by court after death of one party

(1) Where a maintenance agreement within the meaning of section 34 above provides for the continuation of payment under the agreement after the death of one of the parties and that party dies domiciled in England and Wales, the surviving party or the personal representatives of the deceased party may, subject to subsection (2) and (3) below, apply to the High Court or a county court for an order under section 35 above.

(2) An application under this section shall not, except with the permission of the High Court or a county court, be made after the end of the period of six months from the date on which representation in regard to the estate of the deceased is first taken out.

(3) A county court shall not entertain an application under this section, or an application for permission to make an application under this section, unless it would have jurisdiction by virtue of section 22 of the Inheritance (Provision for Family and Dependants) Act 1975 (which confers jurisdiction on county courts in proceedings under that Act if the value of the property mentioned in that section does not exceed £5,000 or such larger sum as may be fixed by order of the Lord Chancellor) to hear and determine proceedings for an order under section 2 of that Act in relation to the deceased's estate.

(4) If a maintenance agreement is altered by a court on an application made in pursuance of subsection (1) above, the like consequences shall ensue as if the alteration had been made immediately before the death by agreement between the parties and for valuable consideration.

(5) The provisions of this section shall not render the personal representatives of the decreased liable for having distributed any part of the estate of the deceased after the expiration of the period of six months referred to in subsection (2) above on the ground that they ought to have taken into account the possibility that a court might permit an application by virtue of this section to be made by the surviving party after that period; but this subsection shall not prejudice any power to recover any part of the estate so distributed arising by virtue of the making of an order in pursuance of this section.

(6) Section 31(9) above shall apply for the purposes of subsection (2) above as it applies for the purposes of subsection (6) of section 31.

(7) Subsection (3) of section 22 of the Inheritance (Provision for Family and Dependants) Act 1975 (which enables rules of court to provide for the transfer from a county court to the High Court or from the High Court to a county court of proceedings for an order under section 2 of that Act) and paragraphs (a) and (b) of subsection (4) of that section (provisions relating to

proceedings commenced in county court before coming into force of order of the Lord Chancellor under that section) shall apply in relation to proceedings consisting of any such application as is referred to in subsection (3) above as they apply in relation to proceedings for an order under section 2 of that Act.

37 Avoidance of transactions intended to prevent or reduce financial relief

(1) For the purposes of this section 'financial relief' means relief under any of the provisions of sections 22, 23, 24, 27, 31 (except subsection (6)) and 35 above, and any reference in this section to defeating a person's claim for financial relief is a reference to preventing financial relief from being granted to that person, or to that person for the benefit of a child of the family, or reducing the amount of any financial relief which might be so granted, or frustrating or impeding the enforcement of any order which might be or has been made at his instance under any of those provisions.

(2) Where proceedings for financial relief are brought by one person against another, the court may, on the application of the first-mentioned person –

(a) if it is satisfied that the other party to the proceedings is, with the intention of defeating the claim for financial relief, about to make any disposition or to transfer out of the jurisdiction or otherwise deal with any property, make such order as it thinks fit for restraining the other party from so doing or otherwise for protecting the claim;

(b) if it is satisfied that the other party has, with that intention, made a reviewable disposition and that if the disposition were set aside financial relief or different financial relief would be granted to the applicant, make an order setting aside the disposition;

(c) if it is satisfied, in a case where an order has been obtained under any of the provisions mentioned in subsection (1) above by the applicant against the other party, that the other party has, with that intention, made a reviewable disposition, make an order setting aside the disposition;

and an application for the purposes of paragraph (b) above shall be made in the proceedings for the financial relief in question.

(3) Where the court makes an order under subsection (2)(b) or (c) above setting aside a disposition it shall give such consequential directions as it thinks fit for giving effect to the order (including directions requiring the making of any payments or the disposal of any property).

(4) Any disposition made by the other party to the proceedings for financial

relief in question (whether before or after the commencement of those proceedings) is a reviewable disposition for the purposes of subsection (2)(b) and (c) above unless it was made for valuable consideration (other than marriage) to a person who, at the time of the disposition, acted in relation to it in good faith and without notice of any intention on the part of the other party to defeat the applicant's claim for financial relief.

(5) Where an application is made under this section with respect to a disposition which took place less than three years before the date of the application or with respect to a disposition or other dealing with property which is about to take place and the court is satisfied –

(a) in a case falling within subsection (2)(a) or (b) above, that the disposition or other dealing would (apart from this section) have the consequence, or

(b) in a case falling within subsection (2)(c) above, that the disposition has had the consequence,

of defeating the applicant's claim for financial relief, it shall be presumed, unless the contrary is shown, that the person who disposed of or is about to dispose of or deal with the property did so or, as the case may be, is about to do so, with the intention of defeating the applicant's claim for financial relief.

(6) In this claim 'disposition' does not include any provision contained in a will or codicil but, with that exception, includes any conveyance, assurance or gift of property of any description, whether made by an instrument or otherwise.

(7) This section does not apply to a disposition made before 1 January 1968.

38   Order for repayment in certain cases of sums paid after cessation of order by reason of remarriage

(1) Where –

(a) a periodical payments or secured periodical payments order in favour of a party to a marriage (hereafter in this section referred to as 'a payments order') has ceased to have effect by reason of the remarriage of that party, and

(b) the person liable to make payments under the order or his or her personal representatives made payments in accordance with it in respect of a period after the date of the remarriage in the mistaken belief that the order was still subsisting,

the person so liable or his or her personal representatives shall not be entitled to bring proceedings in respect of a cause of action arising out of the circumstances mentioned in paragraphs (a) and (b) above against the person entitled to payments under the order or her or his personal representatives, but may instead make an application against that person or her or his personal representatives under this section.

(2) On an application under this section the court may order the respondent to pay to the applicant a sum equal to the amount of the payments made in respect of the period mentioned in subsection (1)(b) above or, if it appears to the court that it would be unjust to make that order, it may either order the respondent to pay to the applicant such lesser sum as it thinks fit or dismiss the application.

(3) An application under this section may be made in proceedings in the High Court or a county court for leave to enforce, or the enforcement of, payment of arrears under the order in question, but when not made in such proceedings shall be made to a county court; and accordingly references in this section to the court are references to the High Court or a county court, as the circumstances require.

(4) The jurisdiction conferred on a county court by this section shall be exercisable notwithstanding that by reason of the amount claimed in the application the jurisdiction would not but for this subsection be exercisable by a county court.

(5) An order under this section for the payment of any sum may provide for the payment of that sum by instalments of such amount as may be specified in the order.

(6) The clerk of a magistrates' court to whom any payments under a payments order are required to be made, and the collecting officer under an attachment of earnings order made to secure payments under a payments order, shall not be liable –

(a) in the case of the clerk, for any act done by him in pursuance of the payments order after the date on which that order ceased to have effect by reason of the remarriage of the person entitled to payments under it, and

(b) in the case of the collecting officer, for any act done by him after that date in accordance with any enactment or rule of court specifying how payments made to him in compliance with the attachment of earnings order are to be dealt with,

if, but only if, the act was one which he would have been under a duty to do had the payments order not so ceased to have effect and the act was done before notice in writing of the fact that the person so entitled had remarried was given to him by or on behalf of that person, the person liable to make payments under the payments order or the personal representatives of either of those persons.

(7) In this section 'collecting officer', in relation to an attachment of earnings order, means the officer of the High Court, the registrar of a county court or the clerk of a magistrates' court to whom a person makes payments in compliance with the order.

39 Settlement, etc made in compliance with a property adjustment order may be avoided on bankruptcy of settlor

The fact that a settlement or transfer of property had to be made in order to comply with a property adjustment order shall not prevent that settlement or transfer from being a transaction in respect of which an order may be made under section 339 or section 340 of the Insolvency Act 1986 (transactions at an undervalue and preferences).

41 Restrictions on decrees for dissolution, annulment or separation affecting children

(1) In any proceedings for a decree of divorce or nullity of marriage, or a decree of judicial separation, the court shall consider –

(a) whether there are any children of the family to whom this section applies; and

(b) where there are any such children, whether (in the light of the arrangements which have been, or are proposed to be, made for their upbringing and welfare) it should exercise any of its powers under the Children Act 1989 with respect to any of them.

(2) Where, in any case to which this section applies, it appears to the court that –

(a) the circumstances of the case require it, or are likely to require it, to exercise any of its powers under the Act of 1989 with respect to any such child;

(b) it is not in a position to exercise that power or (as the case may be) those powers without giving further consideration to the case; and

(c) there are exceptional circumstances which make it desirable in the interests of the child that the court should give a direction under this section,

it may direct that the decree of divorce or nullity is not to be made absolute, or that the decree of judicial separation is not to be granted, until the court orders otherwise.

(3) This section applies to –

(a) any child of the family who has not reached the age of sixteen at the date when the court considers the case in accordance with the requirements of this section; and

(b) any child of the family who has reached that age at that date and in relation to whom the court directs that this section shall apply.

47 Matrimonial relief and declarations of validity in respect of polygamous marriages

(1) A court in England and Wales shall not be precluded from granting matrimonial relief or making a declaration concerning the validity of a marriage by reason only that either party to the marriage is, or has during the subsistence of the marriage been, married to more than one person.

(2) In this section 'matrimonial relief' means –

(a) any decree under Part I of this Act;

(b) a financial provision order under section 27 above;

(c) an order under section 35 above altering a maintenance agreement;

(d) an order under any provision of this Act which confers a power exercisable in connection with, or in connection with proceedings for, any such decree or order as is mentioned in paragraphs (a) to (c) above;

(dd) an order under Part III of the Matrimonial and Family Proceedings Act 1984;

(e) an order under Part I of the Domestic Proceedings and Magistrates' Courts Act 1978.

(3) In this section 'a declaration concerning the validity of a marriage' means any declaration under Part III of the Family Law Act 1986 involving a determination as to the validity of a marriage.

(4) Provision may be made by rules of court –

(a) for requiring notice of proceedings brought by virtue of this section to be served on any additional spouse of a party to the marriage in question; and

(b) for conferring on any such additional spouse the right to be heard in the proceedings,

in such cases as may be specified in the rules.

48 Evidence

(1) The evidence of a husband or wife shall be admissible in any proceedings to prove that marital intercourse did or did not take place between them during any period.

(2) In any proceedings for nullity of marriage, evidence on the question of sexual capacity shall be heard in camera unless in any case the judge is satisfied that in the interests of justice any such evidence ought to be heard in open court.

49 Parties to proceedings under this Act

(1) Where in a petition for divorce or judicial separation, or in any other pleading praying for either form of relief, one party to a marriage alleges that the other has committed adultery, he or she shall make the person alleged to have committed adultery with the other party to the marriage a party to the proceedings unless excused by the open court on special grounds from doing so.

(2) Rules of court may, either generally or in such case as may be prescribed by the rules, exclude the application of subsection (1) above where the person alleged to have committed adultery with the other party to the marriage is not named in the petition or other pleading.

(3) Where in pursuance of subsection (1) above a person is made a party to proceedings for divorce or judicial separation, the court may, if after the close of the evidence on the part of the person making the allegation of adultery it is of opinion that there is not sufficient evidence against the person so made a party, dismiss him or her from the suit.

(4) Rules of court may make provision, in cases not falling within subsection (1) above, with respect to the joinder as parties to proceedings under this Act of persons involved in allegations of adultery or other improper conduct made in those proceedings, and with respect to the dismissal from such proceedings of any parties so joined; and rules of court made by virtue of this subsection may make different provision for different cases.

(5) In every case in which adultery with any party to a suit is alleged against any person not made a party to the suit or in which the court considers, in the interest of any person not already a party to the suit, that that person should be made a party to the suit, the court may if it thinks fit allow that person to intervene upon such terms, if any, as the court thinks just.

52 Interpretation

(1) In this Act –

'child', in relation to one or both of the parties to a marriage, includes an illegitimate child of that party or, as the case may be, of both parties;

'child of the family', in relation to the parties to a marriage, means –

(a) a child of both those parties; and

(b) any other child, not being a child who is placed with those parties as foster parents by a local authority or voluntary organisation, who has been treated by both of those parties as a child of their family;

'education' includes training.

'maintenance assessment' has the same meaning as it has in the Child Support Act 1991 by virtue of section 54 of that Act as read with any regulations in force under that section.

(3) For the avoidance of doubt it is hereby declared that references in this Act to remarriage include references to a marriage which is by law void or voidable

NB Sections 25B(3)–(7) and 25C, above, do not affect the powers of the court under s31, above, in relation to any order made before 1 August 1996: s166(6) of the Pensions Act 1995.

As amended by the Domicile and Matrimonial Proceedings Act 1973, ss6(1)(4), 17(2), Schedule 6; Inheritance (Provision for Family and Dependants) Act 1975, s26(1), 89(2)(a), Schedule 2, para 39; Children Act 1975, s108(1)(b), Schedule 4, Pt I; Domestic Proceedings and Magistrates' Courts Act 1978, ss62, 63, 89(2)(a), (b), Schedule 2, para 38, Schedule 3; Matrimonial Homes and Property Act 1981, s7, 8(2); Administration of Justice Act 1982, ss16, 51; Matrimonial Homes Act 1983, s12, Schedule 2; Mental Health Act 1983, s148, Schedule 4, para 34; Matrimonial and Family Proceedings Act 1984, ss1, 2, 3, 5(1)-(3), (4), 6, 7, 46(1), Schedule 1, paras 10, 11, 12, 13, 15; Insolvency Act 1985, s235(1), Schedule 8, para 23; Insolvency Act 1986, s439(2), Schedule 14; Family Law Act 1986, s68(1), Schedule 1, para 14; Marriage (Prohibited Degrees of Relationship) Act 1986, s6(4); Family Law Reform Act 1987, s33(1), Schedule 2, para 52; Children Act 1989, s108(4), (7), Schedule 12, paras 31, 33, Schedule 15; Maintenance Orders (Backdating) Order 1993, art 2, Schedule 1, paras 1–4; Private International Law (Miscellaneous Provisions) Act 1995, s8(2), Schedule, para 2(1)–(3); Pensions Act 1995, s166; Justices of the Peace Act 1997, s73(2), Schedule 5, para 14.

DOMICILE AND MATRIMONIAL PROCEEDINGS ACT 1973
(1973 c 45)

1   Abolition of wife's dependent domicile

(1) Subject to subsection (2) below, the domicile of a married woman as at any time after the coming into force of this section shall, instead of being the same as her husband's by virtue only of marriage, be ascertained by reference to the same factors as in the case of any other individual capable of having an independent domicile.

(2) Where immediately before this section came into force a woman was married and then had her husband's domicile by dependence, she is to be treated as retaining that domicile (as a domicile of choice, if it is not also her domicile of origin) unless and until it is changed by acquisition or revival of another domicile either on or after the coming into force of this section.

(3) This section extends to England and Wales, Scotland and Northern Ireland.

3   Age at which independent domicile can be acquired

(1) The time at which a person first becomes capable of having an independent domicile shall be when he attains the age of sixteen or marries under that age; and in the case of a person who immediately before 1 January 1974 was incapable of having an independent domicile, but had then attained the age of sixteen or been married, it shall be that date.

(2) This section extends to England and Wales and Northern Ireland (but not to Scotland).

4   Dependent domicile of child not living with his father

(1) Subsection (2) of this section shall have effect with respect to the dependent domicile of a child as at any time after the coming into force of this section when his father and mother are alive but living apart.

(2) The child's domicile as at that time shall be that of his mother if –

(a) he then has his home with her and has no home with his father; or

(b) he has at any time had her domicile by virtue of paragraph (a) above and has not since had a home with his father.

(3) As at any time after the coming into force of this section, the domicile of a child whose mother is dead shall be that which she last had before she died if at her death he had her domicile by virtue of subsection (2) above and he has not since had a home with his father.

(4) Nothing in this section prejudices any existing rule of law as to the cases in which a child's domicile is regarded as being, by dependence, that of his mother.

(5) In this section, 'child' means a person incapable of having an independent domicile.

(6) This section extends to England and Wales, Scotland and Northern Ireland.

5   Jurisdiction of High Court and county courts

(1) Subsections (2) to (5) below shall have effect, subject to section 6(3) and (4) of this Act, with respect to the jurisdiction of the court to entertain –

(a) proceedings for divorce, judicial separation or nullity of marriage; and

(b) proceedings for death to be presumed and a marriage to be dissolved in pursuance of section 19 of the Matrimonial Causes Act 1973;

and in this Part of this Act 'the court' means the High Court and a divorce county court within the meaning of Part V of the Matrimonial and Family Proceedings Act 1984.

(2) The court shall have jurisdiction to entertain proceedings for divorce or judicial separation if (and only if) either of the parties to the marriage –

(a) is domiciled in England and Wales on the date when the proceedings are begun; or

(b) was habitually resident in England and Wales throughout the period of one year ending with that date.

(3) The court shall have jurisdiction to entertain proceedings for nullity of marriage if (and only if) either of the parties to the marriage –

(a) is domiciled in England and Wales on the date when the proceedings are begun; or

(b) was habitually resident in England and Wales throughout the period of one year ending with that date; or

(c) died before that date and either –

(i) was at death domiciled in England and Wales, or

(ii) had been habitually resident in England and Wales throughout the period of one year ending with the date of death.

(4) The court shall have jurisdiction to entertain proceedings for death to be presumed and a marriage to be dissolved if (and only if) the petitioner –

(a) is domiciled in England and Wales on the date when the proceedings are begun; or

(b) was habitually resident in England and Wales throughout the period of one year ending with that date.

(5) The court shall, at any time when proceedings are pending in respect of which it has jurisdiction by virtue of subsection (2) or (3) above (or of this subsection), also have jurisdiction to entertain other proceedings, in respect of the same marriage, for divorce, judicial separation or nullity of marriage, notwithstanding that jurisdiction would not be exercisable under subsection (2) or (3).

(6) Schedule 1 to this Act shall have effect as to the cases in which matrimonial proceedings in England and Wales are to be, or may be, stayed by the court where there are concurrent proceedings elsewhere in respect of the same marriage, and as to the other matters dealt with in that Schedule; but nothing in the Schedule –

(a) requires or authorises a stay of proceedings which are pending when this section comes into force; or

(b) prejudices any power to stay proceedings which is exercisable by the court apart from the Schedule.

SCHEDULE 1

1. The following five paragraphs have effect for the interpretation of this Schedule.

2. 'Matrimonial proceedings' means any proceedings so far as they are one or more of the five following kinds, namely, proceedings for –

divorce,

judicial separation,

nullity of marriage,

a declaration as to the validity of a marriage of the petitioner, and

a declaration as to the subsistence of such a marriage.

3. (1) 'Another jurisdiction' means any country outside England and Wales.

(2) 'Related jurisdiction' means any of the following countries, namely, Scotland, Northern Ireland, Jersey, Guernsey and the Isle of Man (the reference to Guernsey being treated as including Alderney and Sark).

4. (1) References to the trial or first trial in any proceedings do not include references to the separate trial of an issue as to jurisdiction only.

(2) For purposes of this Schedule, proceedings in the court are continuing if they are pending and not stayed.

5. Any reference in this Schedule to proceedings in another jurisdiction is to proceedings in a court of that jurisdiction, and to any other proceedings in that jurisdiction, which are of a description prescribed for the purposes of this paragraph; and provision may be made by rules of court as to when proceedings of any description in another jurisdiction are continuing for the purposes of this Schedule.

6. 'Prescribed' means prescribed by rules of court.

7. While matrimonial proceedings are pending in the court in respect of a marriage and the trial or first trial in those proceedings has not begun, it shall be the duty of any person who is a petitioner in the proceedings, or is a respondent and has in his answer included a prayer for relief to furnish, in such manner and to such persons and on such occasions as may be prescribed, such particulars as may be prescribed of any proceedings which –

(a) he knows to be continuing in another jurisdiction; and

(b) are in respect of that marriage or capable of affecting its validity or subsistence.

8. (1) Where before the beginning of the trial or first trial in any proceedings for divorce which are continuing in the court it appears to the court on the application of a party to the marriage –

(a) that in respect of the same marriage proceedings for divorce or nullity of marriage are continuing in a related jurisdiction; and

(b) that the parties to the marriage have resided together after its celebration; and

(c) that the place where they resided together when the proceedings in the court were begun or, if they did not then reside together, where they last resided together before those proceedings were begun, is in that jurisdiction; and

(d) that either of the said parties was habitually resident in that jurisdiction throughout the year ending with the date on which they last resided together before the date on which the proceedings in the court were begun,

it shall be the duty of the court, subject to paragraph 10(2) below, to order that the proceedings in the court be stayed.

(2) References in sub-paragraph (1) above to the proceedings in the court are, in the case of proceedings which are not only proceedings for divorce, to the proceedings so far as they are proceedings for divorce.

9. (1) Where before the beginning of the trial or first trial in any matrimonial proceedings which are continuing in the court it appears to the court –

(a) that any proceedings in respect of the marriage in question, or capable of affecting its validity or subsistence, are continuing in another jurisdiction; and

(b) that the balance of fairness (including convenience) as between the parties to the marriage is such that it is appropriate for the proceedings in that jurisdiction to be disposed of before further steps are taken in the proceedings in the court or in those proceedings so far as they consist of a particular kind of matrimonial proceedings,

the court may then, if it thinks fit, order that the proceedings in the court be stayed or, as the case may be, that those proceedings be stayed so far as they consist of proceedings of that kind.

(2) In considering the balance of fairness and convenience for the purposes of sub-paragraph (1)(b) above, the court shall have regard to all factors appearing to be relevant, including the convenience of witnesses and any delay or expense which may result from the proceedings being stayed, or not being stayed.

(3) In the case of any proceedings so far as they are proceedings for divorce, the court shall not exercise the power conveyed on it by sub-paragraph (1) above while an application under paragraph 8 above in respect of the proceedings is pending.

(4) If, at any time after the beginning of the trial or first trial in any matrimonial proceedings which are pending in the court, the court declares

by order that it is satisfied that a person has failed to perform the duty imposed on him in respect of the proceedings by paragraph 7 above, sub-paragraph (1) above shall have effect in relation to those proceedings, and to the other proceedings by reference to which the declaration is made, as if the words 'before the beginning of the trial or first trial' were omitted; but no action shall lie in respect of the failure of a person to perform such a duty.

As amended by the Children Act 1975, s108(1)(b), Schedule 4, Pt I; Matrimonial and Family Proceedings Act 1984, s46(1), Schedule 1, para 17.

INHERITANCE (PROVISON FOR FAMILY AND DEPENDANTS) ACT 1975

(1975 c 63)

1   Application for financial provision from deceased's estate

(1) Where after the commencement of this Act a person dies domiciled in England and Wales and is survived by any of the following persons –

(a) the wife or husband of the deceased;

(b) a former wife or former husband of the deceased who has not remarried;

(ba) any person (not being a person included in paragraph (a) or (b) above) to whom subsection (1A) below applies;

(c) a child of the deceased;

(d) any person (not being a child of the deceased) who, in the case of any marriage to which the deceased was at any time a party, was treated by the deceased as a child of the family in relation to that marriage;

(e) any person (not being a person included in the foregoing paragraphs of this subsection) who immediately before the death of the deceased was being maintained, either wholly or partly, by the deceased;

that person may apply to the court for an order under section 2 of this Act on the ground that the disposition of the deceased's estate effected by his will or the law relating to intestacy, or the combination of his will and that law, is not such as to make reasonable financial provision for the applicant.

(1A) This subsection applies to a person if the deceased died on or after 1st January 1996 and, during the whole of the period of two years ending immediately before the date when the deceased died, the person was living –

(a) in the same household as the deceased, and

(b) as the husband or wife of the deceased.

(2) In this Act 'reasonable financial provision' –

(a) in the case of an application made by virtue of subsection (1)(a) above by the husband or wife of the deceased (except where the marriage with the deceased was the subject of a decree of judicial separation and at the date of death the decree was in force and the separation was continuing), means such financial provision as it would be reasonable in all the circumstances of the case for a husband or wife to receive, whether or not that provision is required for his or her maintenance;

(b) in the case of any other application made by virtue of subsection (1) above, means such financial provision as it would be reasonable in all the circumstances of the case for the applicant to receive for his maintenance.

(3) For the purposes of subsection (1)(e) above, a person shall be treated as being maintained by the deceased, either wholly or partly, as the case may be, if the deceased, otherwise than for full valuable consideration, was making a substantial contribution in money or money's worth towards the reasonable needs of that person.

2 Powers of court to make orders

(1) Subject to the provisions of this Act, where an application is made for an order under this section, the court may, if it is satisfied that the disposition of the deceased's estate effected by his will or the law relating to intestacy, or the combination of his will and that law, is not such as to make reasonable financial provision for the applicant, make any one or more of the following orders –

(a) an order for the making to the applicant out of the net estate of the deceased of such periodical payments and for such term as may be specified in the order;

(b) an order for the payment to the applicant out of that estate of a lump sum of such amount as may be so specified;

(c) an order for the transfer to the applicant of such property comprised in that estate as may be so specified;

(d) an order for the settlement for the benefit of the applicant of such property comprised in that estate as may be so specified;

(e) an order for the acquisition out of property comprised in that estate of such property as may be so specified and for the transfer of the property so acquired to the applicant or for the settlement thereof for his benefit;

(f) an order varying any ante-nuptial or post-nuptial settlement (including such a settlement made by will) made on the parties to a marriage to which the deceased was one of the parties, the variation being for the benefit of the surviving party to that marriage, or any child of that marriage, or any person who was treated by the deceased as a child of the family in relation to that marriage.

(2) An order under subsection (1)(a) above providing for the making out of the net estate of the deceased of periodical payments may provide for –

(a) payments of such amount as may be specified in the order,

(b) payments equal to the whole of the income of the net estate or of such portion thereof as may be so specified,

(c) payments equal to the whole of the income of such part of the net estate as the court may direct to be set aside or appropriated for the making out of the income thereof of payments under this section,

or may provide for the amount of the payments or any of them to be determined in any other way the court thinks fit.

(3) Where an order under subsection (1)(a) above provides for the making of payments of an amount specified in the order, the order may direct that such part of the net estate as may be so specified shall be set aside or appropriated for the making out of the income thereof of those payments; but no larger part of the net estate shall be so set aside or appropriated than is sufficient, at the date of the order, to produce by the income thereof the amount required for the making of those payments.

(4) An order under this section may contain such consequential and supplemental provisions as the court thinks necessary or expedient for the purpose of giving effect to the order or for the purpose of securing that the order operates fairly as between one beneficiary of the estate of the deceased and another and may, in particular, but without prejudice to the generality of this subsection –

(a) order any person who holds any property which forms part of the net estate of the deceased to make such payment or transfer such property as may be specified in the order;

(b) vary the disposition of the deceased's estate effected by the will or the law relating to intestacy, or by both the will and the law relating to intestacy, in such manner as the court thinks fair and reasonable having regard to the provisions of the order and all the circumstances of the case;

(c) confer on the trustees of any property which is the subject of an order under this section such powers as appears to the court to be necessary or expedient.

3 Matters to which court is to have regard in exercising powers under s2

(1) Where an application is made for an order under section 2 of this Act, the court shall, in determining whether the disposition of the deceased's estate

effected by his will or the law relating to intestacy, or the combination of his will and that law, is such as to make reasonable financial provision for the applicant and, if the court considers that reasonable financial provision has not been made, in determining whether and in what manner it shall exercise its powers under that section, have regard to the following matters, that is to say –

(a) the financial resources and financial needs which the applicant has or is likely to have in the foreseeable future;

(b) the financial resources and financial needs which any other applicant for an order under section 2 of this Act has or is likely to have in the foreseeable future;

(c) the financial resources and financial needs which any beneficiary of the estate of the deceased has or is likely to have in the foreseeable future;

(d) any obligations and responsibilities which the deceased had towards any applicant for an order under the said section 2 or towards any beneficiary of the estate of the deceased;

(e) the size and nature of the net estate of the deceased;

(f) any physical or mental disability of any applicant for an order under the said section 2 or any beneficiary of the estate of the deceased;

(g) any other matter, including the conduct of the applicant or any other person, which in the circumstances of the case the court may consider relevant.

(2) Without prejudice to the generality of paragraph (g) of subsection (1) above, where an application for an order under section 2 of this Act is made by virtue of section 1(1)(a) or 1(1)(b) of this Act, the court shall, in addition to the matters specifically mentioned in paragraphs (a) to (f) of that subsection, have regard to –

(a) the age of the applicant and the duration of the marriage;

(b) the contribution made by the applicant to the welfare of the family of the deceased, including any contribution made by looking after the home or caring for the family;

and, in the case of an application by the wife or husband of the deceased, the court shall also, unless at the date of death a decree of judicial separation was in force and the separation was continuing, have regard to the provision which the applicant might reasonably have expected to receive if on the day on which the deceased died the marriage, instead of being terminated by death, had been terminated by a decree of divorce.

(2A) Without prejudice to the generality of paragraph (g) of subsection (1) above, where an application for an order under section 2 of this Act is made by virtue of section 1(1)(ba) of this Act, the court shall in addition to the matters specifically mentioned in paragraphs (a) to (f) of that subsection, have regard to –

(a) the age of the applicant and the length of the period during which the applicant lived as the husband or wife of the deceased and in the same household as the deceased;

(b) the contribution made by the applicant to the welfare of the family of the deceased, including any contribution made by looking after the home or caring for the family.

(3) Without prejudice to the generality of paragraph (g) of subsection (1) above, where an application for an order under section 2 of this Act is made by virtue of section 1(1)(c) or 1(1)(d) of this Act, the court shall, in addition to the matters specifically mentioned in paragraphs (a) to (f) of that subsection, have regard to the manner in which the applicant was being or in which he might expect to be educated or trained, and where the application is made by virtue of section 1(1)(d) the court shall also have regard –

(a) to whether the deceased had assumed any responsibility for the applicant's maintenance and, if so, to the extent to which and the basis upon which the deceased assumed that responsibility and to the length of time for which the deceased discharged that responsibility;

(b) to whether in assuming and discharging that responsibility the deceased did so knowing that the applicant was not his own child;

(c) to the liability of any other person to maintain the applicant.

(4) Without prejudice to the generality of paragraph (g) of subsection (1) above, where an application for an order under section 2 of this Act is made by virtue of section 1(1)(e) of this Act, the court shall, in addition to the matters specifically mentioned in paragraphs (a) to (f) of that subsection, have regard to the extent to which and the basis upon which the deceased assumed responsibility for the maintenance of the applicant, and to the length of time for which the deceased discharged that responsibility.

(5) In considering the matters to which the court is required to have regard under this section, the court shall take into account the facts as known to the court at the date of the hearing.

(6) In considering the financial resources of any person for the purposes of this section the court shall take into account his earning capacity, and in considering the financial needs of any person for the purposes of this section the court shall take into account his financial obligations and responsibilities.

4   Time-limit for applications

An application for an order under section 2 of this Act shall not, except with the permission of the court, be made after the end of the period of six months from the date on which representation with respect to the estate of the deceased is first taken out.

5   Interim orders

(1) Where on an application for an order under section 2 of this Act it appears to the court –

(a) that the applicant is in immediate need of financial assistance, but it is not yet possible to determine what order (if any) should be made under that section; and

(b) that property forming part of the net estate of the deceased is or can be made available to meet the need of the applicant;

the court may order that, subject to such conditions or restrictions, if any, as the court may impose and to any further order of the court, there shall be paid to the applicant out of the net estate of the deceased such sum or sums and (if more than one) at such intervals as the court thinks reasonable; and the court may order that, subject to the provisions of this Act, such payments are to be made until such date as the court may specify, not being later than the date on which the court either makes an order under the said section 2 or decides not to exercise its powers under that section.

(2) Subsections (2), (3) and (4) of section 2 of this Act shall apply in relation to an order under this section as they apply in relation to an order under that section.

(3) In determining what order, if any, should be made under this section the court shall, so far as the urgency of the case admits, have regard to the same matters as those to which the court is required to have regard under section 3 of this Act.

(4) An order made under section 2 of this Act may provide that any sum paid to the applicant by virtue of this section shall be treated to such an extent and in such manner as may be provided by that order as having been paid on account of any payment provided for by that order.

6   Variation, discharge, etc of orders for periodical payments

(1) Subject to the provisions of this Act, where the court has made an order under section 2(1)(a) of this Act (in this section referred to as 'the original

order') for the making of periodical payments to any person (in this section referred to as 'the original recipient'), the court, on an application under this section, shall have power by order to vary or discharge the original order or to suspend any provision of it temporarily and to revive the operation of any provision so suspended.

(2) Without prejudice to the generality of subsection (1) above, an order made on an application for the variation of the original order may –

(a) provide for the making out of any relevant property of such periodical payments and for such term as may be specified in the order to any person who has applied, or would but for section 4 of this Act be entitled to apply, for an order under section 2 of this Act (whether or not, in the case of any application, an order was made in favour of the applicant);

(b) provide for the payment out of any relevant property of a lump sum of such amount as may be so specified to the original recipient or to any such person as is mentioned in paragraph (a) above;

(c) provide for the transfer of the relevant property, or such part thereof as may be so specified, to the original recipient or to any such person as is so mentioned.

(3) Where the original order provides that any periodical payments payable thereunder to the original recipient are to cease on the occurrence of an event specified in the order (other than the remarriage of a former wife or former husband) or on the expiration of a period so specified, then, if, before the end of the period of six months from the date of the occurrence of that event or of the expiration of that period, an application is made for an order under this section, the court shall have power to make any order which it would have had power to make if the application had been made before the date (whether in favour of the original recipient or any such person as is mentioned in subsection (2)(a) above and whether having effect from that date or from such later date as the court may specify).

(4) Any reference in this section to the original order shall include a reference to an order made under this section and any reference in this section to the original recipient shall include a reference to any person to whom periodical payments are required to be made by virtue of an order under this section.

(5) An application under this section may be made by any of the following persons, that is to say –

(a) any person who by virtue of section 1(1) of this Act has applied, or would but for section 4 of this Act be entitled to apply, for an order under section 2 of this Act,

(b) the personal representatives of the deceased,

(c) the trustees of any relevant property, and

(d) any beneficiary of the estate of the deceased.

(6) An order under this section may only affect –

(a) property the income of which is at the date of the order applicable wholly or in part for the making of periodical payments to any person who has applied for an order under this Act, or

(b) in the case of an application under subsection (3) above in respect of payments which have ceased to be payable on the occurrence of an event or the expiration of a period, property the income of which was so applicable immediately before the occurrence of that event or the expiration of that period, as the case may be,

and any such property as is mentioned in paragraph (a) or (b) above is in subsections (2) and (5) above referred to as 'relevant property'.

(7) In exercising the powers conferred by this section the court shall have regard to all the circumstances of the case, including any change in any of the matters to which the court was required to have regard when making the order to which the application relates.

(8) Where the court makes an order under this section, it may give such consequential directions as it thinks necessary or expedient having regard to the provisions of the order.

(9) No such order as is mentioned in section 2(1)(d), (e) or (f), 9, 10 or 11 of this Act shall be made on an application under this section.

(10) For the avoidance of doubt it is hereby declared that, in relation to an order which provides for the making of periodical payments which are to cease on the occurrence of an event specified in the order (other than the remarriage of a former wife or former husband) or on the expiration of a period so specified, the power to vary an order includes power to provide for the making of periodical payments after the expiration of that period or the occurrence of that event.

7   Payment of lump sums by instalments

(1) An order under section 2(1)(b) or 6(2)(b) of this Act for the payment of a lump sum may provide for the payment of that sum by instalments of such amount as may be specified in the order.

(2) Where an order is made by virtue of subsection (1) above, the court shall have power, on an application made by the person to whom the lump sum is payable, by the personal representatives of the deceased or by the trustees

of the property out of which the lump sum is payable, to vary that order by varying the number of instalments payable, the amount of any instalment and the date on which any instalment becomes payable.

8   Property treated as part of 'net estate'

(1) Where a deceased person has in accordance with the provisions of any enactment nominated any person to receive any sum of money or other property on his death and that nomination is in force at the time of his death, that sum of money, after deducting therefrom any inheritance tax payable in respect thereof, or that other property, to the extent of the value thereof at the date of the death of the deceased after deducting therefrom any inheritance tax so payable, shall be treated for the purposes of this Act as part of the net estate of the deceased; but this subsection shall not render any person liable for having paid that sum or transferred that other property to the person named in the nomination in accordance with the directions given in the nomination.

(2) Where any sum of money or other property is received by any person as a donatio mortis causa made by a deceased person, that sum of money, after deducting therefrom any inheritance tax payable thereon, or that other property, to the extent of the value thereof at the date of the death of the deceased after deducting therefrom any inheritance tax so payable, shall be treated for the purposes of this Act as part of the net estate of the deceased; but this subsection shall not render any person liable for having paid that sum or transferred that other property in order to give effect to that donatio mortis causa.

(3) The amount of inheritance tax to be deducted for the purposes of this section shall not exceed the amount of that tax which has been borne by the person nominated by the deceased or, as the case may be, the person who has received a sum of money or other property as a donatio mortis causa.

9   Property held on a joint tenancy

(1) Where a deceased person was immediately before his death beneficially entitled to a joint tenancy of any property, then, if, before the end of the period of six months from the date on which representation with respect to the estate of the deceased was first taken out, an application is made for an order under section 2 of this Act, the court for the purpose of facilitating the making of financial provision for the applicant under this Act may order that the deceased's severable share of that property, at the value thereof immediately before his death, shall, to such extent as appears to the court to

be just in all the circumstances of the case, be treated for the purposes of this Act as part of the net estate of the deceased.

(2) In determining the extent to which any severable share is to be treated as part of the net estate of the deceased by virtue of an order under subsection (1) above, the court shall have regard to any inheritance tax payable in respect of that severable share.

(3) Where an order is made under subsection (1) above, the provisions of this section shall not render any person liable for anything done by him before the order was made.

(4) For the avoidance of doubt it is hereby declared that for the purposes of this section there may be a joint tenancy of a chose in action.

10 Dispositions intended to defeat applications for financial provision

(1) Where an application is made to the court for an order under section 2 of this Act, the applicant may, in the proceedings on that application, apply to the court for an order under subsection (2) below.

(2) Where on an application under subsection (1) above the court is satisfied –

(a) that, less than six years before the date of the death of the deceased, the deceased with the intention of defeating an application for financial provision under this Act made a disposition, and

(b) that full valuable consideration for that disposition was not given by the person to whom or for the benefit of whom the disposition was made (in this section referred to as 'the donee') or by any other person, and

(c) that the exercise of the powers conferred by this section would facilitate the making of financial provision for the applicant under this Act,

then, subject to the provisions of this section and of sections 12 and 13 of this Act, the court may order the donee (whether or not at the date of the order he holds any interest in the property disposed of to him or for his benefit by the deceased) to provide, for the purpose of the making of that financial provision, such sum of money or other property as may be specified in the order.

(3) Where an order is made under subsection (2) above as respects any disposition made by the deceased which consisted of the payment of money to or for the benefit of the donee, the amount of any sum of money or the value of any property ordered to be provided under that subsection shall not exceed the amount of the payment made by the deceased after deducting

therefrom any inheritance tax borne by the donee in respect of that payment.

(4) Where an order is made under subsection (2) above as respects any disposition made by the deceased which consisted of the transfer of property (other than a sum of money) to or for the benefit of the donee, the amount of any sum of money or the value of any property ordered to be provided under that subsection shall not exceed the value at the date of the death of the deceased of the property disposed of by him to or for the benefit of the donee (or if that property has been disposed of by the person to whom it was transferred by the deceased, the value at the date of that disposal thereof) after deducting therefrom any inheritance tax borne by the donee in respect of the transfer of that property by the deceased.

(5) Where an application (in this subsection referred to as 'the original application') is made for an order under subsection (2) above in relation to any disposition, then, if on an application under this subsection by the donee or by any applicant for an order under section 2 of this Act the court is satisfied –

  (a) that, less than six years before the date of the death of the deceased, the deceased with the intention of defeating an application for financial provision under this Act made a disposition other than the disposition which is the subject of the original application, and

  (b) that full valuable consideration for that other disposition was not given by the person to whom or for the benefit of whom that other disposition was made or by any other person,

the court may exercise in relation to the person to whom or for the benefit of whom that other disposition was made the powers which the court would have had under subsection (2) above if the original application had been made in respect of that other disposition and the court had been satisfied as to the matters set out in paragraphs (a), (b) and (c) of that subsection; and where any application is made under this subsection, any reference in this section (except in subsection (2)(b)) to the donee shall include a reference to the person to whom or for the benefit of whom that other disposition was made.

(6) In determining whether and in what manner to exercise its powers under this section, the court shall have regard to the circumstances in which any disposition was made and any valuable consideration which was given therefor, the relationship, if any, of the donee to the deceased, the conduct and financial resources of the donee and all the other circumstances of the case.

(7) In this section 'disposition' does not include –

(a) any provision in a will, any such nomination as is mentioned in section 8(1) of this Act or any donatio mortis causa, or

(b) any appointment of property made, otherwise than by will, in the exercise of a special power of appointment,

but, subject to these exceptions, includes any payment of money (including the payment of a premium under a policy of assurance) and any conveyance, assurance, appointment or gift of property of any description, whether made by an instrument or otherwise.

(8) The provisions of this section do not apply to any disposition made before the commencement of this Act.

11   Contracts to leave property by will

(1) Where an application is made to a court for an order under section 2 of this Act, the applicant may, in the proceedings on that application, apply to the court for an order under this section.

(2) Where on an application under subsection (1) above the court is satisfied –

(a) that the deceased made a contract by which he agreed to leave by his will a sum of money or other property to any person or by which he agreed that a sum of money or other property would be paid or transferred to any person out of his estate, and

(b) that the deceased made that contract with the intention of defeating an application for financial provision under this Act, and

(c) that when the contract was made full valuable consideration for that contract was not given or promised by the person with whom or for the benefit of whom the contract was made (in this section referred to as 'the donee') or by any other person, and

(d) that the exercise of the powers conferred by this section would facilitate the making of financial provision for the applicant under this Act,

then, subject to the provisions of this section and of sections 12 and 13 of this Act, the court may make any one or more of the following orders, that is to say –

(i) if any money has been paid or any other property has been transferred to or for the benefit of the donee in accordance with the contract, an order directing the donee to provide, for the purpose of the making of that financial provision, such sum of money or other property as may be specified in the order;

(ii) if the money or all the money has not been paid or the property or all the property has not been transferred in accordance with the contract, an order directing the personal representatives not to make any payment or transfer any property, or not to make any further payment or transfer any further property, as the case may be, in accordance therewith or directing the personal represent-atives only to make such payment or transfer such property as may be specified in the order.

(3) Notwithstanding anything in subsection (2) above, the court may exercise its powers thereunder in relation to any contract made by the deceased only to the extent that the court considers that the amount of any sum of money paid or to be paid or the value of any property transferred or to be transferred in accordance with the contract exceeds the value of any valuable consideration given or to be given for that contract, and for this purpose the court shall have regard to the value of property at the date of the hearing.

(4) In determining whether and in what manner to exercise its powers under this section, the court shall have regard to the circumstances in which the contract was made, the relationship, if any, of the donee to the deceased, the conduct and financial resources of the donee and all the other circumstances of the case.

(5) Where an order has been made under subsection (2) above in relation to any contract, the rights of any person to enforce that contract or to recover damages or to obtain other relief for the breach thereof shall be subject to any adjustment made by the court under section 12(3) of this Act and shall survive to such extent only as is consistent with giving effect to the terms of that order.

(6) The provisions of this section do not apply to a contract made before the commencement of this Act.

12 Provisions supplementary to ss10 and 11

(1) Where the exercise of any of the powers conferred by section 10 or 11 of this Act is conditional on the court being satisfied that a disposition or contract was made by a deceased person with the intention of defeating an application for financial provision under this Act, that condition shall be fulfilled if the court is of the opinion that, on a balance of probabilities, the intention of the deceased (though not necessarily his sole intention) in making the disposition or contract was to prevent an order for financial provision being made under this Act or to reduce the amount of the provision which might otherwise be granted by an order thereunder.

(2) Where an application is made under section 11 of this Act with respect to

any contract made by the deceased and no valuable consideration was given or promised by any person for that contract then, notwithstanding anything in subsection (1) above, it shall be presumed, unless the contrary is shown, that the deceased made that contract with the intention of defeating an application for financial provision under this Act.

(3) Where the court makes an order under section 10 or 11 of this Act it may give such consequential directions as it thinks fit (including directions requiring the making of any payment or the transfer of any property) for giving effect to the order or for securing a fair adjustment of the rights of the persons affected thereby.

(4) Any power conferred in the court by the said section 10 or 11 to order the donee, in relation to any disposition or contract, to provide any sum of money or other property shall be exercisable in like manner in relation to the personal representative of the donee, and –

(a) any reference in section 10(4) to the disposal of property by the donee shall include a reference to disposal by the personal representative of the donee, and

(b) any reference in section 10(5) to an application by the donee under that subsection shall include a reference to an application by the personal representative of the donee;

but the court shall not have power under the said section 10 or 11 to make an order in respect of any property forming part of the estate of the donee which has been distributed by the personal representative; and the personal representative shall not be liable for having distributed any such property before he has notice of the making of an application under the said section 10 or 11 on the ground that he ought to have taken into account the possibility that such an application would be made.

13 Provisions as to trustees in relation to ss10 and 11

(1) Where an application is made for –

(a) an order under section 10 of this Act in respect of a disposition made by the deceased to any person as a trustee, or

(b) an order under section 11 of this Act in respect of any payment made or property transferred, in accordance with a contract made by the deceased, to any person as a trustee,

the powers of the court under the said section 10 or 11 to order that trustee to provide a sum of money or other property shall be subject to the following limitation (in addition, in a case of an application under section 10, to any provision regarding the deduction of inheritance tax) namely, that the amount of any sum of money or the value of any property ordered to be provided –

(i) in the case of an application in respect of a disposition which consisted of the payment of money or an application in respect of the payment of money in accordance with a contract, shall not exceed the aggregate of so much of that money as is at the date of the order in the hands of the trustee and the value at that date of any property which represents that money or is derived therefrom and is at that date in the hands of the trustee;

(ii) in the case of an application in respect of a disposition which consisted of the transfer of property (other than a sum of money) or an application in respect of the transfer of property (other than a sum of money) in accordance with a contract, shall not exceed the aggregate of the value at the date of the order of so much of that property as is at that date in the hands of the trustee and the value at that date of any property which represents the first mentioned property or is derived therefrom and is at that date in the hands of the trustee.

(2) Where any such application is made in respect of a disposition made to any person as a trustee or in respect of any payment made or property transferred in pursuance of a contract to any person as a trustee, the trustee shall not be liable for having distributed any money or other property on the ground that he ought to have taken into account the possibility that such an application would be made.

(3) Where any such application is made in respect of a disposition made to any person as a trustee or in respect of any payment made or property transferred in accordance with a contract to any person as a trustee, any reference in the said section 10 or 11 to the donee shall be construed as including a reference to the trustee or trustees for the time being of the trust in question and any reference in subsection (1) or (2) above to a trustee shall be construed in the same way.

14 Provision as to cases where no financial relief was granted in divorce proceedings, etc

(1) Where, within twelve months from the date on which a decree of divorce or nullity of marriage has been made absolute or a decree of judicial separation has been granted, a party to the marriage dies and –

(a) an application for a financial provision order under section 23 of the Matrimonial Causes Act 1973 or a property adjustment order under section 24 of that Act has not been made by the other party to that marriage, or

(b) such an application has been made but the proceedings thereon have not been determined at the time of the death of the deceased,

then, if an application for an order under section 2 of this Act is made by that other party, the court shall, notwithstanding anything in section 1 or section 3 of this Act, have power, if it thinks it just to do so, to treat that party for the purposes of that application as if the decree of divorce or nullity of marriage had not been made absolute or the decree of judicial separation had not been granted, as the case may be.

(2) This section shall not apply in relation to a decree of judicial separation unless at the date of the death of the deceased the decree was in force and the separation was continuing.

15 Restriction imposed in divorce proceedings, etc on application under this Act

(1) On the grant of a decree of divorce, a decree of nullity of marriage or a decree of judicial separation or at any time thereafter the court, if it considers it just to do so, may, on the application of either party to the marriage, order that the other party to the marriage shall not on the death of the applicant be entitled to apply for an order under section 2 of this Act.

In this subsection 'the court' means the High Court or, where a county court has jurisdiction by virtue of Part V of the Matrimonial and Family Proceedings Act 1984, a county court.

(2) In the case of a decree of divorce or nullity of marriage an order may be made under subsection (1) above before or after the decree is made absolute, but if it is made before the decree is made absolute it shall not take effect unless the decree is made absolute.

(3) Where an order made under subsection (1) above on the grant of a decree of divorce or nullity of marriage has come into force with respect to a party to a marriage, then, on the death of the other party to this marriage, the court shall not entertain any application for an order under section 2 of this Act made by the first-mentioned party.

(4) Where an order made under subsection (1) above on the grant of a decree of judicial separation has come into force with respect to any party to a marriage, then, if the other party to that marriage dies while the decree is in force and the separation is continuing, the court shall not entertain any application for an order under section 2 of this Act made by the first-mentioned party.

15A Restriction imposed in proceedings under Matrimonial and Family Proceedings Act 1984 on application under this Act

(1) On making an order under section 17 of the Matrimonial and Family Proceedings Act 1984 (orders for financial provision and property adjustment following overseas divorces, etc) the court, if it considers it just to do so, may, on the application of either party to the marriage, order that the other party to the marriage shall not on the death of the applicant be entitled to apply for an order under section 2 of this Act.

In this subsection 'the court' means the High Court or, where a county court has jurisdiction by virtue of Part V of the Matrimonial and Family Proceedings Act 1984, a county court.

(2) Where an order under subsection (1) above has been made with respect to a party to a marriage which has been dissolved or annulled, then, on the death of the other party to that marriage, the court shall not entertain an application under section 2 of this Act made by the first-mentioned party.

(3) Where an order under subsection (1) above has been made with respect to a party to a marriage the parties to which have been legally separated, then, if the other party to the marriage dies while the legal separation is in force, the court shall not entertain an application under section 2 of this Act made by the first-mentioned party.

19   Effect, duration and form of orders

(1) Where an order is made under section 2 of this Act then for all purposes, including the purposes of the enactments relating to inheritance tax, the will or the law relating to intestacy, or both the will and the law relating to intestacy, as the case may be, shall have effect and be deemed to have had effect as from the deceased's death subject to the provisions of the order.

(2) Any order made under section 2 or 5 of this Act in favour of –

(a) an applicant who was the former husband or former wife of the deceased, or

(b) an applicant who was the husband or wife of the deceased in a case where the marriage with the deceased was the subject of a decree of judicial separation and at the date of death the decree was in force and the separation was continuing,

shall, in so far as it provides for the making of periodical payments, cease to have effect on the remarriage of the applicant, except in relation to any arrears due under the order on the date of the remarriage.

(3) A copy of the every order made under this Act, other that an order made under section 15(1) of this Act, shall be sent to the principal registry of the Family Division for entry and filing, and a memorandum of the order shall be endorsed on, or permanently annexed to, the probate or letters of administration under which the estate is being administered.

20 Provisions as to personal representatives

(1) The provisions of this Act shall not render the personal representative of a deceased person liable for having distributed any part of the estate of the deceased, after the end of the period of six months from the date on which representation with respect to the estate of the deceased is first taken out, on the ground that he ought to have taken into account the possibility –

(a) that the court might permit the making of an application for an order under section 2 of this Act after the end of that period, or

(b) that, where an order has been made under the said section 2, the court might exercise in relation thereto the powers conferred on it by section 6 of this Act,

but this subsection shall not prejudice any power to recover, by reason of the making of an order under this Act, any part of the estate so distributed.

(2) Where the personal representative of a deceased person pays any sum directed by an order under section 5 of this Act to be paid out of the deceased's net estate, he shall not be under any liability by reason of that estate not being sufficient to make the payment, unless at the time of making the payment he has reasonable cause to believe that the estate is not sufficient.

(3) Where a deceased person entered into a contract by which he agreed to leave by his will any sum of money or other property to any person or by which he agreed that a sum of money or other property would be paid or transferred to any person out of his estate, then, if the personal representative of the deceased has reason to believe that the deceased entered into the contract with the intention of defeating an application for financial provision under this Act, he may, notwithstanding anything in that contract, postpone the payment of that sum of money or the transfer of that property until the expiration of the period of six months from the date on which representation with respect to the estate of the deceased is first taken out or, if during that period an application is made for an order under section 2 of this Act, until the determination of the proceedings on that application.

23 Determination of date on which representation was first taken out

In considering for the purpose of this Act when representation with respect to the estate of a deceased person was first taken out, a grant limited to settled land or to trust property shall be left out of account, and a grant limited to real estate or to personal estate shall be left out of account unless a grant limited to the remainder of the estate has previously been made or is made at the same time.

24 Effect of this Act on s46(1)(vi) of Administration of Estates Act 1925

Section 46(1)(vi) of the Administration of Estates Act 1925, in so far as it provides for the devolution of property on the Crown, the Duchy of Lancaster or the Duke of Cornwall as bona vacantia, shall have effect subject to the provisions of this Act.

25 Interpretation

(1) In this Act –

'beneficiary', in relation to the estate of a deceased person, means –

> (a) a person who under the will of the deceased or under the law relating to intestacy is beneficially interested in the estate or would be so interested if an order had not been made under this Act, and

> (b) a person who has received any sum of money or other property which by virtue of section 8(1) or 8(2) of this Act is treated as part of the net estate of the deceased or would have received that sum or other property if an order had not been made under this Act;

'child' includes an illegitimate child and a child en ventre sa mere at the death of the deceased;

'the court', unless the context otherwise requires, means the High Court, or where a county court has jurisdiction by virtue of section 22 of this Act, a county court;

'former wife' or 'former husband' means a person whose marriage with the deceased was during the lifetime of the deceased either –

> (a) dissolved or annulled by a decree of divorce or a decree of nullity of marriage granted under the law of any part of the British Islands, or

> (b) dissolved or annulled in any country or territory outside the British

Islands by a divorce or annulment which is entitled to be recognised as valid by the law of England and Wales;

'net estate', in relation to a deceased person, means –

(a) all property of which the deceased had power to dispose by his will (otherwise than by virtue of a special power of appointment) less the amount of his funeral, testamentary and administration expenses, debts and liabilities, including any inheritance tax payable out of his estate on his death;

(b) any property in respect of which the deceased held a general power of appointment (not being a power exercisable by will) which has not been exercised;

(c) any sum of money or other property which is treated for the purposes of this Act as part of the net estate of the deceased by virtue of section 8(1) or (2) of this Act;

(d) any property which is treated for the purposes of this Act as part of the net estate of the deceased by virtue of an order made under section 9 of the Act;

(e) any sum of money or other property which is, by reason of a disposition or contract made by the deceased, ordered under section 10 or 11 of this Act to be provided for the purpose of the making of financial provision under this Act;

'property' includes any chose in action;

'reasonable financial provision' has the meaning assigned to it by section 1 of this Act;

'valuable consideration' does not include marriage or a promise of marriage;

'will' includes codicil.

(2) For the purposes of paragraph (a) of the definition of 'net estate' in subsection (1) above a person who is not of full age and capacity shall be treated as having power to dispose by will of all property of which he would have had power to dispose by will if he had been of full age and capacity.

(3) Any reference in this Act to provision out of the net estate of a deceased person includes a reference to provision extending to the whole of that estate.

(4) For the purpose of this Act any reference to a wife or husband shall be treated as including a reference to a person who in good faith entered into a void marriage with the deceased unless either –

(a) the marriage of the deceased and that person was dissolved or annulled during the lifetime of the deceased and the dissolution or annulment is recognised by the law of England and Wales, or

(b) that person has during the lifetime of the deceased entered into a later marriage.

(5) Any reference in this Act to remarriage or to a person who has remarried includes a reference to a marriage which is by law void or voidable or to a person who has entered into such a marriage, as the case may be, and a marriage shall be treated for the purposes of this Act as a remarriage, in relation to any party thereto, notwithstanding that the previous marriage of that party was void or voidable.

(6) Any reference in this Act to an order or decree made under the Matrimonial Causes Act 1973 or under any section of that Act shall be construed as including a reference to an order or decree which is deemed to have been made under that Act or under that section thereof, as the case may be.

(7) Any reference in this Act to any enactment is a reference to that enactment as amended by or under any subsequent enactment.

As amended by the Administration of Justice Act 1982, s52; Matrimonial and Family Proceedings Act 1984, ss8, 25; Law Reform (Succession) Act 1995, s2(1)–(4); Civil Evidence Act 1995, s15(2), Schedule 2.

LEGITIMACY ACT 1976
(1976 c 31)

1 Legitimacy of children of certain void marriages

(1) The child of a void marriage, whenever born, shall, subject to subsection (2) below and Schedule 1 to this Act, be treated as the legitimate child of his parents if at the time of the insemination resulting in the birth or, where there was no such insemination, the child's conception (or at the time of the celebration of the marriage if later) both or either of the parties reasonably believed that the marriage was valid.

(2) This section only applies where the father of the child was domiciled in England and Wales at the time of the birth or, if he died before the birth, was so domiciled immediately before his death.

(3) It is hereby declared for the avoidance of doubt that subsection (1) above applies notwithstanding that the belief that the marriage was valid was due to a mistake as to law.

(4) In relation to a child born after the coming into force of section 28 of the Family Law Reform Act 1987, it shall be presumed for the purposes of subsection (1) above, unless the contrary is shown, that one of the parties to the void marriage reasonably believed at the time of the insemination resulting in the birth or, where there was no such insemination, the child's conception (or at the time of the celebration of the marriage if later) that the marriage was valid.

2 Legitimation by subsequent marriage of parents

Subject to the following provisions of this Act, where the parents of an illegitimate person marry one another, the marriage shall, if the father of the illegitimate person is at the date of marriage domiciled in England and Wales, render that person, if living, legitimate from the date of the marriage.

3 Legitimation by extraneous law

Subject to the following provisions of this Act, where the parents of an illegitimate person marry one another and the father of the illegitimate person is not at the time of the marriage domiciled in England and Wales but is domiciled in a country by the law of which the illegitimate person becomes legitimated by virtue of such subsequent marriage, that person, if living, shall in England and Wales be recognised as having been so legitimated from the date of the marriage notwithstanding that, at the time of his birth, his father was domiciled in a country the law of which did not permit legitimation by subsequent marriage.

4 Legitimation of adopted child

(1) Section 39 of the Adoption Act 1976 does not prevent an adopted child being legitimated under section 2 or 3 above if either natural parent is the sole adoptive parent.

(2) Where an adopted child (with a sole adoptive parent) is legitimated –

(a) subsection (2) of the said section 39 shall not apply after the legitimation to the natural relationship with the other natural parent, and

(b) revocation of the adoption order in consequence of the legitimation shall not affect sections 39, 41 or 42 of the Adoption Act 1976 as it applies to any instrument made before the date of legitimation.

5 Rights of legitimated persons and others to take interests in property

(1) Subject to any contrary indication, the rules of construction contained in this section apply to any instrument other than an existing instrument, so far as the instrument contains a disposition of property.

(2) For the purposes of this section, provisions of the law of intestate succession applicable to the estate of a deceased person shall be treated as if contained in an instrument executed by him (while of full capacity) immediately before his death.

(3) A legitimated person, and any other person, shall be entitled to take any interest as if the legitimated person had been born legitimate.

(4) A disposition which depends on the date of birth of a child or children of the parent or parents shall be construed as if –

(a) a legitimated child had been born on the date of legitimation,

(b) two or more legitimated children legitimated on the same date had been born on that date in the order of their actual births,

but this does not affect any reference to the age of a child.

(5) Examples of phrases in wills on which subsection (4) above can operate are –

1. Children of A 'living at my death or born afterwards'.

2. Children of A 'living at my death or born afterwards before any one of such children for the time being in existence attains a vested interest, and who attain the age of 21 years'.

3. As in example 1 or 2, but referring to grandchildren of A, instead of children of A.

4. A for life 'until he has a child' and then to his child or children.

Note. Subsection (4) above will not affect the reference to the age of 21 years in example 2.

(6) If an illegitimate person or a person adopted by one of his natural parents dies, or has died before the commencement of this Act, and –

(a) after his death his parents marry or have married; and

(b) the deceased would, if living at the time of the marriage, have become a legitimated person,

this section shall apply for the construction of the instrument so far as it relates to the taking of interests by, or in succession to, his spouse, children and remoter issue as if he had been legitimated by virtue of the marriage.

(7) In this section 'instrument' includes a private Act settling property, but not any other enactment.

6   Dispositions depending on date of birth

(1) Where a disposition depends on the date of birth of a child who was born illegitimate and who is legitimated (or, if deceased, is treated as legitimated), section 5(4) above does not affect entitlement under Part II of the Family Law Reform Act 1969 (illegitimate children).

(2) Where a disposition depends on the date of birth of an adopted child who is legitimated (or, if deceased, is treated as legitimated) section 5(4) above does not affect entitlement by virtue of section 42(2) of the Adoption Act 1976.

(3) This section applies for example where –

(a) a testator dies in 1976 bequeathing a legacy to his eldest grandchild living at a specified time,

(b) a daughter has an illegitimate child in 1977 who is the first grandchild,

(c) his married son has a child in 1978,

(d) subsequently the illegitimate child is legitimated,

and in all those cases the daughter's child remains the eldest grandchild of the testator throughout.

8 Personal rights and obligations

A legitimated person shall have the same rights, and shall be under the same obligations in respect of the maintenance and support of himself or of any other person, as if he had been born legitimate, and, subject to the provisions of this Act, the provisions of any Act relating to claims for damages, compensation, allowance, benefit or otherwise by or in respect of a legitimate child shall apply in like manner in the case of a legitimated person.

9 Re-registration of birth of legitimated person

(1) It shall be the duty of the parents of a legitimated person or, in cases where re-registration can be effected on information furnished by one parent and one of the parents is dead, of the surviving parent to furnish to the Registrar General information with a view to obtaining the re-registration of the birth of that person within three months after the date of the marriage by virtue of which he was legitimated.

(2) The failure of the parents or either of them to furnish information as required by subsection (1) above in respect of any legitimated person shall not affect the legitimation of that person.

(3) This section does not apply in relation to a person who was legitimated otherwise than by virtue of the subsequent marriage of his parents.

(4) Any parent who fails to give information as required by this section shall be liable on summary conviction to a fine not exceeding level 1 on the standard scale.

As amended by the Adoption Act 1976, s73(2), Schedule 3, paras 23, 24; Criminal Law Act 1977, s31; Criminal Justice Act 1982, s46; Family Law Reform Act 1987, s28.

ADOPTION ACT 1976
(1976 c 36)

1   Establishment of Adoption Service

(1) It is the duty of every local authority to establish and maintain within their area a service designed to meet the needs, in relation to adoption, of –

    (a) children who have been or may be adopted,

    (b) parents and guardians of such children, and

    (c) persons who have adopted or may adopt a child,

    and for that purpose to provide the requisite facilities, or secure that they are provided by approved adoption societies.

(2) The facilities to be provided as part of the service maintained under subsection (1) include –

    (a) temporary board and lodging where needed by pregnant women, mothers or children;

    (b) arrangements for assessing children and prospective adopters and placing children for adoption;

    (c) counselling for persons with problems relating to adoption.

(3) The facilities of the service maintained under subsection (1) shall be provided in conjunction with the local authority's other social services and with approved adoption societies in their area, so that help may be given in a coordinated manner without duplication, omission or avoidable delay.

(4) The services maintained by local authorities under subsection (1) may be collectively referred to as 'the Adoption Service', and a local authority or approved adoption society may be referred to as an adoption agency.

2   Local authorities' social services

The social services referred to in section 1(3) are the functions of a local authority which stand referred to the authority's social services committee, including, in particular but without prejudice to the generality of the foregoing, a local authority's functions –

(a) under the Children Act 1989, relating to family assistance orders, local authority support for children and families, care and supervision and emergency protection of children, community homes, voluntary homes and organisations, registered children's homes, private arrangements for fostering children, childminding and day care for young children and children accommodated by Health Authorities, Special Health Authorities, National Health Service trusts and local education authorities or in residential care, nursing or mental nursing homes or in independent schools; and

(b) under the National Health Service Act 1977, relating to the provision of care for expectant and nursing mothers.

6 Duty to promote welfare of child

In reaching any decision relating to the adoption of a child a court or adoption agency shall have regard to all the circumstances, first consideration being given to the need to safeguard and promote the welfare of the child throughout his childhood; and shall so far as practicable ascertain the wishes and feelings of the child regarding the decision and give due consideration to them, having regard to his age and understanding.

7 Religious upbringing of adopted child

An adoption agency shall in placing a child for adoption have regard (so far as is practicable) to any wishes of a child's parents and guardians as to the religious upbringing of the child.

11 Restriction on arranging adoptions and placing of children

(1) A person other than an adoption agency shall not make arrangements for the adoption of a child, or place a child for adoption, unless –

(a) the proposed adopter is a relative of the child, or

(b) he is acting in pursuance of an order of the High Court.

(3) A person who –

(a) takes part in the management or control of a body of persons which exists wholly or partly for the purpose of making arrangements for the adoption of children and which is not an adoption agency; or

(b) contravenes subsection (1); or

(c) receives a child placed with him in contravention of subsection (1), shall be guilty of an offence and liable on summary conviction to imprisonment for a term not exceeding three months or to a fine not exceeding level 5 on the standard scale or to both.

(4) In any proceedings for an offence under paragraph (a) of subsection (3), proof of things done or of words written, spoken or published (whether or not in the presence of any party to the proceedings) by any person taking part in the management or control of a body of persons, or in making arrangements for the adoption of children on behalf of the body, shall be admissible as evidence of the purpose for which that body exists.

12   Adoption orders

(1) An adoption order is an order giving parental responsibility for a child to the adopters, made on their application by an authorised court.

(2) The order does not affect parental responsibility so far as it relates to any period before the making of the order.

(3) The making of an adoption order operates to extinguish –

(a) the parental responsibility which any person has for the child immediately before the making of the order;

(aa) any order under the Children Act 1989;

(b) any duty arising by virtue of an agreement or the order of a court to make payments, so far as the payments are in respect of the child's maintenance or upbringing for any period after the making of the order.

(4) Subsection (3)(b) does not apply to a duty arising by virtue of an agreement –

(a) which constitutes a trust, or

(b) which expressly provides that the duty is not to be extinguished by the making of an adoption order.

(5) An adoption order may not be made in relation to a child who is or has been married.

(6) An adoption order may contain such terms and conditions as the court thinks fit.

(7) An adoption order may be made notwithstanding that the child is already an adopted child.

13   Child to live with adopters before order is made

(1) Where –

(a) the applicant, or one of the applicants, is a parent, step-parent or relative of the child, or

(b) the child was placed with the applicants by an adoption agency or in pursuance of an order of the High Court,

an adoption order shall not be made unless the child is at least 19 weeks old and at all times during the preceding 13 weeks had his home with the applicants or one of them.

(2) Where subsection (1) does not apply, an adoption order shall not be made unless the child is at least 12 months old and at all times during the preceding 12 months had his home with the applicants or one of them.

(3) An adoption order shall not be made unless the court is satisfied that sufficient opportunities to see the child with the applicant, or, in the case of an application by a married couple, both applicants together in the home environment have been afforded –

(a) where the child was placed with the applicant by an adoption agency, to that agency, or

(b) in any other case, to the local authority within whose area the home is.

14   Adoption by married couple

(1) An adoption order shall not be made on the application of more than one person except in the circumstances specified in subsections (1A) and (1B).

(1A) An adoption order may be made on the application of a married couple where both the husband and the wife have attained the age of 21 years.

(1B) An adoption order may be made on the application of a married couple where –

(a) the husband or the wife –

(i) is the father or mother of the child; and

(ii) has attained the age of 18 years; and

(b) his or her spouse has attained the age of 21 years.

(2) An adoption order shall not be made on the application of a married couple unless –

(a) at least one of them is domiciled in a part of the United Kingdom, or in the Channel Islands or the Isle of Man, or

(b) the application is for a Convention adoption order and section 17 is complied with.

15 Adoption by one person

(1) An adoption order may be made on the application of one person where he has attained the age of 21 years and –

(a) is not married, or

(b) is married and the court is satisfied that –

(i) his spouse cannot be found, or

(ii) the spouses have separated and are living apart, and the separation is likely to be permanent, or

(iii) his spouse is by reason of ill-health, whether physical or mental, incapable of making an application for an adoption order.

(2) An adoption order shall not be made on the application of one person unless –

(a) he is domiciled in a part of the United Kingdom, or in the Channel Islands or the Isle of Man, or

(b) the application is for a Convention adoption order and section 17 is complied with.

(3) An adoption order shall not be made on the application of the mother or father of the child alone unless the court is satisfied that –

(a) the other natural parent is dead or cannot be found or, by virtue of section 28 of the Human Fertilisation and Embryology Act 1990, there is no other parent, or

(b) there is some other reason justifying the exclusion of the other natural parent,

and where such an order is made the reason justifying the exclusion of the other natural parent shall be recorded by the court.

16 Parental agreement

(1) An adoption order shall not be made unless –

(a) the child is free for adoption by virtue of an order made –

(i) in England and Wales, under section 18; or

(b) in the case of each parent or guardian of the child the court is satisfied that –

(i) he freely, and with full understanding of what is involved, agrees unconditionally to the making of an adoption order (whether or not he knows the identity of the applicants); or

(ii) his agreement to the making of the adoption order should be dispensed with on a ground specified in subsection (2).

(2) The grounds mentioned in subsection (1)(b)(ii) are that the parent or guardian –

(a) cannot be found or is incapable of giving agreement;

(b) is withholding his agreement unreasonably;

(c) has persistently failed without reasonable cause to discharge his parental responsibility for the child;

(d) has abandoned or neglected the child;

(e) has persistently ill-treated the child;

(f) has seriously ill-treated the child (subject to subsection (5)).

(3) Subsection (1) does not apply in any case where the child is not a United Kingdom national and the application for the adoption order is for a Convention adoption order.

(4) Agreement is ineffective for the purposes of subsection (1)(b)(i) if given by the mother less than six weeks after the child's birth.

(5) Subsection (2)(f) does not apply unless (because of the ill-treatment or for other reasons) the rehabilitation of the child within the household of the parent or guardian is unlikely.

18   Freeing child for adoption

(1) Where, on an application by an adoption agency, an authorised court is satisfied in the case of each parent or guardian of the child that –

(a) he freely, and with full understanding of what is involved, agrees generally and unconditionally to the making of an adoption order, or

(b) his agreement to the making of an adoption order should be dispensed with on a ground specified in section 16(2),

the court shall make an order declaring the child free for adoption.

(2) No application shall be made under subsection (1) unless –

(a) it is made with the consent of a parent or guardian of a child, or

(b) the adoption agency is applying for dispensation under subsection (1)(b) of the agreement of each parent or guardian of the child, and the child is in the care of the adoption agency.

(2A) For the purposes of subsection (2) a child is in the care of an adoption agency if the adoption agency is a local authority and he is in their care.

(3) No agreement required under subsection (1)(a) shall be dispensed with under subsection (1)(b) unless the child is already placed for adoption or the court is satisfied that it is likely that the child will be placed for adoption.

(4) An agreement by the mother of the child is ineffective for the purposes of this section if given less than six weeks after the child's birth.

(5) On the making of an order under this section, parental responsibility for the child is given to the adoption agency, and subsections (2) to (4) of section 12 apply as if the order were an adoption order and the agency were the adopters.

(6) Before making an order under this section, the court shall satisfy itself, in relation to each parent or guardian of the child who can be found, that he has been given an opportunity of making, if he so wishes, a declaration that he prefers not to be involved in future questions concerning the adoption of the child; and any such declaration shall be recorded by the court.

(7) Before making an order under this section in the case of a child whose father does not have parental responsibility for him, the court shall satisfy itself in relation to any person claiming to be the father that –

(a) he has no intention of applying for –

(i) an order under section 4(1) of the Children Act 1989, or
(ii) a residence order under section 10 of that Act, or

(b) if he did make any such application, it would be likely to be refused.

(8) Subsections (5) and (7) of section 12 apply in relation to the making of an order under this section as they apply in relation to the making of an order under that section.

19 Progress reports to former parents

(1) This section and section 20 apply to any person ('the former parent') who was required to be given an opportunity of making a declaration under section 18(6) but did not do so.

(2) Within the 14 days following the date 12 months after the making of the order under section 18 the adoption agency to which parental responsibility was given on the making of the order, unless it has previously by notice to the former parent informed him that an adoption order has been made in respect of the child, shall by notice to the former parent inform him –

(a) whether an adoption order has been made in respect of the child, and (if not)

(b) whether the child has his home with a person with whom he has been placed for adoption.

(3) If at the time when the former parent is given notice under subsection (2) an adoption order has not been made in respect of the child, it is thereafter the duty of the adoption agency to give notice to the former parent of the making of an adoption order (if and when made), and meanwhile to give the former parent notice whenever the child is placed for adoption or ceases to have his home with a person with whom he has been placed for adoption.

(4) If at any time the former parent by notice makes a declaration to the adoption agency that he prefers not to be involved in future questions concerning the adoption of the child –

(a) the agency shall secure that the declaration is recorded by the court which made the order under section 18, and

(b) the agency is released from the duty of complying further with subsection (3) as respects that former parent.

20 Revocation of s18 order

(1) The former parent, at any time more than 12 months after the making of the order under section 18 when –

(a) no adoption order has been made in respect of the child, and

(b) the child does not have his home with a person with whom he has been placed for adoption,

may apply to the court which made the order for a further order revoking it on the ground that he wishes to resume parental responsibility.

(2) While the application is pending the adoption agency having parental responsibility shall not place the child for adoption without the leave of the court.

(3) The revocation of an order under section 18 ('a section 18 order') operates –

(a) to extinguish the parental responsibility given to the adoption agency under the section 18 order;

(b) to give parental responsibility for the child to –

(i) the child's mother; and

(ii) where the child's father and mother were married to each other at the time of his birth, the father; and

(c) to revive –

(i) any parental responsibility agreement,

(ii) any order under section 4(1) of the Children Act 1989, and

(iii) any appointment of a guardian in respect of the child (whether made by a court or otherwise),

extinguished by the making of the section 18 order.

(3A) Subject to subsection (3)(c), the revocation does not –

(a) operate to revive –

(i) any order under the Children Act 1989, or

(ii) any duty referred to in section 12(3)(b),

extinguished by the making of the section 18 order; or

(b) affect any person's parental responsibility so far as it relates to the period between the making of the section 18 order and the date of revocation of that order.

(4) Subject to subsection (5), if the application is dismissed on the ground that to allow it would contravene the principle embodied in section 6 –

(a) the former parent who made the application shall not be entitled to make any further application under subsection (1) in respect of the child, and

(b) the adoption agency is released from the duty of complying further with section 19(3) as respects that parent.

(5) Subsection (4)(a) shall not apply where the court which dismissed the application gives leave to the former parent to make a further application under subsection (1), but such leave shall not be given unless it appears to the court that because of a change in circumstances or for any other reason it is proper to allow the application to be made.

22   Notification to local authority of adoption application

(1) An adoption order shall not be made in respect of a child who was not placed with the applicant by an adoption agency unless the applicant has, at least three months before the date of the order, given notice to the local authority within whose area he has his home of his intention to apply for the adoption order.

(1A) An application for such an adoption order shall not be made unless the person wishing to make the application has, within the period of two years preceding the making of the application, given notice as mentioned in subsection (1).

(1B) In subsection (1) and (1A) the references to the area in which the applicant or persons has his home are references to the area in which he has his home at the time of giving the notice.

(2) On receipt of such a notice the local authority shall investigate the matter and submit to the court a report of their investigation.

(3) Under subsection (2), the local authority shall in particular investigate –

(a) so far as is practicable, the suitability of the applicant, and any other matters relevant to the operation of section 6 in relation to the application; and

(b) whether the child was placed with the applicant in contravention of section 11.

(4) A local authority which received notice under subsection (1) in respect of a child whom the authority know to be looked after by another local authority shall, not more than seven days after the receipt of the notice, inform that other local authority in writing, that they have received the notice.

23   Reports where child placed by agency

Where an application for an adoption order relates to a child placed by an adoption agency, the agency shall submit to the court a report on the suitability of the applicants and any other matters relevant to the operation of section 6, and shall assist the court in any manner the court may direct.

24   Restrictions on making adoption orders

(1) The court shall not proceed to hear an application for an adoption order in relation to a child where a previous application for a British adoption

order made in relation to the child by the same persons was refused by any court unless –

(a) in refusing the previous application the court directed that this subsection should not apply, or

(b) it appears to the court that because of a change in circumstances or for any other reason it is proper to proceed with the application.

(2) The court shall not make an adoption order in relation to a child unless it is satisfied that the applicants have not, as respects the child, contravened section 57.

25 Interim orders

(1) Where on an application for an adoption order the requirements of sections 16(1) and 22(1) are complied with, the court may postpone the determination of the application and make an order giving parental responsibility for the child to the applicants for a probationary period not exceeding two years upon such terms for the maintenance of the child and otherwise as the court thinks fit.

(2) Where the probationary period specified in an order under subsection (1) is less than two years, the court may by a further order extend the period to a duration not exceeding two years in all.

27 Restrictions on removal where adoption agreed or application made under s18

(1) While an application for an adoption is pending in a case where a parent or guardian of the child has agreed to the making of the adoption order (whether or not he knows the identity of the applicant), the parent or guardian is not entitled, against the will of the person with whom the child has his home, to remove the child from the home of that person except with the leave of the court.

(2) While an application is pending for an order freeing a child for adoption and –

(a) the child is in the care of the adoption agency making the application, and

(b) the application was not made with the consent of each parent or guardian of the child,

no parent or guardian of the child is entitled, against the will of the person with whom the child has his home, to remove the child from the home of that person except with the leave of the court.

(2A) For the purposes of subsection (2) a child is in the care of an adoption agency if the adoption agency is a local authority and he is in their care.

(3) Any person who contravenes subsection (1) or (2) shall be guilty of an offence and liable on summary conviction to imprisonment for a term not exceeding three months or a fine not exceeding level 5 on the standard scale or both.

28   Restrictions on removal where applicant has provided home for five years

(1) While an application for an adoption order in respect of a child made by the person with whom the child has had his home for the five years preceding the application is pending, no person is entitled, against the will of the applicant, to remove the child from the applicant's home except with the leave of the court or under authority conferred by any enactment or on the arrest of the child.

(2) Where a person ('the prospective adopter') gives notice to the local authority within whose area he has his home that he intends to apply for an adoption order in respect of a child who for the preceding five years has had his home with the prospective adopter, no person is entitled, against the will of the prospective adopter, to remove the child from the prospective adopter's home, except with the leave of a court or under authority conferred by any enactment or on the arrest of the child, before –

(a) the prospective adopter applies for the adoption order, or

(b) the period of three months from the receipt of the notice by the local authority expires,

whichever occurs first.

(2A) The reference in subsections (1) and (2) to any enactment does not include a reference to sections 20(8) of the Children Act 1989.

(3) In any case where subsection (1) or (2) applies and –

(a) the child was being looked after by a local authority before he began to have his home with the applicant or, as the case may be, the prospective adopter, and

(b) the child is still being looked after by a local authority,

the authority which are looking after the child shall not remove him from the home of the applicant or the prospective adopter except in accordance with section 30 or 31 or with the leave of a court.

(4) In subsections (2) and (3) 'a court' means a court with jurisdiction to make adoption orders.

(5) A local authority which receive such notice as is mentioned in subsection (2) in respect of a child whom the authority know to be looked after by another local authority shall, not more than seven days after the receipt of the notice, inform that other authority, in writing, that they have received the notice.

(6) Subsection (2) does not apply to any further notice served by the prospective adopter on any local authority in respect of the same child during the period referred to in paragraph (b) of that subsection or within 28 days after its expiry.

(7) Any person who contravenes subsection (1) or (2) shall be guilty of an offence and liable on summary conviction to imprisonment for a term not exceeding three months or a fine not exceeding level 5 on the standard scale or both.

(10) The Secretary of State may by order amend subsection (1) or (2) to substitute a different period for the period of five years mentioned in that subsection (or the period which, by a previous order under this subsection, was substituted for that period).

33 Duty of local authorities to secure well-being of protected children

(1) It shall be the duty of every local authority to secure that protected children within their area are visited from time to time by officers of the authority, who shall satisfy themselves as to the well-being of the children and give such advice as to their care and maintenance as may appear to be needed.

(2) Any officer of a local authority authorised to visit protected children may, after producing, if asked to do so, some duly authenticated document showing that he is so authorised, inspect any premises in the area of the authority in which such children are to be or are being kept.

39 Status conferred by adoption

(1) An adopted child shall be treated in law –

(a) where the adopters are a married couple, as if he had been born as a child of the marriage (whether or not he was in fact born after the marriage was solemnised);

(b) in any other case, as if he had been born to the adopter in wedlock (but not as a child of any actual marriage of the adopter).

(2) An adopted child shall, subject to subsection (3), be treated in law as if he were not the child of any person other than the adopters or adopter.

(3) In the case of a child adopted by one of its natural parents as sole adoptive parent, subsection (2) has no effect as respects entitlement to property depending on relationship to that parent, or as respects anything else depending on that relationship.

(4) It is hereby declared that this section prevents an adopted child from being illegitimate.

(5) This section has effect –

(a) in the case of an adoption before 1 January 1976, from that date, and

(b) in the case of any other adoption, from the date of the adoption.

(6) Subject to the provisions of this Part, this section –

(a) applies for the construction of enactments or instruments passed or made before the adoption or later, and so applies subject to any contrary indication; and

(b) has effect as respects things done, or events occurring, after the adoption, or after 31 December 1975, whichever is the later.

41   Adoptive relatives

(1) A relationship existing by virtue of section 39 may be referred to as an adoptive relationship, and –

(a) a male adopter may be referred to as the adoptive father;

(b) a female adopter may be referred to as the adoptive mother;

(c) any other relative of any degree under an adoptive relationship may be referred to as an adoptive relative of that degree,

but this section does not prevent the term 'parent', or any other term not qualified by the word 'adoptive', being treated as including an adoptive relative.

47   Miscellaneous enactments

(1) Section 39 does not apply for the purposes of the table of kindred and affinity in Schedule 1 to the Marriage Act 1949 or sections 10 and 11 (incest) of the Sexual Offences Act 1956.

50 Adopted Children Register

(1) The Registrar General shall maintain at the General Register Office a register, to be called the Adopted Children Register, in which shall be made such entries as may be directed to be made therein by adoption orders, but no other entries.

(2) A certified copy of an entry in the Adopted Children Register, if purporting to be sealed or stamped with the seal of the General Register Office, shall, without any further or other proof of that entry, be received as evidence of the adoption to which it relates and, where the entry contains a record of the date of the birth or the country or the district and sub-district of the birth of the adopted person, shall also be received as aforesaid as evidence of that date or country or district and sub-district in all respects as if the copy were a certified copy of an entry in the Registers of Births.

(3) The Registrar General shall cause an index of the Adopted Children Register to be made and kept in the General Register Office; and every person shall be entitled to search that index and to have a certified copy of any entry in the Adopted Children Register in all respects upon and subject to the same terms, conditions and regulations as to payment of fees and otherwise as are applicable under the Births and Deaths Registration Act 1953, and the Registration Service Act 1953, in respect of searches in other indexes kept in the General Register Office and in respect of the supply from that office of certified copies of entries in the certified copies of the Registers of Births and Deaths.

(4) The Registrar General shall, in addition to the Adopted Children Register and the index thereof, keep such other registers and books, and make such entries therein, as may be necessary to record and make traceable the connection between any entry in the Registers of Births which has been marked 'Adopted' and any corresponding entry in the Adopted Children Register.

(5) The registers and books kept under subsection (4) shall not be, nor shall any index thereof be, open to public inspection or search, and the Registrar General shall not furnish any person with any information contained in or with any copy or extract from any such registers or books except in accordance with section 51 or under an order of any of the following courts, that is to say –

(a) the High Court;

(b) the Westminster County Court or such other county court as may be prescribed; and

(c) the court by which an adoption order was made in respect of the person to whom the information, copy or extract relates.

(6) In relation to an adoption order made by a magistrates' court, the reference in paragraph (c) of subsection (5) to the court by which the order was made includes a reference to a court acting for the same petty sessions area.

51 Disclosure of birth records of adopted children

(1) Subject to what follows, the Registrar General shall on an application made in the prescribed manner by an adopted person a record of whose birth is kept by the Registrar General and who has attained the age of 18 years supply to that person on payment of the prescribed fee (if any) such information as is necessary to enable that person to obtain a certified copy of the record of his birth.

(2) On an application made in the prescribed manner by an adopted person under the age of 18 years, a record of whose birth is kept by the Registrar General and who is intending to be married in England or Wales, and on payment of the prescribed fee (if any), the Registrar General shall inform the applicant whether or not it appears from information contained in the registers of live births or other records that the applicant and the person whom he intends to marry may be within the prohibited degrees of relationship for the purposes of the Marriage Act 1949.

(3) Before supplying any information to an applicant under subsection (1), the Registrar General shall inform the applicant that counselling services are available to him –

(a) if he is in England and Wales –

(i) at the General Register Office;

(ii) from the local authority in whose area he is living;

(iii) where the adoption order relating to him was made in England and Wales, from the local authority in whose area the court which made the order sat; or

(iv) from any other local authority;

(d) if he is in the United Kingdom and his adoption was arranged by an adoption society –

(i) approved under section 3,

(ii) approved under section 3 of the Adoption (Scotland) Act 1978,

(iii) registered under Article 4 of the Adoption (Northern Ireland) Order 1987,

from that society.

(4) Where an adopted person who is in England and Wales – applies for information under subsection (1) it shall be the duty of the persons and bodies mentioned in subsection (5) to provide counselling for him if asked by him to do so.

(5) The persons and bodies are –

(a) the Registrar General;

(b) any local authority falling within subsection (3)(a)(ii) to (iv);

(c) any adoption society falling within subsection (3)(d) in so far as it is acting as an adoption society in England and Wales.

(6) If the applicant chooses to receive counselling from a person or body falling within subsection (3), the Registrar General shall send to the person or body the information to which the applicant is entitled under subsection (1).

(7) Where a person –

(a) was adopted before 12 November 1975, and

(b) applies for information under subsection (1),

the Registrar General shall not supply the information to him unless he has attended an interview with a counsellor arranged by a person or body from whom counselling services are available as mentioned in subsection (3).

51A Adoption Contact Register

(1) The Registrar General shall maintain at the General Register Office a register to be called the Adoption Contact Register.

(2) The register shall be in two parts –

(a) Part I: Adopted Persons; and

(b) Part II: Relatives.

(3) The Registrar General shall, on payment of such fees as may be prescribed, enter in Part I of the register the name and address of any adopted person who fulfils the conditions in subsection (4) and who gives notice that he wishes to contact any relative of his.

(4) The conditions are that –

(a) a record of the adopted person's birth is kept by the Registrar General; and

(b) the adopted person has attained the age of 18 years and –

(i) has been supplied by the Registrar General with information under section 51; or

(ii) has satisfied the Registrar General that he has such information as is necessary to enable him to obtain a certified copy of the record of his birth.

(5) The Registrar General shall, on payment of such fee as may be prescribed, enter in Part II of the register the name and address of any person who fulfils the conditions in subsection (6) and who gives notice that he wishes to contact an adopted person.

(6) The conditions are that –

(a) a record of the adopted person's birth is kept by the Registrar General; and

(b) the person giving notice under subsection (5) has attained the age of 18 years and has satisfied the Registrar General that –

(i) he is a relative of the adopted person; and

(ii) he has such information as is necessary to enable him to obtain a certified copy of the record of the adopted person's birth.

(7) The Registrar General shall, on receiving notice from any person named in an entry in the register that he wishes the entry to be cancelled, cancel the entry.

(8) Any notice given under this section must be in such form as may be determined by the Registrar General.

(9) The Registrar General shall transmit to an adopted person whose name is entered in Part I of the register the name and address of any relative in respect of whom there is an entry in Part II of the register.

(10) Any entry cancelled under subsection (7) ceases from the time of cancellation to be an entry for the purposes of subsection (9).

(11) The register shall not be open to public inspection or search and the Registrar General shall not supply any person with information entered in the register (whether in an uncancelled or a cancelled entry) except in accordance with this section.

(12) The register may be kept by means of a computer.

(13) In this section –

(a) 'relative' means any person (other than an adoptive relative) who is related to the adopted person by blood (including half-blood) or marriage;

(b) 'address' includes any address at or through which the person concerned may be contacted; and

(c) 'prescribed' means prescribed by the Secretary of State.

52 Revocation of adoptions on legitimation

(1) Where any person adopted by his father or mother alone has subsequently become a legitimated person on the marriage of his father and mother, the court by which the adoption order was made may, on the application of any of the parties concerned, revoke that order.

(2) Where any person legitimated by virtue of section 1 of the Legitimacy Act 1959 had been adopted by his father and mother before the commencement of that Act, the court by which the adoption order was made may, on the application of any of the parties concerned, revoke that order.

(3) Where a person adopted by his father or mother alone by virtue of a regulated adoption has subsequently become a legitimated person on the marriage of his father and mother, the High Court may, upon an application under this subsection by the parties concerned, by order revoke the adoption.

(4) In relation to an adoption order made by a magistrates' court, the reference in subsections (1) and (2) to the court by which the order was made includes a reference to a court acting for the same petty sessions area.

57 Prohibition on certain payments

(1) Subject to the provisions of this section, it shall not be lawful to make or give to any person any payment or reward for or in consideration of –

(a) the adoption by that person of a child;

(b) the grant by that person of any agreement or consent required in connection with the adoption of a child;

(c) the handing over of a child by that person with a view to the adoption of the child; or

(d) the making by that person of any arrangements for the adoption of a child.

(2) Any person who makes or gives, or agrees or offers to make or give, any payment or reward prohibited by this section, or who receives or agrees to receive or attempts to obtain any such payment or reward, shall be guilty of an offence and liable on summary conviction to imprisonment for a term

not exceeding three months or to a fine not exceeding level 5 on the standard scale or to both.

(3) This section does not apply to any payment made to an adoption agency by a parent or guardian of a child or by a person who adopts or proposes to adopt a child, being a payment in respect of expenses reasonably incurred by the agency in connection with the adoption of the child, or to any payment or reward authorised by the court to which an application for an adoption order in respect of a child is made.

(3A) This section does not apply to –

(a) any payment made by an adoption agency to a person who has applied or proposes to apply to a court for an adoption order or an order under section 55 (adoption of children abroad), being a payment of or towards any legal or medical expenses incurred or to be incurred by that person in connection with the application; or

(b) any payment made by an adoption agency to another adoption agency in consideration of the placing of a child with any person with a view to the child's adoption; or

(c) any payment made by an adoption agency to a voluntary organisation for the time being approved for the purposes of this paragraph by the Secretary of State as a fee for the services of that organisation in putting that adoption agency into contact with another adoption agency with a view to the making of arrangements between the adoption agencies for the adoption of a child.

In paragraph (c) 'voluntary organisation' means a body, other than a public or local authority, the activities of which are not carried on for profit.

57A Permitted allowances

(1) The Secretary of State may make regulations for the purpose of enabling adoption agencies to pay allowances to persons who have adopted, or intend to adopt, children in pursuance of arrangements made by the agencies.

(2) Section 57(1) shall not apply to any payment made by an adoption agency in accordance with the regulations.

(3) The regulations may, in particular, make provision as to –

(a) the procedure to be followed by any agency in determining whether a person should be paid an allowance;

(b) the circumstances in which an allowance may be paid;

(c) the factors to be taken into account in determining the amount of an allowance;

(d) the procedure for review, variation and termination of allowances; and

(e) the information about allowances to be supplied by any agency to any person who is intending to adopt a child.

58   Restriction on advertisements

(1) It shall not be lawful for any advertisement to be published indicating –

(a) that the parent or guardian of a child desires to cause a child to be adopted; or

(b) that a person desires to adopt a child; or

(c) that any person (not being an adoption agency) is willing to make arrangements for the adoption of a child.

(2) Any person who causes to be published or knowingly publishes an advertisement in contravention of the provisions of this section shall be guilty of an offence and liable on summary conviction to a fine not exceeding level 5 on the standard scale.

61   Evidence of agreement and consent

(1) Any agreement or consent which is required by this Act to be given to the making of an order or application for an order (other than an order to which section 17(6) applies) may be given in writing, and, if the document signifying the agreement or consent is witnessed in accordance with rules, it shall be admissible in evidence without further proof of the signature of the person by whom it was executed.

(2) A document signifying such agreement or consent which purports to be witnessed in accordance with rules shall be presumed to be so witnessed, and to have been executed and witnessed on the date and at the place specified in the document, unless the contrary is proved.

62   Courts

(1) In this Act, 'authorised court', as respects an application for an order relating to a child, shall be construed as follows.

(2) Subject to subsections (4) to (6), if the child is in England and Wales when the application is made, the following are authorised courts –

(a) the High Court;

(c) any other county court prescribed by rules made under section 75 of the County Courts Act 1984;

(d) a magistrates' court within whose area the child is, and, in the case of an application for an order freeing the child for adoption, a magistrates' court within whose area a parent or guardian of the child is.

(3) If, in the case of an application for an adoption order or for an order freeing a child for adoption, the child is not in Great Britain when the application is made, the High Court is the authorised court.

(4) In the case of an application for a Convention adoption order, paragraphs (b), (c) and (d) of subsection (2) do not apply.

63 Appeals, etc

(2) Subject to subsection (3), where on an application to a magistrates' court under this Act the court makes or refuses to make an order, an appeal shall lie to the High Court.

(3) Where an application is made to a magistrates' court under this Act, and the court considers that the matter is one which would more conveniently be dealt with by the High Court, the magistrates' court shall refuse to make an order, and in that case no appeal shall lie to the High Court.

64 Proceedings to be private

Proceedings under this Act –

(a) in the High Court, may be disposed of in chambers;

(b) in the county court, shall be heard and determined in camera.

65 Guardians ad litem and reporting officers

(1) For the purpose of any application for an adoption order or an order freeing a child for adoption or an order under section 20 or 55 rules shall provide for the appointment, in such cases as are prescribed –

(a) of a person to act as guardian ad litem of the child upon the hearing of the application, with the duty of safeguarding the interests of the child in the prescribed manner;

(b) of a person to act as reporting officer for the purpose of witnessing agreements to adoption and performing such other duties as the rules may prescribe.

(2) A person who is employed –

(a) in the case of an application for an adoption order, by the adoption agency by whom the child was placed; or

(b) in the case of an application for an order freeing a child for adoption, by the adoption agency by whom the application was made; or

(c) in the case of an application under section 20, by the adoption agency with the parental rights and duties relating to the child,

shall not be appointed to act as guardian ad litem or reporting officer for the purposes of the application but, subject to that, the same person may if the court thinks fit be both guardian ad litem and reporting officer.

72   Interpretation

(1) In this Act, unless the context otherwise requires –

'child', except where used to express a relationship, means a person who has not attained the age of 18 years;

'guardian' has the same meaning as in the Children Act 1989;

'local authority' means the council of a county (other than a metropolitan county), a metropolitan district, a London borough or the Common Council of the City of London but, in relation to Wales, means the council of a county or county borough;

'notice' means a notice in writing;

'parent' means, in relation to a child, any parent who has parental responsibility for the child under the Children Act 1989;

'parental responsibility' and 'parental responsibility agreement' have the same meaning as in the Children Act 1989;

'relative' in relation to a child means a grandparent, brother, sister, uncle or aunt, whether of the full blood or half-blood or by affinity, and includes, where the child is illegitimate, the father of the child and any person who would be a relative within the meaning of this definition if the child were the legitimate child of his mother and father;

(1A) In this Act, in determining with what person, or where, a child has his home, any absence of the child at a hospital or boarding school and any other temporary absence shall be disregarded.

(1B) In this Act, references to a child who is in the care of or looked after by a local authority have the same meaning as in the Children Act 1989.

(3) For the purposes of this Act, a person shall be deemed to make arrangements for the adoption of a child if he enters into or makes any agreement or arrangement for, or for facilitating, the adoption of the child by any other person, whether the adoption is effected, or is intended to be effected, in Great Britain or elsewhere, or if he initiates or takes part in any negotiations of which the purpose or effect is the conclusion of any agreement or the making of any arrangement therefor, and if he causes another person to do so.

As amended by the Criminal Justice Act 1982, ss38, 46; Health and Social Services and Social Security Adjudications Act 1983, ss9, 30, Schedule 2, paras 31, 32, 33, 36, Schedule 10, Pt I; Matrimonial and Family Proceedings Act 1984, s46(3), Schedule 3; Family Law Reform Act 1987, s33(1), Schedule 2, para 67; Children Act 1989, ss88(1), 108(7), Schedule 10, Pt I, paras 1, 3, 4, 5, 6(1), (2), (3), 7, 8, 10, 11, 12(a), (b), 13, 14, 20, 21, 30(1), (2), (3)-(5), (7), (8), (9); Human Fertilisation and Embryology Act 1990, s49(5), Schedule 4, para 4; National Health Service and Community Care Act 1990, s66(1), Schedule 9, para 17; Local Government (Wales) Act 1994, s22(4), Schedule 10, para 9; Health Authorities Act 1995, s2(1), Schedule 1, Pt III, para 101.

DOMESTIC PROCEEDINGS AND MAGISTRATES' COURTS ACT 1978

(1978 c 22)

1 Grounds of application for financial provision

Either party to a marriage may apply to a magistrates' court for an order under section 2 of this Act on the ground that the other party to the marriage –

(a) has failed to provide reasonable maintenance for the applicant; or

(b) has failed to provide, or to make a proper contribution towards, reasonable maintenance for any child of the family; or

(c) has behaved in such a way that the applicant cannot reasonably be expected to live with the respondent; or

(d) has deserted the applicant.

2 Powers of court to make orders for financial provision

(1) Where on an application for an order under this section the applicant satisfies the court of any ground mentioned in section 1 of this Act, the court may ,subject to the provisions of this Part of this Act, make any one or more of the following orders, that is to say –

(a) an order that the respondent shall make to the applicant such periodical payments, and for such term, as may be specified in the order;

(b) an order that the respondent shall pay to the applicant such lump sum as may be so specified;

(c) an order that the respondent shall make to the applicant for the benefit of a child of the family to whom the application relates, or to such a child, such periodical payments, and for such term, as may be so specified;

(d) an order that the respondent shall pay to the applicant for the benefit of a child of the family to whom the application relates, or to such a child, such lump sum as may be so specified.

(2) Without prejudice to the generality of subsection (1)(b) or (d) above, an order under this section for the payment of a lump sum may be made for the purpose of enabling any liability or expenses reasonably incurred in maintaining the applicant, or any child of the family to whom the application relates, before the making of the order to be met.

(3) The amount of any lump sum required to be paid by an order under this section shall not exceed £1,000 or such larger amount as the Lord Chancellor may from time to time by order fix for the purposes of this subsection.

Any order made by the Lord Chancellor under this subsection shall be made by statutory instrument and shall be subject to annulment in pursuance of a resolution of either House of Parliament.

3 Matters to which court is to have regard in exercising its powers under s2

(1) Where an application is made for an order under section 2 of this Act, it shall be the duty of the court, in deciding whether to exercise its powers under that section and, if so, in what manner, to have regard to all the circumstances of the case, first consideration being given to the welfare while a minor of any child of the family who has not attained the age of eighteen.

(2) As regards the exercise of its powers under subsection (1)(a) or (b) of section 2, the court shall in particular have regard to the following matters –

(a) the income, earning capacity, property and other financial resources which each of the parties to the marriage has or is likely to have in the foreseeable future, including in the case of earning capacity any increase in that capacity which it would in the opinion of the court be reasonable to expect a party to the marriage to take steps to acquire;

(b) the financial needs, obligations and responsibilities which each of the parties to the marriage has or is likely to have in the foreseeable future;

(c) the standard of living enjoyed by the parties to the marriage before the occurrence of the conduct which is alleged as the ground of the application;

(d) the age of each party to the marriage and the duration of the marriage;

(e) any physical or mental disability of either of the parties to the marriage;

(f) the contributions which each of the parties has made or is likely in the foreseeable future to make to the welfare of the family, including any contribution by looking after the home or caring for the family;

(g) the conduct of each of the parties, if that conduct is such that it would in the opinion of the court be inequitable to disregard it.

(3) As regards the exercise of its powers under subsection (1)(c) or (d) of section 2, the court shall in particular have regard to the following matters –

(a) the financial needs of the child;

(b) the income, earning capacity (if any), property and other financial resources of the child;

(c) any physical or mental disability of the child;

(d) the standard of living enjoyed by the family before the occurrence of the conduct which is alleged as the ground of the application;

(e) the manner in which the child was being and in which the parties to the marriage expected him to be educated or trained;

(f) the matters mentioned in relation to the parties to the marriage in paragraphs (a) and (b) of subsection (2) above.

(4) As regards the exercise of its powers under section 2 in favour of a child of the family who is not the child of the respondent, the court shall also have regard –

(a) to whether the respondent had assumed any responsibility for the child's maintenance and, if he did, to the extent to which, and the basis on which, he assumed that responsibility and to the length of time during which he discharged that responsibility;

(b) to whether in assuming and discharging that responsibility the respondent did so knowing that the child was not his own child;

(c) to the liability of any other person to maintain the child.

4   Duration of orders for financial provision for a party to a marriage

(1) The term to be specified in any order made under section 2(1)(a) of this Act shall be such term as the court thinks fit except that the term shall not begin earlier than the date of the making of the application for the order and shall not extend beyond the death of either of the parties to the marriage.

(2) Where an order is made under the said section 2(1)(a) and the marriage of the parties affected by the order is subsequently dissolved or annulled but the order continues in force, the order shall, notwithstanding anything in it, cease to have effect on the remarriage of the party in whose favour it was made, except in relation to any arrears due under the order on the date of the remarriage.

5 Age limit on making orders for financial provision for children and duration of such orders

(1) Subject to subsection (3) below, no order shall be made under section 2(1)(c) or (d) of this Act in favour of a child who has attained the age of eighteen.

(2) The term to be specified in an order made under section 2(1)(c) of this Act in favour of a child may begin with the date of the making of an application for the order in question or any later date or a date ascertained in accordance with subsection (5) or (6) below but –

(a) shall not in the first instance extend beyond the date of the birthday of the child next following his attaining the upper limit of the compulsory school age (that is to say, the age that is for the time being that limit by virtue of section 35 of the Education Act 1944 together with any Order in Council made under that section) unless the court considers that in the circumstances of the case the welfare of the child requires that it should extend to a later date; and

(b) shall not in any event, subject to subsection (3) below, extend beyond the date of the child's eighteenth birthday.

(3) The court –

(a) may make an order under section 2(1)(c) or (d) of this Act in favour of a child who has attained the age of eighteen, and

(b) may include in an order made under section 2(1)(c) of this Act in relation to a child who has not attained that age a provision for extending beyond the date when the child will attain that age the term for which by virtue of the order any payments are to be made to or for the benefit of that child,

if it appears to the court –

(i) that the child is, or will be, or if such an order or provision were made would be, receiving instruction at an educational establishment or undergoing training for a trade, profession or vocation, whether or not he is also, or will also be, in gainful employment; or

(ii) that there are special circumstances which justify the making of the order or provision.

(4) Any order made under section 2(1)(c) of this Act in favour of a child shall, notwithstanding anything in the order, cease to have effect on the death of the person liable to make payments under the order.

(5) Where –

(a) a maintenance assessment ('the current assessment') is in force with respect to a child; and

(b) an application is made for an order under section 2(1)(c) of this Act

(i) in accordance with section 8 of the Child Support Act 1991; and

(ii) before the end of the period of 6 months beginning with the making of the current assessment,

the term to be specified in any such order made on that application may be expressed to begin on, or at any time after, the earliest permitted date.

(6) For the purposes of subsection (5) above, 'the earliest permitted date' is whichever is the later of –

(a) the date 6 months before the application is made; or

(b) the date on which the current assessment took effect or, where successive maintenance assessments have been continuously in force with respect to a child, on which the first of those assessments took effect.

(7) Where –

(a) a maintenance assessment ceases to have effect or is cancelled by or under any provision of the Child Support Act 1991; and

(b) an application is made, before the end of the period of 6 months beginning with the relevant date, for an order under section 2(1)(c) of this Act in relation to a child with respect to whom that maintenance assessment was in force immediately before it ceased to have effect or was cancelled,

the term to be specified in any such order, or in any interim order under section 19 of this Act, made on that application, may begin with the date on which that maintenance assessment ceased to have effect or, as the case may be, the date with effect from which it was cancelled, or any later date.

(8) In subsection (7)(b) above –

(a) where the maintenance assessment ceased to have effect, the relevant date is the date on which it so ceased; and

(b) where the maintenance assessment was cancelled, the relevant date is the later of –

(i) the date on which the person who cancelled it did so, and

(ii) the date from which the cancellation first had effect.

6   Orders for payments which have been agreed by the parties

(1) Either party to a marriage may apply to a magistrates' court for an order under this section on the ground that either the party making the application or the other party to the marriage has agreed to make such financial provision as may be specified in the application and, subject to subsection (3) below, the court on such an application may, if –

(a) it is satisfied that the applicant or the respondent, as the case may be, has agreed to make that provision, and

(b) it has no reason to think that it would be contrary to the interests of justice to exercise its powers hereunder,

order that the applicant or the respondent, as the case may be, shall make the financial provision specified in the application.

(2) In this section 'financial provision' means the provision mentioned in any one or more of the following paragraphs, that is to say –

(a) the making of periodical payments by one party to the other,

(b) the payment of a lump sum by one party to the other,

(c) the making of periodical payments by one party to a child of the family or to the other party for the benefit of such a child,

(d) the payment by one party of a lump sum to a child of the family or to the other party for the benefit of such a child,

and any reference in this section to the financial provision specified in an application made under subsection (1) above or specified by the court under subsection (5) below is a reference to the type of provision specified in the application or by the court, as the case may be, to the amount so specified as the amount of any payment to be made thereunder and, in the case of periodical payments, to the term so specified as the term for which the payments are to be made.

(3) Where the financial provision specified in an application under subsection (1) above includes or consists of provision in respect of a child of the family, the court shall not make an order under that subsection unless it considers that the provision which the applicant or the respondent, as the case may be, has agreed to make in respect of that child provides for, or makes a proper contribution towards, the financial needs of the child.

(4) A party to a marriage who has applied for an order under section 2 of this Act shall not be precluded at any time before the determination of that application from applying for an order under this section; but if an order is made under this section on the application of either party and either of them has also made an application for an order under section 2 of this Act,

the application made for the order under section 2 shall be treated as if it had been withdrawn.

(5) Where on an application under subsection (1) above the court decides –

(a) that it would be contrary to the interests of justice to make an order for the making of the financial provision specified in the application, or

(b) that any financial provision which the applicant or the respondent, as the case may be, has agreed to make in respect of a child of the family does not provide for, or make a proper contribution towards, the financial needs of that child,

but is of the opinion –

(i) that it would not be contrary to the interests of justice to make an order for the making of some other financial provision specified by the court, and

(ii) that, in so far as that other financial provision contains any provisions for a child of the family, it provides for, or makes a proper contribution towards, the financial needs of that child,

then, if both the parties agree, the court may order that the applicant or the respondent, as the case may be, shall make that other financial provision.

(6) Subject to subsection (8) below, the provisions of section 4 of this Act shall apply in relation to an order under this section which requires periodical payments to be made to a party to a marriage for his own benefit as they apply in relation to an order under section 2(1)(a) of this Act.

(7) Subject to subsection (8) below, the provisions of section 5 of this Act shall apply in relation to an order under this section for the making of financial provision in respect of a child of the family as they apply in relation to an order under section 2(1)(c) or (d) of this Act.

(8) Where the court makes an order under this section which contains provision for the making of periodical payments and, by virtue of subsection (4) above, an application for an order under section 2 of this Act is treated as if it had been withdrawn, then the term which may be specified as the term for which the payments are to be made may begin with the date of the making of the application for the order under section 2 or any later date.

(9) Where the respondent is not present or represented by counsel or solicitor at the hearing of an application for an order under subsection (1) above, the court shall not make an order under this section unless there is produced to the court such evidence as may be prescribed by rules of –

(a) the consent of the respondent to the making of the order,

(b) the financial resources of the respondent, and

(c) in a case where the financial provision specified in the application includes or consists of provision in respect of a child of the family to be made by the applicant to the respondent for the benefit of the child or to the child, the financial resources of the child.

7   Powers of court where parties are living apart by agreement

(1) Where the parties to a marriage have been living apart for a continuous period exceeding three months, neither party having deserted the other, and one of the parties has been making periodical payments for the benefit of the other party or of a child of the family, that other party may apply to a magistrates' court for an order under this section, and any application made under this subsection shall specify the aggregate amount of the payments so made during the period of three months immediately preceding the date of the making of the application.

(2) Where on an application for an order under this section the court is satisfied that the respondent has made the payments specified in the application, the court may, subject to the provisions of this Part of this Act, make one or both of the following orders, that is to say –

(a) an order that the respondent shall make to the applicant such periodical payments, and for such term, as may be specified in the order;

(b) an order that the respondent shall make to the applicant for the benefit of a child of the family to whom the application relates, or to such a child, such periodical payments, and for such term, as may be so specified.

(3) The court in the exercise of its powers under this section –

(a) shall not require the respondent to make payments which exceed in aggregate during any period of three months the aggregate amount paid by him for the benefit of the applicant or a child of the family during the period of three months immediately preceding the date of the making of the application;

(b) shall not require the respondent to make payments to or for the benefit of any person which exceed in amount the payments which the court considers that it would have required the respondent to make to or for the benefit of that person on an application under section 1 of this Act;

(c) shall not require payments to be made to or for the benefit of a child of the family who is not a child of the respondent unless the court considers that it would have made an order in favour of that child on an application under section 1 of this Act.

(4) Where on an application under this section the court considers that the orders which it has the power to make under this section –

(a) would not provide reasonable maintenance for the applicant, or

(b) if the application relates to a child of the family, would not provide, or make a proper contribution towards, reasonable maintenance for that child,

the court shall refuse to make an order under this section, but the court may treat the application as if it were an application for an order under section 2 of this Act.

(5) The provisions of section 3 of this Act shall apply in relation to an application for an order under this section as they apply in relation to an application for an order under section 2 of this Act subject to the modification that for the reference in subsection (2)(c) of the said section 3 to the occurrence of the conduct which is alleged as the ground of the application there shall be substituted a reference to the living apart of the parties to the marriage.

(6) The provisions of section 4 of this Act shall apply in relation to an order under this section which requires periodical payments to be made to the applicant for his own benefit as they apply in relation to an order under section 2(1)(a) of this Act.

(7) The provisions of section 5 of this Act shall apply in relation to an order under this section for the making of periodical payments in respect of a child of the family as they apply in relation to an order under section 2(1)(c) of this Act.

8   Restrictions on making of orders under this Act: welfare of children

Where an application is made by a party to a marriage for an order under section 2, 6 or 7 of this Act, then, if there is a child of the family who is under the age of eighteen, the court shall not dismiss or make a final order on the application until it has decided whether to exercise any of its powers under the Children Act 1989 with respect to the child.

25   Effect on certain orders of parties living together

(1) Where –

periodical payments are required to be made to one of the parties to a marriage (whether for his own benefit or for the benefit of a child of the family) by an order made under section 2 or 6 of this Act or by an interim maintenance order made under section 19 of this Act (otherwise than on an application under section 7 of this Act),

the order shall be enforceable notwithstanding that the parties to the marriage are living with each other at the date of the making of the order or that, although they are not living with each other at that date, they subsequently resume living with each other; but the order shall cease to have effect if after that date the parties continue to live with each other, or resume living with each other, for a continuous period exceeding six months.

(2) Where any of the following orders is made under this Part of this Act, that is to say –

(a) an order under section 2 or 6 of this Act which requires periodical payments to be made to a child of the family, or

(b) an interim maintenance order under section 19 of this Act (otherwise than on an application under section 7 of this Act) which requires periodical payments to be made to a child of the family,

then, unless the court otherwise directs, the order shall continue to have effect and be enforceable notwithstanding that the parties to the marriage in question are living with each other at the date of the making of the order or that, although they are not living with each other at that date, they subsequently resume living with each other.

(3) Any order made under section 7 of this Act, and any interim maintenance order made on an application for an order under that section, shall cease to have effect if the parties to the marriage resume living with each other.

(4) Where an order made under this Part of this Act ceases to have effect by virtue of subsection (1) or (3) above or by virtue of a direction given under subsection (2) above, a magistrates' court may, on an application made by either party to the marriage, make an order declaring that the first mentioned order ceased to have effect from such date as the court may specify.

26 Reconciliation

(1) Where an application is made for an order under section 2 of this Act the court, before deciding whether to exercise its powers under that section, shall consider whether there is any possibility of reconciliation between the parties to the marriage in question; and if at any stage of the

proceedings on that application it appears to the court that there is a reasonable possibility of such a reconciliation, the court may adjourn the proceedings for such period as it thinks fit to enable attempts to be made to effect a reconciliation.

(2) Where the court adjourns any proceedings under subsection (1) above, it may request a probation officer or any other person to attempt to effect a reconciliation between the parties to the marriage, and where any such request is made, the probation officer or that other person shall report in writing to the court whether the attempt has been successful or not, but shall not include in that report any other information.

27 Refusal of order in case more suitable for High Court

Where on hearing an application for an order under section 2 of this Act a magistrates' court is of the opinion that any of the matters in question between the parties would be more conveniently dealt with by the High Court, the magistrates' court shall refuse to make any order on the application, and no appeal shall lie from that refusal; but if in any proceedings in the High Court relating to or comprising the same subject matter as that application the High Court so orders, the application shall be reheard and determined by a magistrates' court acting for the same petty sessions area as the first mentioned court.

28 Powers of High Court and county court in relation to certain orders under Part I

(1) Where after the making by a magistrates' court of an order under this Part of this Act proceedings between, and relating to the marriage of, the parties to the proceedings in which that order was made have been commenced in the High Court or a county court, then, except in the case of an order for the payment of a lump sum, the court in which the proceedings or any application made therein are or is pending may, if it thinks fit, direct that the order made by a magistrates' court shall cease to have effect on such date as may be specified in the direction.

(3) Nothing in this section shall be taken as prejudicing the effect of any order made by the High Court or a county court so far as it implicitly supersedes or revokes an order or part of an order made by a magistrates' court.

29 Appeals

(1) Subject to section 27 of this Act, where a magistrates' court makes or refuses to make, varies or refuses to vary, revokes or refuses to revoke an

order (other than an interim maintenance order) under this Part of this Act, an appeal shall lie to the High Court.

30 Provisions as to jurisdiction and procedure

(1) A magistrates' court shall, subject to section 2 of the Family Law Act 1986 and section 70 of the Magistrates' Courts Act 1980 and any determination of a magistrates' courts committee thereunder, have jurisdiction to hear an application for an order under this Part of this Act if at the date of the making of the application either the applicant or the respondent ordinarily resides within the commission area for which the court is appointed.

(5) It is hereby declared that any jurisdiction conferred on a magistrates' court by this Part of this Act is exercisable notwithstanding that any party to the proceedings is not domiciled in England.

88 Interpretation

(1) In this Act –

'child', in relation to one or both of the parties to a marriage, includes a child whose father and mother were not married to each other at the time of his birth;

'child of the family', in relation to the parties to a marriage, means –

> (a) a child of both of those parties; and
>
> (b) any other child, not being a child who is placed with those parties as foster parents by a local authority or voluntary organisation, who has been treated by both of those parties as a child of their family; ...

'magistrates' court maintenance order' has the same meaning as in section 150(1) of the Magistrates' Courts Act 1980 [ie, a maintenance order enforceable by a magistrates' court];

'maintenance assessment' has the same meaning as it has in the Child Support Act 1991 by virtue of section 54 of that Act as read with any regulations in force under that section; ...

(2) References in this Act to the parties to a marriage living with each other shall be construed as references to their living with each other in the same household.

(3) For the avoidance of doubt it is hereby declared that references in this Act to remarriage include references to a marriage which is by law void or voidable.

As amended by the Magistrates' Courts Act 1980, s154, Schedule 7, paras 159, 163; Matrimonial Homes Act 1983, s12, Schedule 2; Matrimonial and Family Proceedings Act 1984, ss9, 10, 46(1), Schedule 1, paras 21, 22; Family Law Act 1986, s68(1), Schedule 1, para 24; Family Law Reform Act 1987, s33(1), Schedule 2, para 7; Children Act 1989, s108(5), (7), Schedule 13, paras 3-36, 41, s92(1), (11), Schedule 11, Pt II, para 6, Schedule 15; Courts and Legal Services Act 1990, s125(3), (7), Schedule 18, para 21, Schedule 20; Maintenance Orders (Backdating) Order 1993, art 2, Schedule 1, paras 4, 5, 9; Police and Magistrates' Courts Act 1994, s91(1), Schedule 8, Pt II, para 29; Family Law Act 1996, s66(3), Schedule 10.

INTERPRETATION ACT 1978
(1978 C 30)

5   Definitions

In any Act, unless the contrary intention appears, words and expressions listed in Schedule 1 to this Act are to be construed according to that Schedule.

SCHEDULE 1

'British Islands' means the United Kingdom, the Channel Islands and the Isle of Man. ...

'United Kingdom' means Great Britain and Northern Ireland. ...

MARRIAGE ACT 1983
(1983 c 32)

1 Marriages of house-bound and detained persons in England and Wales

(1) Subject to the provisions of this Act and the Marriage Act 1949, the marriage of a person who is house-bound or is a detained person may be solemnised in England and Wales, on the authority of a superintendent registrar's certificate issued under Part III of the Marriage Act 1949, at the place where that person usually resides.

(2) For the purposes of this section a person is house-bound if –

(a) the notice of his or her marriage given in accordance with section 27 of the Marriage Act 1949 is accompanied by a statement, made in a form prescribed under that Act by a registered medical practitioner not more than fourteen days before that notice is given, that in his opinion –

(i) by reason of illness or disability, he or she ought not to move or be moved from his or her home or the other place where he or she is at that time, and

(ii) it is likely that it will be the case for at least the three months following the date on which the statement is made that by reason of the illness or disability he or she ought not to move or be moved from that place; and

(b) he or she is not a detained person.

(3) For the purposes of this section, a person is a detained person if he or she is for the time being detained –

(a) otherwise than by virtue of section 2, 4, 5, 35, 36 or 136 of the Mental Health Act 1983 (short term detentions), as a patient in a hospital; or

(b) in a prison or other place to which the Prison Act 1952 applies.

(4) In subsection (3) above 'hospital' and 'patient' have the same meanings as in Part II of the Mental Health Act 1983.

(5) For the purposes of this section, a person who is house-bound or is a

detained person shall be taken, if he or she would not otherwise be, to be usually resident at the place where he or she is for the time being.

(6) Nothing in the preceding provisions of this section shall be taken to relate or have any reference to any marriage according to the usages of the Society of Friends or any marriage between two persons professing the Jewish religion according to the usages of the Jews. ...

CHILD ABDUCTION ACT 1984
(1984 c 37)

1   Offence of abduction of child by parent, etc

(1) Subject to subsections (5) and (8) below, a person connected with a child under the age of sixteen commits an offence if he takes or sends the child out of the United Kingdom without the appropriate consent.

(2) A person is connected with a child for the purposes of this section if –

(a) he is a parent of the child; or

(b) in the case of a child whose parents were not married to each other at the time of his birth, there are reasonable grounds for believing that he is the father of the child; or

(c) he is a guardian of the child; or

(d) he is a person in whose favour a residence order is in force with respect to the child; or

(e) he has custody of the child.

(3) In this section 'the appropriate consent', in relation to a child, means –

(a) the consent of each of the following –

(i) the child's mother;

(ii) the child's father, if he has parental responsibility for him;

(iii) any guardian of the child;

(iv) any person in whose favour a residence order is in force with respect to the child;

(v) any person who has custody of the child; or

(b) the leave of the court granted under or by virtue of any provision of Part II of the Children Act 1989; or

(c) if any person has custody of the child, the leave of the court which awarded custody to him.

(4) A person does not commit an offence under this section by taking or sending a child out of the United Kingdom without obtaining the appropriate consent if –

(a) he is a person in whose favour there is a residence order in force with respect to the child, and

(b) he takes or sends him out of the United Kingdom for the period of less than one month.

(4A) Subsection (4) above does not apply if the person taking or sending the child out of the United Kingdom does so in breach of an order under Part II of the Children Act 1989.

(5) A person does not commit an offence under this section by doing anything without the consent of another person whose consent is required under the foregoing provisions if –

(a) he does it in the belief that the other person –

(i) has consented; or

(ii) would consent if he was aware of all the relevant circumstances; or

(b) he has taken all reasonable steps to communicate with the other person but has been unable to communicate with him; or

(c) the other person has unreasonably refused to consent.

(5A) Subsection (5)(c) above does not apply if –

(a) the person who refused to consent is a person –

(i) in whose favour there is a residence order in force with respect to the child; or

(ii) who has custody of the child; or

(b) the person taking or sending the child out of the United Kingdom is, by so acting, in breach of an order made by a court in the United Kingdom.

(6) Where, in proceedings for an offence under this section, there is sufficient evidence to raise an issue as to the application of subsection (5) above, it shall be for the prosecution to prove that that subsection does not apply.

(7) For the purposes of this section –

(a) 'guardian of a child', 'residence order' and 'parental responsibility' have the same meaning as in the Children Act 1989; and

(b) a person shall be treated as having custody of a child if there is in force an order of a court in the United Kingdom awarding him (whether solely or jointly with another person) custody, legal custody or care and control of the child.

(8) This section shall have effect subject to the provisions of the Schedule to this Act in relation to a child who is in the care of a local authority detained in a place of safety, remanded to a local authority accommodation or the subject of proceedings or an order relating to adoption.

2   Offence of abduction of child by other persons

(1) Subject to subsection (3) below, a person, other than one mentioned in subsection (2) below, commits an offence if, without lawful authority or reasonable excuse, he takes or detains a child under the age of sixteen –

(a) so as to remove him from the lawful control of any person having lawful control of the child; or

(b) so as to keep him out of the lawful control of any person entitled to lawful control of the child.

(2) The persons are –

(a) where the father and mother of the child in question were married to each other at the time of his birth, the child's father and mother;

(b) where the father and mother of the child in question were not married to each other at the time of his birth, the child's mother; and

(c) any other person mentioned in section 1(2)(c) to (e) above.

(3) In proceedings against any person for an offence under this section, it shall be a defence for that person to prove –

(a) where the father and mother of the child in question were not married to each other at the time of his birth –

(i) that he is the child's father; or

(ii) that, at the time of the alleged offence, he believed, on reasonable grounds, that he was the child's father; or

(b) that, at the time of the alleged offence, he believed that the child had attained the age of sixteen.

3   Construction of references to taking, sending and detaining

For the purposes of this Part of this Act –

(a) a person shall be regarded as taking a child if he causes or induces the child to accompany him or any other person or causes the child to be taken;

(b) a person shall be regarded as sending a child if he causes the child to be sent;

(c) a person shall be regarded as detaining a child if he causes the child to be detained or induces the child to remain with him or any other person; and

(d) references to a child's parents and to a child whose parents were (or were not) married to each other at the time of his birth shall be construed in accordance with section 1 of the Family Law Reform Act 1987 (which extends their meaning).

4   Penalties and prosecutions

(1) A person guilty of an offence under this Part of this Act shall be liable –

(a) on summary conviction, to imprisonment for a term not exceeding six months or to a fine not exceeding the statutory maximum or to both such imprisonment and fine;

(b) on conviction on indictment, to imprisonment for a term not exceeding seven years.

(2) No prosecution for an offence under section 1 above shall be instituted except by or with the consent of the Director of Public Prosecutions.

5   Restriction on prosecutions for offence of kidnapping

Except by or with the consent of the Director of Public Prosecutions shall be instituted for an offence of kidnapping if it was committed –

(a) against a child under the age of sixteen; and

(b) by a person connected with the child, within the meaning of s1 above.

SCHEDULE

MODIFICATIONS OF SECTION 1 FOR CHILDREN
IN CERTAIN CASES

Children in care in local authorities and voluntary organisations

1. (1) This paragraph applies in the case of a child who is in the care of a local authority within the meaning of the Children Act 1989 in England or Wales.

(2) Where this paragraph applies, section 1 of this Act shall have effect as if –

(a) the reference in subsection (1) to the appropriate consent were a reference to the consent of the local authority in whose care the child is; and

(b) subsections (3) to (6) were omitted.

Children in places of safety

2. (1) This paragraph applies in the case of a child who is –

(a) detained in a place of safety under section 16(3) of the Children and Young Persons Act 1969; or

(b) remanded to local authority accommodation under section 23 of that Act.

(2) Where this paragraph applies, section 1 of this Act shall have effect as if –

(a) the reference in subsection (1) to the appropriate consent were a reference to the leave of any magistrates' court acting for the area in which the place of safety is; and

(b) subsections (3) to (6) were omitted.

Adoption and custodianship

3. (1) This paragraph applies in the case of a child –

(a) who is the subject of an order under section 18 of the Adoption Act 1976 freeing him for adoption; or

(b) who is the subject of a pending application for such an order; or

(c) who is the subject of a pending application for an adoption order; or

(d) who is the subject of an order under section 55 of the Adoption Act 1976 relating to adoption abroad or of a pending application for such an order.

(2) Where this paragraph applies, s1 of this Act shall have effect as if –

(a) the reference in subsection (1) to the appropriate consent were a reference –

(i) in a case within sub-para (1)(a) above, to the consent of the adoption agency which made the application for the section 18 order or, if the section 18 order has been varied under section 21 of that Act so as to give parental responsibility to another agency, to the consent of that other agency;

    (ii) in a case within sub-para (1)(b) or (c) above, to the leave of the court to which the application was made; and

    (iii) in a case within sub-para (1)(d) above, to the leave of the court which made the order or, as the case may be, to which the application was made; and

  (b) subsections (3) to (6) were omitted.

(3) Sub-paragraph (2) above shall be construed as if the references to the court included, in any case where the court is a magistrates' court, a reference to any magistrates' court acting for the same area as that court.

Cases within paragraphs 1 and 3

4. In the case of a child falling within both paragraph 1 and paragraph 3 above, the provisions of paragraph 3 shall apply to the exclusion of those in paragraph 1.

Interpretation

5. In this Schedule –

  (a) 'adoption agency' and 'adoption order' have the same meaning as in the Adoption Act 1976; and

  (b) 'area', in relation to a magistrates' court, means the petty sessions area (within the meaning of the Justices of the Peace Act 1979) for which the court is appointed.

As amended by the Family Law Act 1986, s65; Children Act 1989, s108(4), (7), Schedule 12, paras 37(1)-(5), 38, 39, 40(1)-(7), Schedule 15; Statute Law (Repeals) Act 1993; Justices of the Peace Act 1997, s73(2), Schedule 5, para 20.

SURROGACY ARRANGEMENTS ACT 1985
(1985 c 49)

1 Meaning of 'surrogate mother', 'surrogacy arrangement' and other terms

(1) The following provisions shall have effect for the interpretation of this Act.

(2) 'Surrogate mother' means a woman who carries a child in pursuance of an arrangement –

(a) made before she began to carry the child, and

(b) made with a view to any child carried in pursuance of it being handed over to, and the parental responsibility being met (so far as practicable) by, another person or other persons.

(3) An arrangement is a surrogacy arrangement if, were a woman to whom the arrangement relates to carry a child in pursuance of it, she would be a surrogate mother.

(4) In determining whether an arrangement is made with such a view as is mentioned in subsection (2) above regard may be had to the circumstances as a whole (and, in particular, where there is a promise or understanding that any payment will or may be made to the woman or for her benefit in respect of the carrying of any child in pursuance of the arrangement, to that promise or understanding).

(5) An arrangement may be regarded as made with such a view though subject to conditions relating to the handing over of any child.

(6) A woman who carries a child is to be treated for the purposes of subsection (2)(a) above as beginning to carry it at the time of the insemination, or of the placing in her of an embryo, of an egg in the process of fertilisation or of sperm and eggs, as the case may be, that results in her carrying the child.

(7) 'Body of persons' means a body of persons corporate or unincorporate.

(8) 'Payment' means payment in money or money's worth.

(9) This Act applies to arrangements whether or not they are lawful.

1A Surrogacy arrangements unenforceable

No surrogacy arrangement is enforceable by or against any of the persons making it.

2 Negotiating surrogacy arrangements on a commercial basis, etc

(1) No person shall on a commercial basis do any of the following acts in the United Kingdom, that is –

(a) initiate or take part in any negotiations with a view to the making of a surrogacy arrangement,

(b) offer or agree to negotiate the making of a surrogacy arrangement, or

(c) compile any information with a view to its use in making, or negotiating the making of, surrogacy arrangements;

and no person shall in the United Kingdom knowingly cause another to do any of those acts on a commercial basis.

(2) A person who contravenes subsection (1) above is guilty of an offence; but it is not a contravention of that subsection –

(a) for a woman, with a view to becoming a surrogate mother herself, to do any act mentioned in that subsection or to cause such an act to be done, or

(b) for any person, with a view to a surrogate mother carrying a child for him, to do such an act or to cause such an act to be done.

(3) For the purposes of this section, a person does an act on a commercial basis (subject to subsection (4) below) if –

(a) any payment is at any time received by himself or another in respect of it, or

(b) he does it with a view to any payment being received by himself or another in respect of making, or negotiating or facilitating the making of, any surrogacy arrangement.

In this subsection 'payment' does not include payment to or for the benefit of a surrogate mother or prospective surrogate mother.

(4) In proceedings against a person for an offence under subsection (1)

above, he is not to be treated as doing an act on a commercial basis by reason of any payment received by another in respect of the act if it is proved that –

(a) in a case where the payment was received before he did the act, he did not do the act knowing or having reasonable cause to suspect that any payment had been received in respect of the act; and

(b) in any other case, he did not do the act with a view to any payment being received in respect of it.

(5) Where –

(a) a person acting on behalf of a body of persons takes any part in negotiating or facilitating the making of a surrogacy arrangement in the United Kingdom, and

(b) negotiating or facilitating the making of surrogacy arrangements is an activity of the body,

then, if the body at any time receives any payment made by or on behalf of –

(i) a woman who carries a child in pursuance of the arrangement,

(ii) the person or persons for whom she carries it, or

(iii) any person connected with the woman or with that person or those persons,

the body is guilty of an offence.

For the purpose of this subsection, a payment received by a person connected with a body is to be treated as received by the body.

(6) In proceedings against a body for an offence under subsection (5) above, it is a defence to prove that the payment concerned was not made in respect of the arrangement mentioned in paragraph (a) of that subsection.

(7) A person who in the United Kingdom takes part in the management or control –

(a) of any body of persons, or

(b) of any of the activities of any body of persons,

is guilty of an offence if the activity described in subsection (8) below is an activity of the body concerned.

(8) The activity referred to in subsection (7) above is negotiating or facilitating the making of surrogacy arrangements in the United Kingdom, being –

(a) arrangements the making of which is negotiated or facilitated on a commercial basis, or

(b) arrangements in the case of which payments are received (or treated for the purposes of subsection (5) above as received) by the body concerned in contravention of subsection (5) above.

(9) In proceedings against a person for an offence under subsection (7) above, it is a defence to prove that he neither knew nor had reasonable cause to suspect that the activity described in subsection (8) above was an activity of the body concerned; and for the purposes of such proceedings any arrangement falling within subsection (8)(b) above shall be disregarded if it is proved that the payment concerned was not made in respect of the arrangement.

3   Advertisements about surrogacy

(1) This section applies to any advertisement containing an indication (however expressed) –

(a) that any person is or may be willing to enter into a surrogacy arrangement or to negotiate or facilitate the making of a surrogacy arrangement, or

(b) that any person is looking for a woman willing to become a surrogate mother or for persons wanting a woman to carry a child as a surrogate mother.

(2) Where a newspaper or periodical containing an advertisement to which this section applies is published in the United Kingdom, any proprietor, editor or publisher of the newspaper or periodical is guilty of an offence.

(3) Where an advertisement to which this section applies is conveyed by means of a telecommunication system so as to be seen or heard (or both) in the United Kingdom, any person who in the United Kingdom causes it to be so conveyed knowing it to contain such an indication as is mentioned in subsection (1) above is guilty of an offence.

(4) A person who publishes or causes to be published in the United Kingdom an advertisement to which this section applies (not being an advertisement contained in a newspaper or periodical or conveyed by means of a telecommunication system) is guilty of an offence.

(5) A person who distributes or causes to be distributed in the United Kingdom an advertisement to which this section applies (not being an advertisement contained in a newspaper or periodical published outside the United Kingdom or an advertisement conveyed by means of a

telecommunication system) knowing it to contain such an indication as is mentioned in subsection (1) above is guilty of an offence.

(6) In this section 'telecommunication system' has the same meaning as in the Telecommunications Act 1984.

4   Offences

(1) A person guilty of an offence under this Act shall be liable on summary conviction –

(a) in the case of an offence under section 2 to a fine not exceeding level 5 on the standard scale or to imprisonment for a term not exceeding three months or both,

(b) in the case of an offence under section 3 to a fine not exceeding level 5 on the standard scale.

(2) No proceedings for an offence under this Act shall be instituted –

(a) in England and Wales, except by or with the consent of the Director of Public Prosecutions; and

(b) in Northern Ireland, except by or with the consent of the Director of Public Prosecutions for Northern Ireland.

(3) Where an offence under this Act committed by a body corporate is proved to have been committed with the consent or connivance of, or to be attributable to any neglect on the part of, any director, manager, secretary or other similar officer of the body corporate or any person who was purporting to act in any such capacity, he as well as the body corporate is guilty of the offence and is liable to be proceeded against and punished accordingly.

(4) Where the affairs of a body corporate are managed by its members, subsection (3) above shall apply in relation to the acts and defaults of a member in connection with his functions of management as if he were a director of the body corporate.

(5) In any proceedings for an offence under subsection 2 of this Act, proof of things done or of words written, spoken or published (whether or not in the presence of any party to the proceedings) by any person taking part in the management or control of a body of persons or of any of the activities of the body, or by any person doing any of the acts mentioned in subsection (1)(a) to (c) of that section on behalf of the body, shall be admissible as evidence of the activities of the body.

(6) In relation to an offence under this Act, section 127(1) of the Magistrates'

Courts Act 1980 (information must be laid within six months of commission of offence), section 136(1) of the Criminal Procedure (Scotland) Act 1995 (proceedings must be commenced within that time) and Article 19(1) of the Magistrates' Courts (Northern Ireland) Order 1981 (complaint must be made within that time) shall have effect as if for the reference to six months there were substituted a reference to two years.

As amended by the Children Act 1989, s108(5), Schedule 13, para 56; Human Fertilisation and Embryology Act 1990, s36(1), (2); Statute Law (Repeals) Act 1993; Criminal Procedure (Consequential Provisions) (Scotland) Act 1995, ss4, 5, Schedule 3, Schedule 4, para 57.

MARRIAGE (PROHIBITED DEGREES OF RELATIONSHIP) ACT 1986

(1986 c 16)

1 Marriage between certain persons related by affinity not to be void

(1) A marriage solemnised after the commencement of this Act between a man and a woman who is the daughter or granddaughter of a former spouse of his (whether the former spouse is living or not) or who is the former spouse of his father or grandfather (whether his father or grandfather is living or not) shall not be void by reason only of that relationship if both the parties have attained the age of twenty-one at the time of the marriage and the younger party has not at any time before attaining the age of eighteen been a child of the family in relation to the other party.

(2) A marriage solemnised after the commencement of this Act between a man and a woman who is the grandmother of a former spouse of his (whether the former spouse is living or not) or is a former spouse of his grandson (whether the grandson is living or not) shall not be void by reason only of that relationship.

(3) A marriage solemnised after the commencement of this Act between a man and a woman who is the mother of a former spouse of his shall not be void by reason only of that relationship if the marriage is solemnised after the death of both that spouse and the father of that spouse and after both the parties to the marriage have attained the age of twenty-one.

(4) A marriage solemnised after the commencement of this Act between a man and a woman who is a former spouse of his son shall not be void by reason only of that relationship if the marriage is solemnised after the death of both his son and the mother of his son and after both the parties to the marriage have attained the age of twenty-one.

(5) In this section 'child of the family' in relation to any person means a child who has lived in the same household as that person and been treated by that person as a child of his family.

(6) The Marriage Act 1949 shall have effect subject to the amendments

specified in the Schedule to this Act, being amendments consequential on the preceding provisions of this section.

(7) Where, apart from this Act, any matter affecting the validity of a marriage would fall to be determined (in accordance with the rules of private international law) by reference to the law of a country outside England and Wales nothing in this Act shall preclude the determination of that matter in accordance with that law.

(8) Nothing in this section shall affect any marriage solemnised before the commencement of this Act.

INSOLVENCY ACT 1986
(1986 c 45)

313 Charge on bankrupt's home

(1) Where any property consisting of an interest in a dwelling house which is occupied by the bankrupt or by his spouse or former spouse is comprised in the bankrupt's estate and the trustee is, for any reason, unable for the time being to realise that property, the trustee may apply to the court for an order imposing a charge on the property for the benefit of the bankrupt's estate.

(2) If on an application under this section the court imposes a charge on any property, the benefit of that charge shall be comprised in the bankrupt's estate and is enforceable, up to the value from time to time of the property secured, for the payment of any amount which is payable otherwise than to the bankrupt out of the estate and of interest on that amount at the prescribed rate.

(3) An order under this section made in respect of property vested in the trustee shall provide, in accordance with the rules, for the property to cease to be comprised in the bankrupt's estate and, subject to the charge (and any prior charge), to vest in the bankrupt.

(4) Subsections (1) and (2) and (4) to (6) of section 3 of the Charging Orders Act 1979 (supplemental provisions with respect to charging orders) have effect in relation to orders under this section as in relation to charging orders under that Act.

336 Rights of occupation, etc of bankrupt's spouse

(1) Nothing occurring in the initial period of the bankruptcy (that is to say, the period beginning with the day of the presentation of the petition for the bankruptcy order and ending with the vesting of the bankrupt's estate in a trustee) is to be taken as having given rise to any matrimonial home rights under Part IV of the Family Law Act 1996 in relation to a dwelling house comprised in the bankrupt's estate.

(2) Where a spouse's matromonial home rights under the Act of 1996 are a

charge on the estate or interest of the other spouse, or of trustees for the other spouse, and the other spouse is adjudged bankrupt –

(a) the charge continues to subsist notwithstanding the bankruptcy and, subject to the provisions of that Act, binds the trustee of the bankrupt's estate and persons deriving title under that trustee, and

(b) any application for an order under section 3 of that Act shall be made to the court having jurisdiction in relation to the bankruptcy.

(4) On such an application as is mentioned in subsection (2) the court shall make such order under section 33 of the Act of 1996 or as it thinks just and reasonable having regard to –

(a) the interests of the bankrupt's creditors,

(b) the conduct of the spouse or former spouse, so far as contributing to the bankruptcy,

(c) the needs and financial resources of the spouse or former spouse,

(d) the needs of any children, and

(e) all the circumstances of the case other than the needs of the bankrupt.

(5) Where such an application is made after the end of the period of one year beginning with the first vesting under Chapter IV of this Part of the bankrupt's estate in a trustee, the court shall assume, unless the circumstances of the case are exceptional, that the interests of the bankrupt's creditors outweigh all other considerations.

337 Rights of occupation of bankrupt

(1) This section applies where –

(a) a person who is entitled to occupy a dwelling house by virtue of a beneficial estate or interest is adjudged bankrupt, and

(b) any persons under the age of 18 with whom that person had at some time occupied that dwelling house had their home with that person at the time when the bankruptcy petition was presented and at the commencement of the bankruptcy.

(2) Whether or not the bankrupt's spouse (if any) has matrimonial home rights under Part IV of the Family Law Act 1996 –

(a) the bankrupt has the following rights as against the trustee of his estate –

(i) if in occupation, a right not to be evicted or excluded from the dwelling house or any part of it, except with the leave of the court,

(ii) if not in occupation, a right with the leave of the court to enter into and occupy the dwelling house, and

(b) the bankrupt's rights are a charge, having the like priority as an equitable interest created immediately before the commencement of the bankruptcy, on so much of his estate or interest in the dwelling house as vests in the trustee.

(3) The Act of 1996 has effect, with the necessary modifications, as if –

(a) the rights conferred by paragraph (a) of subsection (2) were matrimonial home rights under that Act,

(b) any application for such leave as is mentioned in that paragraph were an application for an order under section 33 of that Act, and

(c) any charge under paragraph (b) of that subsection on the estate or interest of the trustee were a charge under that Act on the estate or interest of a spouse.

(4) Any application for leave such as is mentioned in subsection (2)(a) or otherwise by virtue of this section for an order under section 33 of the Act of 1996 shall be made to the court having jurisdiction in relation to the bankruptcy.

(5) On such an application the court shall make such order under section 33 of the Act of 1996 as it thinks just and reasonable having regard to the interests of the creditors, to the bankrupt's financial resources, to the needs of the children and to all the circumstances of the case other than the needs of the bankrupt.

(6) Where such an application is made after the end of the period of one year beginning with the first vesting (under chapter IV of this Part) of the bankrupt's estate in a trustee, the court shall assume, unless the circumstances of the case are exceptional, that the interests of the bankrupt's creditors outweigh all other considerations.

339 Transactions at an undervalue

(1) Subject as follows in this section and sections 341 and 342, where an individual is adjudged bankrupt and he has at a relevant time (defined in section 341) entered into a transaction with any person at an undervalue, the trustee of the bankrupt's estate may apply to the court for an order under this section.

(2) The court shall, on such an application, make such order as it thinks fit for restoring the position to what it would have been if that individual had not entered into that transaction.

(3) For the purposes of this section and sections 341 and 342, an individual enters into a transaction with a person at an undervalue if –

(a) he makes a gift to that person or he otherwise enters into a transaction with that person on terms that provide for him to receive no consideration,

(b) he enters into a transaction with that person in consideration of marriage, or

(c) he enters into a transaction with that person for a consideration the value of which, in money or money's worth, is significantly less than the value, in money or money's worth, of the consideration provided by the individual.

340 Preferences

(1) Subject as follows in this and the next two sections, where an individual is adjudged bankrupt and he has at a relevant time (defined in section 341) given a preference to any person, the trustee of the bankrupt's estate may apply to the court for an order under this section.

(2) The court shall, on such an application, make such order as it thinks fit for restoring the position to what it would have been if that individual had not given that preference.

(3) For the purposes of this and the next two sections, an individual gives a preference to a person if –

(a) that person is one of the individual's creditors or a surety or guarantor for any of his debts or other liabilities, and

(b) the individual does anything or suffers anything to be done which (in either case) has the effect of putting that person into a position which, in the event of the individual's bankruptcy, will be better than the position he would have been in if that thing had not been done.

(4) The court shall not make an order under this section in respect of a preference given to any person unless the individual who gave the preference was influenced in deciding to give it by a desire to produce in relation to that person the effect mentioned in subsection (3)(b) above.

(5) An individual who has given a preference to a person who, at the time the preference was given, was an associate of his (otherwise than by reason only of being his employee) is presumed, unless the contrary is shown, to have been influenced in deciding to give it by such a desire as is mentioned in subsection (4).

(6) The fact that something has been done in pursuance of the order of a

court does not, without more, prevent the doing or suffering of that thing from constituting the giving of a preference.

341 'Relevant time' under ss339, 340

(1) Subject as follows, the time at which an individual enters into a transaction at an undervalue or gives a preference is a relevant time if the transaction is entered into or the preference given –

(a) in the case of a transaction at an undervalue, at a time in the period of five years ending with the day of the presentation of the bankruptcy petition on which the individual is adjudged bankrupt,

(b) in the case of a preference which is not a transaction at an undervalue and is given to a person who is an associate of the individual (otherwise than by reason only of being his employee), at a time in the period of two years ending with that day, and

(c) in any other case of a preference which is not a transaction at an undervalue, at a time in the period of six months ending with that day.

(2) Where an individual enters into a transaction at an undervalue or gives a preference at a time mentioned in paragraph (a), (b) or (c) of subsection (1) (not being, in the case of a transaction at an undervalue, a time less than two years before the end of the period mentioned in paragraph (a)), that time is not a relevant time for the purpose of sections 339 and 340 unless the individual –

(a) is insolvent at that time, or

(b) becomes insolvent in consequence of the transaction or preference;

but the requirements of this subsection are presumed to be satisfied, unless the contrary is shown, in relation to any transaction at an undervalue which is entered into by an individual with a person who is an associate of his (otherwise than by reason only of being his employee).

(3) For the purposes of subsection (2), an individual is insolvent if –

(a) he is unable to pay his debts as they fall due, or

(b) the value of his assets is less than the amount of his liabilities, taking into account his contingent and prospective liabilities.

(4) A transaction entered into or preference given by a person who is subsequently adjudged bankrupt on a petition under section 264(1)(d) (criminal bankruptcy) is to be treated as having been entered into or given at a relevant time for the purposes of sections 339 or 340 if it was entered into or given at any time on or after the date specified for the purposes of

this subsection in the criminal bankruptcy order on which the petition was based.

(5) No order shall be made under section 339 or 340 by virtue of subsection (4) of this section where an appeal is pending (within the meaning of section 277) against the individual's conviction of an offence by virtue of which the criminal bankruptcy order was made.

342 Orders under ss339, 340

(1) Without prejudice to the generality of section 339(2) or 340(2), an order under either of those sections with respect to a transaction or preference entered into or given by an individual who is subsequently adjudged bankrupt may (subject as follows) –

(a) require any property transferred as part of the transaction, or in connection with the giving of the preference, to be vested in the trustee of the bankrupt's estate as part of that estate;

(b) require any property to be so vested if it represents in any person's hands the application either of the proceeds of sale of property so transferred or of money so transferred;

(c) release or discharge (in whole or in part) any security given by the individual;

(d) require any person to pay, in respect of benefits received by him from the individual, such sums to the trustee of his estate as the court may direct;

(e) provide for any surety or guarantor whose obligations to any person were released or discharged (in whole or in part) under the transaction or by the giving of the preference to be under such new or revived obligations to that person as the court thinks appropriate;

(f) provide for security to be provided for the discharge of any obligation imposed by or arising under the order, for such an obligation to be charged on any property and for the security or charge to have the same priority as a security or charge released or discharged (in whole or in part) under the transaction or by the giving of the preference; and

(g) provide for the extent to which any person whose property is vested by the order in the trustee of the bankrupt's estate, or on whom obligations are imposed by the order, is to be able to prove in the bankruptcy for debts or other liabilities which arose from, or were released or discharged (in whole or in part) under or by, the transaction or the giving of the preference.

(2) An order under section 339 or 340 may affect the property of, or impose

any obligation on, any person whether or not he is the person with whom the individual in question entered into the transaction or, as the case may be, the person to whom the preference was given; but such an order –

(a) shall not prejudice any interest in property which was acquired from a person other than that individual and was acquired in good faith and for value, or prejudice any interest deriving from such an interest, and

(b) shall not require a person who received a benefit from the transaction or preference in good faith and for value to pay a sum to the trustee of the bankrupt's estate, except where he was a party to the transaction or the payment is to be in respect of a preference given to that person at a time when he was a creditor of that individual.

(2A) Where a person has acquired an interest in property from a person other than the individual in question, or has received a benefit from the transaction or preference, and at the time of that acquisition or receipt –

(a) he had notice of the relevant surrounding circumstances and of the relevant proceedings, or

(b) he was an associate of, or was connected with, either the individual in question or the person with whom that individual entered into the transaction or to whom that individual gave the preference,

then, unless the contrary is shown, it shall be presumed for the purposes of paragraph (a) or (as the case may be) paragraph (b) of subsection (2) that the interest was acquired or the benefit was received otherwise than in good faith.

(3) Any sums required to be paid to the trustee in accordance with an order under section 339 or 340 shall be comprised in the bankrupt's estate.

(4) For the purposes of subsection (2A)(a), the relevant surrounding circumstances are (as the case may require) –

(a) the fact that the individual in question entered into the transaction at an undervalue; or

(b) the circumstances which amounted to the giving of the preference by the individual in question.

(5) For the purposes of subsection (2A)(a), a person has notice of the relevant proceedings if he has notice –

(a) of the fact that the petition on which the individual in question is adjudged bankrupt has been presented; or

(b) of the fact that the individual in question has been adjudged bankrupt.

(6) Section 249 in Part VII of this Act shall apply for the purposes of subsection (2A)(b) as it applies for the purposes of the first Group of Parts.

As amended by the Insolvency (No 2) Act 1994, s2; Trusts of Land and Appointment of Trustees Act 1996, s25(2), Schedule 4; Family Law Act 1996, s66(1), Schedule 8, Pt III, paras 57, 58.

FAMILY LAW ACT 1986
(1986 c 55)

PART I

CHILD CUSTODY

1   Orders to which Part I applies

(1) Subject to the following provisions of this section, in this Part 'Part I order' means –

(a) a section 8 order made by a court in England and Wales under the Children Act 1989, other than an order varying or discharging such an order; ...

(d) an order made by a court in England and Wales in the exercise of the inherent jurisdiction of the High Court with respect to children –

(i) so far as it gives care of a child to any person or provides for contact with, or the education of, a child; but

(ii) excluding an order varying or revoking such an order. ...

(3) In this Part, 'Part I order' –

(a) includes any order which would have been a custody order by virtue of this section in any form in which it was in force at any time before its amendment by the Children Act 1989 ...; and

(b) (subject to section 32 and 40 of this Act) excludes any order which would have been excluded from being a custody order by virtue of this section in any such form. ...

2   Jurisdiction: general

(1) A court in England and Wales shall not have jurisdiction to make a section 1(1)(a) order with respect to a child in or in connection with matrimonial proceedings in England and Wales unless the condition in section 2A of this Act is satisfied.

(2) A court in England and Wales shall not have jurisdiction to make a section 1(1)(a) order in a non-matrimonial case (that is to say, where the condition in section 2A of this Act is not satisfied) unless the condition in section 3 of this Act is satisfied.

(3) A court in England and Wales shall not have jurisdiction to make a section 1(1)(d) order unless –

(a) the condition in section 3 of this Act is satisfied, or

(b) the child concerned is present in England and Wales on the relevant date and the court considers that the immediate exercise of its powers is necessary for his protection.

2A Jurisdiction in or in connection with matrimonial proceedings

(1) The condition referred to in section 2(1) of this Act is that the matrimonial proceedings are proceedings in respect of the marriage of the parents of the child concerned and –

(a) the proceedings –

(i) are proceedings for divorce or nullity of marriage, and
(ii) are continuing;

(b) the proceedings –

(i) are proceedings for judicial separation, and
(ii) are continuing,

and the jurisdiction of the court is not excluded by subsection (2) below; or

(c) the proceedings have been dismissed after the beginning of the trial but –

(i) the section 1(1)(a) order is being made forthwith, or
(ii) the application for the order was made on or before the dismissal. ...

(4) Where a court –

(a) has jurisdiction to make a section 1(1)(a) order in or in connection with matrimonial proceedings, but

(b) considers that it would be more appropriate for Part I matters relating to the child to be determined outside England and Wales,

the court may by order direct that, while the order under this subsection is in force, no section 1(1)(a) order shall be made by any court in or in connection with those proceedings.

3   Habitual residence or presence of child

(1) The condition referred to in section 2(2) of this Act is that on the relevant date the child concerned –

(a) is habitually resident in England and Wales, or

(b) is present in England and Wales and is not habitually resident in any part of the United Kingdom or a specified dependent territory,

and, in either case, the jurisdiction of the court is not excluded by subsection (2) below.

(2) For the purposes of subsection (1) above, the jurisdiction of the court is excluded if, on the relevant date, matrimonial proceedings are continuing in a court in Scotland, Northern Ireland or a specified dependent territory in respect of the marriage of the parents of the child concerned.

(3) Subsection (2) above shall not apply if the court in which the other proceedings there referred to are continuing has made –

(a) an order under section 13(6) or 19A(4) of this Act (not being an order made by virtue of section 13(6)(a)(i)), or a corresponding dependent territory order, or

(b) an order under section 14(2) or 22(2) of this Act which is recorded as made for the purpose of enabling Part I proceedings with respect to the child concerned to be taken in England and Wales,

and that order is in force.

5   Power of court to refuse application or stay proceedings

(1) A court in England and Wales which has jurisdiction to make a Part I order may refuse an application for the order in any case where the matter in question has already been determined in proceedings outside England and Wales.

(2) Where, at any stage of the proceedings on an application made to a court in England and Wales for a Part I order, or for the variation of a Part I order, it appears to the court –

(a) that proceedings with respect to the matters to which the application relates are continuing outside England and Wales, or

(b) that it would be more appropriate for those matters to be determined in proceedings to be taken outside England and Wales,

the court may stay the proceedings on the application.

(3) The court may remove a stay granted in accordance with subsection (2) above if it appears to the court that there has been unreasonable delay in the taking or prosecution of the other proceedings referred to in that subsection, or that those proceedings are stayed, sisted or concluded.

(4) Nothing in this section shall affect any power exercisable apart from this section to refuse an application or to grant or remove a stay.

6   Duration and variation of Part I orders

(1) If a Part I order made by a court in Scotland, Northern Ireland or a specified dependent territory (or a variation of such an order) comes into force with respect to a child at a time when a Part I order made by a court in England and Wales has effect with respect to him, the latter order shall cease to have effect so far as it makes provision for any matter for which the same or different provision is made by (or by the variation of) the order made by the court in Scotland, Northern Ireland or the territory.

(2) Where by virtue of subsection (1) above a Part I order has ceased to have effect so far as it makes provision for any matter, a court in England or Wales shall not have jurisdiction to vary that order so as to make provision for that matter.

(3) A court in England and Wales shall not have jurisdiction to vary a Part I order if, on the relevant date, matrimonial proceedings are continuing in Scotland, Northern Ireland or a specified dependent territory in respect of the marriage of the parents of the child concerned.

(3A) Subsection (3) above shall not apply if –

(a) the Part I order was made in or in connection with proceedings for divorce or nullity in England and Wales in respect of the marriage of the parents of the child concerned; and

(b) those proceedings are continuing.

(3B) Subsection (3) above shall not apply if –

(a) the Part I order was made in or in connection with proceedings for judicial separation in England and Wales;

(b) those proceedings are continuing; and

(c) the decree of judicial separation has not yet been granted.

(4) Subsection (3) above shall not apply if the court in which the proceedings there referred to are continuing has made –

(a) an order under section 13(6) or 19A(4) of this Act (not being an order made by virtue of section 13(6)(a)(i)), or a corresponding dependent territory order, or

(b) an order under section 14(2) or 22(2) of this Act, or a corresponding dependent territory order, which is recorded as made for the purpose of enabling Part I proceedings with respect to the child concerned to be taken in England and Wales,

and that order is in force.

(5) Subsection (3) above shall not apply in the case of a variation of a section 1(1)(d) order if the child concerned is present in England and Wales on the relevant date and the court considers that the immediate exercise of its powers is necessary for his protection.

(6) Subsection (7) below applies where a Part I order which is –

(a) a residence order (within the meaning of the Children Act 1989) in favour of a person with respect to a child,

(b) an order made in the exercise of the High Court's inherent jurisdiction with respect to children by virtue of which a person has care of a child, or

(c) an order –

(i) of a kind mentioned in section 1(3)(a) of this Act

(ii) under which a person is entitled to the actual possession of a child,

ceases to have effect in relation to that person by virtue of subsection (1) above.

(7) Where this subsection applies, any family assistance order made under section 16 of the Children Act 1989 with respect to the child shall also cease to have effect.

(8) For the purposes of subsection (7) above the reference to a family assistance order under section 16 of the Children Act 1989 shall be deemed to include a reference to an order for the supervision of a child made under –

(a) section 7(4) of the Family Law Reform Act 1969,

(b) section 44 of the Matrimonial Causes Act 1973,

(c) section 2(2)(a) of the Guardianship Act 1973,

(d) section 34(5) or 36(3)(b) of the Children Act 1975, or

(e) section 9 of the Domestic Proceedings and Magistrates' Courts Act 1978;

but this subsection shall cease to have effect once all such orders for the supervision of children have ceased to have effect in accordance with Schedule 14 to the Children Act 1989.

7 Interpretation of Chapter II

In this Chapter –

(a) 'child' means a person who has not attained the age of eighteen;

(b) 'matrimonial proceedings' means proceedings for divorce, nullity or marriage or judicial separation;

(c) 'the relevant date' means, in relation to the making or variation of an order –

(i) where an application is made for an order to be made or varied, the date of the application (or first application, if two or more are determined together), and

(ii) where no such application is made, the date on which the court is considering whether to make or, as the case may be, vary the order; and

(d) 'section 1(1)(a) order' and 'section 1(1)(d) order' means orders falling within section 1(1)(a) and (d) of this Act respectively.

25 Recognition of Part I orders: general

(1) Where a Part I order made by a court in any part of the United Kingdom or in a specified dependent territory is in force with respect to a child who has not attained the age of sixteen, then, subject to subsection (2) below, the order shall be recognised in any other part or, in the case of a dependent territory order, any part of the United Kingdom as having the same effect in that part as if it had been made by the appropriate court in that part and as if that court had had jurisdiction to make it.

(2) Where a Part I order includes provision as to the means by which rights conferred by the order are to be enforced, subsection (1) above shall not apply to that provision.

(3) A court in a part of the United Kingdom in which a Part I order is recognised in accordance with subsection (1) above shall not enforce the order unless it has been registered in that part of the United Kingdom under section 27 of this Act and proceedings for enforcement are taken in accordance with section 29 of this Act.

27   Registration

(1) Any person on whom any rights are conferred by a Part I order may apply to the court which made it for the order to be registered in another part of the United Kingdom under this section, or in a specified dependent territory under a corresponding provision.

(2) An application under this section shall be made in the prescribed manner and shall contain the prescribed information and be accompanied by such documents as may be prescribed.

(3) On receiving an application under this section the court which made the Part I order shall, unless it appears to the court that the order is no longer in force, cause the following documents to be sent to the appropriate court in the part of the United Kingdom or dependent territory specified in the application, namely –

  (a) a certified copy of the order, and

  (b) where the order has been varied, prescribed particulars of any variation which is in force, and

  (c) a copy of the application and of any accompanying documents.

(4) Where the prescribed officer of the appropriate court in any part of the United Kingdom receives a certified copy of a Part I order under subsection (3) above or under a corresponding dependent territory provision, he shall forthwith cause the order, together with particulars of any variation, to be registered in that court in the prescribed manner.

(5) An order shall not be registered under this section in respect of a child who has attained the age of sixteen, and the registration of an order in respect of a child who has not attained the age of sixteen shall cease to have effect on the attainment by the child of that age.

28   Cancellation and variation of registration

(1) A court which revokes, recalls or varies an order registered under section 27 of this Act shall cause notice of the revocation, recall or variation to be given in the prescribed manner to the prescribed officer of the court in which it is registered and, on receiving the notice, the prescribed officer –

  (a) in the case of the revocation or recall of the order, shall cancel the registration, and

  (b) in the case of the variation of the order, shall cause particulars of the variation to be registered in the prescribed manner.

(2) Where –

(a) an order registered under section 27 of this Act ceases (in whole or in part) to have effect in the part of the United Kingdom or in a specified dependent territory in which it was made, otherwise than because of its revocation, recall or variation, or

(b) an order registered under section 27 of this Act in Scotland ceases (in whole or in part) to have effect there as a result of the making of an order in proceedings outside the United Kingdom and any specified dependent territory,

the court in which the order is registered may, of its own motion or on the application of any person who appears to the court to have an interest in the matter, cancel the registration (or, if the order has ceased to have effect in part, cancel the registration so far as it relates to the provisions which have ceased to have effect).

29 Enforcement

(1) Where a Part I order has been registered under section 27 of this Act, the court in which it is registered shall have the same powers for the purpose of enforcing the order as it would have if it had itself made the order and had jurisdiction to make it; and proceedings for or with respect to enforcement may be taken accordingly.

(2) Where an application has been made to any court for the enforcement of an order registered in that court under section 27 of this Act, the court may, at any time before the application is determined, give such interim directions as it thinks fit for the purpose of securing the welfare of the child concerned or of preventing changes in the circumstances relevant to the determination of the application.

(3) The references in subsection (1) above to a Part I order do not include references to any provision of the order as to the means by which rights conferred by the order are to be enforced.

30 Staying or sisting of enforcement proceedings

(1) Where in accordance with section 29 of this Act proceedings are taken in any court for the enforcement of an order registered in that court, any person who appears to the court to have an interest in the matter may apply for the proceedings to be stayed or sisted on the ground that he has taken or intends to take other proceedings (in the United Kingdom or elsewhere) as a result of which the order may cease to have effect, or may have a different effect, in the part of the United Kingdom in which it is registered.

(2) If after considering an application under subsection (1) above the court

considers that the proceedings for enforcement should be stayed or sisted in order that other proceedings may be taken or concluded, it shall stay or sist the proceedings for enforcement accordingly.

(3) The court may remove a stay or recall of sist granted in accordance with subsection (2) above if it appears to the court –

(a) that there has been unreasonable delay in the taking or prosecution of the other proceedings referred to in that subsection, or

(b) that those other proceedings are concluded and that the registered order, or a relevant part of it, is still in force.

(4) Nothing in this section shall affect any power exercisable apart from this section to grant, remove or recall a stay or sist.

31 Dismissal of enforcement proceedings

(1) Where in accordance with section 29 of this Act proceedings are taken in any court for the enforcement of an order registered in that court, any person who appears to the court to have an interest in the matter may apply for those proceedings to be dismissed on the ground that the order has (in whole or in part) ceased to have effect in the part of the United Kingdom or specified dependent territory in which it was made.

(2) Where in accordance with section 29 of this Act proceedings are taken in the Court of Session for the enforcement of an order registered in that court, any person who appears to the court to have an interest in the matter may apply for those proceedings to be dismissed on the ground that the order has (in whole or in part) ceased to have effect in Scotland as a result of the making of an order in proceedings outside the United Kingdom and any specified dependent territory.

(3) If, after considering an application under subsection (1) or (2) above, the court is satisfied that the registered order has ceased to have effect, it shall dismiss the proceedings for enforcement (or, if it is satisfied that the order has ceased to have effect in part, it shall dismiss the proceedings so far as they relate to the enforcement of provisions which have ceased to have effect).

32 Interpretation of Chapter V

(1) In this Chapter –

'the appropriate court', in relation to England and Wales or Northern Ireland, means the High Court and, in relation to Scotland, means the Court of Session and, in relation to a specified dependent territory, means the corresponding court in that territory;

'Part I order' includes (except where the context otherwise requires) any order within section 1(3) of this Act which, on the assumptions mentioned in subsection (3) below –

(a) could have been made notwithstanding the provisions of this Part or the corresponding dependent territory provisions;

(b) would have been a Part I order for the purposes of this Part; and

(c) would not have ceased to have effect by virtue of section 6, 15 or 23 of this Act.

(2) In the application of this Chapter to Scotland, 'Part I order' also includes (except where the context otherwise requires) any order within section 1(3) of this Act which, on the assumptions mentioned in subsection (3) below –

(a) would have been a Part I order for the purposes of this Part; and

(b) would not have ceased to have effect by virtue of section 6 or 23 of this Act,

and which, but for the provisions of this Part, would be recognised in Scotland under any rule of law.

(3) The said assumptions are –

(a) that this Part or the corresponding dependent territory provisions, as the case may be, had been in force at all material times; and

(b) that any reference in section 1 of this Act to any enactment included a reference to any corresponding enactment previously in force.

33   Power to order disclosure of child's whereabouts

(1) Where in proceedings for or relating to a Part I order in respect of a child there is not available to the court adequate information as to where the child is, the court may order any person who it has reason to believe may have relevant information to disclose it to the court.

(2) A person shall not be excused from complying with an order under subsection (1) above by reason that to do so may incriminate him or his spouse of an offence; but a statement or admission made in compliance with such an order shall not be admissible in evidence against either of them in proceedings for any offence other than perjury.

(3) A court in Scotland before which proceedings are pending for the enforcement of an order for the custody of a child made outside the United

Kingdom and any specified dependent territory which is recognised in Scotland shall have the same powers as it would have under subsection (1) above if the order were its own.

34 Power to order recovery of child

(1) Where –

(a) a person is required by a Part I order, or an order for the enforcement of a Part I order, to give up a child to another person ('the person concerned'), and

(b) the court which made the order imposing the requirement is satisfied that the child has not been given up in accordance with the order,

the court may make an order authorising an officer of the court or a constable to take charge of the child and deliver him to the person concerned.

(2) The authority conferred by subsection (1) above includes authority –

(a) to enter and search any premises where the person acting in pursuance of the order has reason to believe the child may be found, and

(b) to use such force as may be necessary to give effect to the purpose of the order.

(3) Where by virtue of –

(a) section 14 of the Children Act 1989, or

(b) Article 14 (enforcement of residence orders) of the Children (Northern Ireland) Order 1995,

a Part I order (or a provision of a Part I order) may be enforced as if it were an order requiring a person to give up a child to another person, subsection (1) above shall apply as if the Part I order had included such a requirement.

(4) This section is without prejudice to any power conferred on a court by or under any other enactment or rule of law.

35 Powers to restrict removal of child from jurisdiction

(3) A court in Scotland –

(a) at any time after the commencement of proceedings in connection with which the court would have jurisdiction to make a Part I order, or

(b) in any proceedings in which it would be competent for the court to grant an interdict prohibiting the removal of a child from its jurisdiction,

may, on an application by any of the persons mentioned in subsection (4) below, grant interdict or interim interdict prohibiting the removal of the child from the United Kingdom or any part of the United Kingdom or any specified dependent territory or out of the control of the person in whose custody the child is.

(4) The said persons are –

(a) any party to the proceedings,

(b) the guardian of the child concerned, and

(c) any other person who has or wishes to obtain the custody or care of the child.

(5) In subsection (3) above 'the court' means the Court of Session or the sheriff; and for the purposes of subsection (3)(a) above, proceedings shall be held to commence –

(a) in the Court of Session, when a summons is signeted or a petition is presented;

(b) in the sheriff court, when the warrant of citation is signed.

36   Effect of orders restricting removal

(1) This section applies to any order made by a court in the United Kingdom or any specified dependent territory prohibiting the removal of a child from the United Kingdom or from any specified part of it or from any such territory.

(2) An order to which this section applies, made by a court in one part of the United Kingdom or in a specified dependent territory, shall have effect in each other part, or, in the case of an order made in a dependent territory, each part of the United Kingdom –

(a) as if it had been made by the appropriate court in that part, and

(b) in the case of an order which has the effect of prohibiting the child's removal to that part, as if it had included a prohibition on his further removal to any place except one to which he could be removed consistently with the order.

(3) The references in subsections (1) and (2) above to prohibitions on a child's removal include references to prohibitions subject to exceptions; and in a case where removal is prohibited except with the consent of the court,

nothing in subsection (2) above shall be construed as affecting the identity of the court whose consent is required.

(4) In this section 'child' means a person who has not attained the age of sixteen; and this section shall cease to apply to an order relating to a child when he attains the age of sixteen.

37 Surrender of passports

(1) Where there is in force an order prohibiting or otherwise restricting the removal of a child from the United Kingdom or from any specified part of it or from a specified dependent territory, the court by which the order was in fact made, or by which it is treated under section 36 of this Act as having been made, may require any person to surrender any United Kingdom passport which has been issued to, or contains particulars of, the child.

(2) In this section 'United Kingdom passport' means a current passport issued by the Government of the United Kingdom.

38 Automatic restriction on removal of wards of court

(1) The rule of law which (without any order of the court) restricts the removal of a ward of court from the jurisdiction of the court shall, in a case to which this section applies, have effect subject to the modifications in subsection (3) below.

(2) This section applies in relation to a ward of court if –

(a) proceedings for divorce, nullity or judicial separation in respect of the marriage of his parents are continuing in a court in another part of the United Kingdom (that is to say, in a part of the United Kingdom) outside the jurisdiction of the court of which he is a ward), or in a specified dependent territory, or

(b) he is habitually resident in another part of the United Kingdom or in a specified dependent territory,

except where that other part is Scotland and he has attained the age of sixteen.

(3) Where this section applies, the rule referred to in subsection (1) above shall not prevent –

(a) the removal of the ward of court, without the consent of any court, to the other part of the United Kingdom or the specified dependent territory mentioned in subsection (2) above, or

(b) his removal to any other place with the consent of either the appropriate court in that other part of the United Kingdom or the specified dependent territory or the court mentioned in subsection (2)(a) above.

39   Duty to furnish particulars of other proceedings

Parties to proceedings for or relating to a Part I order shall, to such extent and in such manner as may be prescribed, give particulars of other proceedings known to them which relate to the child concerned (including proceedings instituted abroad and proceedings which are no longer continuing).

40   Interpretation of Chapter VI

(1) In this Chapter –

'the appropriate court' has the same meaning as in Chapter V;

'Part I order' includes (except where the context otherwise requires) any such order as is mentioned in section 32(1) of this Act.

(2) In the application of this chapter to Scotland, 'Part I order' also includes (except where the context otherwise requires) any such order as is mentioned in section 32(2) of this Act.

41   Habitual residence after removal without consent, etc

(1) Where a child who –

(a) has not attained the age of sixteen, and

(b) is habitually resident in a part of the United Kingdom or in a specified dependent territory,

becomes habitually resident outside that part of the United Kingdom or that territory in consequence of circumstances of the kind specified in subsection (2) below, he shall be treated for the purposes of this Part as continuing to be habitually resident in that part of the United Kingdom or that territory for the period of one year beginning with the date on which those circumstances arise.

(2) The circumstances referred to in subsection (1) above exist where the child is removed from or retained outside, or himself leaves or remains outside, the part of the United Kingdom or the territory in which he was habitually resident before his change of residence –

(a) without the agreement of the person or all the persons having, under the law of that part of the United Kingdom or that territory, the right to determine where he is to reside, or

(b) in contravention of an order made by a court in any part of the United Kingdom or in a specified dependent territory.

(3) A child shall cease to be treated by virtue of subsection (1) above as habitually resident in a part of the United Kingdom or a specified dependent territory if, during the period there mentioned –

(a) he attains the age of sixteen, or

(b) he becomes habitually resident outside that part of the United Kingdom or that territory with the agreement of the person or persons mentioned in subsection (2)(a) above and not in contravention of an order made by a court in any part of the United Kingdom or in any specified dependent territory.

42 General interpretation of Part I

(1) In this Part –

'certified copy', in relation to an order of any court, means a copy certified by the prescribed officer of the court to be a true copy of the order or of the official record of the order;

'corresponding dependent territory order', 'corresponding dependent territory provision' and similar expressions, in relation to a specified dependent territory, shall be construed in accordance with Schedule 3 to the Family Law Act 1986 (Dependent Territories) Order 1991 as from time to time in force; 'dependent territory' has the meaning given by section 43(2) of this Act.

'part of the United Kingdom' means England and Wales, Scotland or Northern Ireland;

'prescribed' means prescribed by rules of court or act of sederunt;

'specified dependent territory' means a dependent territory for the time being specified in Schedule 1 to the said order of 1991.

(2) For the purposes of this Part proceedings in England and Wales, Northern Ireland or a specified dependent territory for divorce, nullity or judicial separation in respect of the marriage of the parents of a child shall, unless they have been dismissed, be treated as continuing until the child concerned attains the age of eighteen (whether or not a decree has been granted and whether or not, in the case of a decree of divorce or nullity of marriage, that decree has been made absolute).

(3) For the purposes of this Part, matrimonial proceedings in a court in Scotland which has jurisdiction in those proceedings to make a Part I order with respect to a child shall, unless they have been dismissed or decree of absolvitor has been granted therein, be treated as continuing until the child concerned attains the age of sixteen.

(4) Any reference in this Part to proceedings in respect of the marriage of the parents of a child shall, in relation to a child who, although not a child of both parties to the marriage, is a child of the family of those parties, be construed as a reference to proceedings in respect of that marriage; and for this purpose 'child of the family' –

(a) if the proceedings are in England and Wales, means any child who has been treated by both parties as a child of their family, except a child who is placed with those parties as foster parents by a local authority or a voluntary organisation;

(b) if the proceedings are in Scotland, means any child of one of the parties who has been accepted as one of the family by the other party;

(c) if the proceedings are in Northern Ireland, means any child who has been treated by both parties as a child of their family, except a child who is placed with those parties as foster parents by an authority within the meaning of the Children (Northern Ireland) Order 1995 or a voluntary organisation;

(d) if the proceedings are in a specified dependent territory, means any child who has been treated by both parties as a child of their family, except a child who has been placed with those parties as foster parents by a public authority in that territory.

(5) References in this Part to Part I orders include (except where the context otherwise requires) references to Part I orders as varied.

(6) For the purposes of this Part each of the following orders shall be treated as varying the Part I order to which it relates –

(a) an order which provides for a person to be allowed contact with or to be given access to a child who is the subject of a Part I order, or which makes provision for the education of such a child,

(7) In this Part –

(a) references to Part I proceedings in respect of a child are references to any proceedings for a Part I order or an order corresponding to a Part I order and include, in relation to proceedings outside the United Kingdom and any specified dependent territory, references to proceedings before a tribunal or other authority having power under the law having effect there to determine Part I matters; and

(b) references to Part I matters are references to matters that might be determined by a Part I order or an order corresponding to a Part I order.

43 Application of Part I to dependent territories

(1) Her Majesty may by Order in Council make provision corresponding to or applying any of the foregoing provisions of this Part, with such modifications as appear to Her Majesty to be appropriate, for the purpose of regulating –

(a) in any dependent territory;

(b) as between any dependent territory and any part of the United Kingdom; or

(c) as between any dependent territory and any other such territory,

the jurisdiction of courts to make Part I orders, or orders corresponding to Part I orders, and the recognition and enforcement of such orders.

(2) In subsection (1) above 'dependent territory' means any of the following territories –

(a) the Isle of Man,

(b) any of the Channel Islands, and

(c) any colony. ...

PART II

RECOGNITION OF DIVORCES, ANNULMENTS AND LEGAL SEPARATIONS

44 Recognition in United Kingdom of divorces, annulments and judicial separations granted in the British Islands

(1) Subject to section 52(4) and (5)(a) of this Act, no divorce or annulment obtained in any part of the British Islands shall be regarded as effective in any part of the United Kingdom unless granted by a court of civil jurisdiction.

(2) Subject to section 51 of this Act, the validity of any divorce, annulment or judicial separation granted by a court of civil jurisdiction in any part of the British Islands shall be recognised throughout the United Kingdom.

45 Recognition in the United Kingdom of overseas divorces, annulments and legal separations

Subject to sections 51 and 52 of this Act, the validity of a divorce, annulment or legal separation obtained in a country outside the British Islands (in this Part referred to as an overseas divorce, annulment or legal separation) shall be recognised in the United Kingdom if, and only if, it is entitled to recognition –

(a) by virtue of sections 46 to 49 of this Act, or

(b) by virtue of any enactment other than this Part.

46 Grounds for recognition

(1) The validity of an overseas divorce, annulment or legal separation obtained by means of proceedings shall be recognised if –

(a) the divorce, annulment or legal separation is effective under the law of the country in which it was obtained; and

(b) at the relevant date either party to the marriage –

(i) was habitually resident in the country in which the divorce, annulment or legal separation was obtained; or

(ii) was domiciled in that country; or

(iii) was a national of that country.

(2) The validity of an overseas divorce, annulment or legal separation obtained otherwise than by means of proceedings shall be recognised if –

(a) the divorce, annulment or legal separation is effective under the law of the country in which it was obtained;

(b) at the relevant date –

(i) each party to the marriage was domiciled in that country; or

(ii) either party to the marriage was domiciled in that country and the other party was domiciled in a country under whose law the divorce, annulment or legal separation is recognised as valid; and

(c) neither party to the marriage was habitually resident in the United Kingdom throughout the period of one year immediately preceding that date.

(3) In this section 'the relevant date' means –

(a) in the case of an overseas divorce, annulment or legal separation obtained by means of proceedings, the date of the commencement of the proceedings;

(b) in the case of an overseas divorce, annulment or legal separation obtained otherwise than by means of proceedings, the date on which it was obtained.

(4) Where in the case of an overseas annulment, the relevant date fell after the death of either party to the marriage, any reference in subsection (1) or (2) above to that date shall be construed in relation to that party as a reference to the date of death.

(5) For the purpose of this section, a party to a marriage shall be treated as domiciled in a country if he was domiciled in that country either according to the law of that country in family matters or according to the law of the part of the United Kingdom in which the question of recognition arises.

47   Cross-proceedings and divorces following legal separations

(1) Where there have been cross-proceedings, the validity of an overseas divorce, annulment or legal separation obtained either in the original proceedings or in the cross-proceedings shall be recognised if –

(a) the requirements of section 46(1)(b)(i), (ii) or (iii) of this Act are satisfied in relation to the date of the commencement either of the original proceedings or of the cross-proceedings, and

(b) the validity of the divorce, annulment or legal separation is otherwise entitled to recognition by virtue of the provisions of this Part.

(2) Where a legal separation, the validity of which is entitled to recognition by virtue of the provisions of section 46 of this Act or of subsection (1) above, is converted, in the country in which it was obtained, into a divorce which is effective under the law of that country, the validity of the divorce shall be recognised whether or not it would itself be entitled to recognition by virtue of those provisions.

48   Proof of facts relevant to recognition

(1) For the purpose of deciding whether an overseas divorce, annulment or legal separation obtained by means of proceedings is entitled to recognition by virtue of section 46 and 47 of this court, any finding of fact made (whether expressly or by implication) in the proceedings and on the basis of which jurisdiction was assumed in the proceedings shall –

(a) if both parties to the marriage took part in the proceedings, be conclusive evidence of the fact found; and

(b) in any other case, be sufficient proof of that fact unless the contrary be shown.

(2) In this section 'finding of fact' includes a finding that either party to the marriage –

(a) was habitually resident in the country in which the divorce, annulment or legal separation was obtained; or

(b) was under the law of that country domiciled there; or

(c) was a national of that country.

(3) For the purposes of subsection (1)(a) above, a party to the marriage who has appeared in judicial proceedings shall be treated as having taken part in them.

49 Modifications of Part II in relation to countries comprising territories having different systems of law

(1) In relation to a country comprising territories in which different systems of law are in force in matters of divorce, annulment or legal separation, the provisions of this Part mentioned in subsections (2) to (5) below shall have effect subject to the modifications there specified.

(2) In a case of a divorce, annulment or legal separation the recognition of the validity of which depends on whether the requirements of subsection (1)(b)(i) or (ii) of section 46 of this Act are satisfied, that section and, in the case of a legal separation, section 47(2) of this Act shall have effect as if each territory were a separate country.

(3) In the case of a divorce, annulment or legal separation the recognition of the validity of which depends on whether the requirements of subsection (1)(b)(iii) of section 46 of this Act are satisfied –

(a) that section shall have effect as if for paragraph (a) of subsection (1) there were substituted the following paragraph –

'(a) the divorce, annulment or legal separation is effective throughout the country in which it was obtained;'; and

(b) in the case of a legal separation, section 47(2) of this Act shall have effect as if for the words 'is effective under the law of that country' there were substituted the words 'is effective throughout that country'.

(4) In the case of a divorce, annulment or legal separation the recognition of the validity of which depends on whether the requirements of subsection (2)(b) of section 46 of this Act are satisfied, that section and section 52(3) and

(4) of this Act and, in the case of a legal separation, section 47(2) of this Act shall have effect as if each territory were a separate country.

(5) Paragraphs (a) and (b) of section 48(2) of this Act shall each have effect as if each territory were a separate country.

50 Non-recognition of divorce or annulment in another jurisdiction no bar to remarriage

Where, in any part of the United Kingdom –

(a) a divorce or annulment has being granted by a court of civil jurisdiction, or

(b) the validity of a divorce or annulment is recognised by virtue of this Part,

the fact that the divorce or annulment would not be recognised elsewhere shall not preclude either party to the marriage from remarrying in that part of the United Kingdom or cause the remarriage of either party (wherever the remarriage takes place) to be treated as invalid in that part.

51 Refusal of recognition

(1) Subject to section 52 of this Act, recognition of the validity of –

(a) a divorce, annulment or judicial separation granted by a court of civil jurisdiction in any part of the British Islands, or

(b) an overseas divorce, annulment or legal separation,

may be refused in any part of the United Kingdom if the divorce, annulment or separation was granted or obtained at a time when it was irreconcilable with a decision determining the question of the subsistence or validity of the marriage of the parties previously given (whether before or after the commencement of this Part) by a court of civil jurisdiction in that part of the United Kingdom or by a court elsewhere and recognised or entitled to be recognised in that part of the United Kingdom.

(2) Subject to section 52 of this Act, recognition of the validity of –

(a) a divorce or judicial separation granted by a court of civil jurisdiction in any part of the British Island, or

(b) an overseas divorce or legal separation,

may be refused in any part of the United Kingdom if the divorce or separation was granted or obtained at a time when, according to the law of that part of the United Kingdom (including its rules of private international law and the provisions of this Part), there was no subsisting marriage between the parties.

(3) Subject to section 52 of this Act, recognition by virtue of section 45 of this Act of the validity of the overseas divorce, annulment or legal separation may be refused if –

> (a) in the case of a divorce, annulment or legal separation obtained by means of proceedings, it was obtained –
>
> > (i) without such steps having been taken for giving notice of the proceedings to a party to the marriage as, having regard to the nature of the proceedings and all the circumstances, should reasonably have been taken; or
> >
> > (ii) without a party to the marriage having been given (for any reason other than lack of notice) such opportunity to take part in the proceedings as, having regard to those matters, he should reasonably have been given; or
>
> (b) in the case of a divorce, annulment or legal separation obtained otherwise than by means of proceedings –
>
> > (i) there is no official document certifying that the divorce, annulment or legal separation is effective under the law of the country in which it was obtained; or
> >
> > (ii) where either party to the marriage was domiciled in another country at the relevant date, there is no official document certifying that the divorce, annulment or legal separation is recognised as valid under the law of that other country; or
>
> (c) in either case, recognition of the divorce, annulment or legal separation would be manifestly contrary to public policy.

(4) In this section –

'official', in relation to a document certifying that a divorce, annulment or legal separation is effective, or is recognised as valid, under the law of any country, means issued by a person or body appointed or recognised for the purpose under that law;

'the relevant date' has the same meaning as in section 46 of this Act;

and subsection (5) of that section shall apply for the purposes of this section as it applies for the purposes of that section.

(5) Nothing in this Part shall be construed as requiring the recognition of any finding of fault made in any proceedings for divorce, annulment or

separation or of any maintenance, custody or other ancillary order made in any such proceedings.

52 Provisions as to divorces, annulments, etc obtained before commencement of Part II

(1) The provisions of this Part shall apply –

(a) to a divorce, annulment or judicial separation granted by a court of civil jurisdiction in the British Islands before the date of the commencement of this Part, and

(b) to an overseas divorce, annulment or legal separation obtained before that date,

as well as to one granted or obtained on or after that date.

(2) In the case of such a divorce, annulment or separation as is mentioned in subsection (1)(a) or (b) above, the provisions of this Part shall require or, as the case may be, preclude the recognition of its validity in relation to any time before that date as well as in relation to any subsequent time, but those provisions shall not –

(a) affect any property to which any person became entitled before that date, or

(b) affect the recognition of the validity of the divorce, annulment or separation if that matter has been decided by any competent court in the British Islands before that date.

(3) Subsections (1) and (2) above shall apply in relation to any divorce or judicial separation granted by a court of civil jurisdiction in the British Islands before the date of the commencement of this Part whether granted before or after the commencement of section 1 of the Recognition of Divorces and Legal Separations Act 1971.

(4) The validity of any divorce, annulment or legal separation mentioned in subsection (5) below shall be recognised in the United Kingdom whether or not it is entitled to recognition by virtue of any of the foregoing provisions of this Part.

(5) The divorces, annulments and legal separations referred to in subsection (4) above are –

(a) a divorce which was obtained in the British Islands before 1 January 1974 and was recognised as valid under rules of law applicable before that date;

(b) an overseas divorce which was recognised as valid under the

Recognition of Divorces and Legal Separations Act 1971 and was not affected by section 16(2) of the Domicile and Matrimonial Proceedings Act 1973 (proceedings otherwise than in a court of law where both parties resident in the United Kingdom);

(c) a divorce of which the decree was registered under section 1 of the Indian and Colonial Divorce Jurisdiction Act 1926;

(d) a divorce or annulment which was recognised as valid under section 4 of the Matrimonial Causes (War Marriages) Act 1944; and

(e) an overseas legal separation which was recognised as valid under the Recognition of Divorces and Legal Separations Act 1971.

54 Interpretation of Part II

(1) In this Part –

'annulment' includes any decree or declarator of nullity of marriage, however expressed;

'part of the United kingdom' means England Wales, Scotland or Northern Ireland;

'proceedings' means judicial or other proceedings.

(2) I this Part 'country' includes a colony or other dependent territory of the United Kingdom but for the purposes of this Part a person shall be treated as a national of such a territory only if it has a law of citizenship or nationality separate from that of the United Kingdom and he is a citizen or national of that territory under that law.

Part III

DECLARATIONS OF STATUS

55 Declarations as to marital status

(1) Subject to the following provisions of this section, any person may apply to the court for one or more of the following declarations in relation to a marriage specified in the application, that is to say –

(a) a declaration that the marriage was at its inception a valid marriage;

(b) a declaration that the marriage subsisted on a date specified in the application;

(c) a declaration that the marriage did not subsist on a date so specified;

(d) a declaration that the validity of a divorce, annulment or legal separation obtained in any country outside England and Wales in respect of the marriage is entitled to recognition in England and Wales;

(e) a declaration that the validity of a divorce, annulment or legal separation so obtained in respect of the marriage is not entitled to recognition in England and Wales.

(2) A court shall have jurisdiction to entertain an application under subsection (1) above if, and only if, either of the parties to the marriage to which the application relates –

(a) is domiciled in England and Wales on the date of the application, or

(b) has been habitually resident in England and Wales throughout the period of one year ending with that date, or

(c) died before that date and either –

(i) was at death domiciled in England and Wales, or

(ii) had been habitually resident in England and Wales throughout the period of one year ending with the date of death.

(3) Where an application under section (1) above is made by any person other than a party to the marriage to which the application relates, the court shall refuse to hear the application if it considers that the applicant does not have a sufficient interest in the determination of that application.

56   Declarations of parentage, legitimacy or legitimation

(1) Any person may apply to the court for a declaration –

(a) that a person named in the application is or was his parent; or

(b) that he is the legitimate child of his parents.

(2) Any person may apply to the court for one (or for one or, in the alternative, the other) of the following declarations, that is to say –

(a) a declaration that he has become a legitimated person;

(b) a declaration that he has not become a legitimated person.

(3) A court shall have jurisdiction to entertain an application under this section if, and only if, the applicant –

(a) is domiciled in England and Wales on the date of the application, or

(b) has been habitually resident in England and Wales throughout the period of one year ending with that date.

(4) Where a declaration is made on an application under subsection (1) above, the prescribed officer of the court shall notify the Registrar General,

in such a manner and within such period as may be prescribed, of the making of that declaration.

(5) In this section 'legitimated person' means a person legitimated or recognised as legitimated –

(a) under section 2 or 3 of the Legitimacy Act 1976;

(b) under section 1 or 8 of the Legitimacy Act 1926; or

(c) by a legitimation (whether or not by virtue of the subsequent marriage of his parents) recognised by the law of England and Wales and effected under the law of another country.

57 Declarations as to adoptions effected overseas

(1) Any person whose status as an adopted child of any person depends on whether he has been adopted by that person by either –

(a) an overseas adoption as defined by section 72(2) of the Adoption Act 1976, or

(b) an adoption recognised by the law of England and Wales and effected under the law of any country outside the British Islands,

may apply to the court for one (or for one or, in the alternative, the other) of the declarations mentioned in subsection (2) below.

(2) The said declarations are –

(a) a declaration that the applicant is for the purposes of section 39 of the Adoption Act 1976 the adopted child of that person;

(b) a declaration that the applicant is not for the purposes of that section the adopted child of that person.

(3) A court shall have jurisdiction to entertain an application under subsection (1) above if, and only if, the applicant –

(a) is domiciled in England and Wales on the date of the application, or

(b) has been habitually resident in England and Wales throughout the period of one year ending with that date.

58 General provisions as to the making and effect of declarations

(1) Where on an application for a declaration under this Part the truth of the proposition to be declared is proved to the satisfaction of the court, the court shall make that declaration unless to do so would manifestly be contrary to public policy.

(2) Any declaration made under this Part shall be binding on Her Majesty and all other persons.

(3) The court, on the dismissal of an application for a declaration under this Part, shall not have power to make any declaration for which an application has not been made.

(4) No declaration which may be applied for under this Part may be made otherwise than under this Part by any court.

(5) No declaration may be made by any court, whether under this Part or otherwise –

(a) that a marriage was at its inception void;

(b) that any person is or was illegitimate.

(6) Nothing in this section shall affect the powers of any court to grant a decree of nullity of marriage.

59   Provisions relating to the Attorney-General

(1) On an application for a declaration under this Part the court may at any stage of the proceedings, of its own motion or on the application of any party to the proceedings, direct that all necessary papers in the matter be sent to the Attorney-General.

(2) The Attorney-General, whether or not he is sent papers in relation to an application for a declaration under this Part, may –

(a) intervene in the proceedings on that application in such manner as he thinks necessary or expedient, and

(b) argue before the court any question in relation to the application which the court considers it necessary to have fully argued.

(3) Where any costs are incurred by the Attorney-General in connection with any application for a declaration under this Part, the court may make such order as it considers just as to the payment of those costs by parties to the proceedings.

60   Supplementary provisions as to declarations

(1) Any declaration made under this Part, and any application for such a declaration, shall be in the form prescribed by rules of court.

(2) Rules of court may make provision –

(a) as to the information required to be given by any applicant for a declaration under this Part;

(b) as to the persons who are to be parties to proceedings on an application under this Part;

(c) requiring notice of an application under this Part to be served on the Attorney-General and on persons who may be affected by any declaration applied for.

(3) No proceedings under this Part shall affect any final judgment or decree already pronounced or made by any court of competent jurisdiction.

(4) The court hearing an application under this Part may direct that the whole or any part of the proceedings shall be heard in camera, and an application for a direction under this subsection shall be heard in camera unless the court otherwise directs.

63   Interpretation of Part III

In this Part 'the court' means the High Court or a county court.

As amended by the Family Law Reform Act 1987, ss22, 33(1), Schedule 2, para 96; Children Act 1989, s108(5), (7), Schedule 13, paras 62(1), (2)(a), (b), (3), 63, 64, 65, 66(1), (2), (3), 70, 71, Schedule 15; Age of Legal Capacity (Scotland) Act 1991, s10(1), Schedule 10, para 47; Family Law Act 1986 (Dependent Territories) Order 1991; Family Law Act (Dependent Territories) Order 1994; Children (Northern Ireland) Order 1995, art 185(2), Schedule 10; Children (Northern Ireland Consequential Amendments) Order 1995, art 12(1), (3), (4), (5)(b), (c), 15, Schedule.

FAMILY LAW REFORM ACT 1987
(1987 c 42)

1 General principle

(1) In this Act and enactments passed and instruments made after the coming into force of this section, references (however expressed) to any relationship between two persons shall, unless the contrary intention appears, be construed without regard to whether or not the father and mother of either of them, or the father and mother of any person through whom the relationship is deduced, have or had been married to each other at any time.

(2) In this Act and enactments passed after the coming into force of this section, unless the contrary intention appears –

(a) references to a person whose father and mother were married to each other at the time of his birth include; and

(b) references to a person whose father and mother were not married to each other at the time of his birth do not include,

references to any person to whom subsection (3) below applies, and cognate references shall be construed accordingly.

(3) This subsection applies to any person who –

(a) is treated as legitimate by virtue of section 1 of the Legitimacy Act 1976;

(b) is a legitimated person within the meaning of section 10 of that Act;

(c) is an adopted child within the meaning of Part IV of the Adoption Act 1976; or

(d) is otherwise treated in law as legitimate.

(4) For the purpose of construing references falling within subsection (2) above, the time of a person's birth shall be taken to include any time during the period beginning with –

(a) the insemination resulting in his birth; or

(b) where there was no such insemination, his conception,

and (in either case) ending with his birth.

27 Artificial insemination

(1) Where after the coming into force of this section a child is born in England and Wales as the result of the artificial insemination of a woman who –

(a) was at the time of the insemination a party to a marriage (being a marriage which had not at that time been dissolved or annulled); and

(b) was artificially inseminated with the semen of some person other than the other party to that marriage,

then, unless it is proved to the satisfaction of any court by which the matter has to be determined that the other party to that marriage did not consent to the insemination, the child shall be treated in law as the child of the parties to that marriage and shall not be treated as the child of any person other than the parties to that marriage.

(2) Any reference in this section to a marriage includes a reference to a void marriage if at the time of the insemination resulting in the birth of the child both or either of the parties reasonably believed that the marriage was valid; and for the purposes of this section it shall be presumed, unless the contrary is shown, that one of the parties so believed at that time that the marriage was valid.

(3) Nothing in this section shall affect the succession to any dignity or title of honour or render any person capable of succeeding to or transmitting a right to succeed to any such dignity or title.

CHILDREN ACT 1989
(1989 c 41)

PART I

INTRODUCTORY

1 Welfare of the child

(1) When a court determines any question with respect to –

(a) the upbringing of a child; or

(b) the administration of a child's property or the application of any income arising from it,

the child's welfare shall be the court's paramount consideration.

(2) In any proceedings in which any question with respect to the upbringing of a child arises, the court shall have regard to the general principle that any delay in determining the question is likely to prejudice the welfare of the child.

(3) In the circumstances mentioned in subsection (4), a court shall have regard in particular to –

(a) the ascertainable wishes and feelings of the child concerned (considered in the light of his age and understanding);

(b) his physical, emotional and educational needs;

(c) the likely effect on him of any change in his circumstances;

(d) his age, sex, background and any characteristics of his which the court considers relevant;

(e) any harm which he has suffered or is at risk of suffering;

(f) how capable each of his parents, and any other person in relation to whom the court considers the question to be relevant, is of meeting his needs;

(g) the range of powers available to the court under this Act in the proceedings in question.

(4) The circumstances are that –

(a) the court is considering whether to make, vary or discharge a section 8 order, and the making, variation or discharge of the order is opposed by any party to the proceedings; or

(b) the court is considering whether to make, vary or discharge an order under Part IV.

(5) Where a court is considering whether or not to make one or more orders under this Act with respect to a child, it shall not make the order or any of the orders unless it considers that doing so would be better for the child than making no order at all.

2   Parental responsibility for children

(1) Where a child's father and mother were married to each other at the time of his birth, they shall each have parental responsibility for the child.

(2) Where a child's father and mother were not married to each other at the time of his birth –

(a) the mother shall have parental responsibility for the child;

(b) the father shall not have parental responsibility for the child, unless he acquires it in accordance with the provisions of this Act.

(3) References in this Act to a child whose father and mother were, or (as the case may be) were not, married to each other at the time of his birth must be read with section 1 of the Family Law Reform Act 1987 (which extends their meaning).

(4) The rule of law that a father is the natural guardian of his legitimate child is abolished.

(5) More than one person may have parental responsibility for the same child at the same time.

(6) A person who has parental responsibility for a child at any time shall not cease to have that responsibility solely because some other person subsequently acquires parental responsibility for the child.

(7) Where more than one person has parental responsibility for a child, each of them may act alone and without the other (or others) in meeting that responsibility; but nothing in this Part shall be taken to affect the operation of any enactment which requires the consent of more than one person in a matter affecting the child.

(8) The fact that a person has parental responsibility for a child shall not

entitle him to act in any way which would be incompatible with any order made with respect to the child under this Act.

(9) A person who has parental responsibility for a child may not surrender or transfer any part of that responsibility to another but may arrange for some or all of it to be met by one or more persons acting on his behalf.

(10) The person with whom any such arrangement is made may himself be a person who already has parental responsibility for the child concerned.

(11) The making of any such arrangement shall not affect any liability of the person making it which may arise from any failure to meet any part of his parental responsibility for the child concerned.

3   Meaning of 'parental responsibility'

(1) In this Act 'parental responsibility' means all the rights, duties, powers, responsibilities and authority which by law a parent of a child has in relation to the child and his property.

(2) It also includes the rights, powers and duties which a guardian of the child's estate (appointed, before the commencement of section 5, to act generally) would have had in relation to the child and his property.

(3) The rights referred to in subsection (2) include, in particular, the right of the guardian to receive or recover in his own name, for the benefit of the child, property of whatever description and wherever situated which the child is entitled to receive or recover.

(4) The fact that a person has, or does not have, parental responsibility for a child shall not affect –

(a) any obligation which he may have in relation to the child (such as a statutory duty to maintain the child); or
(b) any rights which, in the event of the child's death, he (or any other person) may have in relation to the child's property.

(5) A person who –

(a) does not have parental responsibility for a particular child; but
(b) has care of the child,

may (subject to the provisions of this Act) do what is reasonable in all the circumstances of the case for the purpose of safeguarding or promoting the child's welfare.

4 Acquisition of parental responsibility by father

(1) Where a child's father and mother were not married to each other at the time of his birth –

(a) the court may, on the application of the father, order that he shall have parental responsibility for the child; or

(b) the father and mother may by agreement ('a parental responsibility agreement') provide for the father to have parental responsibility for the child.

(2) No parental responsibility agreement shall have effect for the purposes of this Act unless –

(a) it is made in the form prescribed by regulations made by the Lord Chancellor; and

(b) where regulations are made by the Lord Chancellor prescribing the manner in which such agreements must be recorded, it is recorded in the prescribed manner.

(3) Subject to section 12(4), an order under subsection (1)(a), or a parental responsibility agreement, may only be brought to an end by an order of the court made on the application –

(a) of any person who has parental responsibility for the child; or

(b) with leave of the court, of the child himself.

(4) The court may only grant leave under subsection (3)(b) if it is satisfied that the child has sufficient understanding to make the proposed application.

5 Appointment of guardians

(1) Where an application with respect to a child is made to the court by any individual, the court may by order appoint that individual to be the child's guardian if –

(a) the child has no parent with parental responsibility for him; or

(b) a residence order has been made with respect to the child in favour of a parent or guardian of his who has died while the order was in force.

(2) The power conferred by subsection (1) may also be exercised in any family proceedings if the court considers that the order should be made even though no application has been made for it.

(3) A parent who has parental responsibility for his child may appoint another individual to be the child's guardian in the event of his death.

(4) A guardian of a child may appoint another individual to take his place as the child's guardian in the event of his death.

(5) An appointment under subsection (3) or (4) shall not have effect unless it is made in writing, is dated and is signed by the person making the appointment or –

  (a) in the case of an appointment made by a will which is not signed by the testator, is signed at the direction of the testator in accordance with the requirements of section 9 of the Wills Act 1837; or

  (b) in any other case, is signed at the direction of the person making the appointment, in his presence and in the presence of two witnesses who each attest the signature.

(6) A person appointed as a child's guardian under this section shall have parental responsibility for the child concerned.

(7) Where –

  (a) on the death of any person making an appointment under subsection (3) or (4), the child concerned has no parent with parental responsibility for him; or

  (b) immediately before the death of any person making such an appointment, a residence order in his favour was in force with respect to the child,

the appointment shall take effect on the death of that person.

(8) Where, on the death of any person making an appointment under subsection (3) or (4) –

  (a) the child concerned has a parent with parental responsibility for him; and

  (b) subsection (7)(b) does not apply,

the appointment shall take effect when the child no longer has a parent who has parental responsibility for him.

(9) Subsections (1) and (7) do not apply if the residence order referred to in paragraph (b) of those subsections was also made in favour of a surviving parent of the child.

(10) Nothing in this section shall be taken to prevent an appointment under subsection (3) or (4) being made by two or more persons acting jointly.

(11) Subject to any provision made by rules of court, no court shall exercise the High Court's inherent jurisdiction to appoint a guardian of the estate of any child.

(12) Where rules of court are made under subsection (11) they may prescribe the circumstances in which, and conditions subject to which, an appointment of such a guardian may be made.

(13) A guardian of a child may only be appointed in accordance with the provisions of this section.

6 Guardians: revocation and disclaimer

(1) An appointment under section 5(3) or (4) revokes an earlier such appointment (including one made in an unrevoked will or codicil) made by the same person in respect of the same child, unless it is clear (whether as the result of an express provision in the later appointment or by any necessary implication) that the purpose of the later appointment is to appoint an additional guardian.

(2) An appointment under section 5(3) or (4) (including one made in an unrevoked will or codicil) is revoked if the person who made the appointment revokes it by a written and dated instrument which is signed –

(a) by him; or

(b) at his direction, in his presence and in the presence of two witnesses who each attest the signature.

(3) An appointment under section 5(3) or (4) (other than one made in a will or codicil) is revoked if, with the intention of revoking the appointment, the person who made it –

(a) destroys the instrument by which it was made; or

(b) has some other person destroy that instrument in his presence.

(3A) An appointment under section 5(3) or (4) (including one made in an unrevoked will or codicil) is revoked if the person appointed is the spouse of the person who made the appointment and either –

(a) a decree of a court of civil jurisdiction in England and Wales dissolves or annuls the marriage, or

(b) the marriage is dissolved or annulled and the divorce or annulment is entitled to recognition in England and Wales by virtue of Part II of the Family Law Act 1986,

unless a contrary intention appears by the appointment.

(4) For the avoidance of doubt, an appointment under section 5(3) or (4) made in a will or codicil is revoked if the will or codicil is revoked.

(5) A person who is appointed as a guardian under section 5(3) or (4) may

disclaim his appointment by an instrument in writing signed by him and made within a reasonable time of his first knowing that the appointment has taken effect.

(6) Where regulations are made by the Lord Chancellor prescribing the manner in which such disclaimers must be recorded, no such disclaimer shall have effect unless it is recorded in the prescribed manner.

(7) Any appointment of a guardian under section 5 may be brought to an end at any time by order of the court –

(a) on the application of any person who has parental responsibility for the child;

(b) on the application of the child concerned, with leave of the court; or

(c) in any family proceedings, if the court considers that it should be brought to an end even though no application has been made.

7   Welfare reports

(1) A court considering any question with respect to a child under this Act may –

(a) ask a probation officer; or

(b) ask a local authority to arrange for –

(i) an officer of the authority; or

(ii) such other person (other than a probation officer) as the authority considers appropriate,

to report to the court on such matters relating to the welfare of that child as are required to be dealt with in the report.

(2) The Lord Chancellor may make regulations specifying matters which, unless the court orders otherwise, must be dealt with in any report under this section.

(3) The report may be made in writing, or orally, as the court requires.

(4) Regardless of any enactment or rule of law which would otherwise prevent it from doing so, the court may take account of –

(a) any statement contained in the report; and

(b) any evidence given in respect of the matters referred to in the report,

in so far as the statement or evidence is, in the opinion of the court, relevant to the question which it is considering.

(5) It shall be the duty of the authority or probation officer to comply with any request for a report under this section.

PART II

ORDERS WITH RESPECT TO CHILDREN IN FAMILY PROCEEDINGS

8   Residence, contact and other orders with respect to children

(1) In this Act –

'a contact order' means an order requiring the person with whom a child lives, or is to live, to allow the child to visit or stay with the person named in the order, or for that person and the child otherwise to have contact with each other;

'a prohibited steps order' means an order that no step which could be taken by a parent in meeting his parental responsibility for a child, and which is of a kind specified in the order, shall be taken by any person without the consent of the court;

'a residence order' means an order settling the arrangements to be made as to the person with whom a child is to live; and

'a specific issue order' means an order giving directions for the purpose of determining a specific question which has arisen, or which may arise, in connection with any aspect of parental responsibility for a child.

(2) In this Act 'a section 8 order' means any of the orders mentioned in subsection (1) and any order varying or discharging such an order.

(3) For the purposes of this Act 'family proceedings' means any proceedings –

    (a) under the inherent jurisdiction of the High Court in relation to children; and

    (b) under the enactments mentioned in subsection (4),

but does not include proceedings on an application for leave under section 100(3).

(4) The enactments are –

    (a) Parts I, II and IV of this Act;

    (b) the Matrimonial Causes Act 1973;

    (d) the Adoption Act 1976;

(e) the Domestic proceedings and Magistrates' Courts Act 1978;

(g) Part III of the Matrimonial and Family Proceedings Act 1984;

(h) the Family Law Act 1996.

9 Restrictions on making section 8 orders

(1) No court shall make any section 8 order, other than a residence order, with respect to a child who is in the care of a local authority.

(2) No application may be made by a local authority for a residence order or contact order and no court shall make such an order in favour of a local authority.

(3) A person who is, or was at any time within the last six months, a local authority foster parent of a child may not apply for leave to apply for a section 8 order with respect to the child unless –

(a) he had the consent of the authority;

(b) he is a relative of the child; or

(c) the child has lived with him for at least three years preceding the application.

(4) The period of three years mentioned in subsection (3)(c) need not be continuous but must have begun not more than five years before the making of the application.

(5) No court shall exercise its powers to make a specific issue order or prohibited steps order –

(a) with a view to achieving a result which could be achieved by making a residence or contact order; or

(b) in any way which is denied to the High Court (by section 100(2)) in the exercise of its inherent jurisdiction with respect to children.

(6) No court shall make any section 8 order which is to have effect for a period which will end after the child has reached the age of sixteen unless it is satisfied that the circumstances of the case are exceptional.

(7) No court shall make any section 8 order, other than one varying or discharging such an order, with respect to a child who has reached the age of sixteen unless it is satisfied that the circumstances of the case are exceptional.

10   Power of court to make section 8 orders

(1) In any family proceedings in which a question arises with respect to the welfare of any child, the court may make a section 8 order with respect to the child if –

  (a) an application for the order has been made by a person who –

   (i) is entitled to apply for a section 8 order with respect to the child; or

   (ii) has obtained the leave of the court to make the application; or

  (b) the court considers that the order should be made even though no such application has been made.

(2) The court may also make a section 8 order with respect to any child on the application of a person who –

  (a) is entitled to apply for a section 8 order with respect to the child; or

  (b) has obtained the leave of the court to make the application.

(3) This section is subject to the restrictions imposed by section 9.

(4) The following persons are entitled to apply to the court for any section 8 order with respect to a child –

  (a) any parent or guardian of the child;

  (b) any person in whose favour a residence order is in force with respect to the child.

(5) The following persons are entitled to apply for a residence or contact order with respect to a child –

  (a) any party to a marriage (whether or not subsisting) in relation to whom the child is a child of the family;

  (b) any person with whom the child has lived for a period of at least three years;

  (c) any person who –

   (i) in any case where a residence order is in force with respect to the child, has the consent of each of the persons in whose favour the order was made;

   (ii) in any case where the child is in the care of a local authority, has the consent of that authority; or

   (iii) in any other case, has the consent of each of those (if any) who have parental responsibility for the child.

(6) A person who would not otherwise be entitled (under the previous provisions of this section) to apply for the variation or discharge of a section 8 order shall be entitled to do so if –

(a) the order was made on his application; or

(b) in the case of a contact order, he is named in the order.

(7) Any person who falls within a category of person prescribed by rules of court is entitled to apply for any such section 8 order as may be prescribed in relation to that category of person.

(8) Where the person applying for leave to make an application for a section 8 order is the child concerned, the court may only grant leave if it is satisfied that he has sufficient understanding to make the proposed application for the section 8 order.

(9) Where the person applying for leave to make an application for a section 8 order is not the child concerned, the court shall, in deciding whether or not to grant leave, have particular regard to –

(a) the nature of the proposed application for the section 8 order;

(b) the applicant's connection with the child;

(c) any risk there might be of that proposed application disrupting the child's life to such an extent that he would be harmed by it; and

(d) where the child is being looked after by a local authority –

(i) the authority's plans for the child's future; and

(ii) the wishes and feelings of the child's parents.

(10) The period of three years mentioned in subsection (5)(b) need not be continuous but must not have begun more than five years before, or ended more than three months before, the making of the application.

11   General principles and supplementary provisions

(1) In proceedings in which any question of making a section 8 order, or any other question with respect to such an order, arises, the court shall (in the light of any rules made by virtue of subsection (2)) –

(a) draw up a timetable with a view to determining the question without delay; and

(b) give such directions as it considers appropriate for the purpose of ensuring, so far as is reasonably practicable, that that timetable is adhered to.

(2) Rules of court may –

(a) specify periods within which specified steps must be taken in relation to proceedings in which such questions arise; and

(b) make other provision with respect to such proceedings for the purpose of ensuring, so far as is reasonably practicable, that such questions are determined without delay.

(3) Where a court has power to make a section 8 order, it may do so at any time during the course of the proceedings in question even though it is not in a position to dispose finally of those proceedings.

(4) Where a residence order is made in favour of two or more persons who do not themselves all live together, the order may specify the periods during which the child is to live in the different households concerned.

(5) Where –

(a) a residence order has been made with respect to a child; and

(b) as a result of the order the child lives, or is to live, with one of two parents who each have parental responsibility for him,

the residence order shall cease to have effect if the parents live together for a continuous period of more than six months.

(6) A contact order which requires the parent with whom a child lives to allow the child to visit, or otherwise have contact with, his other parent shall cease to have effect if the parents live together for a continuous period of more than six months.

(7) A section 8 order may –

(a) contain directions about how it is to be carried into effect;

(b) impose conditions which must be complied with by any person –

(i) in whose favour the order is made;

(ii) who is a parent of the child concerned;

(iii) who is not a parent of his but who has parental responsibility for him; or

(iv) with whom the child is living,

and to whom the conditions are expressed to apply;

(c) be made to have effect for a specified period, or contain provisions which are to have effect for a specified period;

(d) make such incidental, supplemental or consequential provision as the court thinks fit.

12   Residence orders and parental responsibility

(1) Where the court makes a residence order in favour of the father of a child it shall, if the father would not otherwise have parental responsibility for the child, also make an order under section 4 giving him that responsibility.

(2) Where the court makes a residence order in favour of any person who is not the parent or guardian of the child concerned that person shall have parental responsibility for the child while the residence order remains in force.

(3) Where a person has parental responsibility for a child as a result of subsection (2), he shall not have the right –

(a) to consent, or refuse to consent, to the making of an application with respect to the child under section 18 of the Adoption Act 1976;

(b) to agree, or refuse to agree, to the making of an adoption order, or an order under section 55 of the Act 1976, with respect to the child; or

(c) to appoint a guardian for the child.

(4) Where subsection (1) requires the court to make an order under section 4 in respect of the father of a child, the court shall not bring that order to an end at any time while the residence order concerned remains in force.

13   Change of child's name or removal from jurisdiction

(1) Where a residence order is in force with respect to a child, no person may –

(a) cause the child to be known by a new surname; or

(b) remove him from the United Kingdom;

without either the written consent of every person who has parental responsibility for the child or the leave of the court.

(2) Subsection (1)(b) does not prevent the removal of a child, for a period of less than one month, by the person in whose favour the residence order is made.

(3) In making a residence order with respect to a child the court may grant the leave required by subsection (1)(b), either generally or for specified purposes.

14   Enforcement of residence orders

(1) Where –

(a) a residence order is in force with respect to a child in favour of any person; and

(b) any other person (including one in whose favour the order is also in force) is in breach of the arrangements settled by that order,

the person mentioned in paragraph (a) may, as soon as the requirement in subsection (2) is complied with, enforce the order under section 63(3) of the Magistrates' Courts Act 1980 as if it were an order requiring the other person to produce the child to him.

(2) The requirement is that a copy of the residence order has been served on the other person.

(3) Subsection (1) is without prejudice to any other remedy open to the person in whose favour the residence order is in force.

15   Orders for financial relief with respect to children

(1) Schedule 1 ... makes provision in relation to financial relief for children. ...

16   Family assistance orders

(1) Where, in any family proceedings, the court has power to make an order under this Part with respect to any child, it may (whether or not it makes such an order) make an order requiring –

(a) a probation officer to be made available; or

(b) a local authority to make an officer of the authority available,

to advise, assist and (where appropriate) befriend any person named in the order.

(2) The persons who may be named in an order under this section ('a family assistance order') are –

(a) any parent or guardian of the child;

(b) any person with whom the child is living or in whose favour a contact order is in force with respect to the child;

(c) the child himself.

(3) No court may make a family assistance order unless –

(a) it is satisfied that the circumstances of the case are exceptional; and

(b) it has obtained the consent of every person to be named in the order other than the child.

(4) A family assistance order may direct –

(a) the person named in the order; or

(b) such of the persons named in the order as may be specified in the order,

to take such steps as may be so specified with a view to enabling the officer concerned to be kept informed of the address of any person named in the order and to be allowed to visit any such person.

(5) Unless it specifies a shorter period, a family assistance order shall have effect for a period of six months beginning with the day on which it is made.

(6) Where –

(a) a family assistance order is in force with respect to a child; and

(b) a section 8 order is also in force with respect to the child,

the officer concerned may refer to the court the question whether the section 8 order should be varied or discharged.

(7) A family assistance order shall not be made so as to require a local authority to make an officer of theirs available unless –

(a) the authority agree; or

(b) the child concerned lives or will live within their area.

(8) Where a family assistance order requires a probation officer to be made available, the officer shall be selected in accordance with arrangements made by the probation committee for the area in which the child lives or will live.

(9) If the selected probation officer is unable to carry out his duties, or dies, another probation officer shall be selected in the same manner.

PART III

LOCAL AUTHORITY SUPPORT FOR CHILDREN AND FAMILIES

20 Provision of accommodation for children: general

(1) Every local authority shall provide accommodation for any child in need within their area who appears to them to require accommodation as a result of –

(a) there being no person who has parental responsibility for him;

(b) his being lost or having been abandoned; or

(c) the person who has been caring for him being prevented (whether or not permanently, and for whatever reason) from providing him with suitable accommodation or care.

(2) Where a local authority provide accommodation under subsection (1) for a child who is ordinarily resident in the area of another local authority, that other local authority may take over the provision of accommodation for the child within –

(a) three months of being notified in writing that the child is being provided with accommodation; or

(b) such other longer period as may be prescribed.

(3) Every local authority shall provide accommodation for any child in need within their area who has reached the age of sixteen and whose welfare the authority consider is likely to be seriously prejudiced if they do not provide him with accommodation.

(4) A local authority may provide accommodation for any child within their area (even though a person who has parental responsibility for him is able to provide him with accommodation) if they consider that to do so would safeguard or promote the child's welfare.

(5) A local authority may provide accommodation for any person who has reached the age of sixteen but is under twenty-one in any community home which takes children who have reached the age of sixteen if they consider that to do so would safeguard or promote his welfare.

(6) Before providing accommodation under this section, a local authority shall, so far as is reasonably practicable and consistent with the child's welfare –

(a) ascertain the child's wishes regarding the provision of accommodation; and

(b) give due consideration (having regard to his age and understanding) to such wishes of the child as they have been able to ascertain.

(7) A local authority may not provide accommodation under this section for any child if any person who –

(a) has parental responsibility for him; and

(b) is willing and able to –

(i) provide accommodation for him; or

(ii) arrange for accommodation to be provided for him,

objects.

(8) Any person who has parental responsibility for a child may at any time remove the child from accommodation provided by or on behalf of the local authority under this section.

(9) Subsections (7) and (8) do not apply while any person –

(a) in whose favour a residence order is in force with respect to the child; or

(b) who has care of the child by virtue of an order made in the exercise of the High Court's inherent jurisdiction with respect to children,

agrees to the child being looked after in accommodation provided by or on behalf of the local authority.

(10) Where there is more than one such person as is mentioned in subsection (9), all of them must agree.

(11) Subsections (7) and (8) do not apply where a child who has reached the age of sixteen agrees to being provided with accommodation under this section.

22 General duty of local authority in relation to children looked after by them

(1) In this Act, any reference to a child who is looked after by a local authority is a reference to a child who is –

(a) in their care; or

(b) provided with accommodation by the authority in the exercise of any functions (in particular those under this Act) which stand referred to their social services committee under the Local Authority Social Services Act 1970.

(2) In subsection (1) 'accommodation' means accommodation which is provided for a continuous period of more than 24 hours.

(3) It shall be the duty of a local authority looking after any child –

(a) to safeguard and promote his welfare; and

(b) to make such use of services available for children cared for by their own parents as appears to the authority reasonable in his case.

(4) Before making any decision with respect to a child whom they are looking after, or proposing to look after, a local authority shall, so far as is reasonably practicable, ascertain the wishes and feelings of –

(a) the child;

(b) his parents;

(c) any person who is not a parent of his but who has parental responsibility for him; and

(d) any other person whose wishes and feelings the authority consider to be relevant,

regarding the matter to be decided.

(5) In making any such decision a local authority shall give due consideration –

(a) having regard to his age and understanding, to such wishes and feelings of the child as they have been able to ascertain;

(b) to such wishes and feelings of any person mentioned in subsection (4)(b) to (d) as they have been able to ascertain; and

(c) to the child's religious persuasion, racial origin and cultural and linguistic background.

(6) If it appears to a local authority that it is necessary, for the purpose of protecting members of the public from serious injury, to exercise their powers with respect to a child whom they are looking after in a manner which may not be consistent with their duties under this section, they may do so.

(7) If the Secretary of State considers it necessary, for the purpose of protecting members of the public from serious injury, to give directions to a local authority with respect to the exercise of their powers with respect to a child whom they are looking after, he may give such directions to the authority.

(8) Where any such directions are given to an authority they shall comply with them even though doing so is inconsistent with their duties under this section.

PART IV

CARE AND SUPERVISION

31 Care and supervision orders

(1) On the application of any local authority or authorised person, the court may make an order –

(a) placing the child with respect to whom the application is made in the care of a designated local authority; or

(b) putting him under the supervision of a designated local authority or of a probation officer.

(2) A court may only make a care order or supervision order if it is satisfied –

(a) that the child concerned is suffering, or is likely to suffer, significant harm; and

(b) that the harm, or likelihood of harm, is attributable to –

(i) the care given to the child, or likely to be given to him if the order were not made, not being what it would be reasonable to expect a parent to give to him; or

(ii) the child's being beyond parental control.

(3) No care order or supervision order may be made with respect to a child who has reached the age of seventeen (or sixteen, in the case of a child who is married).

(4) An application under this section may be made on its own or in any other family proceedings.

(5) The court may –

(a) on an application for a care order, make a supervision order;

(b) on an application for a supervision order, make a care order.

(6) Where an authorised person proposes to make an application under this section he shall –

(a) if it is reasonably practicable to do so; and

(b) before making the application,

consult the local authority appearing to him to be the authority in whose area the child concerned is ordinarily resident.

(7) An application made by an authorised person shall not be entertained by the court if, at the time when it is made, the child concerned is –

(a) the subject of an earlier application for a care order, or supervision order, which has not been disposed of; or

(b) subject to –

(i) a care order or supervision order;

(ii) an order under section 7(7)(b) of the Children and Young Persons Act 1969; or

(iii) a supervision requirement within the meaning of the Social Work (Scotland) Act 1968.

(8) The local authority designated in a care order must be –

(a) the authority within whose area the child is ordinarily resident; or

(b) where the child does not reside in the area of a local authority, the authority within whose area any circumstances arose in consequence of which the order is being made.

(9) In this section –

'authorised person' means –

(a) the National Society for the Prevention of Cruelty to Children and any of its officers; and

(b) any person authorised by order of the Secretary of State to bring proceedings under this section and any officer of a body which is so authorised;

'harm' means ill-treatment or the impairment of health or development;

'development' means physical, intellectual, emotional, social or behavioural development;

'health' means physical or mental health; and

'ill-treatment' includes sexual abuse and forms of ill-treatment which are not physical.

(10) Where the question of whether harm suffered by a child is significant turns on the child's health or development, his health or development shall be compared with that which could reasonably be expected of a similar child.

(11) In this Act –

'a care order' means (subject to section 105(1)) an order under subsection (1)(a) and (except where express provision to the contrary is made) includes an interim care order made under section 38; and

'a supervision order' means an order under subsection (1)(b) and (except where express provision to the contrary is made) includes an interim supervision order made under section 38.

32   Period within which application for order under this Part must be disposed of

(1) A court hearing an application for an order under this Part shall (in the light of any rules made by virtue of subsection (2)) –

(a) draw up a timetable with a view to disposing of the application without delay; and

(b) give such directions as it considers appropriate for the purpose of ensuring, so far as is reasonably practicable, that that timetable is adhered to.

(2) Rules of court may –

(a) specify periods within which specified steps must be taken in relation to such proceedings; and

(b) make other provision with respect to such proceedings for the purpose of ensuring, so far as is reasonably practicable, that they are disposed of without delay.

33 Effect of care order

(1) Where a care order is made with respect to a child it shall be the duty of the local authority designated by the order to receive the child into their care and to keep him in their care while the order remains in force.

(2) Where –

(a) a care order has been made with respect to a child on the application of an authorised person; but

(b) the local authority designated by the order was not informed that that person proposed to make the application,

the child may be kept in the care of that person until received into the care of the authority.

(3) While a care order is in force with respect to a child, the local authority designated by the order shall –

(a) have parental responsibility for the child; and

(b) have the power (subject to the following provisions of this section) to determine the extent to which a parent or guardian of the child may meet his parental responsibility for him.

(4) The authority may not exercise the power in subsection (3)(b) unless they are satisfied that it is necessary to do so in order to safeguard or promote the child's welfare.

(5) Nothing in subsection (3)(b) shall prevent a parent or guardian of the child who has care of him from doing what is reasonable in all the circumstances of the case for the purpose of safeguarding or promoting his welfare.

(6) While a care order is in force with respect to a child, the local authority designated by the order shall not –

(a) cause the child to be brought up in any religious persuasion other than that in which he would have been brought up if the order had not been made; or

(b) have the right –

(i) to consent or refuse to consent to the making of an application with respect to the child under section 18 of the Adoption Act 1976;

(ii) to agree or refuse to agree to the making of an adoption order, or an order under section 55 of the Act of 1976, with respect to the child; or

(iii) to appoint a guardian for the child.

(7) While a care order is in force with respect to a child, no person may –

(a) cause the child to be known by a new surname; or

(b) remove him from the United Kingdom,

without either the written consent of every person who has parental responsibility for the child or the leave of the court.

(8) Subsection (7)(b) does not –

(a) prevent the removal of such a child, for a period of less than one month, by the authority in whose care he is; or

(b) apply to arrangements for such a child to live outside England and Wales (which are governed by paragraph 19 of Schedule 2).

(9) The power in subsection (3)(b) is subject (in addition to being subject to the provisions of this section) to any right, duty, power, responsibility or authority which a parent or guardian of the child has in relation to the child and his property by virtue of any other enactment.

34 Parental contact, etc with children in care

(1) Where a child is in the care of a local authority, the authority shall (subject to the provisions of this section) allow the child reasonable contact with –

(a) his parents;

(b) any guardian of his;

(c) where there was a residence order in force with respect to the child immediately before the care order was made, the person in whose favour the order was made; and

(d) where, immediately before the care order was made, a person had care of the child by virtue of an order made in the exercise of the High Court's inherent jurisdiction with respect to children, that person.

(2) On an application made by the authority or the child, the court may make such order as it considers appropriate with respect to the contact which is to be allowed between the child and any named person.

(3) On an application made by –

(a) any person mentioned in paragraphs (a) to (d) of subsection (1); or

(b) any person who has obtained the leave of the court to make the application,

the court may make such order as it considers appropriate with respect to the contact which is to be allowed between the child and that person.

(4) On an application made by the authority or the child, the court may make an order authorising the authority to refuse to allow contact between the child and any person who is mentioned in paragraphs (a) to (d) of subsection (1) and named in the order.

(5) When making a care order with respect to a child, or in any family proceedings in connection with a child who is in the care of a local authority, the court may make an order under this section, even though no application for such an order has been made with respect to the child, if it considers that the order should be made.

(6) An authority may refuse to allow the contact that would otherwise be required by virtue of subsection (1) or an order under this section if –

(a) they are satisfied that it is necessary to do so in order to safeguard or promote the child's welfare; and

(b) the refusal –

(i) is decided upon as a matter of urgency; and

(ii) does not last for more than seven days.

(7) An order under this section may impose such conditions as the court considers appropriate.

(8) The Secretary of State may by regulations make provision as to –

(a) the steps to be taken by a local authority who have exercised their powers under subsection (6);

(b) the circumstances in which, and conditions subject to which, the terms of any order under this section may be departed from by agreement between the local authority and the person in relation to whom the order is made;

(c) notification by a local authority of any variation or suspension of arrangements made (otherwise than under an order under this section) with a view to affording any person contact with a child to whom this section applies.

(9) The court may vary or discharge any order made under this section on the application of the authority, the child concerned or the person named in the order.

(10) An order under this section may be made either at the same time as the care order itself or later.

(11) Before making a care order with respect to any child the court shall –

(a) consider the arrangements which the authority have made, or propose to make, for affording any person contact with a child to whom this section applies; and

(b) invite the parties to the proceedings to comment on those arrangements.

35 Supervision orders

(1) While a supervision order is in force it shall be the duty of the supervisor –

(a) to advise, assist and befriend the supervised child;

(b) to take such steps as are reasonably necessary to give effect to the order; and

(c) where –

(i) the order is not wholly complied with; or

(ii) the supervisor considers that the order may no longer be necessary,

to consider whether or not to apply to the court for its variation or discharge.

(2) Parts I and II of Schedule 3 make further provision with respect to supervision orders.

36 Education supervision orders

(1) On the application of any local education authority, the court may make an order putting the child with respect to whom the application is made under the supervision of a designated local education authority.

(2) In this Act 'an education supervision order' means an order under subsection (1).

(3) A court may only make an education supervision order if it is satisfied that the child concerned is of compulsory school age and is not being properly educated.

(4) For the purposes of this section, a child is being properly educated only if he is receiving efficient full-time education suitable to his age, ability and aptitude and any special educational needs he may have.

(5) Where a child is –

(a) the subject of a school attendance order which is in force under section 437 of the Education Act 1996 and which has not been complied with; or

(b) a registered pupil at a school which he is not attending regularly within the meaning of section 444 of that Act,

then, unless it is proved that he is being properly educated, it shall be assumed that he is not.

(6) An education supervision order may not be made with respect to a child who is in the care of a local authority.

(7) The local education authority designated in an education supervision order must be –

(a) the authority within whose area the child concerned is living or will live; or

(b) where –

(i) the child is a registered pupil at a school; and

(ii) the authority mentioned in paragraph (a) and the authority within whose area the school is situated agree,

the latter authority.

(8) Where a local education authority propose to make an application for an education supervision order they shall, before making the application, consult the appropriate local authority.

(9) The appropriate local authority is –

(a) in the case of a child who is being provided with accommodation by, or on behalf of, a local authority, that authority; and

(b) in any other case, the local authority within whose area the child concerned lives, or will live.

(10) Part III of Schedule 3 make further provision with respect to education supervision orders.

37 Powers of court in certain family proceedings

(1) Where, in any family proceedings in which a question arises with respect to the welfare of any child, it appears to the court that it may be appropriate for a care or supervision order to be made with respect to him, the court may direct the appropriate authority to undertake an investigation of the child's circumstances.

(2) Where the court gives a direction under this section the local authority concerned shall, when undertaking the investigation, consider whether they should –

(a) apply for a care order or for a supervision order with respect to the child;

(b) provide services or assistance for the child or his family; or

(c) take any other action with respect to the child.

(3) Where a local authority undertake an investigation under this section, and decide not to apply for a care order or supervision order with respect to the child concerned, they shall inform the court of –

(a) their reasons for so deciding;

(b) any service or assistance which they have provided, or intend to provide, for the child and his family; and

(c) any other action which they have taken, or propose to take, with respect to the child.

(4) The information shall be given to the court before the end of the period of eight weeks beginning with the date of the direction, unless the court otherwise directs.

(5) The local authority named in a direction under subsection (1) must be –

(a) the authority in whose area the child is ordinarily resident; or

(b) where the child is not ordinarily resident in the area of a local authority, the authority within whose area any circumstances arose in consequence of which the direction is being given.

(6) If, on the conclusion of any investigation or review under this section, the authority decide not to apply for a care order or supervision order with respect to the child –

(a) they shall consider whether it would be appropriate to review the case at a later date; and

(b) if they decide that it would be, they shall determine the date on which that review is to begin.

38   Interim orders

(1) Where –

(a) in any proceedings on an application for a care order or supervision order, the proceedings are adjourned; or

(b) the court gives a direction under section 37(1),

the court may make an interim care order or an interim supervision order with respect to the child concerned.

(2) A court shall not make an interim care order or interim supervision order under this section unless it is satisfied that there are reasonable grounds for believing that the circumstances with respect to the child are as mentioned in section 31(2).

(3) Where, in any proceedings on an application for a care order or supervision order, a court makes a residence order with respect to the child concerned, it shall also make an interim supervision order with respect to him unless satisfied that his welfare will be satisfactorily safeguarded without an interim order being made.

(4) An interim order made under or by virtue of this section shall have effect for such period as may be specified in the order, but shall in any event cease to have effect on whichever of the following events first occurs –

(a) the expiry of the period of eight weeks beginning with the date on which the order is made;

(b) if the order is the second or subsequent such order made with respect to the same child in the same proceedings, the expiry of the relevant period;

(c) in a case which falls within subsection (1)(a), the disposal of the application;

(d) in a case which falls within subsection (1)(b), on the disposal of an application for a care order or supervision order made by the authority with respect to the child;

(e) in a case which falls within subsection (1)(b) and in which –

(i) the court has given a direction under section 37(4), but

(ii) no application for a care order or supervision order has been made with respect to the child, the expiry of the period fixed by that direction.

(5) In subsection (4)(b) 'the relevant period' means –

(a) the period of four weeks beginning with the date on which the order in question is made; or

(b) the period of eight weeks beginning with the date on which the first order was made if that period ends later than the period mentioned in paragraph (a).

(6) Where the court makes an interim care order, or interim supervision order, it may give such directions (if any) as it considers appropriate with regard to the medical or psychiatric examination or other assessment of the child; but if the child is of sufficient understanding to make an informed decision he may refuse to submit to the examination or other assessment.

(7) A direction under subsection (6) may be to the effect that there is to be –

(a) no such examination or assessment; or

(b) no such examination or assessment unless the court directs otherwise.

(8) A direction under subsection (6) may be –

(a) given when the interim order is made or at any time while it is in force; and

(b) varied at any time on the application of any person falling within any class of person prescribed by rules of court for the purposes of this subsection.

(10) Where a court makes an order under or by virtue of this section it shall, in determining the period for which the order is to be in force, consider whether any party who was, or might have been, opposed to the making of the order was in a position to argue his case against the order in full.

38A Power to include exclusion requirement in interim care order

(1) Where –

(a) on being satisfied that there are reasonable grounds for believing that the circumstances with respect to a child are as mentioned in section 31(2)(a) and (b)(i), the court makes an interim care order with respect to a child, and

(b) the conditions mentioned in subsection (2) are satisfied,

the court may include an exclusion requirement in the interim care order.

(2) The conditions are –

(a) that there is reasonable cause to believe that, if a person ('the relevant person') is excluded from a dwelling-house in which the child lives, the child will cease to suffer, or cease to be likely to suffer, significant harm, and

(b) that another person living in the dwelling-house (whether a parent of the child or some other person) –

(i) is able and willing to give to the child the care which it would be reasonable to expect a parent to give him, and

(ii) consents to the inclusion of the exclusion requirement.

(3) For the purposes of this section an exclusion requirement is any one or more of the following –

(a) a provision requiring the relevant person to leave a dwelling-house in which he is living with the child,

(b) a provision prohibiting the relevant person from entering a dwelling-house in which the child lives, and

(c) a provision excluding the relevant person from a defined area in which a dwelling-house in which the child lives is situated.

(4) The court may provide that the exclusion requirement is to have effect for a shorter period than the other provisions of the interim care order.

(5) Where the court makes an interim care order containing an exclusion requirement, the court may attach a power of arrest to the exclusion requirement.

(6) Where the court attaches a power of arrest to an exclusion requirement of an interim care order, it may provide that the power of arrest is to have effect for a shorter period than the exclusion requirement.

(7) Any period specified for the purposes of subsection (4) or (6) may be extended by the court (on one or more occasions) on an application to vary or discharge the interim care order.

(8) Where a power of arrest is attached to an exclusion requirement of an interim care order by virtue of subsection (5), a constable may arrest without warrant any person whom he has reasonable cause to believe to be in breach of the requirement.

(9) Sections 47(7), (11) and (12) and 48 of, and Schedule 5 to, the Family Law Act 1996 shall have effect in relation to a person arrested under subsection (8) of this section as they have effect in relation to a person arrested under section 47(6) of that Act.

(10) If, while an interim care order containing an exclusion requirement is in force, the local authority have removed the child from the dwelling-house from which the relevant person is excluded to other accommodation for a continuous period of more than 24 hours, the interim care order shall cease to have effect in so far as it imposes the exclusion requirement.

38B Undertakings relating to interim care orders

(1) In any case where the court has power to include an exclusion requirement in an interim care order, the court may accept an undertaking from the relevant person.

(2) No power of arrest may be attached to any undertaking given under subsection (1).

(3) An undertaking given to a court under subsection (1) –

    (a) shall be enforceable as if it were an order of the court, and

    (b) shall cease to have effect if, while it is in force, the local authority have removed the child from the dwelling-house from which the relevant person is excluded to other accommodation for a continuous period of more than 24 hours.

(4) This section has effect without prejudice to the powers of the High Court and county court apart from this section.

(5) In this section "exclusion requirement" and "relevant person" have the same meaning as in section 38A.

39 Discharge and variation, etc of care orders and supervision orders

(1) A care order may be discharged by the court on the application of –

    (a) any person who has parental responsibility for the child;

    (b) the child himself; or

    (c) the local authority designated by the order.

(2) A supervision order may be varied or discharged by the court on the application of –

    (a) any person who has parental responsibility for the child;

    (b) the child himself; or

    (c) the supervisor.

(3) On the application of a person who is not entitled to apply for the order to be discharged, but who is a person with whom the child is living, a supervision order may be varied by the court in so far as it imposes a requirement which affects that person.

(3A) On the application of a person who is not entitled to apply for the order to be discharged, but who is a person to whom an exclusion requirement contained in the order applies, an interim care order may be varied or discharged by the court in so far as it imposes the exclusion requirement.

(3B) Where a power of arrest has been attached to an exclusion requirement of an interim care order, the court may, on the application of any person entitled to apply for the discharge of the order so far as it imposes the exclusion requirement, vary or discharge the order in so far as it confers a power of arrest (whether or not any application has been made to vary or discharge any other provision of the order).

(4) Where a care order is in force with respect to a child the court may, on the application of any person entitled to apply for the order to be discharged, substitute a supervision order for the care order.

(5) When a court is considering whether to substitute one order for another under subsection (4) any provision of this Act which would otherwise require section 31(2) to be satisfied at the time when the proposed order is substituted or made shall be disregarded.

41   Representation of child and of his interests in certain proceedings

(1) For the purpose of any specified proceedings, the court shall appoint a guardian ad litem for the child concerned unless satisfied that it is not necessary to do so in order to safeguard his interests.

(2) The guardian ad litem shall –

(a) be appointed in accordance with rules of court; and

(b) be under a duty to safeguard the interests of the child in the manner prescribed by such rules.

(3) Where –

(a) the child concerned is not represented by a solicitor; and

(b) any of the conditions mentioned in subsection (4) is satisfied,

the court may appoint a solicitor to represent him.

(4) The conditions are that –

(a) no guardian ad litem has been appointed for the child;

(b) the child has sufficient understanding to instruct a solicitor and wishes to do so;

(c) it appears to the court that it would be in the child's best interests for him to be represented by a solicitor.

(5) Any solicitor appointed under or by virtue of this section shall be appointed, and shall represent the child, in accordance with rules of court.

(6) In this section 'specified proceedings' means any proceedings –

(a) on an application for a care order or supervision order;

(b) in which the court has given a direction under section 37(1) and has made, or is considering whether to make, an interim care order;

(c) on an application for the discharge of a care order or the variation or discharge of a supervision order;

(d) on an application under section 39(4);

(e) in which the court is considering whether to make a residence order with respect to a child who is the subject of a care order;

(f) with respect to contact between a child who is the subject of a care order and any other person;

(g) under Part V;

(h) on an appeal against –

(i) the making of, or refusal to make, a care order, supervision order or any order under section 34;

(ii) the making of, or refusal to make, a residence order with respect to a child who is the subject of a care order; or

(iii) the variation or discharge, or refusal of an application to vary or discharge, an order of a kind mentioned in sub-paragraph (i) or (ii);

(iv) the refusal of an application under section 39(4);

(v) the making of, or refusal to make, an order under Part V; or

(i) which are specified for the time being, for the purposes of this section, by rules of court.

(7) The Secretary of State may by regulations provide for the establishment of panels of persons from whom guardians ad litem appointed under this section must be selected.

(8) Subsection (7) shall not be taken to prejudice the power of the Lord Chancellor to confer or impose duties on the Official Solicitor under section 90(3) of the Supreme Court Act 1981.

(11) Regardless of any enactment or rule of law which would otherwise prevent it from doing so, the court may take account of –

(a) any statement contained in a report made by a guardian ad litem who is appointed under this section for the purpose of the proceedings in question; and

(b) any evidence given in respect of the matters referred to in the report,

in so far as the statement or evidence is, in the opinion of the court, relevant to the question which the court is considering.

42 Right of guardian ad litem to have access to local authority records

(1) Where a person has been appointed as a guardian ad litem under this Act he shall have the right at all reasonable times to examine and take copies of –

(a) any records of, or held by, a local authority or an authorised person which were compiled in connection with the making, or proposed making, by any person of any application under this Act with respect to the child concerned;

(b) any records of, or held by, a local authority which were compiled in connection with any functions which stand referred to their social services committee under the Local Authority Social Services Act 1970, so far as those records relate to that child; or

(c) any records of, or held by, an authorised person which were compiled in connection with the activities of that person, so far as those records relate to that child.

(2) Where a guardian ad litem takes a copy of any record which he is entitled to examine under this section, that copy or any part of it shall be admissible as evidence of any matter referred to in any –

(a) report which he makes to the court in the proceedings in question; or

(b) evidence which he gives in those proceedings.

(3) Subsection (2) has effect regardless of any enactment or rule of law which would otherwise prevent the record in question being admissible in evidence.

(4) In this section 'authorised person' has the same meaning as in section 31.

PART V

PROTECTION OF CHILDREN

43 Child assessment orders

(1) On the application of a local authority or authorised person for an order to be made under this section with respect to a child, the court may make the order if, but only if, it is satisfied that –

(a) the applicant has reasonable cause to suspect that the child is suffering, or is likely to suffer, significant harm;

(b) an assessment of the state of the child's health or development, or of the way in which he has been treated, is required to enable the applicant to determine whether or not the child is suffering, or is likely to suffer, significant harm; and

(c) it is unlikely that such an assessment will be made, or be satisfactory, in the absence of an order under this section.

(2) In this Act 'a child assessment order' means an order under this section.

(3) A court may treat an application under this section as an application for an emergency protection order.

(4) No court shall make a child assessment order if it is satisfied –

(a) that there are grounds for making an emergency protection order with respect to the child; and

(b) that it ought to make such an order rather than a child assessment order.

(5) A child assessment order shall –

(a) specify the date by which the assessment is to begin; and

(b) have effect for such period, not exceeding seven days beginning with that date, as may be specified in the order.

(6) Where a child assessment order is in force with respect to a child it shall be the duty of any person who is in a position to produce the child –

(a) to produce him to such person as may be named in the order; and

(b) to comply with such directions relating to the assessment of the child as the court thinks fit to specify in the order.

(7) A child assessment order authorises any person carrying out the assessment, or any part of the assessment, to do so in accordance with the terms of the order.

(8) Regardless of subsection (7), if the child is of sufficient understanding to make an informed decision he may refuse to submit to a medical or psychiatric examination or other assessment.

(9) The child may only be kept away from home –

(a) in accordance with directions specified in the order;

(b) if it is necessary for the purposes of the assessment; and

(c) for such period or periods as may be specified in the order.

(10) Where the child is to be kept away from home, the order shall contain such directions as the court thinks fit with regard to the contact that he must be allowed to have with other persons while away from home.

(11) Any person making an application for a child assessment order shall take such steps as are reasonably practicable to ensure that notice of the application is given to –

(a) the child's parents;

(b) any person who is not a parent of his but who has parental responsibility for him;

(c) any other person caring for the child;

(d) any person in whose favour a contact order is in force with respect to the child;

(e) any person who is allowed to have contact with the child by virtue of an order under section 34; and

(f) the child,

before the hearing of the application.

(12) Rules of court may make provision as to the circumstances in which –

(a) any of the persons mentioned in subsection (11); or

(b) such other person as may be specified in the rules,

may apply to the court for a child assessment order to be varied or discharged.

(13) In this section 'authorised person' means a person who is an authorised person for the purposes of section 31.

44   Orders for emergency protection of children

(1) Where any person ('the applicant') applies to the court for an order to be made under this section with respect to a child, the court may make the order if, but only if it is satisfied that –

(a) there is reasonable cause to believe that the child is likely to suffer significant harm if –

(i) he is not removed to accommodation provided by or on behalf of the applicant; or

(ii) he does not remain in the place in which he is then being accommodated;

(b) in the case of an application made by a local authority –

(i) enquiries are being made with respect to the child under section 47(1)(b); and

(ii) those enquiries are being frustrated by access to the child being unreasonably refused to a person authorised to seek access and that the applicant has reasonable cause to believe that access to the child is required as a matter of urgency; or

(c) in the case of an application made by an authorised person –

(i) the applicant has reasonable cause to suspect that a child is suffering, or is likely to suffer, significant harm;

(ii) the applicant is making enquiries with respect to the child's welfare; and

(iii) those enquiries are being frustrated by access to the child being unreasonably refused to a person authorised to seek access and the applicant has reasonable cause to believe that access to the child is required as a matter of urgency.

(2) In this section –

(a) 'authorised person' means a person who is an authorised person for the purposes of section 31; and

(b) 'a person authorised to seek access' means –

(i) in the case of an application by a local authority, an officer of the local authority or a person authorised by the authority to act on their behalf in connection with the enquiries; or

(ii) in the case of an application by an authorised person, that person.

(3) Any person –

(a) seeking access to a child in connection with enquiries of a kind mentioned in subsection (1); and

(b) purporting to be a person authorised to do so,

shall, on being asked to do so, produce some duly authenticated document as evidence that he is such a person.

(4) While an order under this section ('an emergency protection order') is in force it –

(a) operates as a direction to any person who is in a position to do so to comply with any request to produce the child to the applicant;

(b) authorises –

(i) the removal of the child at any time to accommodation provided by or on behalf of the applicant and his being kept there; or

(ii) the prevention of the child's removal from any hospital, or other place, in which he was being accommodated immediately before the making of the order; and

(c) gives the applicant parental responsibility for the child.

(5) Where an emergency protection order is in force with respect to a child, the applicant –

(a) shall only exercise the power given by virtue of subsection (4)(b) in order to safeguard the welfare of the child;

(b) shall take, and shall only take, such action in meeting his parental responsibility for the child as is reasonably required to safeguard or promote the welfare of the child (having regard in particular to the duration of the order); and

(c) shall comply with the requirements of any regulations made by the Secretary of State for the purposes of this subsection.

(6) Where the court makes an emergency protection order, it may give such directions (if any) as it considers appropriate with respect to –

(a) the contact which is, or is not, to be allowed between the child and any named person;

(b) the medical or psychiatric examination or other assessment of the child.

(7) Where any direction is given under subsection (6)(b), the child may, if he is of sufficient understanding to make an informed decision, refuse to submit to the examination or other assessment.

(8) A direction under subsection (6)(a) may impose conditions and one under subsection (6)(b) may be to the effect that there is to be –

(a) no such examination or assessment; or

(b) no such examination or assessment unless the court directs otherwise.

(9) A direction under subsection (6) may be –

(a) given when the emergency protection order is made or at any time while it is in force; and

(b) varied at any time on the application of any person falling within any class of person prescribed by rules of court for the purposes of this subsection.

(10) Where an emergency protection order is in force with respect to a child and –

(a) the applicant has exercised the power given by subsection (4)(b)(i) but it appears to him that it is safe for the child to be returned; or

(b) the applicant has exercised the power given by subsection (4)(b)(ii) but it appears to him that it is safe for the child to be allowed to be removed from the place in question,

he shall return the child or (as the case may be) allow him to be removed.

(11) Where he is required by subsection (10) to return the child the applicant shall –

(a) return him to the care of the person from whose care he was removed; or

(b) if that is not reasonably practicable, return him to the care of –

(i) a parent of his;

(ii) any person who is not a parent of his but who has parental responsibility for him; or

(iii) such other person as the applicant (with the agreement of the court) considers appropriate.

(12) Where the applicant has been required by subsection (10) to return the child, or to allow him to be removed, he may again exercise his powers with respect to the child (at any time while the emergency protection order remains in force) if it appears to him that a change in the circumstances of the case makes it necessary for him to do so.

(13) Where an emergency protection order has been made with respect to a child, the applicant shall, subject to any direction given under subsection (6), allow the child reasonable contact with –

(a) his parents;

(b) any person who is not a parent of his but who has parental responsibility for him;

(c) any person with whom he was living immediately before the making of the order;

(d) any person in whose favour a contact order is in force with respect to him;

(e) any person who is allowed to have contact with the child by virtue of an order under section 34; and

(f) any person acting on behalf of any of those persons.

(14) Wherever it is reasonably practicable to do so, an emergency protection order shall name the child; and where it does not name him it shall describe him as clearly as possible.

(15) A person shall be guilty of an offence if he intentionally obstructs any person exercising the power under subsection (4)(b) to remove, or prevent the removal of, a child.

(16) A person guilty of an offence under subsection (15) shall be liable on summary conviction to a fine not exceeding level 3 on the standard scale.

44A Power to include exclusion requirement in emergency protection order

(1) Where –

(a) on being satisfied as mentioned in section 44(1)(a), (b) or (c), the court makes an emergency protection order with respect to a child, and

(b) the conditions mentioned in subsection (2) are satisfied,

the court may include an exclusion requirement in the emergency protection order.

(2) The conditions are –

(a) that there is reasonable cause to believe that, if a person ("the relevant person") is excluded from a dwelling-house in which the child lives, then –

(i) in the case of an order made on the ground mentioned in section 44(1)(a), the child will not be likely to suffer significant harm, even though the child is not removed as mentioned in section 44(1)(a)(i) or does not remain as mentioned in section 44(1)(a)(ii), or

(ii) in the case of an order made on the ground mentioned in paragraph (b) or (c) of section 44(1), the enquiries referred to in that paragraph will cease to be frustrated, and

(b) that another person living in the dwelling-house (whether a parent of the child or some other person) –

(i) is able and willing to give to the child the care which it would be reasonable to expect a parent to give him, and

(ii) consents to the inclusion of the exclusion requirement.

(3) For the purposes of this section an exclusion requirement is any one or more of the following –

(a) a provision requiring the relevant person to leave a dwelling-house in which he is living with the child,

(b) a provision prohibiting the relevant person from entering a dwelling-house in which the child lives, and

(c) a provision excluding the relevant person from a defined area in which a dwelling-house in which the child lives is situated.

(4) The court may provide that the exclusion requirement is to have effect for a shorter period than the other provisions of the order.

(5) Where the court makes an emergency protection order containing an exclusion requirement, the court may attach a power of arrest to the exclusion requirement.

(6) Where the court attaches a power of arrest to an exclusion requirement of an emergency protection order, it may provide that the power of arrest is to have effect for a shorter period than the exclusion requirement.

(7) Any period specified for the purposes of subsection (4) or (6) may be extended by the court (on one or more occasions) on an application to vary or discharge the emergency protection order.

(8) Where a power of arrest is attached to an exclusion requirement of an emergency protection order by virtue of subsection (5), a constable may arrest without warrant any person whom he has reasonable cause to believe to be in breach of the requirement.

(9) Sections 47(7), (11) and (12) and 48 of, and Schedule 5 to, the Family Law Act 1996 shall have effect in relation to a person arrested under subsection (8) of this section as they have effect in relation to a person arrested under section 47(6) of that Act.

(10) If, while an emergency protection order containing an exclusion requirement is in force, the applicant has removed the child from the dwelling-house from which the relevant person is excluded to other accommodation for a continuous period of more than 24 hours, the order shall cease to have effect in so far as it imposes the exclusion requirement.

44B Undertakings relating to emergency protection orders

(1) In any case where the court has power to include an exclusion requirement in an emergency protection order, the court may accept an undertaking from the relevant person.

(2) No power of arrest may be attached to any undertaking given under subsection (1).

(3) An undertaking given to a court under subsection (1) –

(a) shall be enforceable as if it were an order of the court, and

(b) shall cease to have effect if, while it is in force, the applicant has removed the child from the dwelling-house from which the relevant person is excluded to other accommodation for a continuous period of more than 24 hours.

(4) This section has effect without prejudice to the powers of the High Court and county court apart from this section.

(5) In this section "exclusion requirement" and "relevant person" have the same meaning as in section 44A.

45 Duration of emergency protection orders and other supplemental provisions

(1) An emergency protection order shall have effect for such period, not exceeding eight days, as may be specified in the order.

(2) Where –

(a) the court making an emergency protection order would, but for this subsection, specify a period of eight days as the period for which the order is to have effect; but

(b) the last of those eight days is a public holiday (that is to say, Christmas Day, Good Friday, a bank holiday or a Sunday),

the court may specify a period which ends at noon on the first later day which is not such a holiday.

(3) Where an emergency protection order is made on an application under section 46(7), the period of eight days mentioned in subsection (1) shall begin with the first day on which the child was taken into police protection under section 46.

(4) Any person who –

(a) has parental responsibility for a child as the result of an emergency protection order; and

(b) is entitled to apply for a care order with respect to the child,

may apply to the court for the period during which the emergency protection order is to have effect to be extended.

(5) On an under subsection (4) the court may extend the period during which the order is to have effect by such period, not exceeding seven days, as it thinks fit, but may do so only if it has reasonable cause to believe that the child concerned is likely to suffer significant harm if the order is not extended.

(6) An emergency protection order may only be extended once.

(7) Regardless of any enactment or rule of law which would otherwise prevent it from doing so, a court hearing an application for, or with respect to, an emergency protection order may take account of –

(a) any statement contained in any report made to the court in the course of, or in connection with, the hearing; or

(b) any evidence given during the hearing,

which is, in the opinion of the court, relevant to the application.

(8) Any of the following may apply to the court for an emergency protection order to be discharged –

(a) the child;

(b) a parent of his;

(c) any person who is not a parent of his but who has parental responsibility for him; or

(d) any person with whom he was living immediately before the making of the order.

(8A) On the application of a person who is not entitled to apply for the order to be discharged, but who is a person to whom an exclusion requirement contained in the order applies, an emergency protection order may be varied or discharged by the court in so far as it imposes the exclusion requirement.

(8B) Where a power of arrest has been attached to an exclusion requirement of an emergency protection order, the court may, on the application of any person entitled to apply for the discharge of the order so far as it imposes the exclusion requirement, vary or discharge the order in so far as it confers a power of arrest (whether or not any application has been made to vary or discharge any other provision of the order).

(9) No application for the discharge of an emergency protection order shall be heard by the court before the expiry of the period of 72 hours beginning with the making of the order.

(10) No appeal may be made against –

(a) the making of, or refusal to make, an emergency protection order;

(b) the extension of, or refusal to extend, the period during which such an order is to have effect;

(c) the discharge of, or refusal to discharge, such an order; or

(d) the giving of, or refusal to give, any direction in connection with such an order.

(11) Subsection (8) does not apply –

(a) where the person who would otherwise be entitled to apply for the emergency protection order to be discharged –

(i) was given notice (in accordance with rules of court) of the hearing at which the order was made; and

(ii) was present at that hearing; or

(b) to any emergency protection order the effective period of which has been extended under subsection (5).

(12) A court making an emergency protection order may direct that the applicant may, in exercising any powers which he has by virtue of the order, be accompanied by a registered medical practitioner, registered nurse or registered health visitor, if he so chooses.

46 Removal and accommodation of children by police in cases of emergency

(1) Where a constable has reasonable cause to believe that a child would otherwise be likely to suffer significant harm, he may –

(a) remove the child to suitable accommodation and keep him there; or

(b) take such steps as are reasonable to ensure that the child's removal from any hospital, or other place in which he is then being accommodated, is prevented.

(2) For the purposes of this Act, a child with respect to whom a constable has exercised his powers under this section is referred to as having been taken into police protection.

(3) As soon as is reasonably practicable after taking a child into police protection, the constable concerned shall –

(a) inform the local authority within whose area the child was found of the steps that have been, and are proposed to be, taken with respect to the child under this section and the reasons for taking them;

(b) give details to the authority within whose area the child is ordinarily resident ('the appropriate authority') of the place at which the child is being accommodated;

(c) inform the child (if he appears capable of understanding) –

(i) of the steps that have been taken with respect to him under this section and of the reasons for taking them; and

(ii) of the further steps that may be taken with respect to him under this section;

(d) take such steps as are reasonably practicable to discover the wishes and feelings of the child;

(e) secure that the case is inquired into by an officer designated for the purposes of this section by the chief officer of the police area concerned; and

(f) where the child was taken into police protection by being removed to accommodation which is not provided –

(i) by or on behalf of a local authority; or

(ii) as a refuge, in compliance with the requirements of section 51,

secure that he is moved to accommodation which is so provided.

(4) As soon as is reasonably practicable after taking a child into police protection, the constable concerned shall take such steps as are reasonably practicable to inform –

(a) the child's parents;

(b) every person who is not a parent of his but who has parental responsibility for him; and

(c) any other person with whom the child was living immediately before being taken into police protection,

of the steps that he has taken under this section with respect to the child, the reasons for taking them and the further steps that may be taken with respect to him under this section.

(5) On completing any inquiry under subsection (3)(e), the officer conducting it shall release the child from police protection unless he considers that there is still reasonable cause for believing that the child would be likely to suffer significant harm if released.

(6) No child may be kept in police protection for more than 72 hours.

(7) While a child is being kept in police protection, the designated officer may apply on behalf of the appropriate authority for an emergency protection order to be made under section 44 with respect to the child.

(8) An application may be made under subsection (7) whether or not the authority know of it or agree to its being made.

(9) While a child is being kept in police protection –

(a) neither the constable concerned nor the designated officer shall have parental responsibility for him; but

(b) the designated officer shall do what is reasonable in all the circumstances of the case for the purpose of safeguarding or promoting the child's welfare (having regard in particular to the length of the period during which the child will be so protected).

(10) Where a child has been taken into police protection, the designated officer shall allow –

(a) the child's parents;

(b) any person who is not a parent of the child but who has parental responsibility for him;

(c) any person with whom the child was living immediately before he was taken into police protection;

(d) any person in whose favour a contact order is in force with respect to the child;

(e) any person who is allowed to have contact with the child by virtue of an order under section 34; and

(f) any person acting on behalf of any of those persons,

to have such contact (if any) with the child as, in the opinion of the designated officer, is both reasonable and in the child's best interests.

(11) Where a child who has been taken into police protection is in accommodation provided by, or on behalf of, the appropriate authority, subsection (1) shall have effect as if it referred to the authority rather than to the designated officer.

47 Local authority's duty to investigate

(1) Where a local authority –

(a) are informed that a child who lives, or is found, in their area –

(i) is the subject of an emergency protection order; or

(ii) is in police protection; or

(b) have reasonable cause to suspect that a child who lives, or is found, in their area is suffering, or is likely to suffer, significant harm,

the authority shall make, or cause to be made, such enquiries as they consider necessary to enable them to decide whether they should take any action to safeguard or promote the child's welfare.

(2) Where a local authority have obtained an emergency protection order with respect to a child, they shall make, or cause to be made, such enquiries as they consider necessary to enable them to decide what action they should take to safeguard or promote the child's welfare.

(3) The enquiries shall, in particular, be directed towards establishing –

(a) whether the authority should make any application to the court, or exercise any of their other powers under this Act, with respect to the child;

(b) whether, in the case of a child –

(i) with respect to whom an emergency protection order has been made; and

(ii) who is not in accommodation provided by or on behalf of the authority,

it would be in the child's best interests (while an emergency protection order remains in force) for him to be in such accommodation; and

(c) whether, in the case of a child who has been taken into police protection, it would be in the child's best interests for the authority to ask for an application to be made under section 46(7).

(4) Where enquiries are being made under subsection (1) with respect to a child, the local authority concerned shall (with a view to enabling them to determine what action, if any, to take with respect to him) take such steps as are reasonably practicable –

(a) to obtain access to him; or

(b) to ensure that access to him is obtained, on their behalf, by a person authorised by them for the purpose,

unless they are satisfied that they already have sufficient information with respect to him.

(5) Where, as a result of any such enquiries, it appears to the authority that there are matters connected with the child's education which should be investigated, they shall consult the relevant local education authority.

(6) Where, in the course of enquiries made under this section –

(a) any officer of the local authority concerned; or

(b) any person authorised by the authority to act on their behalf in connection with those enquiries –

(i) is refused access to the child concerned; or

(ii) is denied information as to his whereabouts,

the authority shall apply for an emergency protection order, a child assessment order, a care order or a supervision order with respect to the child unless they are satisfied that his welfare can be satisfactorily safeguarded without their doing so.

(7) If, on the conclusion of any enquiries or review made under this section, the authority decide not to apply for an emergency protection order, a child assessment order, a care order or a supervision order they shall –

(a) consider whether it would be appropriate to review the case at a later date; and

(b) if they decide that it would be, determine the date on which that review is to begin.

(8) Where, as a result of complying with this section, a local authority conclude that they should take action to safeguard or promote the child's welfare they shall take that action (so far as it is both within their power and reasonably practicable for them to do so).

(9) Where a local authority are conducting enquiries under this section, it shall be the duty of any person mentioned in subsection (11) to assist them with those enquiries (in particular by providing relevant information and advice) if called upon by the authority to do so.

(10) Subsection (9) does not oblige any person to assist a local authority where doing so would be unreasonable in all the circumstances of the case.

(11) The persons are –

(a) any local authority;

(b) any local education authority;

(c) any local housing authority;

(d) any Health Authority, Special Health Authority or National Health Service trust; and

(e) any person authorised by the Secretary of State for the purposes of this section.

(12) Where a local authority are making enquiries under this section with respect to a child who appears to them to be ordinarily resident within the

area of another authority, they shall consult that other authority, who may undertake the necessary enquiries in their place.

48 Powers to assist in discovery of children who may be in need of emergency protection

(1) Where it appears to a court making an emergency protection order that adequate information as to the child's whereabouts –

(a) is not available to the applicant for the order; but

(b) is available to another person,

it may include in the order a provision requiring that other person to disclose, if asked to do so by the applicant, any information that he may have as to the child's whereabouts.

(2) No person shall be excused from complying with such a requirement on the ground that complying might incriminate him or his spouse of an offence; but a statement or admission made in complying shall not be admissible in evidence against either of them in proceedings for any offence other than perjury.

(3) An emergency protection order may authorise the applicant to enter premises specified by the order and search for the child with respect to whom the order is made.

(4) Where the court is satisfied that there is reasonable cause to believe that there may be another child on those premises with respect to whom an emergency protection order ought to be made, it may make an order authorising the applicant to search for that other child on those premises.

(5) Where –

(a) an order has been made under subsection (4);

(b) the child concerned has been found on the premises; and

(c) the applicant is satisfied that the grounds for making an emergency protection order exist with respect to him,

the order shall have effect as if it were an emergency protection order.

(6) Where an order has been made under subsection (4), the applicant shall notify the court of its effect.

(7) A person shall be guilty of an offence if he intentionally obstructs any person exercising the power of entry and search under subsection (3) or (4).

(8) A person guilty of an offence under subsection (7) shall be liable on summary conviction to a fine not exceeding level 3 on the standard scale.

(9) Where, on an application made by any person for a warrant under this section, it appears to the court –

(a) that a person attempting to exercise powers under an emergency protection order has been prevented from doing so by being refused entry to the premises concerned or access to the child concerned; or

(b) that any such person is likely to be so prevented from exercising any such powers,

it may issue a warrant authorising any constable to assist the person mentioned in paragraph (a) or (b) in the exercise of those powers, using reasonable force if necessary.

(10) Every warrant issued under this section shall be addressed to, and executed by, a constable who shall be accompanied by the person applying for the warrant if –

(a) that person so desires; and

(b) the court by whom the warrant is issued does not direct otherwise.

(11) A court granting an application for a warrant under this section may direct that the constable concerned may, in executing the warrant, be accompanied by a registered medical practitioner, registered nurse or registered health visitor if he so chooses.

(12) An application for a warrant under this section shall be made in the manner and form prescribed by rules of court.

(13) Wherever it is reasonably practicable to do so, an order under subsection (4), an application for a warrant under this section and any such warrant shall name the child; and where it does not name him it shall describe him as clearly as possible.

49 Abduction of children in care, etc

(1) A person shall be guilty of an offence if, knowingly and without lawful authority or reasonable excuse, he –

(a) takes a child to whom this section applies away from the responsible person;

(b) keeps such a child away from the responsible person; or

(c) induces, assists or incites such a child to run away or stay away from the responsible person.

(2) This section applies in relation to a child who is –

(a) in care;

(b) the subject of an emergency protection order; or

(c) in police protection,

and in this section 'the responsible person' means any person who for the time being has care of him by virtue of the care order, the emergency protection order, or section 46, as the case may be.

(3) A person guilty of an offence under this section shall be liable on summary conviction to imprisonment for a term not exceeding six months, or to a fine not exceeding level 5 on the standard scale, or to both.

50 Recovery of abducted children, etc

(1) Where it appears to the court that there is reason to believe that a child to whom this section applies

(a) has been unlawfully taken away or is being unlawfully kept away from the responsible person;

(b) has run away or is staying away from the responsible person; or

(c) is missing,

the court may make an order under this section ('a recovery order').

(2) This section applies to the same children to whom section 49 applies and in this section 'the responsible person' has the same meaning as in section 49.

(3) A recovery order –

(a) operates as a direction to any person who is in a position to do so to produce the child on request to any authorised person;

(b) authorises the removal of the child by any authorised person;

(c) requires any person who has information as to the child's whereabouts to disclose that information, if asked to do so, to a constable or an officer of the court;

(d) authorises a constable to enter any premises specified in the order and search for the child, using reasonable force if necessary.

(4) The court may make a recovery order only on the application of –

(a) any person who has parental responsibility for the child by virtue of a care order or emergency protection order; or

(b) where the child is in police protection, the designated officer.

(5) A recovery order shall name the child and –

    (a) any person who has parental responsibility for the child by virtue of a care order or emergency protection order; or

    (b) where the child is in police protection, the designated officer.

(6) Premises may only be specified under subsection (3)(d) if it appears to the court that there are reasonable grounds for believing the child to be on them.

PART XII

MISCELLANEOUS AND GENERAL

91 Effect and duration of orders, etc

(1) The making of a residence order with respect to a child who is the subject of a care order discharges the care order.

(2) The making of a care order with respect to a child who is the subject of any section 8 order discharges that order.

(3) The making of a care order with respect to a child who is the subject of a supervision order discharges that other order.

(4) The making of a care order with respect to a child who is a ward of court brings that wardship to an end.

(5) The making of a care order with respect to a child who is the subject of a school attendance order made under section 437 of the Education Act 1996 discharges the school attendance order.

(6) Where an emergency protection order is made with respect to a child who is in care, the care order shall have effect subject to the emergency protection order.

(7) Any order made under section 4(1) or 5(1) shall continue in force until the child reaches the age of eighteen, unless it is brought to an end earlier.

(8) Any –

    (a) agreement under section 4; or

    (b) appointment under section 5(3) or (4),

shall continue in force until the child reaches the age of eighteen, unless it is brought to an end earlier.

(9) An order under Schedule 1 has effect as specified in that Schedule.

(10) A section 8 order shall, if it would otherwise still be in force, cease to have effect when the child reaches the age of sixteen, unless it is to have effect beyond that age by virtue of section 9(6).

(11) Where a section 8 order has effect with respect to a child who has reached the age of sixteen, it shall, if it would otherwise still be in force, cease to have effect when he reaches the age of eighteen.

(12) Any care order, other than an interim care order, shall continue in force until the child reaches the age of eighteen, unless it is brought to an end earlier.

(13) Any order made under any other provision of this Act in relation to a child shall, if it would otherwise still be in force, cease to have effect when he reaches the age of eighteen.

(14) On disposing of any application for an order under this Act, the court may (whether or not it makes any other order in response to the application) order that no application for an order under this Act of any specified kind may be made with respect to the child concerned by any person named in the order without leave of the court.

(15) Where an application ('the previous application') has been made for –

    (a) the discharge of a care order;

    (b) the discharge of a supervision order;

    (c) the discharge of an education supervision order;

    (d) the substitution of a supervision order for a care order; or

    (e) a child assessment order,

no further application of a kind mentioned in paragraphs (a) to (e) may be made with respect to the child concerned, without leave of the court, unless the period between the disposal of the previous application and the making of the further application exceeds six months.

(16) Subsection (15) does not apply to applications made in relation to interim orders.

(17) Where –

    (a) a person has made an application for an order under section 34;

    (b) the application has been refused; and

    (c) a period of less than six months has elapsed since the refusal, that person may not make a further application for such an order with respect to the same child, unless he has obtained the leave of the court.

94 Appeals

(1) Subject to any express provisions to the contrary made by or under this Act, an appeal shall lie to the High Court against –

(a) the making by a magistrates' court of any order under this Act; or

(b) any refusal by a magistrates' court to make such an order.

(2) Where a magistrates' court has power, in relation to any proceedings under this Act, to decline jurisdiction because it considers that the case can more conveniently be dealt with by another court, no appeal shall lie against any exercise by that magistrates' court of that power.

98 Self-incrimination

(1) In any proceedings in which a court is hearing an application for an order under Part IV or V, no person shall be excused from –

(a) giving evidence on any matter; or

(b) answering any question put to him in the course of his giving evidence,

on the ground that doing so might incriminate him or his spouse of an offence.

(2) A statement or admission made in such proceedings shall not be admissible in evidence against the person making it or his spouse in proceedings for an offence other than perjury.

100 Restrictions on use of wardship jurisdiction

(1) Section 7 of the Family Law Reform Act 1969 (which gives the High Court power to place a ward of court in the care, or under the supervision, of a local authority) shall cease to have effect.

(2) No court shall exercise the High Court's inherent jurisdiction with respect to children –

(a) so as to require a child to be placed in the care, or put under the supervision, of a local authority;

(b) so as to require a child to be accommodated by or on behalf of a local authority;

(c) so as to make a child who is the subject of a care order a ward of court; or

(d) for the purpose of conferring on any local authority power to determine any question which has arisen, or which may arise, in connection with any aspect of parental responsibility for a child.

(3) No application for any exercise of the court's inherent jurisdiction with respect to children may be made by a local authority unless the authority have obtained the leave of the court.

(4) The court may only grant leave if it is satisfied that –

(a) the result which the authority wish to achieve could not be achieved through the making of any order of a kind to which subsection (5) applies; and

(b) there is reasonable cause to believe that if the court's inherent jurisdiction is not exercised with respect to the child he is likely to suffer significant harm.

(5) This subsection applies to any order –

(a) made otherwise than in the exercise of the court's inherent jurisdiction; and

(b) which the local authority is entitled to apply for (assuming, in the case of any application which may only be made with leave, that leave is granted).

105 Interpretation

(1) In this Act – ...

'child' means, subject to paragraph 16 of Schedule 1, a person under the age of eighteen; ...

'child of the family', in relation to the parties to a marriage means –

(a) a child of both of those parties;

(b) any other child, not being a child who is placed with those parties as foster parents by a local authority or voluntary organisation, who has been treated by both of those parties as a child of their family; ...

"dwelling-house" includes –

(a) any building or part of a building which is occupied as a dwelling;

(b) any caravan, house-boat or structure which is occupied as a dwelling;

and any yard, garden, garage or outhouse belonging to it and occupied with it; ...

'relative', in relation to a child, means a grandparent, brother, sister, uncle or aunt (whether of the full blood or half blood or by affinity) or step-parent; ...

'upbringing', in relation to any child, includes the care of the child but not his maintenance.

(2) References in this Act to a child whose father and mother were, or (as the case may be) were not, married to each other at the time of his birth must be read with section 1 of the Family Law Reform Act 1987 (which extends the meaning of such references).

(3) References in this Act to –

(a) a person with whom a child lives, or is to live, as the result of a residence order; or

(b) a person in whose favour a residence order is in force,

shall be construed as references to the person named in the order as the person with whom the child is to live.

(6) In determining the 'ordinary residence' of a child for any purpose of this Act, there shall be disregarded any period in which he lives in any place –

(a) which is a school or other institution;

(b) in accordance with the requirements of a supervision order under this Act or an order under section 7(7)(b) of the Children and Young Persons Act 1969; or

(c) while he is being provided with accommodation by or on behalf of a local authority.

SCHEDULE 1

FINANCIAL PROVISION FOR CHILDREN

Orders for financial relief against parents

1. (1) On an application made by a parent or guardian of a child, or by any person in whose favour a residence order is in force with respect to a child, the court may –

(a) in the case of an application to the High Court or a county court, make one or more of the orders mentioned in sub-paragraph (2);

(b) in the case of an application to a magistrates' court, make one or both of the orders mentioned in paragraphs (a) and (c) of that sub-paragraph.

(2) The orders referred to in sub-paragraph (1) are –

(a) an order requiring either or both parents of a child –

(i) to make to the applicant for the benefit of the child; or
(ii) to make to the child himself,

such periodical payments, for such term, as may be specified in the order;

(b) an order requiring either or both parents of a child –

(i) to secure to the applicant for the benefit of the child; or
(ii) to secure to the child himself,

such periodical payments, for such term, as may be so specified;

(c) an order requiring either or both parents of a child –

(i) to pay to the applicant for the benefit of the child; or
(ii) to pay to the child himself,

such lump sum as may be so specified;

(d) an order requiring a settlement to be made for the benefit of the child, and to the satisfaction of the court, of property –

(i) to which either parent is entitled (either in possession or in reversion); and
(ii) which is specified in the order;

(e) an order requiring either or both parents of a child –

(i) to transfer to the applicant, for the benefit of the child; or
(ii) to transfer to the child himself,

such property to which the parent is, or the parents are, entitled (either in possession or in reversion) as may be specified in the order.

(3) The powers conferred by this paragraph may be exercised at any time.

(4) An order under sub-paragraph (2)(a) or (b) may be varied or discharged by a subsequent order made on the application of any person by or to whom payments were required to be made under the previous order.

(5) Where a court makes an order under this paragraph –

(a) it may at any time make a further such order under sub-paragraph (2)(a), (b) or (c) with respect to the child concerned if he has not reached the age of eighteen;

(b) it may not make more than one order under sub-paragraph (2)(d) or (e) against the same person in respect of the same child.

(6) On making, varying or discharging a residence order the court may exercise any of its powers under this Schedule even though no application has been made to it under this Schedule.

(7) Where a child is a ward of court, the court may exercise any of its powers under this Schedule even though no application has been made to it.

Orders for financial relief for persons over eighteen

2. (1) If, on an application by a person who has reached the age of eighteen, it appears to the court –

(a) that the applicant is, will be or (if an order were made under this paragraph) would be receiving instruction at an educational establishment or undergoing training for a trade, profession or vocation, whether or not while in gainful employment; or

(b) that there are special circumstances which justify the making of an order under this paragraph,

the court may make one or both of the orders mentioned in sub-paragraph (2).

(2) The orders are –

(a) an order requiring either or both of the applicant's parents to pay to the applicant such periodical payments, for such term, as may be specified in the order;

(b) an order requiring either or both of the applicant's parents to pay to the applicant such lump sum as may be so specified.

(3) An application may not be made under this paragraph by any person if, immediately before he reached the age of sixteen, a periodical payments order was in force with respect to him.

(4) No order shall be made under this paragraph at a time when the parents of the applicant are living with each other in the same household.

(5) An order under sub-paragraph (2)(a) may be varied or discharged by a subsequent order made on the application of any person by or to whom payments were required to be made under the previous order.

(6) in sub-paragraph (3) 'periodical payments order' means an order made under –

(a) this Schedule;

(c) section 23 or 27 of the Matrimonial Causes Act 1973;

(d) Part I of the Domestic Proceedings and Magistrates' Courts Act 1978,

for the making or securing of periodical payments.

(7) The powers conferred by this paragraph shall be exercisable at any time.

(8) Where the court makes an order under this paragraph it may from time to time while that order remains in force make a further such order.

Duration of orders for financial relief

3. (1) The term to be specified in an order for periodical payments made under paragraph 1(2)(a) or (b) in favour of a child may begin with the date of the making of an application for the order in question or any later date or a date ascertained in accordance with sub-paragraph (5) or (6) but –

(a) shall not in the first instance extend beyond the child's seventeenth birthday unless the court thinks it right in the circumstances of the case to specify a later date; and

(b) shall not in any event extend beyond the child's eighteenth birthday.

(2) Paragraph (b) of sub-paragraph (1) shall not apply in the case of a child if it appears to the court that –

(a) the child is, or will be or (if an order were made without complying with that paragraph) would be receiving instruction at an educational establishment or undergoing training for a trade, profession or vocation, whether or not while in gainful employment; or

(b) there are special circumstances which justify the making of an order without complying with that paragraph.

(3) An order for periodical payments made under paragraph 1(2)(a) or 2(2)(a) shall, notwithstanding anything in the order, cease to have effect on the death of the person liable to make payments under the order.

(4) Where an order is made under paragraph 1(2)(a) or (b) requiring periodical payments to be made or secured to the parent of a child, the order shall cease to have effect if –

(a) any parent making or securing the payments; and

(b) any parent to whom the payments are made or secured,

live together for a period of more than six months.

(5) Where –

(a) a maintenance assessment ('the current assessment') is in force with respect to a child; and

(b) an application is made for an order under paragraph 1(2)(a) or (b) of this Schedule for periodical payments in favour of that child –

(i) in accordance with section 8 of the Child Support Act 1991; and

(ii) before the end of the period of 6 months beginning with the making of the current assessment,

the term to be specified in any such order made on that application may be expressed to begin on, or at any time after, the earliest permitted date.

(6) For the purposes of subsection (5) above, 'the earliest permitted date' is whichever is the later of –

(a) the date 6 months before the application is made; or

(b) the date on which the current assessment took effect or, where successive maintenance assessments have been continuously in force with respect to a child, on which the first of those assessments took effect.

(7) Where –

(a) a maintenance assessment ceases to have effect or is cancelled by or under any provision of the Child Support Act 1991, and

(b) an application is made, before the end of the period of 6 months beginning with the relevant date, for an order for periodical payments under paragraph 1(2)(a) or (b) in favour of a child with respect to whom that maintenance assessment was in force immediately before it ceased to have effect or was cancelled,

the term to be specified in any such order, or in any interim order under paragraph 9, made on that application may begin with the date on which that maintenance assessment ceased to have effect or, as the case may be, the date with effect from which it was cancelled, or any later date.

(8) In sub-paragraph (7)(b) –

(a) where the maintenance assessment ceased to have effect, the relevant date is the date on which it so ceased; and

(b) where the maintenance assessment was cancelled, the relevant date is the later of –

(i) the date on which the person who cancelled it did so, and

(ii) the date from which the cancellation first had effect.

Matters to which court is to have regard in making
orders for financial relief

4. (1) In deciding whether to exercise its powers under paragraph 1 or 2, and if so in what manner, the court shall have regard to all the circumstances including –

(a) the income, earning capacity, property and other financial resources which each person mentioned in sub-paragraph (4) has or is likely to have in the foreseeable future;

(b) the financial needs, obligations and responsibilities which each person mentioned in sub-paragraph (4) has or is likely to have in the foreseeable future;

(c) the financial needs of the child;

(d) the income, earning capacity (if any), property and other financial resources of the child;

(e) any physical or mental disability of the child;

(f) the manner in which the child was being, or was expected to be, educated or trained.

(2) In deciding whether to exercise its powers under paragraph 1 against a person who is not the mother or father of the child, and if so in what manner, the court shall in addition have regard to –

(a) whether that person had assumed responsibility for the maintenance of the child and, if so, the extent to which and basis on which he assumed that responsibility and the length of the period during which he met that responsibility;

(b) whether he did so knowing that the child was not his child;

(c) the liability of any other person to maintain the child.

(3) Where the court makes an order under paragraph 1 against a person who is not the father of the child, it shall record in the order that the order is made on the basis that the person against whom the order is made is not the child's father.

(4) The persons mentioned in sub-paragraph (1) are –

(a) in relation to a decision whether to exercise its powers under paragraph 1, any parent of the child;

(b) in relation to a decision whether to exercise its powers under paragraph 2, the mother and father of the child;

(c) the applicant for the order;

(d) any other person in whose favour the court proposes to make the order.

Provisions relating to lump sums

5. (1) Without prejudice to the generality of paragraph 1, an order under that paragraph for the payment of a lump sum may be made for the purpose of enabling any liabilities or expenses –

(a) incurred in connection with the birth of the child or in maintaining the child; and

(b) reasonably incurred before the making of the order,

to be met

(2) The amount of any lump sum required to be paid by an order made by a magistrates' court under paragraph 1 or 2 shall not exceed £1,000 or such larger amount as the Lord Chancellor may from time to time by order fix for the purposes of this sub-paragraph.

(3) The power of the court under paragraph 1 or 2 to vary or discharge an order for the making or securing of periodical payments by a parent shall include power to make an order under that provision for the payment of a lump sum by that parent.

(4) The amount of any lump sum which a parent may be required to pay by virtue of sub-paragraph (3) shall not, in the case of an order made by a magistrates' court, exceed the maximum amount that may at the time of the making of the order be required to be paid under sub-paragraph (2), but a magistrates' court may make an order for the payment of a lump sum not exceeding that amount even though the parent was required to pay a lump sum by a previous order under this Act.

(5) An order made under paragraph 1 or 2 for the payment of a lump sum may provide for the payment of that sum by instalments.

(6) Where the court provides for the payment of a lump sum by instalments the court, on an application made either by the person liable to pay or the person entitled to receive that sum, shall have power to vary that order by varying –

(a) the number of instalments payable;

(b) the amount of any instalment payable;

(c) the date on which any instalment becomes payable.

Variation, etc of orders for periodical payments

6. (1) In exercising its powers under paragraph 1 or 2 to vary or discharge an order for the making or securing of periodical payments the court shall have regard to all the circumstances of the case, including any change in any of the matters to which the court was required to have regard when making the order.

(2) The power of the court under paragraph 1 or 2 to vary an order for the making or securing of periodical payments shall include power to suspend any provision of the order temporarily and to revive any provision so suspended.

(3) Where on an application under paragraph 1 or 2 for the variation or discharge of an order for the making or securing of periodical payments the court varies the payments required to be made under that order, the court may provide that the payments as so varied shall be made from such date as the court may specify, except that, subject to sub-paragraph (9), the date shall not be earlier than the date of the making of the application.

(4) An application for the variation of an order made under paragraph 1 for the making or securing of periodical payments to or for the benefit of a child may, if the child has reached the age of sixteen, be made by the child himself.

(5) Where an order for the making or securing of periodical payments made under paragraph 1 ceases to have effect on the date on which the child reaches the age of sixteen, or at any time after that date but before or on the date on which he reaches the age of eighteen, the child may apply to the court which made the order for an order for its revival.

(6) If on such an application it appears to the court that –

(a) the child is, will be or (if an order were made under this sub-paragraph) would be receiving instruction at an educational establishment or undergoing training for a trade, profession or vocation, whether or not while in gainful employment; or

(b) there are special circumstances which justify the making of an order under this paragraph, the court shall have power by order to revive the order from such date as the court may specify, not being earlier than the date of the making of the application.

(7) Any order which is revived by an order under sub-paragraph (5) may be varied or discharged under that provision, on the application of any person by whom or to whom payments are required to be made under the revived order.

(8) An order for the making or securing of periodical payments made under paragraph 1 may be varied or discharged, after the death of either parent, on the application of a guardian of the child concerned.

(9) Where –

(a) an order under paragraph 1(2)(a) or (b) for the making or securing of periodical payments in favour of more than one child ('the order') is in force;

(b) the order requires payments specified in it to be made to or for the benefit of more than one child without apportioning those payments between them;

(c) a maintenance assessment ('the assessment') is made with respect to one or more, but not all, of the children with respect to whom those payments are to be made; and

(d) an application is made, before the end of the period of 6 months beginning with the date on which the assessment was made, for the variation or discharge of the order,

the court may, in exercise of its powers under paragraph 1 to vary or discharge the order, direct that the variation of discharge shall take effect from the date on which the assessment took effect or any later date.

Variation of orders for periodical payments, etc made by magistrates' courts

6A. (1) Subject to sub-paragraphs (7) and (8), the power of a magistrates' court –

(a) under paragraph 1 or 2 to vary an order for the making of periodical payments, or

(b) under paragraph 5(6) to vary an order for the payment of a lump sum by instalments,

shall include power, if the court is satisfied that payment has not been made in accordance with the order, to exercise one of its powers under paragraphs (a) to (d) of section 59(3) of the Magistrates' Courts Act 1980.

(2) In any case where –

(a) a magistrates' court has made an order under this Schedule for the making of periodical payments or for the payment of a lump sum by instalments, and

(b) payments under the order are required to be made by any method of payment falling within section 59(6) of the Magistrates' Courts Act 1980 (standing order, etc),

any person entitled to make an application under this Schedule for the variation of the order (in this paragraph referred to as 'the applicant') may apply to the clerk to the justices for the petty sessions area for which the court is acting for the order to be varied as mentioned in sub-paragraph (3).

(3) Subject to sub-paragraph (5), where an application is made under sub-paragraph (2), the clerk, after giving written notice (by post or otherwise) of the application to any interested party and allowing that party, within the period of 14 days beginning with the date of the giving of that notice, an opportunity to make written representations, may vary the order to provide that payments under the order shall be made to the clerk. ...

Alteration of maintenance agreement

10. (1) In this paragraph and in paragraph 11 'maintenance agreement' means any agreement in writing made with respect to a child, whether before or after the commencement of this paragraph, which –

(a) is or was made between the father and mother of the child; and

(b) contains provision with respect to the making or securing of payments, or the disposition or use of any property, for the maintenance or education of the child,

and any such provisions are in this paragraph, and paragraph 11, referred to as 'financial arrangements'.

(2) Where a maintenance agreement is for the time being subsisting and each of the parties to the agreement is for the time being either domiciled or resident in England and Wales, then either party may apply to the court for an order under this paragraph.

(3) If the court to which the application is made is satisfied either –

(a) that, by reason of a change in the circumstances in the light of which any financial arrangements contained in the agreement were made (including a change foreseen by the parties when making the agreement), the agreement should be altered so as to make different financial arrangements; or

(b) that the agreement does not contain proper financial arrangements with respect to the child,

then that court may by order make such alterations in the agreement by varying or revoking any financial arrangements contained in it as may appear to it to be just having regard to all the circumstances.

(4) If the maintenance agreement is altered by an order under this paragraph, the agreement shall have effect thereafter as if the alteration had been made by agreement between the parties and for valuable consideration.

(5) Where a court decides to make an order under this paragraph altering the maintenance agreement –

(a) by inserting provision for the making or securing by one of the parties to the agreement of periodical payments for the maintenance of the child; or

(b) by increasing the rate of periodical payments required to be made or secured by one of the parties for the maintenance of the child,

then, in deciding the term for which under the agreement as altered by the order the payments or (as the case may be) the additional payments attributable to the increase are to be made or secured for the benefit of the child, the court shall apply the provisions of sub-paragraphs (1) and (2) of paragraph 3 as if the order were an order under paragraph 1(2)(a) or (b).

(6) A magistrates' court shall not entertain an application under sub-paragraph (2) unless both the parties to the agreement are resident in England and Wales and at least one of the parties is resident in the commission area (within the meaning of the Justices of the Peace Act 1979) for which the court is appointed, and shall not have power to make any order on such an application except –

(a) in a case where the agreement contains no provisions for periodical payments by either of the parties, an order inserting provision for the making by one of the parties of periodical payments for the maintenance of the child;

(b) in a case where the agreement includes provision for the making by one of the parties of periodical payments, an order increasing or reducing the rate of, or terminating, any of those payments.

(7) For the avoidance of doubt it is hereby declared that nothing in this paragraph affects any power of a court before which any proceedings between the parties to a maintenance agreement are brought under any other enactment to make an order containing financial arrangements or any right of either party to apply for such an order in such proceedings.

11. (1) Where a maintenance agreement provides for the continuation, after the death of one of the parties, of payments for the maintenance of a child and that party dies domiciled in England and Wales, the surviving party or the personal representatives of the deceased party may apply to the High Court or a county court for an order under paragraph 10.

(2) If a maintenance agreement is altered by a court on an application under this paragraph, the agreement shall have effect thereafter as if the alteration had been made, immediately before the death, by agreement between the parties and for valuable consideration.

(3) An application under this paragraph shall not, except with leave of the High Court or a county court, be made after the end of the period of six months beginning with the day on which representation in regard to the estate of the deceased is first taken out.

(4) In considering for the purposes of sub-paragraph (3) the question when representation was first taken out, a grant limited to settled land or to trust property shall be left out of account and a grant limited to real estate or to personal estate shall be left out of account unless a grant limited to the remainder of the estate has previously been made or is made at the same time.

(5) A county court shall not entertain an application under this paragraph, or an application for leave to make an application under this paragraph, unless it would have jurisdiction to hear and determine proceedings for an order under section 2 of the Inheritance (Provision for Family and Dependants) Act 1975 in relation to the deceased's estate by virtue of section 25 of the County Courts Act 1984 (jurisdiction under the Act of 1975).

(6) The provisions of this paragraph shall not render the personal representatives of the deceased liable for having distributed any part of the estate of the deceased after the expiry of the period of six months referred to in sub-paragraph (3) on the ground that they ought to have taken into account the possibility that a court might grant leave for an application by virtue of this paragraph to be made by the surviving party after that period.

(7) Sub-paragraph (6) shall not prejudice any power to recover any part of the estate so distributed arising by virtue of the making of an order in pursuance of this paragraph.

Interpretation

16. (1) In this Schedule 'child' includes, in any case where an application is made under paragraph 2 or 6 in relation to a person who has reached the age of eighteen, that person.

(2) In this Schedule, except paragraphs 2 and 15, 'parent' includes any party to a marriage (whether or not subsisting) in relation to whom the child concerned is a child of the family; and for this purpose any reference to either parent or both parents shall be construed as references to any parent of his and to all of his parents.

(3) In this Schedule, 'maintenance assessment' has the same meaning as it has in the Child Suport Act 1991 by virtue of section 54 of that Act as read with any regulations in force under that section.

SCHEDULE 3

SUPERVISION ORDERS

Meaning of 'responsible person'

1. In this Schedule, 'the responsible person', in relation to a supervised child, means –

(a) any person who has parental responsibility for the child; and

(b) any other person with whom the child is living.

Power of supervisor to give directions to supervised child

2. (1) A supervision order may require the supervised child to comply with any directions given from time to time by the supervisor which require him to do all or any of the following things –

(a) to live at a place or places specified in the directions for a period or periods so specified;

(b) to present himself to a person or persons specified in the directions at a place or places and on a day or days so specified;

(c) to participate in activities specified in the directions on a day or days so specified.

(2) It shall be for the supervisor to decide whether, and to what extent, he exercises his power to give directions and to decide the form of any directions which he gives.

(3) Sub-paragraph (1) does not confer on a supervisor power to give directions in respect of any medical or psychiatric examination or treatment (which are matters dealt with in paragraphs 4 and 5).

Imposition of obligations on responsible person

3. (1) With the consent of any responsible person, a supervision order may include a requirement –

(a) that he take all reasonable steps to ensure that the supervised child complies with any direction given by the supervisor under paragraph 2;

(b) that he take all reasonable steps to ensure that the supervised child complies with any requirement included in the order under paragraph 4 or 5;

(c) that he comply with any directions given by the supervisor requiring him to attend at a place specified in the directions for the purpose of taking part in activities so specified.

(2) A direction given under sub-paragraph (1)(c) may specify the time at which the responsible person is to attend and whether or not the supervised child is required to attend with him.

(3) A supervision order may require any person who is a responsible person in relation to the supervised child to keep the supervisor informed of his address, if it differs from the child's.

Life of supervision order

6. (1) Subject to sub-paragraph (2) and section 91, a supervision order shall cease to have effect at the end of the period of one year beginning with the date on which it was made.

(2) A supervision order shall also cease to have effect if an event mentioned in section 25(1)(a) or (b) of the Child Abduction and Custody Act 1985 (termination of existing orders) occurs with respect to the child.

(3) Where the supervisor applies to the court to extend, or further extend, a supervision order the court may extend the order for such period as it may specify.

(4) A supervision order may not be extended so as to run beyond the end of the period of three years beginning with the date on which it was made.

EDUCATION SUPERVISION ORDERS

Effect of orders

12. (1) Where an education supervision order is in force with respect to a child, it shall be the duty of the supervisor –

(a) to advise, assist and befriend, and give directions to –

(i) the supervised child; and
(ii) his parents;

in such a way as will, in the opinion of the supervisor, secure that he is properly educated;

(b) where any such directions given to –

(i) the supervised child; or
(ii) a parent of his,

have not been complied with, to consider what further steps to take in the exercise of the supervisor's powers under this Act.

(2) Before giving any directions under sub-paragraph (1) the supervisor shall, so far as is reasonably practicable, ascertain the wishes and feelings of –

(a) the child; and
(b) his parents;

including, in particular, their wishes as to the place at which the child should be educated.

(3) When settling the terms of any such directions, the supervisor shall give due consideration –

(a) having regard to the child's age and understanding, to such wishes and feelings of his as the supervisor has been able to ascertain; and
(b) to such wishes and feelings of the child's parents as he has been able to ascertain.

(4) Directions may be given under this paragraph at any time while the education supervision order is in force.

13. (1) Where an education supervision order is in force with respect to a child, the duties of the child's parents under sections 7 and 444 of the Education Act 1996 (duties to secure education of children and to secure regular attendance of registered pupils) shall be superseded by their duty to comply with any directions in force under the education supervision order.

(2) Where an education supervision order is made with respect to a child –

(a) any school attendance order –

(i) made under section 437 of the Education Act 1996 with respect to the child; and

(ii) in force immediately before the making of the education supervision order,

shall cease to have effect; and

(b) while the education supervision order remains in force, the following provisions shall not apply with respect to the child –

(i) section 437 of that Act (school attendance orders);

(ii) section 9 of that Act (pupils to be educated in accordance with wishes of their parents);

(iii) sections 411 and 423 of that Act (parental preference and appeals against admission decisions);

(c) a supervision order made with respect to the child in criminal proceedings, while the education supervision order is in force, may not include an education requirement of the kind which could otherwise be included under section 12C of the Children and Young Persons Act 1969;

(d) any education requirement of a kind mentioned in paragraph (c), which was in force with respect to the child immediately before the making of the education supervision order, shall cease to have effect.

Duration of orders

15. (1) An education supervision order shall have effect for a period of one year, beginning with the date on which it is made.

(2) An education supervision order shall not expire if, before it would otherwise have expired, the court has (on the application of the authority in whose favour the order was made) extended the period during which it is in force.

(3) Such an application may not be made earlier than three months before the date on which the order would otherwise expire.

(4) The period during which an education supervision order is in force may be extended under sub-paragraph (2) on more than one occasion.

(5) No one extension may be for a period of more than three years.

(6) An education supervision order shall cease to have effect on –

(a) the child's ceasing to be of compulsory school age; or

(b) the making of a care order with respect to the child;

and sub-paragraphs (1) to (4) are subject to this sub-paragraph.

As amended by the Courts and Legal Services Act 1990, ss116, 125(7), Schedule 16, paras 10(2), 18, 19, 20, 23, Schedule 20; Maintenance Enforcement Act 1991, s6; Child Support Act 1991, s58(14); Education Act 1993, s307(1), (3), Schedule 19, para 149, Schedule 21, Pt II; Maintenance Orders (Backdating) Order 1993, at 2, Schedule 1, paras 10-13, 15; Law Reform (Succession) Act 1995, s4(1); Health Authorities Act 1995, s2(1), Schedule 1, Pt III, para 118(1), (7); Education Act 1996, s582(1), Schedule 37, Pt I, paras 85, 90, 93; Family Law Act 1996, ss 52, 66 (1), (3), Schedules 6, 8, Pt III, para 60(1), 10; Justices of the Peace Act 1997, s73(2), Schedule 5, para 27.

HUMAN FERTILISATION AND EMBRYOLOGY ACT 1990
(1990 c 37)

1 Meaning of 'embryo', 'gamete' and associated expressions

(1) In this Act, except where otherwise stated –

(a) embryo means a live human embryo where fertilisation is complete, and

(b) references to an embryo include an egg in the process of fertilisation,

and for this purpose, fertilisation is not complete until the appearance of a two cell zygote.

(2) This Act, so far as it governs bringing about the creation of an embryo, applies only to bringing about the creation of an embryo outside the human body; and in this Act –

(a) references to embryos the creation of which was brought about in vitro (in their application to those where fertilisation is complete) are to those where fertilisation began outside the human body whether or not it was completed there, and

(b) references to embryos taken from a woman do not include embryos whose creation was brought about in vitro.

(3) This Act, so far as it governs the keeping or use of an embryo, applies only to keeping or using an embryo outside the human body.

(4) References in this Act to gametes, eggs or sperm, except where otherwise stated, are to live human gametes, eggs or sperm but references below in this Act to gametes or eggs do not include eggs in the process of fertilisation.

2 Other terms

(1) In this Act –

'the Authority' means the Human Fertilisation and Embryology Authority established under section 5 of this Act, 'directions' means directions under section 23 of this Act,

'licence' means a licence under Schedule 2 to this Act and, in relation to a licence, 'the person responsible' has the meaning given by section 17 of this Act, and

'treatment services' means medical, surgical or obstetric services provided to the public or a section of the public for the purpose of assisting women to carry children.

(2) References in this Act to keeping, in relation to embryos or gametes, include keeping while preserved, whether preserved by cryopreservation or in any other way; and embryos or gametes so kept are referred to in this Act as 'stored' (and 'store' and 'storage' are to be interpreted accordingly).

(3) For the purposes of this Act, a woman is not to be treated as carrying a child until the embryo has become implanted.

3 Prohibitions in connection with embryos

(1) No person shall –

(a) bring about the creation of an embryo, or
(b) keep or use an embryo,

except in pursuance of a licence.

(2) No person shall place in a woman –

(a) a live embryo other than a human embryo, or
(b) any live gametes other than human gametes.

(3) A licence cannot authorise –

(a) keeping or using an embryo after the appearance of the primitive streak,
(b) placing an embryo in any animal,
(c) keeping or using an embryo in any circumstances in which regulations prohibit its keeping or use, or
(d) replacing a nucleus of a cell of an embryo with a nucleus taken from a cell of any person, embryo or subsequent development of an embryo.

(4) For the purposes of subsection (3)(a) above, the primitive streak is to be taken to have appeared in an embryo not later than the end of the period of 14 days beginning with the day when the gametes are mixed, not counting any time during which the embryo is stored.

3A Prohibition in connection with germ cells

(1) No person shall, for the purpose of providing fertility services for any woman, use female germ cells taken or derived from an embryo or a foetus or use embryos created by using such cells.

(2) In this section –

'female germ cells' means cells of the female germ line and includes such cells at any stage of maturity and accordingly includes eggs; and

'fertility services' means medical, surgical or obstetric services provided for the purpose of assisting women to carry children.

4   Prohibitions in connection with gametes

(1) No person shall –

    (a) store any gametes, or
    (b) in the course of providing treatment services for any woman, use the sperm of any man unless the services are being provided for the woman and the man together or use the eggs of any other woman, or
    (c) mix gametes with the live gametes of any animal,

except in pursuance of a licence.

(2) A licence cannot authorise storing or using gametes in any circumstances in which regulations prohibit their storage or use.

(3) No person shall place sperm and eggs in a woman in any circumstances specified in regulations except in pursuance of a licence.

(4) Regulations made by virtue of subsection (3) above may provide that, in relation to licences only to place sperm and eggs in a woman in such circumstances, sections 12 to 22 of this Act shall have effect with such modifications as may be specified in the regulations.

(5) Activities regulated by this section or section 3 of this Act are referred to in this Act as 'activities governed by this Act'.

27 Meaning of 'mother'

(1) The woman who is carrying or has carried a child as a result of the placing in her of an embryo or of sperm and eggs, and no other woman, is to be treated as the mother of the child.

(2) Subsection (1) above does not apply to any child to the extent that the

child is treated by virtue of adoption as not being the child of any person other than the adopter or adopters.

(3) Subsection (1) above applies whether the woman was in the United Kingdom or elsewhere at the time of the placing in her of the embryo or the sperm and eggs.

28   Meaning of 'father'

(1) This section applies in the case of a child who is being or has been carried by a woman as the result of the placing in her of an embryo or of sperm and eggs or her artificial insemination.

(2) If –

(a) at the time of the placing in her of the embryo or the sperm and eggs or of her insemination, the woman was a party to a marriage, and

(b) the creation of the embryo carried by her was not brought about with the sperm of the other party to the marriage,

then, subject to subsection (5) below, the other party to the marriage shall be treated as the father of the child unless it is shown that he did not consent to the placing in her of the embryo or the sperm and eggs or to her insemination (as the case may be).

(3) If no man is treated, by virtue of subsection (2) above, as the father of the child but –

(a) the embryo or the sperm and eggs were placed in the woman, or she was artificially inseminated, in the course of treatment services provided for her and a man together by a person to whom a licence applies, and

(b) the creation of the embryo carried by her was not brought about with the sperm of that man,

then, subject to subsection (5) below, that man shall be treated as the father of the child.

(4) Where a person is treated as the father of the child by virtue of subsection (2) or (3) above, no other person is to be treated as the father of the child.

(5) Subsections (2) and (3) above do not apply –

(a) in relation to England and Wales and Northern Ireland, to any child who, by virtue of the rules of common law, is treated as the legitimate child of the parties to a marriage,

(b) in relation to Scotland, to any child who, by virtue of any enactment or other rule of law, is treated as the child of the parties to a marriage, or

(c) to any child to the extent that the child is treated by virtue of adoption as not being the child of any person other than the adopter or adopters.

(6) Where –

(a) the sperm of a man who has given such consent as is required by paragraph 5 of Schedule 3 to this Act was used for a purpose for which such consent was required, or

(b) the sperm of a man, or an embryo the creation of which was brought about with his sperm, was used after his death,

he is not to be treated as the father of the child.

(7) The references in subsection (2) above to the parties to a marriage at the time there referred to –

(a) are to the parties to a marriage subsisting at that time, unless a judicial separation was then in force, but

(b) include the parties to a void marriage if either or both of them reasonably believed at that time that the marriage was valid; and for the purposes of this subsection it shall be presumed, unless the contrary is shown, that one of them reasonably believed at that time that the marriage was valid.

(8) This section applies whether the woman was in the United Kingdom or elsewhere at the time of the placing in her of the embryo or the sperm and eggs or her artificial insemination.

(9) In subsection (7)(a) above, 'judicial separation' includes a legal separation obtained in a country outside the British Islands and recognised in the United Kingdom.

29   Effect of sections 27 and 28

(1) Where by virtue of section 27 or 28 of this Act a person is to be treated as the mother or father of a child, that person is to be treated in law as the mother or, as the case may be, father of the child for all purposes.

(2) Where by virtue of section 27 or 28 of this Act a person is not to be treated as the mother or father of a child, that person is to be treated in law as not being the mother or, as the case may be, father of the child for any purpose.

(3) Where subsection (1) or (2) above has effect, references to any relationship between two people in any enactment, deed or other instrument or document (whenever passed or made) are to be read accordingly.

(4) In relation to England and Wales and Northern Ireland, nothing in the provisions of section 27(1) or 28(2) to (4), read with this section, affects –

(a) the succession to any dignity or title of honour or renders any person capable of succeeding to or transmitting a right to succeed to any such dignity or title, or

(b) the devolution of any property limited (expressly or not) to devolve (as nearly as the law permits) along with any dignity or title of honour. ...

30 Parental orders in favour of gamete donors

(1) The court may make an order providing for a child to be treated in law as the child of the parties to a marriage (referred to in this section as 'the husband' and 'the wife') if –

(a) the child has been carried by a woman other than the wife as the result of the placing in her of an embryo or sperm and eggs or her artifical insemination,

(b) the gametes of the husband or the wife, or both, were used to bring about the creation of the embryo, and

(c) the conditions in subsection (2) to (7) below are satisfied.

(2) The husband and the wife must apply for the order within six months of the birth of the child or, in the case of a child born before the coming into force of this Act, within six months of such coming into force.

(3) At the time of the application and of the making of the order –

(a) the child's home must be with the husband and the wife, and

(b) the husband or the wife, or both of them, must be domiciled in a part of the United Kingdom or in the Channel Islands or the Isle of Man.

(4) At the time of the making of the order both the husband and the wife must have attained the age of eighteen.

(5) The court must be satisfied that both the father of the child (including a person who is the father by virtue of section 28 of this Act), where he is not the husband, and the woman who carried the child have freely, and with full understanding of what is involved, agreed unconditionally to the making of the order.

(6) Subsection (5) above does not require the agreement of a person who cannot be found or is incapable of giving agreement and the agreement of the woman who carried the child is ineffective for the purposes of that subsection if given by her less than six weeks after the child's birth.

(7) The court must be satisfied that no money or other benefit (other than for expenses reasonably incurred) has been given or received by the husband or the wife for or in consideration of –

(a) the making of the order,

(b) any agreement required by subsection (5) above,

(c) the handing over of the child to the husband and the wife, or

(d) the making of any arrangements with a view to the making of the order,

unless authorised by the court. ...

As amended by the Criminal Justice and Public Order Act 1994, s156(1), (2).

CHILD SUPPORT ACT 1991
(1991 c 48)

1 The duty to maintain

(1) For the purposes of this Act, each parent of a qualifying child is responsible for maintaining him.

(2) For the purposes of this Act, an absent parent shall be taken to have met his responsibility to maintain any qualifying child of his by making periodical payments of maintenance with respect to the child of such amount, and at such intervals, as may be determined in accordance with the provisions of this Act.

(3) Where a maintenance assessment made under this Act requires the making of periodical payments, it shall be the duty of the absent parent with respect to whom the assessment was made to make those payments.

2 Welfare of children: the general principle

Where, in any case which falls to be dealt with under this Act, the Secretary of State or any child support officer is considering the exercise of any discretionary power conferred by this Act, he shall have regard to the welfare of any child likely to be affected by his decision.

3 Meaning of certain terms used in this Act

(1) A child is a 'qualifying child' if –

    (a) one of his parents is, in relation to him, an absent parent; or

    (b) both of his parents are, in relation to him, absent parents.

(2) The parent of any child is an 'absent parent', in relation to him, if –

    (a) that parent is not living in the same household with the child; and

    (b) the child has his home with a person who is, in relation to him, a person with care.

(3) A person is a 'person with care', in relation to any child, if he is a person –

(a) with whom the child has his home;

(b) who usually provides day to day care for the child (whether exclusively or in conjunction with any other person); and

(c) who does not fall within a prescribed category of person.

(4) The Secretary of State shall not, under subsection (3)(c), prescribe as a category –

(a) parents;

(b) guardians;

(c) persons in whose favour residence orders under section 8 of the Children Act 1989 are in force; ...

(5) For the purposes of this Act there may be more than one person with care in relation to the same qualifying child.

(6) Periodical payments which are required to be paid in accordance with a maintenance assessment are referred to in this Act as 'child support maintenance'.

(7) Expressions are defined in this section only for the purposes of this Act.

4   Child support maintenance

(1) A person who is, in relation to any qualifying child or any qualifying children, either the person with care or the absent parent may apply to the Secretary of State for a maintenance assessment to be made under this Act with respect to that child, or any of those children.

(2) Where a maintenance assessment has been made in response to an application under this section the Secretary of State may, if the person with care or absent parent with respect to whom the assessment was made applies to him under this subsection, arrange for –

(a) the collection of the child support maintenance payable in accordance with the assessment;

(b) the enforcement of the obligation to pay child support maintenance in accordance with the assessment.

(3) Where an application under subsection (2) for the enforcement of the obligation mentioned in subsection (2)(b) authorises the Secretary of State to take steps to enforce that obligation whenever he considers it necessary to do so, the Secretary of State may act accordingly.

(4) A person who applies to the Secretary of State under this section shall,

so far as that person reasonably can, comply with such regulations as may be made by the Secretary of State with a view to the Secretary of State or the child support officer being provided with the information which is required to enable –

(a) the absent parent to be traced (where that is necessary);

(b) the amount of child support maintenance payable by the absent parent to be assessed; and

(c) that amount to be recovered from the absent parent.

(5) Any person who has applied to the Secretary of State under this section may at any time request him to cease acting under this section.

(6) It shall be the duty of the Secretary of State to comply with any request made under subsection (5) (but subject to any regulations made under subsection (8)).

(7) The obligation to provide information which is imposed by subsection (4) –

(a) shall not apply in such circumstances as may be prescribed; and

(b) may, in such circumstances as may be prescribed, be waived by the Secretary of State.

(8) The Secretary of State may by regulations make such incidental, supplemental or transitional provision as he thinks appropriate with respect to cases in which he is requested to cease to act under this section.

(9) No application may be made under this section if there is in force with respect to the person with care and absent parent in question a maintenance assessment made in response to an application under section 6.

(10) No application may be made at any time under this section with respect to a qualifying child or any qualifying children if –

(a) there is in force a written maintenance agreement made before 5th April 1993, or a maintenance order, in respect of that child or those children and the person who is, at that time, the absent parent; or

(b) benefit is being paid to, or in respect of, a parent with care of that child or those children.

(11) In subsection (10) 'benefit' means any benefit which is mentioned in, or prescribed by regulations under, section 6(1).

5 Child support maintenance: supplemental provisions

(1) Where –

(a) there is more than one person with care of a qualifying child; and

(b) one or more, but not all, of them have parental responsibility for (or, in Scotland, parental rights over) the child;

no application may be made for a maintenance assessment with respect to the child by any of those persons who do not have parental responsibility for (or, in Scotland, parental rights over) the child.

(2) Where more than one application for a maintenance assessment is made with respect to the child concerned, only one of them may be proceeded with.

(3) The Secretary of State may by regulations make provision as to which of two or more applications for a maintenance assessment with respect to the same child is to be proceeded with.

6 Applications by those receiving benefit

(1) Where income support, an income-based jobseeker's allowance, family credit or any other benefit of a prescribed kind is claimed by or in respect of, or paid to or in respect of, the parent of a qualifying child she shall, if –

(a) she is a person with care of the child; and

(b) she is required to do so by the Secretary of State,

authorise the Secretary of State to take action under this Act to recover child support maintenance from the absent parent.

(2) The Secretary of State shall not require a person ('the parent') to give him the authorisation mentioned in subsection (1) if he considers that there are reasonable grounds for believing that –

(a) if the parent were to be required to give that authorisation; or

(b) if she were to give it,

there would be a risk of her, or of any child living with her, suffering harm or undue distress as a result.

(3) Subsection (2) shall not apply if the parent requests the Secretary of State to disregard it.

(4) The authorisation mentioned in subsection (1) shall extend to all children of the absent parent in relation to whom the parent first mentioned in subsection (1) is a person with care.

(5) That authorisation shall be given, without unreasonable delay, by completing and returning to the Secretary of State an application –

(a) for the making of a maintenance assessment with respect to the qualifying child or qualifying children; and

(b) for the Secretary of State to take action under this Act to recover, on her behalf, the amount of child support maintenance so assessed.

(6) Such an application shall be made on a form ('a maintenance application form') provided by the Secretary of State.

(7) A maintenance application form shall indicate in general terms the effect of completing and returning it.

(8) Subsection (1) has effect regardless of whether any of the benefits mentioned there is payable with respect to any qualifying child.

(9) A person who is under the duty imposed by subsection (1) shall, so far as she reasonably can, comply with such regulations as may be made by the Secretary of State with a view to the Secretary of State or the child support officer being provided with the information which is required to enable –

(a) the absent parent to be traced;

(b) the amount of child support maintenance payable by the absent parent to be assessed; and

(c) that amount to be recovered from the absent parent.

(10) The obligation to provide information which is imposed by subsection (9) –

(a) shall not apply in such circumstances as may be prescribed; and

(b) may, in such circumstances as may be prescribed, be waived by the Secretary of State.

(11) A person with care who has authorised the Secretary of State under subsection (1) but who subsequently ceases to fall within that subsection may request the Secretary of State to cease acting under this section.

(12) It shall be the duty of the Secretary of State to comply with any request made under subsection (11) (but subject to any regulations made under subsection (13)).

(13) The Secretary of State may by regulations make such incidental or transitional provision as he thinks appropriate with respect to cases in which he is requested under subsection (11) to cease to act under this section.

(14) The fact that a maintenance assessment is in force with respect to a person with care shall not prevent the making of a new maintenance

assessment with respect to her in response to an application under this section.

8 Role of the courts with respect to maintenance for children

(1) This subsection applies in any case where a child support officer would have jurisdiction to make a maintenance assessment with respect to a qualifying child and an absent parent of his on an application duly made by a person entitled to apply for such an assessment with respect to that child.

(2) Subsection (1) applies even though the circumstances of the case are such that a child support officer would not make an assessment if it were applied for.

(3) In any case where subsection (1) applies, no court shall exercise any power which it would otherwise have to make, vary or revive any maintenance order in relation to the child and absent parent concerned.

(3A) In any case in which section 4(10) or 7(10) prevents the making of an application for a maintenance assessment, and –

(a) no application has been made for a maintenance assessment under section 6, or

(b) such an application has been made but no maintenance assessment has been made in response to it,

subsection (3) shall have effect with the omission of the word 'vary'

(4) Subsection (3) does not prevent a court from revoking a maintenance order.

(5) The Lord Chancellor or in relation to Scotland the Lord Advocate may by order provide that, in such circumstances as may be specified by the order, this section shall not prevent a court from exercising any power which it has to make a maintenance order in relation to a child if –

(a) a written agreement (whether or not enforceable) provides for the making, or securing, by an absent parent of the child of periodical payments to or for the benefit of the child; and

(b) the maintenance order which the court makes is, in all material respects, in the same terms as that agreement.

(6) This section shall not prevent a court from exercising any power which it has to make a maintenance order in relation to a child if –

(a) a maintenance assessment is in force with respect to the child;

(b) the amount of the child support maintenance payable in accordance with the assessment was determined by reference to the alternative formula mentioned in paragraph 4(3) of Schedule 1; and

(c) the court is satisfied that the circumstances of the case make it appropriate for the absent parent to make or secure the making of periodical payments under a maintenance order in addition to the child support maintenance payable by him in accordance with the maintenance assessment.

(7) This section shall not prevent a court from exercising any power which it has to make a maintenance order in relation to a child if –

(a) the child is, will be or (if the order were to be made) would be receiving instruction at an educational establishment or undergoing training for a trade, profession or vocation (whether or not while in gainful employment); and

(b) the order is made solely for the purposes of requiring the person making or securing the making of periodical payments fixed by the order to meet some or all of the expenses incurred in connection with the provision of the instruction or training.

(8) This section shall not prevent a court from exercising any power which it has to make a maintenance order in relation to a child if –

(a) a disability living allowance is paid to or in respect of him; or

(b) no such allowance is paid but he is disabled,

and the order is made solely for the purpose of requiring the person making or securing the making of periodical payments fixed by the order to meet some or all of any expenses attributable to the child's disability.

(9) For the purposes of subsection (8), a child is disabled if he is blind, deaf or dumb or is substantially and permanently handicapped by illness, injury, mental disorder or congenital deformity or such other disability as may be prescribed.

(10) This section shall not prevent a court from exercising any power which it has to make a maintenance order in relation to a child if the order is made against a person with care of the child.

(11) In this Act 'maintenance order', in relation to any child, means an order which requires the making or securing of periodical payments to or for the benefit of the child and which is made under –

(a) Part II of the Matrimonial Causes Act 1973;

(b) the Domestic Proceedings and Magistrates' Courts Act 1978;

(c) Part III of the Matrimonial and Family Proceedings Act 1984;

(d) the Family Law (Scotland) Act 1985;

(e) Schedule 1 to the Children Act 1989; or

(f) any other prescribed enactment,

and includes any order varying or reviving such an order.

9 Agreements about maintenance

(1) In this section 'maintenance agreement' means any agreement for the making, or for securing the making, of periodical payments by way of maintenance, or in Scotland aliment, to or for the benefit of any child.

(2) Nothing in this Act shall be taken to prevent any person from entering into a maintenance agreement.

(3) Subject to section 4(10)(a) and section 7(10) the existence of a maintenance agreement shall not prevent any party to the agreement, or any other person, from applying for a maintenance assessment with respect to any child to or for whose benefit periodical payments are to be made or secured under the agreement.

(4) Where any agreement contains a provision which purports to restrict the right of any person to apply for a maintenance assessment, that provision shall be void.

(5) Where section 8 would prevent any court from making a maintenance order in relation to a child and an absent parent of his, no court shall exercise any power that it has to vary any agreement so as –

(a) to insert a provision requiring that absent parent to make or secure the making of periodical payments by way of maintenance, or in Scotland aliment, to or for the benefit of that child; or

(b) to increase the amount payable under such a provision.

(6) In any case in which section 4(10) or 7(10) prevents the making of an application for a maintenance assessment, and –

(a) no application has been made for a maintenance assessment under section 6, or

(b) such an application has been made but no maintenance assessment has been made in response to it,

subsection (5) shall have effect with the omission of paragraph (b).

10 Relationship between maintenance assessments and certain court orders and related matters

(1) Where an order of a kind prescribed for the purposes of this subsection is in force with respect to any qualifying child with respect to whom a maintenance assessment is made, the order –

(a) shall, so far as it relates to the making or securing of periodical payments, cease to have effect to such extent as may be determined in accordance with regulations made by the Secretary of State; or

(b) where the regulations so provide, shall, so far as it so relates, have effect subject to such modifications as may be so determined.

(2) Where an agreement of a kind prescribed for the purposes of this subsection is in force with respect to any qualifying child with respect to whom a maintenance assessment is made, the agreement –

(a) shall, so far as it relates to the making or securing of periodical payments, be unenforceable to such extent as may be determined in accordance with regulations made by the Secretary of State; or

(b) where the regulations so provide, shall, so far as it so relates, have effect subject to such modifications as may be so determined. ...

11 Maintenance assessments

(1) Any application for a maintenance assessment made to the Secretary of State shall be referred by him to a child support officer whose duty it shall be to deal with the application in accordance with the provision made by or under this Act.

(1A) Where –

(a) an application for a maintenance assessment is made under section 6, but

(b) the Secretary of State becomes aware, before referring the application to a child support officer, that the claim mentioned in subsection (1) of that section has been disallowed or withdrawn,

he shall, subject to subsection (1B), treat the application as if it had not been made.

(1B) If it appears to the Secretary of State that subsection (10) of section 4 would not have prevented the parent with care concerned from making an application for a maintenance assessment under that section he shall –

(a) notify her of the effect of this subsection, and

(b) if, before the end of the period of 28 days beginning with the day on which notice was sent to her, she asks him to do so, treat the application as having been made not under section 6 but under section 4.

(1C) Where the application is not preserved under subsection (1B) (and so is treated as not having been made) the Secretary of State shall notify –

(a) the parent with care concerned; and

(b) the absent parent (or alleged absent parent), where it appears to him that the person is aware of the application.

(2) The amount of child support maintenance to be fixed by any maintenance assessment shall be determined in accordance with the provisions of Part I of Schedule 1.

(3) Part II of Schedule 1 makes further provision with respect to maintenance assessments.

12 Interim maintenance assessments

(1) This section applies where a child support officer –

(a) is required to make a maintenance assessment;

(b) is proposing to conduct a review under section 16, 17, 18 or 19; or

(c) is conducting such a review.

(1A) If it appears to the child support officer that he does not have sufficient information to enable him –

(a) in a case falling within subsection (1)(a), to make the assessment,

(b) in a case falling within subsection (1)(b), to conduct the proposed review, or

(c) in a case falling within subsection (1)(c), to complete the review,

he may make an interim maintenance assessment.

(2) The Secretary of State may by regulations make provision as to interim maintenance assessments.

(3) The regulations may, in particular, make provision as to –

(a) the procedure to be followed in making an interim maintenance assessment; and

(b) the basis on which the amount of child support maintenance fixed by an interim assessment is to be calculated.

(4) Before making any interim assessment a child support officer shall, if it is reasonably practicable to do so, give written notice of his intention to make such an assessment to –

(a) the absent parent concerned;

(b) the person with care concerned; and

(c) where the application for a maintenance assessment was made under section 7, the child concerned.

(5) Where a child support officer serves notice under subsection (4), he shall not make the proposed interim assessment before the end of such period as may be prescribed.

13   Child support officers

(1) The Secretary of State shall appoint persons (to be known as child support officers) for the purpose of exercising functions –

(a) conferred on them by this Act, or by any other enactment; or

(b) assigned to them by the Secretary of State.

(2) A child support officer may be appointed to perform only such functions as may be specified in his instrument of appointment.

(3) The Secretary of State shall appoint a Chief Child Support Officer.

(4) It shall be the duty of the Chief Child Support Officer to –

(a) advise child support officers on the discharge of their functions in relation to making, reviewing or cancelling maintenance assessments;

(b) keep under review the operation of the provision made by or under this Act with respect to making, reviewing or cancelling maintenance assessments; and

(c) report to the Secretary of State annually, in writing, on the matters with which the Chief Child Support Officer is concerned. ...

14   Information required by Secretary of State

(1) The Secretary of State may make regulations requiring any information or evidence needed for the determination of any application under this Act, or any question arising in connection with such an application, or needed in connection with the collection or enforcement of child support or other maintenance under this Act, to be furnished –

(a) by such persons as may be determined in accordance with regulations made by the Secretary of State; and

(b) in accordance with the regulations. ...

15 Powers of inspectors

(1) Where, in a particular case, the Secretary of State considers it appropriate to do so for the purpose of acquiring information which he or any child support officer requires for the purposes of this Act, he may appoint a person to act as an inspector under this section.

(2) Every inspector shall be furnished with a certificate of his appointment.

(3) Without prejudice to his being appointed to act in relation to any other case, or being appointed to act for a further period in relation to the case in question, an inspector's appointment shall cease at the end of such period as may be specified.

(4) An inspector shall have power –

(a) to enter at all reasonable times –

(i) any specified premises, other than premises used solely as a dwelling-house; and

(ii) any premises which are not specified but which are used by any specified person for the purpose of carrying on any trade, profession, vocation or business; and

(b) to make such examination and enquiry there as he considers appropriate.

(5) An inspector exercising his powers may question any person aged 18 or over whom he finds on the premises.

(6) If required to do so by an inspector exercising his powers, any person who is or has been –

(a) an occupier of the premises in question;

(b) an employer or an employee working at or from those premises;

(c) carrying on at or from those premises any trade, profession, vocation or business;

(d) an employee or agent of any person mentioned in paragraphs (a) to (c),

shall furnish to the inspector all such information and documents as the inspector may reasonably require.

(7) No person shall require under this section to answer any question or to give any evidence tending to incriminate himself or, in the case of a person who is married, his or her spouse.

(8) On applying for admission to any premises in the exercise of his powers, an inspector shall, if so required, produce his certificate. ...

16 Periodical reviews

(1) The Secretary of State shall make such arrangements as he considers necessary to secure that, where any maintenance assessment has been in force for a prescribed period, the amount of child support maintenance fixed by that assessment ('the original assessment') is reviewed by a child support officer under this section as soon as is reasonably practicable after the end of that prescribed period.

(2) Before conducting any review under this section, the child support officer concerned shall give, to such persons as may be prescribed, such notice of the proposed review as may be prescribed.

(3) A review shall be conducted under this section as if a fresh application for a maintenance assessment had been made by the person in whose favour the original assessment was made.

(4) On completing any review under this section, the child support officer concerned shall make a fresh maintenance assessment, unless he is satisfied that the original assessment has ceased to have effect or should be brought to an end. ...

17 Reviews on change of circumstances

(1) Where a maintenance assessment is in force –

   (a) the absent parent or person with care with respect to whom it was made; or
   (b) where the application for the assessment was made under section 7, either of them or the child concerned,

may apply to the Secretary of State for the amount of child support maintenance fixed by that assessment ('the original assessment') to be reviewed under this section.

(2) An application under this section may be made only on the ground that, by reason of a change of circumstance since the original assessment was made, the amount of child support maintenance payable by the absent parent would be significantly different if it were to be fixed by a

maintenance assessment made by reference to the circumstances of the case as at the date of the application.

(2A) The Secretary of State shall refer to a child support officer any application under this section which is duly made.

(3) The child support officer to whom an application under this section has been referred shall not proceed unless, on the information before him, he considers that it is likely that he will be required by subsection (6), or by virtue of subsection (7), to make a fresh maintenance assessment if he conducts a review,

(4) Before conducting any review under this section, the child support officer concerned shall give to such persons as may be prescribed, such notice of the proposed review as may be prescribed.

(4A) Where a child support officer is conducting a review under this section,. and the original assessment has ceased to have effect, he may continue the review as if the application for a review related to the original assessment and any subsequent assessment.

(5) In conducting a review under this section, the child support officer shall take into account a change of circumstance only if –

(a) he has been notified of it in such a manner, and by such person, as may be prescribed; or

(b) it is one which he knows has taken place.

(6) On completing a review of the original assessment under this section, the child support officer concerned shall make a fresh maintenance by reference to the circumstances of the case as at the date of the application under this section, unless –

(a) he is satisfied that the original assessment has ceased to have effect or should be brought to an end; or

(b) the difference between the amount of child support maintenance fixed by the original assessment and the amount that would be fixed if a fresh assessment were to be made as a result of the review is less than such amount as may be prescribed.

(7) On completing a review of any subsequent assessment under this section the child support officer concerned shall make a fresh maintenance assessment except in such circumstances as may be prescribed.

(8) In this section 'subsequent assessment' means a maintenance assessment made after the original assessment with respect to the same persons as the original assessment.

18 Reviews of decisions of child support officers

(1) Where –

(a) an application for a maintenance assessment is refused; or

(b) an application, under section 17, for the review of a maintenance assessment which is in force is refused,

the person who made that application may apply to the Secretary of State for the refusal to be reviewed.

(2) Where a maintenance assessment is in force –

(a) the absent parent or person with care with respect to whom it was made; or

(b) where the application for the assessment was made under section 7, either of them or the child concerned,

may apply to the Secretary of State for the assessment to be reviewed.

(3) Where a maintenance assessment is cancelled the appropriate person may apply to the Secretary of State for the cancellation to be reviewed.

(4) Where an application for the cancellation of a maintenance assessment is refused, the appropriate person may apply to the Secretary of State for the refusal to be reviewed.

(5) An application under this section shall give the applicant's reasons (in writing) for making it.

(6) The Secretary of State shall refer to a child support officer any application under this section which is duly made; and the child support officer shall conduct the review applied for unless in his opinion there are no reasonable grounds for supposing that the refusal, assessment or cancellation in question –

(a) was made in ignorance of a material fact;

(b) was based on a mistake as to a material fact; or

(c) was wrong in law.

(6A) Where a child support officer is conducting a review under this section and the maintenance assessment in question ('the original assessment') is no longer in force, he may continue the review as if the application for a review related to the original assessment and any maintenance assessment made after the original assessment with respect to the same persons as the original assessment.

(7) The Secretary of State shall arrange for a review under this section to

be conducted by a child support officer who played no part in taking the decision which is to be reviewed.

(8) Before conducting any review under this section, the child support officer concerned shall give to such persons as may be prescribed, such notice of the proposed review as may be prescribed.

(9) If a child support officer conducting a review under this section is satisfied that a maintenance assessment or (as the case may be) a fresh maintenance assessment should be made, he shall proceed accordingly.

(10) In making a maintenance assessment by virtue of subsection (9), a child support officer shall, if he is aware of any material change of circumstance since the decision being reviewed was taken, take account of that change of circumstance in making the assessment.

(10A) If a child support officer conducting a under this section is satisfied that the maintenance assessment in question was not validly made he may cancel it with effect from the date on which it took effect. ...

(12) In this section 'appropriate person' means –

(a) the absent parent or person with care with respect to whom the maintenance assessment in question was, or remains, in force; or

(b) where the application for that assessment was made under section 7, either of those persons or the child concerned.

19   Reviews at instigation of child support officers

(1) Where a child support officer is not conducting a review under section 16, 17 or 18, he may nevertheless review –

(a) a refusal to make a maintenance assessment,

(b) a refusal to review a maintenance assessment under section 17,

(c) a maintenance assessment (whether or not in force),

(d) a cancellation of a maintenance assessment, or

(e) a refusal to cancel a maintenance assessment,

if he suspects that it may be defective for one or more of the reasons set out in subsection (2).

(2) The reasons are that the refusal, assessment or cancellation –

(a) was made in ignorance of a material fact;

(b) was based on a mistake as to a material fact; or

(c) was wrong in law.

(3) If, on completing such a review, the child support officer is satisfied that the refusal, assessment or cancellation is defective for one or more of those reasons, he may –

(a) take no further action;

(b) in the case of a maintenance assessment which has been cancelled, set aside the cancellation;

(c) make a maintenance assessment;

(d) make a fresh maintenance assessment;

(e) cancel the maintenance assessment in question.

(4) Where a child support officer sets a cancellation aside under subsection (3), the maintenance assessment in question shall have effect as if it had never been cancelled.

(5) Any cancellation of a maintenance assessment under this section shall have effect from such date as may be determined by the child support officer.

(6) Where a child support officer suspects that if an application for a review of a maintenance assessment were to be made under section 17 it would be appropriate to make one or more fresh maintenance assessments, he may review the maintenance assessment even though no application for its review has been made under that section.

(7) If, on completing a review by virtue of subsection (6), the child support officer is satisfied that it would be appropriate to make one or more fresh maintenance assessments, he may do so.

20 Appeals

(1) Any person who is aggrieved by the decision of a child support officer –

(a) on a review under section 18;

(b) to refuse an application for such a review,

may appeal to a child support appeal tribunal against that decision.

(2) Except with leave of the chairman of a child support appeal tribunal, no appeal under this section shall be brought after the end of the period of 28 days beginning with the date on which notification was given of the decision in question.

(2A) A tribunal hearing an appeal under this section may, at the request of any part to the appeal, take into account –

(a) any later maintenance assessment made with respect to the same parties;

(b) any change in the circumstances of the case.

(3) Where an appeal under this section is allowed, the tribunal shall remit the case to the Secretary of State, who shall arrange for it to be dealt with by a child support officer.

(4) The tribunal may, in remitting any case under this section, give such directions as it considers appropriate.

20A Lapse of appeals

(1) This section applies where –

(a) a person has brought an appeal under section 20; and

(b) before the appeal is heard, the decision appealed against is reviewed under section 19.

(2) If the child support officer conducting the review considers that the decision which he has made on the review is the same as that which would have been made on the appeal had every ground of the appeal succeeded, the appeal shall lapse.

(3) In any other case, the review shall be of no effect and the appeal shall proceed accordingly.

21   Child support appeal tribunals

(1) There shall be tribunals to be known as child support appeal tribunals which shall, subject to any order under section 45, hear and determine appeals under section 20 and have such other functions as are conferred by this Act. ...

22   Child Support Commissioners

(1) Her Majesty may from time to time appoint a Chief Child Support Commissioner and such number of other Child Support Commissioners as she may think fit.

(2) The Chief Child Support Commissioner and the other Child Support Commissioners shall be appointed from among persons who –

(a) have a 10 year general qualification; or

(b) are advocates or solicitors in Scotland of 10 years' standing. ...

24 Appeal to Child Support Commissioner

(1) Any person who is aggrieved by a decision of a child support appeal tribunal, and any child support officer, may appeal to a Child Support Commissioner on a question of law.

(1A) The Secretary of State may appeal to a Child Support Commissioner on a question of law in relation to any decision of a child support appeal tribunal made in connection with an application for a departure direction.

(2) Where, on an appeal under this section, a Child Support Commissioners holds that the decision appealed against was wrong in law he shall set it aside.

(3) Where a decision is set aside under subsection (2), the Child Support Commissioner may –

(a) if he can do so without making fresh or further findings of fact, give the decision which he considers should have been given by the child support appeal tribunal;

(b) if he considers it expedient, make such findings and give such decision as he considers appropriate in the light of those findings; or

(c) on an appeal by the Secretary of State, refer the case to a child support appeal tribunal with directions for its determination; or

(d) on any other appeal, refer the case to a child support officer or, if he considers it appropriate, to a child support appeal tribunal with directions for its determination.

(4) Any reference under subsection (3) to a child support officer shall, subject to any direction of the Child Support Commissioner, to be a child support officer who has taken no part in the decision originally appealed against.

(5) On a reference under subsection (3) to a child support appeal tribunal, the tribunal shall, subject to any direction of the Child Support Commissioner, consist of persons who were not members of the tribunal which gave the decision which has been appealed against.

(6) No appeal lies under this section without the leave –

(a) of the person who was the chairman of the child support appeal tribunal when the decision appealed against was given or of such other chairman of a child support appeal tribunal as may be determined in accordance with regulations made by the Lord Chancellor; or

(b) subject to and in accordance with regulations so made, of a Child Support Commissioner. ...

(8) Where a question which would otherwise fall to be determined by a child

support officer first arises in the course of an appeal to a Child Support Commissioner, he may, if he thinks fit, determine it even though it has not been considered by a child support officer, ...

25 Appeal from Child Support Commissioner on question of law

(1) An appeal on a question of law shall lie to the appropriate court from any decision of a Child Support Commissioner.

(2) No such appeal may be brought except –

(a) with leave of the Child Support Commissioner who gave the decision or, where regulations made by the Lord Chancellor so provide, of a Child Support Commissioner selected in accordance with the regulations; or

(b) if the Child Support Commissioner refuses leave, with the leave of the appropriate court.

(3) An application of leave to appeal under this section against a decision of a Child Support Commissioner ('the appeal decision') may only be made by –

(a) a person who was a party to the proceedings in which the original decision, or appeal decision, was given;

(b) the Secretary of State; or

(c) any other person who is authorised to do so by regulations made by the Lord Chancellor.

(3A) The Child Support Commissioner to whom an application for leave to appeal under this section is made shall specify as the appropriate court either the Court of Appeal or the Court of Session.

(3B) In determining the appropriate court, the Child Support Commissioner shall have regard to the circumstances of the case, and in particular the convenience of the persons who may be parties to the appeal

(4) In this section –

'appropriate court', except in subsections (3A) and (3B), means the court specified in accordance with those subsections;

'original decision' means the decision to which the appeal decision in question relates. ...

26 Disputes about parentage

(1) Where a person who is alleged to be a parent of the child with respect to whom an application for a maintenance assessment has been made ('the

alleged parent') denies that he is one of the child's parents, the child support officer concerned shall not make a maintenance assessment on the assumption that the alleged parent is one of the child's parents unless the case falls within one of those set out in subsection (2).

(2) The Cases are –

CASE A

Where the alleged parent is a parent of the child in question by virtue of having adopted him.

CASE B

Where the alleged parent is a parent of the child in question by virtue of an order under section 30 of the Human Fertilisation and Embryology Act 1990 (parental orders in favour of gamete donors).

CASE C

Where –

(a) either

(i) a declaration that the alleged parent is a parent of the child in question (or a declaration which has that effect) is in force under section 56 of the Family Law Act 1986 (declarations of parentage) ...; and

(b) the child has not subsequently been adopted.

CASE D

Where –

(a) a declaration to the effect that the alleged parent is one of the parents of the child in question has been made under section 27; and

(b) the child has not subsequently been adopted.

CASE F

Where –

(a) the alleged parent has been found, or adjudged, to be the father of the child in question –

(i) in proceedings before any court in England and Wales which are relevant proceedings for the purposes of section 12 of the Civil Evidence Act 1968 ...; or

(ii) in affiliation proceedings before any court in the United Kingdom (whether or not he offered any defence to the allegation of paternity) and that finding or adjudication still subsists; and

(b) the child has not subsequently been adopted.

(3) In this section –

'adopted' means adopted within the meaning of Part IV of the Adoption Act 1976 or, in relation to Scotland, Part IV of the Adoption (Scotland) Act 1978; and

'affiliation proceedings', in relation to Scotland, means any action of affiliation and aliment.

27 Reference to court for declaration of parentage

(1) Subsection (1A) applies in any case where –

(a) an application for a maintenance assessment has been made, or a maintenance assessment is in force, with respect to a person ('the alleged parent') who denies that he is a parent of a child with respect to whom the application or assessment was made; and

(b) a child support officer to whom the case is referred is not satisfied that the case falls within one of those set out in section 26(2).

(1A) In any case where this subsection applies, the Secretary of State or the person with care may apply to the court for a declaration as to whether or not the alleged parent is one of the child's parents (a).

(2) If, on hearing any application under subsection (1A), the court is satisfied that the alleged parent is, or is not, a parent of the child in question it shall make a declaration to that effect.

(3) A declaration under this section shall have effect only for the purposes of –

(a) this Act; and

(b) proceedings in which a court is considering whether to make a maintenance order in the circumstances mentioned in subsection (6), (7) or (8) of section 8.

(4) In this section 'court' means, subject to any provision made under Schedule 11 to the Children Act 1989 (jurisdiction of courts with respect to certain proceedings relating to children) the High Court, a county court or a magistrates' court. ...

28A Application for a departure direction

(1) Where a maintenance assessment ('the current assessment') is in force –

(a) the person with care, or absent parent, with respect to whom is was made, or

(b) where the application for the current assessment was made under section 7, either of those persons or the child concerned,

may apply to the Secretary of State for a direction under section 28F (a 'departure direction').

(2) An application for a departure direction shall state in writing the grounds on which it is made and shall, in particular, state whether it is based on –

(a) the effect of the current assessment; or

(b) a material change in the circumstances of the case since the current assessment was made.

(3) In other respects, an application for a departure direction shall be made in such manner as may be prescribed.

(4) An application made under this section even though –

(a) an application for a review has been made under section 17 or 18 with respect to the current assessment; or

(b) a child support officer is conducting a review of the current assessment under section 16 or 19. ...

28B Preliminary consideration of applications

(1) Where an application for a departure direction has been duly made to the Secretary of State, he may give the application a preliminary consideration.

(2) Where the Secretary of State does so he may, on completing the preliminary consideration, reject the application if it appears to him –

(a) that there are no grounds on which a departure direction could be given in response to the application; or

(b) that the difference between the current amount and the revised amount is less than an amount to be calculated in accordance with regulations made by the Secretary of State for the purposes of this subsection and section 28F(4).

(3) In subsection (2) –

'the current amount' means the amount of the child support maintenance fixed by the current assessment; and

'the revised amount' means the amount of child support maintenance which, but for subsection (2)(b), would be fixed if a fresh maintenance assessment were to be made as a result of a departure direction allowing the departure applied for.

(4) Before completing any preliminary consideration, the Secretary of State may refer the current assessment to a child support officer for it to be reviewed as if an application for a review had been made under section 17 or 18.

(5) A review initiated by a reference under subsection (4) shall be conducted as if subsection (4) of section 17, or (as the case may be) subsection (8) of section 18, were omitted.

(6) Where, as a result of a review of the current assessment under section 16, 17, 18 or 19 (including a review initiated by a reference under subsection (4)), a fresh maintenance assessment is made, the Secretary of State –

(a) shall notify the applicant and such other persons as may be prescribed that the fresh maintenance assessment has been made; and

(b) may direct that the application is to lapse unless, before the end of such period as may be prescribed, the applicant notified the Secretary of State that he wishes it to stand.

28C Imposition of a regular payments condition

(1) Where an application for a departure direction is made by an absent parent, the Secretary of State may impose on him one of the conditions mentioned in subsection (2) ('a regular payments condition').

(2) The conditions are that –

(a) the applicant must make the payments of child support maintenance fixed by the current assessment'

(b) the applicant must make such reduced payments of child support maintenance as may be determined in accordance with regulations made by the Secretary of State.

(3) Where the Secretary of State imposes a regular payments condition, he shall give written notice to the absent parent and person with care concerned of the imposition of the condition and of the effect of failure to comply with it.

(4) A regular payments condition shall cease to have effect on the failure or determination of the application.

(5) For the purposes of subsection (4), an application for a departure direction fails if –

(a) it lapses or is withdrawn; or

(b) the Secretary of State rejects it on completing a preliminary consideration under section 28B.

(6) Where an absent parent has failed to comply with a regular payments condition –

(a) the Secretary of State may refuse to consider the application; and

(b) in prescribed circumstances the application shall lapse.

(7) The question whether an absent parent has failed to comply with a regular payments condition shall be determined by the Secretary of State.

(8) Where the Secretary of State determines that an absent parent has failed to comply with a regular payments condition he shall give that parent, and the person with care concerned, written notice of his decision.

28D Determination of applications

(1) Where an application for a departure direction has not failed, the Secretary of State shall –

(a) determine the application in accordance with the relevant provisions of or made under, this Act; or

(b) refer the application to a child support appeal tribunal for the tribunal to determine it in accordance with those provisions.

(2) For the purposes of subsection (1), an application for a departure direction has failed if –

(a) it has lapsed or been withdrawn; or

(b) the Secretary of State has rejected it on completing a preliminary consideration under section 28B.

(3) In dealing with an application for a departure direction which has been referred to it under subsection (1)(b), a child support appeal tribunal shall

have the same powers, and be subject to the same duties, as would the Secretary of State if he were dealing with the application.

28E Matters to be taken into account

(1) In determining any application for a departure direction, the Secretary of State shall have regard both to the general principles set out in subsection (2) and to such other considerations as may be prescribed.

(2) The general principles are that –

(a) parents should be responsible for maintaining their children whenever they can afford to do so;

(b) where a parent has more than one child, his obligation to maintain any one of them should be no less of an obligation than his obligation to maintain any other of them.

(3) In determining any application for a departure direction, the Secretary of State shall take into account any representations made to him –

(a) by the person with care or absent parent concerned; or

(b) where the application for the current assessment was made under section 7, by either of them or the child concerned.

(4) In determining any application for a departure direction, no account shall be taken of the fact that –

(a) any part of the income of the person with care concerned is, or would be if a departure direction were made, derived from any benefit; or

(b) some or all of any child support maintenance might be taken into account in any manner in relation to any entitlement to benefit.

(5) In this section 'benefit' has such meaning as may be prescribed.

28F Departure directions

(1) The Secretary of State may give a departure direction if –

(a) he is satisfied that the case is one which falls within one or more of the cases set out in Part I of Schedule 4B or in regulations made under that Part; and

(b) it is his opinion that, in all the circumstances of the case, it would be just and equitable to give a departure direction.

(2) In considering whether it would be just and equitable in any case to

give a departure direction, the Secretary of State shall have regard, in particular, to –

(a) the financial circumstances of the absent parent concerned,

(b) the financial circumstances of the person with care concerned, and

(c) the welfare of any child likely to be affected by the direction.

(3) The Secretary of State may by regulations make provision –

(a) for factors which are to be taken into account in determining whether it would be just and equitable to give a departure direction in any case;

(b) for factors which are not to be taken into account in determining such a question.

(4) The Secretary of State shall not give a departure direction if he is satisfied that the difference between the current amount and the revised amount is less than an amount to be calculated in accordance with regulations made by the Secretary of State for the purposes of this subsection and section 28B(2).

(5) In subsection (4) –

'the current amount' means the amount of the child support maintenance fixed by the current assessment, and

'the revised amount' means the amount of child support maintenance which would be fixed if a fresh maintenance assessment were to be made as a result of the departure direction which the Secretary of State would give in response to the application of subsection (4).

(6) A departure direction shall

(a) require a child support officer to make one or more fresh maintenance assessment; and

(b) specify the basis on which the amount of child support maintenance is to be fixed by any assessment made in consequence of the direction. ...

28G Effect and duration of departure directions

(1) Where a departure direction is given, it shall be the duty of the child support officer to whom the case is referred to comply with the direction as soon as is reasonably practicable.

(2) A departure direction may be given so as to have effect –

(a) for a specified period; or

(b) until the occurrence of a specified event. ...

28H Appeals in relation to applications for departure directions

(1) Any qualifying person who is aggrieved by any decision of the Secretary of State on an application for a departure direction may appeal to a child support appeal tribunal against that decision.

(2) In subsection (1), 'qualifying person' means –

(a) the person with care, or absent parent, with respect to whom the current assessment was made, or

(b) where the application for the current assessment was made under section 7, either of those persons or the child concerned.

(3) Except with leave of the chairman of a child support appeal tribunal, no appeal under this section shall be brought after the end of the period of 28 days beginning with the date on which notification was given of the decision in question.

(4) On an appeal under this section, the tribunal shall –

(a) consider the matter –

(i) as if it were exercising the powers of the Secretary of State in relation to the application in question; and

(ii) as if it were subject to the duties imposed on him in relation to that application;

(b) have regard to any representations made to it by the Secretary of State; and

(c) confirm the decision or replace it with such decision as the tribunal considers appropriate.

29 Collection of child support maintenance

(1) The Secretary of State may arrange for the collection of any child support maintenance payable in accordance with a maintenance assessment where –

(a) the assessment is made by virtue of section 6; or

(b) an application has been made to the Secretary of State under section 4(2) or 7(3) for him to arrange for its collection.

(2) Where a maintenance assessment is made under this Act, payments of child support maintenance under the assessment shall be made in accordance with regulations made by the Secretary of State. ...

31   Deduction from earnings orders

(1) This section applies where any person ('the liable person') is liable to make payments of child support maintenance.

(2) The Secretary of State may make an order ('a deduction from earnings order') against a liable person to secure the payment of any amount due under the maintenance assessment in question.

(3) A deduction from earnings order may be made so as to secure the payment of –

(a) arrears of child support maintenance payable under the assessment;

(b) amounts of child support maintenance which will become due under the assessment; or

(c) both such arrears and such future amounts.

(4) A deduction from earnings order –

(a) shall be expressed to be directed at a person ('the employer') who has the liable person in his employment; and

(b) shall have effect from such date as may be specified in the order.

(5) A deduction from earnings order shall operate as an instruction to the employer to –

(a) make deductions from the liable person's earnings; and

(b) pay the amounts deducted to the Secretary of State.

(6) The Secretary of State shall serve a copy of any deduction from earnings order which he makes under this section on –

(a) the person who appears to the Secretary of State to have the liable person in question in his employment; and

(b) the liable person.

(7) Where –

(a) a deduction from earnings order has been made; and

(b) a copy of the order has been served on the liable person's employer,

it shall be the duty of that employer to comply with the order; but he shall not be under any liability for non-compliance before the end of the period of 7 days beginning with the date on which the copy was served on him.

(8) In this section and in section 32 [regulations about deduction from earning orders] 'earning' has such meaning as may be prescribed.

33 Liability orders

(1) This section applies where –

(a) a person who is liable to make payments of child support maintenance ('the liable person') fails to make one or more of those payments; and

(b) it appears to the Secretary of State that –

(i) it is inappropriate to make a deduction from earnings order against him (because, for example, he is not employed); or

(ii) although such an order has been made against him, it has proved ineffective as a means of securing that payments are made in accordance with the maintenance assessment in question.

(2) The Secretary of State may apply to a magistrates' court ... for an order ('a liability order') against the liable person.

(3) Where the Secretary of State applies for a liability order, the magistrates' court ... shall make the order if satisfied that the payments in question have become payable by the liable person and have not been paid.

(4) On an application under subsection (2), the court ... shall not question the maintenance assessment under which the payments of child support maintenance fell to be made. ...

35 Enforcement of liability orders by distress

(1) Where a liability order has been made against a person ('the liable person'), the Secretary of State may levy the appropriate amount by distress and sale of the liable person's goods.

(2) In subsection (1), 'the appropriate amount' means the aggregate of –

(a) the amount in respect of which the order was made, to the extent that it remains unpaid; and

(b) an amount, determined in such manner as may be prescribed, in respect of the charges connected with the distress. ...

36 Enforcement in county courts

(1) Where a liability order has been made against a person, the amount in respect of which the order was made, to the extent that it remains unpaid, shall, if a county court so orders, be recoverable by means of garnishee proceedings or a charging order, as if it were payable under a county court order. ...

40 Commitment to prison

(1) Where the Secretary of State has sought –

(a) to levy an amount by distress under this Act; or

(b) to recover an amount by virtue of section 36,

and that amount, or any portion of it, remains unpaid he may apply to a magistrates' court for the issue of a warrant committing the liable person to prison.

(2) On any such application the court shall (in the presence of the liable person) inquire as to –

(a) the liable person's means; and

(b) whether there has been wilful refusal or culpable neglect on his part.

(3) If, but only if, the court is of the opinion that there has been wilful refusal or culpable neglect on the part of the liable person it may –

(a) issue a warrant of commitment against him; or

(b) fix a term of imprisonment and postpone the issue of the warrant until such time and on such conditions (if any) as it thinks just.

(4) Any such warrant –

(a) shall be made in respect of an amount equal to the aggregate of –

(i) the amount mentioned in section 35(1) or so much of it as remains outstanding; and

(ii) an amount (determined in accordance with regulations made by the Secretary of State) in respect of the costs of commitment; and

(b) shall state that amount.

(5) No warrant may be issued under this section against the person who is under the age of 18.

(6) A warrant issued under this section shall order the liable person –

(a) to be imprisoned for a specified period; but

(b) to be released (unless he is in custody for some other reason) on payment of the amount stated in the warrant.

(7) The maximum period of imprisonment which may be imposed by virtue of subsection (6) ... shall not exceed six weeks. ...

41 Arrears of child support maintenance

(1) This section applies where –

(a) the Secretary of State is authorised under section 4, 6 or 7 to recover child support maintenance payable by an absent parent in accordance with a maintenance assessment; and

(b) the absent parent has failed to make one or more payments of child support maintenance due from him in accordance with that assessment.

(2) Where the Secretary of State recovers any such arrears he may, in such circumstances as may be prescribed and to such extent as may be prescribed, retain them if he is satisfied that the amount of any benefit paid to or in respect of the person with care of the child or children in question would have been less had the absent parent made the payment or payments of child support maintenance in question.

(2A) In determining for the purposes of subsection (2) where the amount of any benefit paid would have been less at any time than the amount which was paid at that time, in a case where the maintenance assessment had effect from a date earlier than that on which it was made, the assessment shall be taken to have been in force at that time.

(3) In such circumstances as may be prescribed, the absent parent shall be liable to make such payments of interest with respect to the arrears of child support maintenance as may be prescribed. ...

41A Arrears: alternative to interest payments

(1) The Secretary of State may by regulations make provision for the payment by absent parents who are in arrears with payments of child support maintenance of sums determined in accordance with the regulations.

(2) A sum payable under any such regulations is referred to in this section as an 'additional sum'.

(3) Any liability of an absent parent to pay an additional sum shall not affect any liability of his to pay the arrears of child support maintenance concerned.

(4) The Secretary of State shall exercise his powers under this section and those under section 41(3) in such a way as to ensure that no absent parent is liable to pay both interest and an additional sum in respect of the same period (except by reference to different maintenance assessments). ...

44 Jurisdiction

(1) A child support officer shall have jurisdiction to make a maintenance assessment with respect to a person who is –

(a) a person with care;

(b) an absent parent; or

(c) a qualifying child,

only if that person is habitually resident in the United Kingdom.

(2) Where the person with care is not an individual, subsection (1) shall have effect as if paragraph (a) were omitted. ...

46 Failure to comply with obligations imposed by section 6

(1) This section applies where any person ('the parent') –

(a) fails to comply with a requirement imposed on her by the Secretary of State under section 6(1); or

(b) fails to comply with any regulation made under section 6(9).

(2) A child support officer may serve written notice on the parent requiring her, before the end of the specified period, either to comply or to give him her reasons for failing to do so.

(3) When the specified period has expired, the child support officer shall consider whether, having regard to any reasons given by the parent, there are reasonable grounds for believing that, if she were to be required to comply, there would be a risk of her or of any children living with her suffering harm or undue distress as a result of complying.

(4) If the child support officer considers that there are such reasonable grounds, he shall –

(a) take no further action under this section in relation to the failure in question; and

(b) notify the parent, in writing, accordingly.

(5) If the child support officer considers that there are no such reasonable grounds, he may, except in prescribed circumstances, give a reduced benefit direction with respect to the parent. ...

(7) Any person who is aggrieved by a decision of a child support officer to give a reduced benefit direction may appeal to a child support appeal tribunal against that decision.

(8) Sections 20(2) to (4) and 21 shall apply in relation to appeals under subsection (7) as they apply in relation to appeals under section 20. ...

(11) In this section – ...

'reduced benefit direction' means a direction, binding on the adjudication officer, that the amount payable by way of any relevant benefit to, or in respect of, the parent concerned be reduced by such amount, and for such period, as may be prescribed;

'relevant benefit' means income support, family credit or any other benefit of a kind prescribed for the purposes of section 6; ...

48   Right of audience

(1) Any officer of the Secretary of State who is authorised by the Secretary of State for the purposes of this section shall have, in relation to any proceedings under this Act before a magistrates' court, a right of audience and the right to conduct litigation.

(2) In this section 'right of audience' and 'right to conduct litigation' have the same meaning as in section 119 of the Courts and Legal Services Act 1990.

54   Interpretation

In this Act –

'absent parent' has the meaning given in section 3(2);

'adjudication officer' has the same meaning as in the benefit Acts; ...

'application for a depature direction' means an application under section 28A; ...

'assessable income' has the meaning given in paragraph 5 of Schedule 1;

'benefit Acts' means the Social Security Contributions and Benefits Act 1992 and the Social Security Administration Act 1992;

'Chief Adjudication Officer' has the same meaning as in the benefit Acts;

'Chief Child Support Officer' has the meaning given in section 13;

'child benefit' has the same meaning as in the Child Benefit Act 1975;

'child support appeal tribunal' means a tribunal appointed under section 21;

'child support maintenance' has the meaning given in section 3(6);

'child support officer' has the meaning given in section 13;

'current assessment', in relation to an application for a departure direction, means (subject to any regulations made under paragraph 10 of Schedule 4A) the maintenance assessment with respect to which the application is made;

'deduction from earnings order' has the meaning given in section 31(2);

'departure direction' has the meaning given in section 28A;

'disability living allowance' has the same meaning as in the benefit Acts;

'family credit' has the same meaning as in the benefit Acts;

'general qualification' shall be construed in accordance with section 71 of the Courts and Legal Services Act 1990 (qualification for judicial appointments);

'income support' has the same meaning as in the benefit Acts;

'income-based jobseeker's allowance' has the same meaning as in the Jobseekers Act 1995;

'interim maintenance assessment' has the meaning given in section 12;

'liability order' has the meaning given in section 33(2);

'maintenance agreement' has the meaning given in section 9(1);

'maintenance assessment' means an assessment of maintenance made under this Act and, except in prescribed circumstances, includes an interim maintenance assessment;

'maintenance order' has the meaning given in section 8(11);

'maintenance requirement' means the amount calculated in accordance with paragraph 1 of Schedule 1;

'parent', in relation to any child, means any person who is in law the mother or father of the child;

'parent with care' means a person who is, in relation to a child, both a parent and a person with care;

'parental responsibility' has the same meaning as in the Children Act 1989;

'parental rights' has the same meaning as in the Law Reform (Parent and Child) (Scotland) Act 1986;

'person with care' has the meaning given in section 3(3);

'prescribed' means prescribed by regulations made by the Secretary of State;

'qualifying child' has the meaning given in section 3(1).

55 Meaning of 'child'

(1) For the purposes of this Act a person is a child if –

(a) he is under the age of 16;
(b) he is under the age of 19 and receiving full-time education (which is not advanced education) –

(i) by attendance at a recognised educational establishment; or
(ii) elsewhere, if the education is recognised by the Secretary of State; or

(c) he does not fall within paragraph (a) or (b) but –

(i) he is under the age of 18, and
(ii) prescribed conditions are satisfied with respect to him.

(2) A person is not a child for the purposes of this Act if he –

(a) is or has been married;
(b) has celebrated a marriage which is void; or
(c) has celebrated a marriage in respect of which a decree of nullity has been granted.

(3) In this section –

'advanced education' means education of a prescribed description; and

'recognised educational establishment' means an establishment recognised by the Secretary of State for the purposes of this section as being, or as comparable to, a university, college or school.

(4) Where a person has reached the age of 16, the Secretary of State may recognise education provided for him otherwise than at a recognised educational establishment only if the Secretary of State is satisfied that education was being so provided for him immediately before he reached the age of 16.

(5) The Secretary of State may provide that in prescribed circumstances education is or is not to be treated for the purposes of this section as being full-time.

(6) In determining whether a person falls within subsection (1)(b), no

account shall be taken of such interruptions in his education as may be prescribed.

(7) The Secretary of State may by regulations provide that a person who ceases to fall within subsection (1) shall be treated as continuing to fall within that subsection for a prescribed period.

(8) No person shall be treated as continuing to fall within subsection (1) by virtue of regulations made under subsection (7) after the end of the week in which he reaches the age of 19.

SCHEDULE 3

CHILD SUPPORT APPEAL TRIBUNALS

The president

(1) (1) The persons appointed as President of the social security appeal tribunals, medical appeal tribunals and disability appeal tribunals shall, by virtue of that appointment, also be President of the child support appeal tribunals. ...

(2) (1) A child support appeal tribunal shall consist of a chairman and two other persons.

(2) The chairman and the other members of the tribunal must not all be of the same sex.

(3) Sub-paragraph (2) shall not apply to any proceedings before a child support appeal tribunal if the chairman of the tribunal rules that it is not reasonably practicable to comply with that sub-paragraph in those proceedings. ...

The chairmen

(3) (1) The chairman of a child support appeal tribunal shall be nominated by the President. ...

(4) (1) The Lord Chancellor may appoint regional and other full-time chairmen for child support appeal tribunals.

(2) A person is qualified to be appointed as a full-time chairman if he has a seven year general qualification ...

Other members of child support appeal tribunals

(5) (1) The members of a child support appeal tribunal other than the chairman shall be drawn from the appropriate panel constituted under this paragraph. ...

(3) The panel for an area shall be composed of persons appearing to the President to have knowledge or experience of conditions in the area and to be representative of persons living or working in the area. ...

SCHEDULE 4A

DEPARTURE DIRECTIONS ...

Anticipation of change of circumstances

(5) (1) A departure direction may be given so as to provide that if the circumstances of the case change in such manner as may be specified in the direction of a fresh maintenance assessment is to be made.

(2) Where any such provision is made, the departure direction may provide for the basis on which the amount of child support maintenance is to be fixed by the fresh maintenance assessment to differ from the basis on which the amount of child support maintenance was fixed by any earlier maintenance assessment made as a result of the direction. ...

As amended by the Social Security (Consequential Provisions) Act 1992, s4, Schedules 1, 2, para 114; Child Support Act 1995, ss1–8, 11–16, 18(1), (3), (4), 19, 20(1)–(4), 22, 30(5), Schedules 1, 3, paras 1–8, 11, 12, 14, 16; Jobseekers Act 1995, s41(4), Schedule 2, para 20(1), (2), (6).

CRIMINAL JUSTICE ACT 1991
(1991 c 53)

20 Statements as to offender's financial circumstances ...

(1B) Before exercising its powers under section 55 of the Children and Young Persons Act 1933 against the parent or guardian of any individual who has been convicted of an offence, the court may make a financial circumstances order with respect to the parent or (as the case may be) guardian.

(1C) In this section 'a financial circumstances order' means, in relation to any individual, an order requiring him to give to the court, within such period as may be specified in the order, such a statement of his financial circumstances as the court may require.

(2) An individual who without reasonable excuse fails to comply with a financial circumstances order shall be liable on summary conviction to a fine not exceeding level 3 on the standard scale. ...

As substituted by the Criminal Justice Act 1993, s65(3), (4), 79(14), Schedule 3, para 2, Schedule 6 and amended by the Criminal Justice and Public Order Act 1994, s168(1), (2), Schedule 9, para 42(1), (3), (5).

SOCIAL SECURITY CONTRIBUTIONS AND BENEFITS ACT 1992

(1992 c 4)

Part VII

INCOME-RELATED BENEFITS

123 Income-related benefits

(1) Prescribed schemes shall provide for the following benefits (in this Act referred to as 'income-related benefits') –

(a) income support;

(b) family credit;

(c) disability working allowance;

(d) housing benefit; and

(e) council tax benefit. ...

124 Income support

(1) A person in Great Britain is entitled to income support if –

(a) he is of or over the age of 16;

(b) he has no income or his income does not exceed the applicable amount;

(c) he is not engaged in remunerative work and, if he is a member of a married or unmarried couple, the other member is not so engaged;

(d) except in such circumstances as may be prescribed, he is not receiving relevant education;

(e) he falls within a prescribed category of person; and

(f) he is not entitled to a jobseeker's allowance and, if he is a member of a married or unmarried couple, the other member of the couple is not entitled to an income-based jobseeker's allowance.

(4) Subject to subsection (5) below, where a person is entitled to income support, then –

(a) if he has no income, the amount shall be the applicable amount; and

(b) if he has income, the amount shall be the difference between his income and the applicable amount.

(5) Where a person is entitled to income support for a period to which this subsection applies, the amount payable for that period shall be calculated in such manner as may be prescribed.

(6) Subsection (5) above applies –

(a) to a period of less than a week which is the whole period for which income support is payable; and

(b) to any other period of less than a week for which it is payable.

128 Family credit

(1) Subject to regulations under section 5(1)(a) of the Administration Act, a person in Great Britain is entitled to family credit if, when the claim for it is made or is treated as made –

(a) his income –

(i) does not exceed the amount which is the applicable amount at such date as may be prescribed; or

(ii) exceeds it, but only by such an amount that there is an amount remaining if the deduction for which subsection (2)(b) below provides is made;

(b) he or, if he is a member of a married or unmarried couple, he or the other member of the couple, is engaged and normally engaged in remunerative work;

(c) except in such circumstances as may be prescribed, neither he nor any member of his family is entitled to a disability working allowance; and

(d) he or, if he is a member of a married or unmarried couple, he or the other member, is responsible for a member of the same household who is a child or a person of a prescribed description.

(2) Where a person is entitled to family credit, then –

(a) if his income does not exceed the amount which is the applicable amount at the date prescribed under subsection (1)(a)(i) above, the amount of the family credit shall be the amount which is the appropriate maximum family credit in his case; and

(b) if his income exceeds the amount which is the applicable amount at that date, the amount of the family credit shall be what remains after the deduction from the appropriate maximum family credit of a prescribed percentage of the excess of his income over the applicable amount.

(3) Family credit shall be payable for a period of 26 weeks or such other period as may be prescribed and, subject to regulations, an award of family credit and the rate at which it is payable shall not be affected by any change of circumstances during that period or by any order under section 150 of the Administration Act. ...

130 Housing benefit

(1) A person is entitled to housing benefit if –

(a) he is liable to make payments in respect of a dwelling in Great Britain which he occupies as his home;

(b) there is an appropriate maximum housing benefit in his case; and

(c) either –

(i) he has no income or his income does not exceed the applicable amount; or

(ii) his income exceeds that amount, but only by so much that there is an amount remaining if the deduction for which subsection (3)(b) below provides is made.

(2) In subsection (1) above 'payments in respect of a dwelling' means such payments as may be prescribed, but the power to prescribe payments does not include power to prescribe –

(a) payments to a billing or levying authority in respect of council tax; or

(b) mortgage payments ...

(3) Where a person is entitled to housing benefit, then –

(a) if he has no income or his income does not exceed the applicable amount, the amount of the housing benefit shall be the amount which is the appropriate maximum housing benefit in his case; and

(b) if his income exceeds the applicable amount, the amount of the housing benefit shall be what remains after the deduction from the appropriate maximum housing benefit of prescribed percentages of the excess of his income over the applicable amount.

(4) Regulations shall prescribe the manner in which the appropriate maximum housing benefit is to be determined in any case. ...

131 Council tax benefit

(1) A person is entitled to council tax benefit in respect of a particular day falling after 31 March 1993 if the following are fulfilled, namely, the condition set out in subsection (3) below and either –

(a) each of the two conditions set out in subsections (4) and (5) below; or

(b) the condition set out in subsection (6) below.

(2) Council tax benefit –

(a) shall not be allowed to a person in respect of any day falling before the day on which his entitlement is to be regarded as commencing for that purpose by virtue of paragraph (1) of section 6(1) of the Administration Act; but

(b) may be allowed to him in respect of not more than 6 days immediately following the day on which his period of entitlement would otherwise come to an end, if his entitlement is to be regarded by virtue of that paragraph as not having ended for that purpose.

(3) The main condition for the purposes of subsection (1) above is that the person concerned –

(a) is for the day liable to pay council tax in respect of a dwelling of which he is a resident; and

(b) is not a prescribed person or a person of a prescribed class.

(4) The first condition for the purposes of subsection (1)(a) above is that there is an appropriate maximum council tax benefit in the case of the person concerned.

(5) The second condition for the purposes of subsection (1)(a) above is that –

(a) the day falls within a week in respect of which the person concerned has no income;

(b) the day falls within a week in respect of which his income does not exceed the applicable amount;

(c) neither paragraph (a) nor paragraph (b) above is fulfilled in his case but amount A exceeds amount B where –

(i) amount A is the appropriate maximum council tax benefit in his case; and

(ii) amount B is a prescribed percentage of the difference between his income in respect of the week in which the day falls and the applicable amount.

(6) The condition for the purposes of subsection (1)(b) above is that –

(a) no other resident of the dwelling is liable to pay rent to the person concerned in respect of the dwelling; and

(b) there is an alternative maximum council tax benefit in the case of that person which is derived from the income or aggregate incomes of one or more residents to whom this subsection applies.

(7) Subsection (6) above applies to any other resident of the dwelling who –

(a) is not a person who, in accordance with Schedule 1 to the Local Government Finance Act 1992, falls to be disregarded for the purposes of discount; and

(b) is not a prescribed person or a person of a prescribed class.

(8) Subject to subsection (9) below, where a person is entitled to council tax benefit in respect of a day, the amount to which he is entitled shall be –

(a) if subsection (5)(a) or (b) above applies, the amount which is the appropriate maximum council tax benefit in his case;

(b) if subsection (5)(c) above applies, the amount found by deducting amount B from amount A, where 'amount A' and 'amount B' have the meanings given by that subsection; and

(c) if subsection (6) above applies, the amount which is the alternative maximum council tax benefit in his case.

(9) Where a person is entitled to council tax benefit in respect of a day, and both subsection (5) and subsection (6) above apply, the amount to which he is entitled shall be whichever is the greater of –

(a) the amount given by paragraph (a) or, as the case may be, paragraph (b) of subsection (8) above; and

(b) the amount given by paragraph (c) of that subsection.

(10) Regulations shall prescribe the manner in which –

(a) the appropriate maximum council tax benefit;

(b) the alternative maximum council tax benefit;

are to be determined in any case.

(11) In this section 'dwelling' and 'resident' have the same meanings as in Part I or II of the Local Government Finance Act 1992.

135 The applicable amount

(1) The applicable amount, in relation to any income-related benefit, shall be such amount or the aggregate of such amounts as may be prescribed in relation to that benefit.

(2) The power to prescribe applicable amounts conferred by subsection (1) above includes power to prescribe nil as an applicable amount.

PART VIII

THE SOCIAL FUND

138 Payments out of the social fund

(1) Payments may be made out of the social fund, in accordance with this Part of this Act –

(a) of prescribed amounts, whether in respect of prescribed items or otherwise, to meet, in prescribed circumstances, maternity expenses and funeral expenses; and

(b) to meet other needs in accordance with directions given or guidance issued by the Secretary of State.

(2) Payments may also be made out of that fund, in accordance with this Part of this Act, of a prescribed amount or a number of prescribed amounts to prescribed descriptions of persons, in prescribed circumstances, to meet expenses for heating which appear to the Secretary of State to have been or to be likely to be incurred in cold weather.

(3) The power to make a payment out of the social fund such as is mentioned in subsection (1)(b) above may be exercised by making a payment to a third party with a view to the third party providing, or arranging for the provision of, goods or services for the applicant.

(4) In this section 'prescribed' means specified in or determined in accordance with regulations.

139 Awards by social fund officers

(1) The questions whether a payment such as is mentioned in section 138(1)(b) above is to be awarded and how much it is to be shall be determined by a social fund officer.

(2) A social fund officer may determine that an award shall be payable in specified instalments at specified times.

(3) A social fund officer may determine that an award is to be repayable.

(4) An award that is to be repayable shall be repayable upon such terms and conditions as before the award is paid the Secretary of State notifies to the person by or on behalf of whom the application for it was made.

(5) Payment of an award shall be made to the applicant unless the social fund officer determines otherwise.

140 Principles of determination

(1) In determining whether to make an award to the applicant or the amount or value to be awarded a social fund officer shall have regard, subject to subsection (2) below, to all the circumstances of the case and, in particular –

    (a) the nature, extent and urgency of the need;

    (b) the existence of resources from which the need may be met;

    (c) the possibility that some other person or body may wholly or partly meet it;

    (d) where the payment is repayable, the likelihood of repayment and the time within which repayment is likely;

    (e) any relevant allocation under section 168(1) to (4) of the Administration Act.

(2) A social fund officer shall determine any question in accordance with any general directions issued by the Secretary of State and in determining any question shall take account of any general guidance issued by him.

PART IX

CHILD BENEFIT

141 Child benefit

A person who is responsible for one or more children in any week shall be entitled, subject to the provisions of this Part of this Act, to a benefit (to be known as 'child benefit') for that week in respect of the child or each of the children for whom he is responsible.

142 Meaning of 'child'

(1) For the purposes of this Part of this Act a person shall be treated as a child for any week in which –

(a) he is under the age of 16; or

(b) he is under the age of 18 and not receiving full-time education and prescribed conditions are satisfied in relation to him; or

(c) he is under the age of 19 and receiving full-time education either by attendance at a recognised educational establishment or, if the education is recognised by the Secretary of State, elsewhere.

(2) The Secretary of State may recognise education provided otherwise than at a recognised educational establishment for a person who, in the opinion of the Secretary of State, could reasonably be expected to attend such an establishment only if the Secretary of State is satisfied that education was being so provided for that person immediately before he attained the age of 16.

143 Meaning of 'person responsible for child'

(1) For the purposes of this Part of this Act a person shall be treated as responsible for a child in any week if –

(a) he has the child living with him in that week; or

(b) he is contributing to the cost of providing for the child at a weekly rate which is not less than the weekly rate of child benefit payable in respect of the child for that week.

(2) Where a person has had a child living with him at some time before a particular week he shall be treated for the purposes of this section as having the child living with him in that week notwithstanding their absence from one another unless, in the 16 weeks preceding that week, they were absent from one another for more than 56 days not counting any day which is to be disregarded under subsection (3) below.

(3) Subject to subsection (4) below, a day of absence shall be disregarded for the purposes of subsection (2) above if it is due solely to the child's –

(a) receiving full-time education by attendance at a recognised educational establishment;

(b) undergoing medical or other treatment as an in-patient in a hospital or similar institution; or

(c) being, in such circumstances as may be prescribed, in residential accommodation pursuant to arrangements made under –

(i) section 21 of the National Assistance Act 1948;

(ii) the Children Act 1989; or

(iii) the Social Work (Scotland) Act 1968.

(4) The number of days that may be disregarded by virtue of subsection (3)(b) or (c) above in the case of any child shall not exceed such number as may be prescribed unless the person claiming to be responsible for the child regularly incurs expenditure in respect of the child.

145 Rate of child benefit

(1) Child benefit shall be payable at such weekly rate as may be prescribed.

(2) Different rates may be prescribed in relation to different cases, whether by reference to the age of the child in respect of whom the benefit is payable or otherwise.

(3) The power to prescribe different rates under subsection (2) above shall be exercised so as to bring different rates into force on such day as the Secretary of State may by order specify.

(4) No rate prescribed in place of a rate previously in force shall be lower than the rate that it replaces.

147 Interpretation of Part IX and supplementary provisions

(1) In this Part of this Act

'prescribed' means prescribed by regulations;

'recognised educational establishment' means an establishment recognised by the Secretary of State as being, or as comparable to, a university, college or school;

'voluntary organisation' means a body, other than a public or local authority, the activities of which are carried on otherwise than for profit; and

'week' means a period of seven days beginning with a Monday.

(2) Subject to any provision made by regulations, references in this Part of this Act to any condition being satisfied or any facts existing in a week shall be construed as references to the condition being satisfied or the facts existing at the beginning of that week.

(3) References in this Part of this Act to a parent, father or mother of a child shall be construed as including references to a step-parent, step-father or step-mother. ...

As amended by the Local Government Finance Act 1992, s103, Schedule 9, paras 1, 3 and 4; Jobseekers Act 1995, s41(4), (5), Schedule 2, para 30, Schedule 3.

SOCIAL SECURITY ADMINISTRATION ACT 1992
(1992 c 5)

78   Recovery of social fund awards

(1) A social fund award which is repayable shall be recoverable by the Secretaty of State.

(2) Without prejudice to any other method of recovery, the Secretary of State may recover an award by deduction from prescribed benefits.

(3) The Secretary of State may recover an award –

(a) from the person to or for the benefit of whom it was made;

(b) where that person is a member of a married or unmarried couple, from the other member of the couple;

(c) from a person who is liable to maintain the person by or on behalf of whom the application for the award was made or any person in relation to whose needs the award was made.

(3A) Where –

(a) a jobseeker's allowance is payable to a person from whom an award is recoverable under subsection (3) above; and

(b) that person is subject to a bankruptcy order,

a sum deducted from that benefit under subsection (2) above shall not be treated as income of his for the purposes of the Insolvency Act 1986. ...

(4) Payments to meet funeral expenses may in all cases be recovered, as if they were funeral expenses, out of the estate of the deceased, and (subject to section 71 above) by no other means.

(5) In this section –

'married couple' means a man and woman who are married to each other and are members of the same household;

'unmarried couple' means a man and woman who are not married to each other but are living together as husband and wife otherwise than in circumstances prescribed under section 132 of the Contributions and Benefits Act.

(6) For the purposes of this section –

(a) a man shall be liable to maintain his wife and any child of whom he is the father;

(b) a woman shall be liable to maintain her husband and any children of whom she is the mother;

(c) a person shall be liable to maintain another person throughout any period in respect of which the first-mentioned person has, on or after 23 May 1980 (the date of the passing of the Social Security Act 1980) and either alone or jointly with a further person, given an undertaking in writing in pursuance of immigration rules within the meaning of the Immigration Act 1971 to be responsible for the maintenance and accommodation of the other person; and

(d) 'child' includes a person who has attained the age of 16 but not the age of 19 and in respect of whom either parent, or some person acting in the place of either parent, is receiving income support or an income-based jobseeker's allowance.

(7) Any reference in subsection (6) above to children of whom the man or the woman is the father or the mother shall be construed in accordance with section 1 of the Family Law Reform Act 1987.

105 Failure to maintain – general

(1) If –

(a) any person persistently refuses or neglects to maintain himself or any person whom he is liable to maintain; and

(b) in consequence of his refusal or neglect income support or an income-based jobseeker's allowance is paid to or in respect of him or such a person,

he shall be guilty of an offence and liable on summary conviction to imprisonment for a term not exceeding three months or to a fine of an amount not exceeding level 4 on the standard scale or to both.

(2) For the purposes of subsection (1) above a person shall not be taken to refuse or neglect to maintain himself or any other person by reason only of anything done or omitted in furtherance of a trade dispute.

(3) Subject to subsection (4) below, subsections (6) to (9) of section 78 above

shall have effect for the purposes of this Part of this Act as they have effect for the purposes of that section.

(4) For the purposes of this section, in its application to an income-based jobseeker's allowance, a person is liable to maintain another if that other person is his or her spouse.

As amended by the Jobseekers Act 1995, s41(4), Schedule 2, paras 51, 53.

CHILD SUPPORT ACT 1995
(1995 c 34)

10   The child maintenance bonus

(1) The Secretary of State may by regulations make provision for the payment, in prescribed circumstances, of sums to persons –

(a) who are or have been in receipt of child maintenance; and

(b) to or in respect of whom income support of a jobseeker's allowance is or has been paid.

(2) A sum payable under the regulations shall be known as 'a child maintenance bonus'.

(3) A child maintenance bonus shall be treated for all purposes as payable by way of income support or (as the case may be) a jobseeker's allowance. ...

18   Deferral of right to apply for maintenance assessment ...

(6) Neither section 4(10) nor section 7(10) of the 1991 Act shall apply in relation to a maintenance order made in the circumstances mentioned in subsection (7) or (8) of section 8 of the 1991 Act. ...

NB Other provisions of this Act make insertions in, or amendments to, the Child Support Act 1991 and they are incorporated in the text of that Act.

PRIVATE INTERNATIONAL LAW (MISCELLANEOUS PROVISIONS) ACT 1995
(1995 c 42)

5 Validity in English law of potentially polygamous marriages

(1) A marriage entered into outside England and Wales between parties neither of whom is already married is not void under the law of England and Wales on the ground that it is entered into under a law which permits polygamy and that either party is domiciled in England and Wales.

(2) This section does not affect the determination of the validity of a marriage by reference to the law of another country to the extent that it falls to be so determined in accordance with the rules of private international law.

6 Application of section 5 to prior marriages

(1) Section 5 above shall be deemed to apply, and always to have applied, to any marriage entered into before commencement which is not excluded by subsection (2) or (3) below.

(2) That section does not apply to a marriage a party to which has (before commencement) entered into a later marriage which either –

(a) is valid apart from this section but would be void if section 5 above applied to the earlier marriage; or
(b) is valid by virtue of this section.

(3) That section does not apply to a marriage which has been annulled before commencement, whether by a decree granted in England and Wales or by an annulment obtained elsewhere and recognised in England and Wales at commencement.

(4) An annulment of a marriage resulting from legal proceedings begun before commencement shall be treated for the purposes of subsection (3) above as having taken effect before that time.

(5) For the purposes of subsections (3) and (4) above a marriage which has been declared to be invalid by a court of competent jurisdiction in any proceedings concerning either the validity of the marriage or any right dependent on its validity shall be treated as having been annulled.

(6) Nothing in section 5 above, in its application to marriages entered into before commencement –

(a) gives or affects any entitlement to an interest –

(i) under the will or codicil of, or on the intestacy of, a person who died before commencement; or

(ii) under a settlement or other disposition of property made before that time (otherwise than by will or codicil);

(b) gives or affects any entitlement to a benefit, allowance, pension or other payment –

(i) payable before, or in respect of a period before, commencement; or

(ii) payable in respect of the death of a person before that time;

(c) affects tax in respect of a period or event before commencement; or

(d) affects the succession to any dignity or title of honour.

(7) In this section 'commencement' means the commencement of this Part [ie on 8 January 1996].

FAMILY LAW ACT 1996
(1996 c 27)

PART I

PRINCIPLES OF PARTS II AND III

1 The general principles underlying Parts II and III

The court and any person, in exercising functions under or in consequence of Parts II and III, shall have regard to the following general principles –

(a) that the institution of marriage is to be supported;

(b) that the parties to a marriage which may have broken down are to be encouraged to take all practicable steps, whether by marriage counselling or otherwise, to save the marriage;

(c) that a marriage which has irretrievably broken down and is being brought to an end should be brought to an end –

(i) with minimum distress to the parties and to the children affected;

(ii) with questions dealt with in a manner designed to promote as good a continuing relationship between the parties and any children affected as is possible in the circumstances; and

(iii) without costs being unreasonably incurred in connection with the procedures to be followed in bringing the marriage to an end; and

(d) that any risk to one of the parties to a marriage, and to any children, of violence from the other party should, so far as reasonably practicable, be removed or diminished.

PART IV

FAMILY HOMES AND DOMESTIC VIOLENCE

30 Rights concerning matrimonial home where one spouse has no estate, etc

(1) This section applies if –

(a) one spouse is entitled to occupy a dwelling-house by virtue of –

(i) a beneficial estate or interest or contract; or

(ii) any enactment giving that spouse the right to remain in occupation; and

(b) the other spouse is not so entitled.

(2) Subject to the provisions of this Part, the spouse not so entitled has the following rights ('matrimonial home rights') –

(a) if in occupation, a right not to be evicted or excluded from the dwelling-house or any part of it by the other spouse except with the leave of the court given by an order under section 33;

(b) if not in occupation, a right with the leave of the court so given to enter into and occupy the dwelling-house.

(3) If a spouse is entitled under this section to occupy a dwelling-house or any part of a dwelling-house, any payment or tender made or other thing done by that spouse in or towards satisfaction of any liability of the other spouse in respect of rent, mortgage payments or other outgoings affecting the dwelling-house is, whether or not it is made or done in pursuance of an order under section 40, as good as if made or done by the other spouse.

(4) A spouse's occupation by virtue of this section –

(a) is to be treated, for the purposes of the Rent (Agriculture) Act 1976 and the Rent Act 1977 (other than Part V and sections 103 to 106 of that Act), as occupation by the other spouse as the other spouse's residence, and

(b) if the spouse occupies the dwelling-house as that spouse's only or principal home, is to be treated, for the purposes of the Housing Act 1985 and Part I of the Housing Act 1988, as occupation by the other spouse as the other spouse's only or principal home.

(5) If a spouse ('the first spouse') –

(a) is entitled under this section to occupy a dwelling-house or any part of a dwelling-house, and

(b) makes any payment in or towards satisfaction of any liability of the other spouse ('the second spouse') in respect of mortgage payments affecting the dwelling-house,

the person to whom the payment is made may treat it as having been made by the second spouse, but the fact that the person has treated any such payment as having been so made does not affect any claim of the first spouse against the second spouse to an interest in the dwelling-house by virtue of the payment.

(6) If a spouse is entitled under this section to occupy a dwelling-house or part of a dwelling-house by reason of an interest of the other spouse under a trust, all the provisions of subsections (3) to (5) apply in relation to the trustees as they apply in relation to the other spouse.

(7) This section does not apply to a dwelling-house which has at no time been, and which was at no time intended by the spouses to be, a matrimonial home of theirs.

(8) A spouse's matrimonial home rights continue –

(a) only so long as the marriage subsists, except to the extent that an order under section 33(5) otherwise provides; and

(b) only so long as the other spouse is entitled as mentioned in subsection (1) to occupy the dwelling-house, except where provision is made by section 31 for those rights to be a charge on an estate or interest in the dwelling-house.

(9) It is hereby declared that a spouse –

(a) who has an equitable interest in a dwelling-house or in its proceeds of sale, but

(b) is not a spouse in whom there is vested (whether solely or as joint tenant) a legal estate in fee simple or a legal term of years absolute in the dwelling-house,

is to be treated, only for the purpose of determining whether he has matrimonial home rights, as not being entitled to occupy the dwelling-house by virtue of that interest.

31 Effect of matrimonial home rights as charge on dwelling-house

(1) Subsections (2) and (3) apply if, at any time during a marriage, one spouse is entitled to occupy a dwelling-house by virtue of a beneficial estate or interest.

(2) The other spouse's matrimonial home rights are a charge on the estate or interest.

(3) The charge created by subsection (2) has the same priority as if it were an equitable interest created at whichever is the latest of the following dates –

(a) the date on which the spouse so entitled acquires the estate or interest;

(b) the date of the marriage; and

(c) 1st January 1968 (the commencement date of the Matrimonial Homes Act 1967).

(4) Subsections (5) and (6) apply if, at any time when a spouse's matrimonial home rights are a charge on an interest of the other spouse under a trust, there are, apart from either of the spouses, no persons, living or unborn, who are or could become beneficiaries under the trust.

(5) The rights are a charge also on the estate or interest of the trustees for the other spouse.

(6) The charge created by subsection (5) has the same priority as if it were an equitable interest created (under powers overriding the trusts) on the date when it arises.

(7) In determining for the purposes of subsection (4) whether there are any persons who are not, but could become, beneficiaries under the trust, there is to be disregarded any potential exercise of a general power of appointment exercisable by either or both of the spouses alone (whether or not the exercise of it requires the consent of another person).

(8) Even though a spouse's matrimonial home rights are a charge on an estate or interest in the dwelling-house, those rights are brought to an end by –

(a) the death of the other spouse, or

(b) the termination (otherwise than by death) of the marriage,

unless the court directs otherwise by an order made under section 33(5).

(9) If –

(a) a spouse's matrimonial home rights are a charge on an estate or interest in the dwelling-house, and

(b) that estate or interest is surrendered to merge in some other estate or interest expectant on it in such circumstances that, but for the merger, the person taking the estate or interest would be bound by the charge,

the surrender has effect subject to the charge and the persons thereafter entitled to the other estate or interest are, for so long as the estate or interest surrendered would have endured if not so surrendered, to be treated for all purposes of this Part as deriving title to the other estate or interest under the other spouse or, as the case may be, under the trustees for the other spouse, by virtue of the surrender.

(10) If the title to the legal estate by virtue of which a spouse is entitled to occupy a dwelling-house (including any legal estate held by trustees for that spouse) is registered under the Land Registration Act 1925 or any enactment replaced by that Act –

(a) registration of a land charge affecting the dwelling-house by virtue of this Part is to be effected by registering a notice under that Act; and

(b) a spouse's matrimonial home rights are not an overriding interest within the meaning of that Act affecting the dwelling-house even though the spouse is in actual occupation of the dwelling-house.

(11) A spouse's matrimonial home rights (whether or not constituting a charge) do not entitle that spouse to lodge a caution under section 54 of the Land Registration Act 1925.

(12) If –

(a) a spouse's matrimonial home rights are a charge on the estate of the other spouse or of trustees of the other spouse, and

(b) that estate is the subject of a mortgage,

then if, after the date of the creation of the mortgage ('the first mortgage'), the charge is registered under section 2 of the Land Charges Act 1972, the charge is, for the purposes of section 94 of the Law of Property Act 1925 (which regulates the rights of mortgagees to make further advances ranking in priority to subsequent mortgages), to be deemed to be a mortgage subsequent in date to the first mortgage.

(13) It is hereby declared that a charge under subsection (2) or (5) is not registrable under subsection (10) or under section 2 of the Land Charges Act 1972 unless it is a charge on a legal estate.

32   Further provisions relating to matrimonial home rights

Schedule 4 re-enacts with consequential amendments and minor modifications provisions of the Matrimonial Homes Act 1983.

33 Occupation orders where applicant has estate or interest, etc or has matrimonial home rights

(1) If –

(a) a person ('the person entitled') –

(i) is entitled to occupy a dwelling-house by virtue of a beneficial estate or interest or contract or by virtue of any enactment giving him the right to remain in occupation, or

(ii) has matrimonial home rights in relation to a dwelling-house, and

(b) the dwelling-house –

(i) is or at any time has been the home of the person entitled and of another person with whom he is associated, or

(ii) was at any time intended by the person entitled and any such other person to be their home,

the person entitled may apply to the court for an order containing any of the provisions specified in subsections (3), (4) and (5).

(2) If an agreement to marry is terminated, no application under this section may be made by virtue of section 62(3)(e) by reference to that agreement after the end of the period of three years beginning with the day on which it is terminated.

(3) An order under this section may –

(a) enforce the applicant's entitlement to remain in occupation as against the other person ('the respondent');

(b) require the respondent to permit the applicant to enter and remain in the dwelling-house or part of the dwelling-house;

(c) regulate the occupation of the dwelling-house by either or both parties;

(d) if the respondent is entitled as mentioned in subsection (1)(a)(i), prohibit, suspend or restrict the exercise by him of his right to occupy the dwelling-house;

(e) if the respondent has matrimonial home rights in relation to the dwelling-house and the applicant is the other spouse, restrict or terminate those rights;

(f) require the respondent to leave the dwelling-house or part of the dwelling-house; or

(g) exclude the respondent from a defined area in which the dwelling-house is included.

(4) An order under this section may declare that the applicant is entitled as mentioned in subsection (1)(a)(i) or has matrimonial home rights.

(5) If the applicant has matrimonial home rights and the respondent is the other spouse, an order under this section made during the marriage may provide that those rights are not brought to an end by –

(a) the death of the other spouse; or

(b) the termination (otherwise than by death) of the marriage.

(6) In deciding whether to exercise its powers under subsection (3) and (if so) in what manner, the court shall have regard to all the circumstances including –

(a) the housing needs and housing resources of each of the parties and of any relevant child;

(b) the financial resources of each of the parties;

(c) the likely effect of any order, or of any decision by the court not to exercise its powers under subsection (3), on the health, safety or well-being of the parties and of any relevant child; and

(d) the conduct of the parties in relation to each other and otherwise.

(7) If it appears to the court that the applicant or any relevant child is likely to suffer significant harm attributable to conduct of the respondent if an order under this section containing one or more of the provisions mentioned in subsection (3) is not made, the court shall make the order unless it appears to it that –

(a) the respondent or any relevant child is likely to suffer significant harm if the order is made; and

(b) the harm likely to be suffered by the respondent or child in that event is as great as, or greater than, the harm attributable to conduct of the respondent which is likely to be suffered by the applicant or child if the order is not made.

(8) The court may exercise its powers under subsection (5) in any case where it considers that in all the circumstances it is just and reasonable to do so.

(9) An order under this section –

(a) may not be made after the death of either of the parties mentioned in subsection (1); and

(b) except in the case of an order made by virtue of subsection (5)(a), ceases to have effect on the death of either party.

(10) An order under this section may, in so far as it has continuing effect,

be made for a specified period, until the occurrence of a specified event or until further order.

34   Effect of order under section 33 where rights are charge on dwelling-house

(1) If a spouse's matrimonial home rights are a charge on the estate or interest of the other spouse or of trustees for the other spouse –

(a) an order under section 33 against the other spouse has, except so far as a contrary intention appears, the same effect against persons deriving title under the other spouse or under the trustees and affected by the charge, and

(b) sections 33(1), (3), (4) and (10) and 30(3) to (6) apply in relation to any person deriving title under the other spouse or under the trustees and affected by the charge as they apply in relation to the other spouse.

(2) The court may make an order under section 33 by virtue of subsection (1)(b) if it considers that in all the circumstances it is just and reasonable to do so.

35   One former spouse with no existing right to occupy

(1) This section applies if –

(a) one former spouse is entitled to occupy a dwelling-house by virtue of a beneficial estate or interest or contract, or by virtue of any enactment giving him the right to remain in occupation;

(b) the other former spouse is not so entitled; and

(c) the dwelling-house was at any time their matrimonial home or was at any time intended by them to be their matrimonial home.

(2) The former spouse not so entitled may apply to the court for an order under this section against the other former spouse ('the respondent').

(3) If the applicant is in occupation, an order under this section must contain provision –

(a) giving the applicant the right not to be evicted or excluded from the dwelling-house or any part of it by the respondent for the period specified in the order; and

(b) prohibiting the respondent from evicting or excluding the applicant during that period.

(4) If the applicant is not in occupation, an order under this section must contain provision –

(a) giving the applicant the right to enter into and occupy the dwelling-house for the period specified in the order; and

(b) requiring the respondent to permit the exercise of that right.

(5) An order under this section may also –

(a) regulate the occupation of the dwelling-house by either or both of the parties;

(b) prohibit, suspend or restrict the exercise by the respondent of his right to occupy the dwelling-house;

(c) require the respondent to leave the dwelling-house or part of the dwelling-house; or

(d) exclude the respondent from a defined area in which the dwelling-house is included.

(6) In deciding whether to make an order under this section containing provision of the kind mentioned in subsection (3) or (4) and (if so) in what manner, the court shall have regard to all the circumstances including –

(a) the housing needs and housing resources of each of the parties and of any relevant child;

(b) the financial resources of each of the parties;

(c) the likely effect of any order, or of any decision by the court not to exercise its powers under subsection (3) or (4), on the health, safety or well-being of the parties and of any relevant child;

(d) the conduct of the parties in relation to each other and otherwise;

(e) the length of time that has elapsed since the parties ceased to live together;

(f) the length of time that has elapsed since the marriage was dissolved or annulled; and

(g) the existence of any pending proceedings between the parties –

(i) for an order under section 23A or 24 of the Matrimonial Causes Act 1973 (property adjustment orders in connection with divorce proceedings etc);

(ii) for an order under paragraph 1(2)(d) or (e) of Schedule 1 to the Children Act 1989 (orders for financial relief against parents); or

(iii) relating to the legal or beneficial ownership of the dwelling-house.

(7) In deciding whether to exercise its power to include one or more of the provisions referred to in subsection (5) ('a subsection (5) provision') and (if so) in what manner, the court shall have regard to all the circumstances including the matters mentioned in subsection (6)(a) to (e).

(8) If the court decides to make an order under this section and it appears to it that, if the order does not include a subsection (5) provision, the applicant or any relevant child is likely to suffer significant harm attributable to conduct of the respondent, the court shall include the subsection (5) provision in the order unless it appears to the court that –

(a) the respondent or any relevant child is likely to suffer significant harm if the provision is included in the order; and

(b) the harm likely to be suffered by the respondent or child in that event is as great as or greater than the harm attributable to conduct of the respondent which is likely to be suffered by the applicant or child if the provision is not included.

(9) An order under this section –

(a) may not be made after the death of either of the former spouses; and

(b) ceases to have effect on the death of either of them.

(10) An order under this section must be limited so as to have effect for a specified period not exceeding six months, but may be extended on one or more occasions for a further specified period not exceeding six months.

(11) A former spouse who has an equitable interest in the dwelling-house or in the proceeds of sale of the dwelling-house but in whom there is not vested (whether solely or as joint tenant) a legal estate in fee simple or a legal term of years absolute in the dwelling-house is to be treated (but only for the purpose of determining whether he is eligible to apply under this section) as not being entitled to occupy the dwelling-house by virtue of that interest.

(12) Subsection (11) does not prejudice any right of such a former spouse to apply for an order under section 33.

(13) So long as an order under this section remains in force, subsections (3) to (6) of section 30 apply in relation to the applicant –

(a) as if he were the spouse entitled to occupy the dwelling-house by virtue of that section; and

(b) as if the respondent were the other spouse.

36 One cohabitant or former cohabitant with no existing right to occupy

(1) This section applies if –

(a) one cohabitant or former cohabitant is entitled to occupy a dwelling-house by virtue of a beneficial estate or interest or contract or by virtue of any enactment giving him the right to remain in occupation;

(b) the other cohabitant or former cohabitant is not so entitled; and

(c) that dwelling-house is the home in which they live together as husband and wife or a home in which they at any time so lived together or intended so to live together.

(2) The cohabitant or former cohabitant not so entitled may apply to the court for an order under this section against the other cohabitant or former cohabitant ('the respondent').

(3) If the applicant is in occupation, an order under this section must contain provision –

(a) giving the applicant the right not to be evicted or excluded from the dwelling-house or any part of it by the respondent for the period specified in the order; and

(b) prohibiting the respondent from evicting or excluding the applicant during that period.

(4) If the applicant is not in occupation, an order under this section must contain provision –

(a) giving the applicant the right to enter into and occupy the dwelling-house for the period specified in the order; and

(b) requiring the respondent to permit the exercise of that right.

(5) An order under this section may also –

(a) regulate the occupation of the dwelling-house by either or both of the parties;

(b) prohibit, suspend or restrict the exercise by the respondent of his right to occupy the dwelling-house;

(c) require the respondent to leave the dwelling-house or part of the dwelling-house; or

(d) exclude the respondent from a defined area in which the dwelling-house is included.

(6) In deciding whether to make an order under this section containing provision of the kind mentioned in subsection (3) or (4) and (if so) in what manner, the court shall have regard to all the circumstances including –

(a) the housing needs and housing resources of each of the parties and of any relevant child;

(b) the financial resources of each of the parties;

(c) the likely effect of any order, or of any decision by the court not to exercise its powers under subsection (3) or (4), on the health, safety or well-being of the parties and of any relevant child;

(d) the conduct of the parties in relation to each other and otherwise;

(e) the nature of the parties' relationship;

(f) the length of time during which they have lived together as husband and wife;

(g) whether there are or have been any children who are children of both parties or for whom both parties have or have had parental responsibility;

(h) the length of time that has elapsed since the parties ceased to live together; and

(i) the existence of any pending proceedings between the parties –

(i) for an order under paragraph 1(2)(d) or (e) of Schedule 1 to the Children Act 1989 (orders for financial relief against parents); or

(ii) relating to the legal or beneficial ownership of the dwelling-house.

(7) In deciding whether to exercise its powers to include one or more of the provisions referred to in subsection (5) ('a subsection (5) provision') and (if so) in what manner, the court shall have regard to all the circumstances including –

(a) the matters mentioned in subsection (6)(a) to (d); and

(b) the questions mentioned in subsection (8).

(8) The questions are –

(a) whether the applicant or any relevant child is likely to suffer significant harm attributable to conduct of the respondent if the subsection (5) provision is not included in the order; and

(b) whether the harm likely to be suffered by the respondent or child if the provision is included is as great as or greater than the harm attributable to conduct of the respondent which is likely to be suffered by the applicant or child if the provision is not included.

(9) An order under this section –

(a) may not be made after the death of either of the parties; and

(b) ceases to have effect on the death of either of them.

(10) An order under this section must be limited so as to have effect for a specified period not exceeding six months, but may be extended on one occasion for a further specified period not exceeding six months.

(11) A person who has an equitable interest in the dwelling-house or in the

proceeds of sale of the dwelling-house but in whom there is not vested (whether solely or as joint tenant) a legal estate in fee simple or a legal term of years absolute in the dwelling-house is to be treated (but only for the purpose of determining whether he is eligible to apply under this section) as not being entitled to occupy the dwelling-house by virtue of that interest.

(12) Subsection (11) does not prejudice any right of such a person to apply for an order under section 33.

(13) So long as the order remains in force, subsections (3) to (6) of section 30 apply in relation to the applicant –

(a) as if he were a spouse entitled to occupy the dwelling-house by virtue of that section; and

(b) as if the respondent were the other spouse.

37   Neither spouse entitled to occupy

(1) This section applies if –

(a) one spouse or former spouse and the other spouse or former spouse occupy a dwelling-house which is or was the matrimonial home; but

(b) neither of them is entitled to remain in occupation –

(i) by virtue of a beneficial estate or interest or contract; or

(ii) by virtue of any enactment giving him the right to remain in occupation.

(2) Either of the parties may apply to the court for an order against the other under this section.

(3) An order under this section may –

(a) require the respondent to permit the applicant to enter and remain in the dwelling-house or part of the dwelling-house;

(b) regulate the occupation of the dwelling-house by either or both of the parties;

(c) require the respondent to leave the dwelling-house or part of the dwelling-house; or

(d) exclude the respondent from a defined area in which the dwelling-house is included.

(4) Subsections (6) and (7) of section 33 apply to the exercise by the court of its powers under this section as they apply to the exercise by the court of its powers under subsection (3) of that section.

(5) An order under this section must be limited so as to have effect for a specified period not exceeding six months, but may be extended on one or more occasions for a further specified period not exceeding six months.

38 Neither cohabitant or former cohabitant entitled to occupy

(1) This section applies if –

(a) one cohabitant or former cohabitant and the other cohabitant or former cohabitant occupy a dwelling-house which is the home in which they live or lived together as husband and wife; but

(b) neither of them is entitled to remain in occupation –

(i) by virtue of a beneficial estate or interest or contract; or

(ii) by virtue of any enactment giving him the right to remain in occupation.

(2) Either of the parties may apply to the court for an order against the other under this section.

(3) An order under this section may –

(a) require the respondent to permit the applicant to enter and remain in the dwelling-house or part of the dwelling-house;

(b) regulate the occupation of the dwelling-house by either or both of the parties;

(c) require the respondent to leave the dwelling-house or part o the dwelling-house; or

(d) exclude the respondent from a defined area in which the dwelling-house is included.

(4) In deciding whether to exercise its powers to include one or more of the provisions referred to in subsection (3) ('a subsection (3) provision') and (if so) in what manner, the court shall have regard to all the circumstances including –

(a) the housing needs and housing resources of each of the parties and of any relevant child;

(b) the financial resources of each of the parties;

(c) the likely effect of any order, or of any decision by the court not to exercise its powers under subsection (3), on the health, safety or well-being of the parties and of any relevant child;

(d) the conduct of the parties in relation to each other and otherwise; and

(e) the questions mentioned in subsection (5).

(5) The questions are –

(a) whether the applicant or any relevant child is likely to suffer significant harm attributable to conduct of the respondent if the subsection (3) provision is not included in the order; and

(b) whether the harm likely to be suffered by the respondent or child if the provision is included is as great as or greater than the harm attributable to conduct of the respondent which is likely to be suffered by the applicant or child if the provision is not included.

(6) An order under this section shall be limited so as to have effect for a specified period not exceeding six months, but may be extended on one occasion for a further specified period not exceeding six months.

39 Supplementary provisions

(1) In this Part an 'occupation order' means an order under section 33, 35, 36, 37 or 38.

(2) An application for an occupation order may be made in other family proceedings or without any other family proceedings being instituted.

(3) If –

(a) an application for an occupation order is made under section 33, 35, 36, 37 or 38, and

(b) the court considers that it has no power to make the order under the section concerned, but that it has power to make an order under one of the other sections,

the court may make an order under that other section.

(4) The fact that a person has applied for an occupation order under sections 35 to 38, or that an occupation order has been made, does not affect the right of any person to claim a legal or equitable interest in any property in any subsequent proceedings (including subsequent proceedings under this Part).

40 Additional provisions that may be included in certain occupation orders

(1) The court may on, or at any time after, making an occupation order under section 33, 35 or 36 –

(a) impose on either party obligations as to –

(i) the repair and maintenance of the dwelling-house; or

(ii) the discharge of rent, mortgage payments or other outgoings affecting the dwelling-house;

(b) order a party occupying the dwelling-house or any part of it (including a party who is entitled to do so by virtue of a beneficial estate or interest or contract or by virtue of any enactment giving him the right to remain in occupation) to make periodical payments to the other party in respect of the accommodation, if the other party would (but for the order) be entitled to occupy the dwelling-house by virtue of a beneficial estate or interest or contract or by virtue of any such enactment;

(c) grant either party possession or use of furniture or other contents of the dwelling-house;

(d) order either party to take reasonable care of any furniture or other contents of the dwelling-house;

(e) order either party to take reasonable steps to keep the dwelling-house and any furniture or other contents secure.

(2) In deciding whether and, if so, how to exercise its powers under this section, the court shall have regard to all the circumstances of the case including –

(a) the financial needs and financial resources of the parties; and

(b) the financial obligations which they have, or are likely to have in the foreseeable future, including financial obligations to each other and to any relevant child.

(3) An order under this section ceases to have effect when the occupation order to which it relates ceases to have effect.

41 Additional considerations if parties are cohabitants or former cohabitants

(1) This section applies if the parties are cohabitants or former cohabitants.

(2) Where the court is required to consider the nature of the parties' relationship, it is to have regard to the fact that they have not given each other the commitment involved in marriage.

42 Non-molestation orders

(1) In this Part a 'non-molestation order' means an order containing either or both of the following provisions –

(a) provision prohibiting a person ('the respondent') from molesting another person who is associated with the respondent;

(b) provision prohibiting the respondent from molesting a relevant child.

(2) The court may make a non-molestation order –

(a) if an application for the order has been made (whether in other family proceedings or without any other family proceedings being instituted) by a person who is associated with the respondent; or

(b) if in any family proceedings to which the respondent is a party the court considers that the order should be made for the benefit of any other party to the proceedings or any relevant child even though no such application has been made.

(3) In subsection (2) 'family proceedings' includes proceedings in which the court has made an emergency protection order under section 44 of the Children Act 1989 which includes an exclusion requirement (as defined in section 44A(3) of that Act).

(4) Where an agreement to marry is terminated, no application under subsection (2)(a) may be made by virtue of section 62(3)(e) by reference to that agreement after the end of the period of three years beginning with the day on which it is terminated.

(5) In deciding whether to exercise its powers under this section and, if so, in what manner, the court shall have regard to all the circumstances including the need to secure the health, safety and well-being –

(a) of the applicant or, in a case falling within subsection (2)(b), the person for whose benefit the order would be made; and

(b) of any relevant child.

(6) A non-molestation order may be expressed so as to refer to molestation in general, to particular acts of molestation, or to both.

(7) A non-molestation order may be made for a specified period or until further order.

(8) A non-molestation order which is made in other family proceedings ceases to have effect if those proceedings are withdrawn or dismissed.

43 Leave of court required for applications by children under sixteen

(1) A child under the age of sixteen may not apply for an occupation order or a non-molestation order except with the leave of the court.

(2) The court may grant leave for the purpose of subsection (1) only if it is satisfied that the child has sufficient understanding to make the proposed application for the occupation order or non-molestation order.

44 Evidence of agreement to marry

(1) Subject to subsection (2), the court shall not make an order under section 33 or 42 by virtue of section 62(3)(e) unless there is produced to it evidence in writing of the existence of the agreement to marry.

(2) Subsection (1) does not apply if the court is satisfied that the agreement to marry was evidenced by –

(a) the gift of an engagement ring by one party to the agreement to the other in contemplation of their marriage, or

(b) a ceremony entered into by the parties in the presence of one or more other persons assembled for the purpose of witnessing the ceremony.

45 Ex parte orders

(1) The court may, in any case where it considers that it is just and convenient to do so, make an occupation order or a non-molestation order even though the respondent has not been given such notice of the proceedings as would otherwise be required by rules of court.

(2) In determining whether to exercise its powers under subsection (1), the court shall have regard to all the circumstances including –

(a) any risk of significant harm to the applicant or a relevant child, attributable to conduct of the respondent, if the order is not made immediately;

(b) whether it is likely that the applicant will be deterred or prevented from pursuing the application if an order is not made immediately; and

(c) whether there is reason to believe that the respondent is aware of the proceedings but is deliberately evading service and that the applicant or a relevant child will be seriously prejudiced by the delay involved –

(i) where the court is a magistrates' court, in effecting service of proceedings; or

(ii) in any other case, in effecting substituted service.

(3) If the court makes an order by virtue of subsection (1) it must afford the respondent an opportunity to make representations relating to the order as soon as just and convenient at a full hearing.

(4) If, at a full hearing, the court makes an occupation order ('the full order'), then –

(a) for the purposes of calculating the maximum period for which the full order may be made to have effect, the relevant section is to apply as if the period for which the full order will have effect began on the date on which the initial order first had effect; and

(b) the provisions of section 36(10) or 38(6) as to the extension of orders are to apply as if the full order and the initial order were a single order.

(5) In this section –

'full hearing' means a hearing of which notice has been given to all the parties in accordance with rules of court;

'initial order' means an occupation order made by virtue of subsection (1); and

'relevant section' means section 33(10), 35(10), 36(10), 37(5) or 38(6).

46   Undertakings

(1) In any case where the court has power to make an occupation order or non-molestation order, the court may accept an undertaking from any party to the proceedings.

(2) No power of arrest may be attached to any undertaking given under subsection (1).

(3) The court shall not accept an undertaking under subsection (1) in any case where apart from this section a power of arrest would be attached to the order.

(4) An undertaking given to a court under subsection (1) is enforceable as if it were an order of the court.

(5) This section has effect without prejudice to the powers of the High Court and the county court apart from this section.

47   Arrest for breach of order

(1) In this section 'a relevant order' means an occupation order or a non-molestation order.

(2) If –

(a) the court makes a relevant order; and

(b) it appears to the court that the respondent has used or threatened violence against the applicant or a relevant child,

it shall attach a power of arrest to one or more provisions of the order unless satisfied that in all the circumstances of the case the applicant or child will be adequately protected without such a power of arrest.

(3) Subsection (2) does not apply in any case where the relevant order is made by virtue of section 45(1), but in such a case the court may attach a power of arrest to one or more provisions of the order if it appears to it –

(a) that the respondent has used or threatened violence against the applicant or a relevant child; and

(b) that there is a risk of significant harm to the applicant or child, attributable to conduct of the respondent, if the power of arrest is not attached to those provisions immediately.

(4) If, by virtue of subsection (3), the court attaches a power of arrest to any provisions of a relevant order, it may provide that the power of arrest is to have effect for a shorter period than the other provisions of the order.

(5) Any period specified for the purposes of subsection (4) may be extended by the court (on one or more occasions) on an application to vary or discharge the relevant order.

(6) If, by virtue of subsection (2) or (3), a power of arrest is attached to certain provisions of an order, a constable may arrest without warrant a person whom he has reasonable cause for suspecting to be in breach of any such provision.

(7) If a power of arrest is attached under subsection (2) or (3) to certain provisions of the order and the respondent is arrested under subsection (6) –

(a) he must be brought before the relevant judicial authority within the period of 24 hours beginning at the time of his arrest; and

(b) if the matter is not then disposed of forthwith, the relevant judicial authority before whom he is brought may remand him.

In reckoning for the purposes of this subsection any period of 24 hours, no account is to be taken of Christmas Day, Good Friday or any Sunday.

(8) If the court has made a relevant order but –

(a) has not attached a power of arrest under subsection (2) or (3) to any provisions of the order, or

(b) has attached that power only to certain provisions of the order,

then, if at any time the applicant considers that the respondent has failed to comply with the order, he may apply to the relevant judicial authority for the issue of a warrant for the arrest of the respondent.

(9) The relevant judicial authority shall not issue a warrant on an application under subsection (8) unless _

(a) the application is substantiated on oath; and

(b) the relevant judicial authority has reasonable grounds for believing that the respondent has failed to comply with the order.

(10) If a person is brought before a court by virtue of a warrant issued under subsection (9) and the court does not dispose of the matter forthwith, the court may remand him.

(11) Schedule 5 (which makes provision corresponding to that applying in magistrates' courts in civil cases under sections 128 and 129 of the Magistrates' Courts Act 1980) has effect in relation to the powers of the High Court and a county court to remand a person by virtue of this section.

(12) If a person remanded under this section is granted bail (whether in the High Court or a county court under Schedule 5 or in a magistrates' court under section 128 or 129 of the Magistrates' Courts Act 1980), he may be required by the relevant judicial authority to comply, before release on bail or later, with such requirements as appear to that authority to be necessary to secure that he does not interfere with witnesses or otherwise obstruct the course of justice.

48 Remand for medical examination and report

(1) If the relevant judicial authority has reason to consider that a medical report will be required, any power to remand a person under section 47(7)(b) or (10) may be exercised for the purpose of enabling a medical examination and report to be made.

(2) If such a power is so exercised, the adjournment must not be for more than 4 weeks at a time unless the relevant judicial authority remands the accused in custody.

(3) If the relevant judicial authority so remands the accused, the adjournment must not be for more than 3 weeks at a time.

(4) If there is reason to suspect that a person who has been arrested –

(a) under section 47(6), or

(b) under a warrant issued on an application made under section 47(8),

is suffering from mental illness or severe mental impairment, the relevant judicial authority has the same power to make an order under section 35 of the Mental Health Act 1983 (remand for report on accused's mental condition) as the Crown Court has under section 35 of the Act of 1983 in the case of an accused person within the meaning of that section.

49 Variation and discharge of orders

(1) An occupation order or non-molestation order may be varied or discharged by the court on an application by –

    (a) the respondent, or

    (b) the person on whose application the order was made.

(2) In the case of a non-molestation order made by virtue of section 42(2)(b), the order may be varied or discharged by the court even though no such application has been made.

(3) If a spouse's matrimonial home rights are a charge on the estate or interest of the other spouse or of trustees for the other spouse, an order under section 33 against the other spouse may also be varied or discharged by the court on an application by any person deriving title under the other spouse or under the trustees and affected by the charge.

(4) If, by virtue of section 47(3), a power of arrest has been attached to certain provisions of an occupation order or non-molestation order, the court may vary or discharge the order under subsection (1) in so far as it confers a power of arrest (whether or not any application has been made to vary or discharge any other provision of the order).

50 Power of magistrates' court to suspend execution of committal order

(1) If, under section 63(3) of the Magistrates' Courts Act 1980, a magistrates' court has power to commit a person to custody for breach of a relevant requirement, the court may by order direct that the execution of the order of committal is to be suspended for such period or on such terms and conditions as it may specify.

(2) In subsection (1) 'a relevant requirement' means –

    (a) an occupation order or non-molestation order;

    (b) an exclusion requirement included by virtue of section 38A of the Children Act 1989 in an interim care order made under section 38 of that Act; or

    (c) an exclusion requirement included by virtue of section 44A of the

Children Act 1989 in an emergency protection order under section 44 of that Act.

51 Power of magistrates' court to order hospital admission or guardianship

(1) A magistrates' court has the same power to make a hospital order or guardianship order under section 37 of the Mental Health Act 1983 or an interim hospital order under section 38 of that Act in the case of a person suffering from mental illness or severe mental impairment who could otherwise be committed to custody for breach of a relevant requirement as a magistrates' court has under those sections in the case of a person convicted of an offence punishable on summary conviction with imprisonment.

(2) In subsection (1) 'a relevant requirement' has the meaning given by section 50(2).

52 Amendments of Children Act 1989

Schedule 6 makes amendments of the provisions of the Children Act 1989 relating to interim care orders and emergency protection orders.

53 Transfer of certain tenancies

Schedule 7 makes provision in relation to the transfer of certain tenancies on divorce etc or on separation of cohabitants.

54 Dwelling-house subject to mortgage

(1) In determining for the purposes of this Part whether a person is entitled to occupy a dwelling-house by virtue of an estate or interest, any right to possession of the dwelling-house conferred on a mortgagee of the dwelling-house under or by virtue of his mortgage is to be disregarded.

(2) Subsection (1) applies whether or not the mortgagee is in possession.

(3) Where a person ('A') is entitled to occupy a dwelling-house by virtue of an estate or interest, a connected person does not by virtue of –

(a) any matrimonial home rights conferred by section 30, or

(b) any rights conferred by an order under section 35 or 36,

have any larger right against the mortgagee to occupy the dwelling-house than A has by virtue of his estate or interest and of any contract with the mortgagee.

(4) Subsection (3) does not apply, in the case of matrimonial home rights, if under section 31 those rights are a charge, affecting the mortgagee, on the estate or interest mortgaged.

(5) In this section 'connected person', in relation to any person, means that person's spouse, former spouse, cohabitant or former cohabitant.

55 Actions by mortgagees: joining connected persons as parties

(1) This section applies if a mortgagee of land which consists of or includes a dwelling-house brings an action in any court for the enforcement of his security.

(2) A connected person who is not already a party to the action is entitled to be made a party in the circumstances mentioned in subsection (3).

(3) The circumstances are that –

(a) the connected person is enabled by section 30(3) or (6) (or by section 30(3) or (6) as applied by section 35(13) or 36(13)), to meet the mortgagor's liabilities under the mortgage;

(b) he has applied to the court before the action is finally disposed of in that court; and

(c) the court sees no special reason against his being made a party to the action and is satisfied –

(i) that he may be expected to make such payments or do such other things in or towards satisfaction of the mortgagor's liabilities or obligations as might affect the outcome of the proceedings; or

(ii) that the expectation of it should be considered under section 36 of the Administration of Justice Act 1970.

(4) In this section 'connected person' has the same meaning as in section 54.

56 Actions by mortgagees: service of notice on certain persons

(1) This section applies if a mortgagee of and which consists, or substantially consists, of a dwelling-house brings an action for the enforcement of his security, and at the relevant time there is –

(a) in the case of unregistered land, a land charge of Class F registered against the person who is the estate owner at the relevant time or any person who, where the estate owner is a trustee, preceded him as trustee during the subsistence of the mortgagee; or

(b) in the case of registered land, a subsisting registration of –

(i) a notice under section 31(10);

(ii) a notice under section 2(8) of the Matrimonial Homes Act 1983; or

(iii) a notice or caution under section 2(7) of the Matrimonial Homes Act 1967.

(2) If the person on whose behalf –

(a) the land charge is registered, or

(b) the notice or caution is entered,

is not a party to the action, the mortgagee must serve notice of the action on him.

(3) If –

(a) an official search has been made on behalf of the mortgagee which would disclose any land charge of Class F, notice or caution within subsection (1)(a) or (b),

(b) a certificate of the result of the search has been issued, and

(c) the action is commenced within the priority period,

the relevant time is the date of the certificate.

(4) In any other case the relevant time is the time when the action is commenced.

(5) The priority period is, for both registered and unregistered land, the period for which, in accordance with section 11(5) and (6) of the Land Charges Act 1972, a certificate on an official search operates in favour of a purchaser.

57 Jurisdiction of courts

(1) For the purposes of this Part 'the court' means the High Court, a county court or a magistrates' court.

(2) Subsection (1) is subject to the provision made by or under the following provisions of this section, to section 59 and to any express provision as to the jurisdiction of any court made by any other provision of this Part.

(3) The Lord Chancellor may by order specify proceedings under this Part which may only be commenced in –

(a) a specified level of court;

(b) a court which falls within a specified class of court; or

(c) a particular court determined in accordance with, or specified in, the order.

(4) The Lord Chancellor may by order specify circumstances in which specified proceedings under this Part may only be commenced in –

(a) a specified level of court;

(b) a court which falls within a specified class of court; or

(c) a particular court determined in accordance with, or specified in, the order.

(5) The Lord Chancellor may by order provide that in specified circumstances the whole, or any specified part of any specified proceedings under this Part is to be transferred to –

(a) a specified level of court;

(b) a court which falls within a specified class of court; or

(c) a particular court determined in accordance with, or specified in, the order.

(6) An order under subsection (5) may provide for the transfer to be made at any stage, or specified stage, of the proceedings and whether or not the proceedings, or any part of them, have already been transferred.

(7) An order under subsection (5) may make such provision as the Lord Chancellor thinks appropriate for excluding specified proceedings from the operation of section 38 or 39 of the Matrimonial and Family Proceedings Act 1984 (transfer of family proceedings) or any other enactment which would otherwise govern the transfer of those proceedings, or any part of them.

(8) For the purposes of subsections (3), (4) and (5), there are three levels of court –

(a) the High Court;

(b) any county court; and

(c) any magistrates' court.

(9) The Lord Chancellor may by order make provision for the principal registry of the Family Division of the High Court to be treated as if it were a county court for specified purposes of this Part, or of any provision made under this Part.

(10) Any order under subsection (9) may make such provision as the Lord Chancellor thinks expedient for the purpose of applying (with or without

modifications) provisions which apply in relation to the procedure in county courts to the principal registry when it acts as if it were a county court.

(11) In this section 'specified' means specified by an order under this section.

58 Contempt proceedings

The powers of the court in relation to contempt of court arising out of a person's failure to comply with an order under this Part may be exercised by the relevant judicial authority.

59 Magistrates' courts

(1) A magistrates' court shall not be competent to entertain any application, or make any order, involving any disputed question as to a party's entitlement to occupy any property by virtue of a beneficial estate or interest or contract or by virtue of any enactment giving him the right to remain in occupation, unless it is unnecessary to determine the question in order to deal with the application or make the order.

(2) A magistrates' court may decline jurisdiction in any proceedings under this Part if it considers that the case can more conveniently be dealt with by another court.

(3) The powers of a magistrates' court under section 63(2) of the Magistrates' Courts Act 1980 to suspend or rescind orders shall not apply in relation to any order made under this Part.

60 Provison for third parties to act on behalf of victims of domestic violence

(1) Rules of court may provide for a prescribed persons, or any person in a prescribed category, ('a representative') to act on behalf of another in relation to proceedings to which this Part applies.

(2) Rules made under this section may, in particular, authorise a representative to apply for an occupation order or for a non-molestation order for which the person on whose behalf the representative is acting could have applied. ...

61 Appeals

(1) An appeal shall lie to the High Court against –

    (a) the making by a magistrates' court of any order under this Part, or

(b) any refusal by a magistrates' court to make such an order,

but no appeal shall lie against any exercise by a magistrates' court of the power conferred by section 59(2).

(2) On an appeal under this section, the High Court may make such orders as may be necessary to give effect to its determination of the appeal.

(3) Where an order is made under subsection (2), the High Court may also make such incidental or consequential orders as appear to it to be just.

(4) Any order of the High Court made on an appeal under this section (other than one directing that an application be re-heard by a magistrates' court) shall, for the purposes –

(a) of the enforcement of the order, and

(b) of any power to vary, revive or discharge orders,

be treated as if it were an order of the magistrates' court from which the appeal was brought and not an order of the High Court.

(5) The Lord Chancellor may by order make provision as to the circumstances in which appeals may be made against decisions taken by courts on questions arising in connection with the transfer, or proposed transfer, of proceedings by virtue of any order under section 57(5).

(6) Except to the extent provided for in any order made under subsection (5), no appeal may be made against any decision of a kind mentioned in that subsection.

62 Meaning of 'cohabitants', 'relevant child' and 'associated persons'

(1) For the purposes of this Part –

(a) 'cohabitants' are a man and a woman who, although not married to each other, are living together as husband and wife; and

(b) 'former cohabitants' is to be read accordingly, but does not include cohabitants who have subsequently married each other.

(2) In this Part, 'relevant child', in relation to any proceedings under this Part, means –

(a) any child who is living with or might reasonably be expected to live with either party to the proceedings;

(b) any child in relation to whom an order under the Adoption Act 1976 or the Children Act 1989 is in question in the proceedings; and

(c) any other child whose interests the court considers relevant.

(3) For the purposes of this Part, a person is associated with another person if –

(a) they are or have been married to each other;

(b) they are cohabitants or former cohabitants;

(c) they live or have lived in the same household, otherwise than merely by reason of one of them being the other's employee, tenant, lodger or boarder;

(d) they are relatives;

(e) they have agreed to marry one another (whether or not that agreement has been terminated);

(f) in relation to any child, they are both persons falling within subsection (4); or

(g) they are parties to the same family proceedings (other than proceedings under this Part).

(4) A person falls within this subsection in relation to a child if –

(a) he is a parent of the child; or

(b) he has or has had parental responsibility for the child.

(5) If a child has been adopted or has been freed for adoption by virtue of any of the enactments mentioned in section 16(1) of the Adoption Act 1976, two persons are also associated with each other for the purposes of this Part if –

(a) one is a natural parent of the child or a parent of such a natural parent; and

(b) the other is the child or any person –

(i) who has become a parent of the child by virtue of an adoption order or has applied for an adoption order, or

(ii) with whom the child has at any time been placed for adoption.

(6) A body corporate and another person are not, by virtue of subsection (3)(f) or (g), to be regarded for the purposes of this Part as associated with each other.

63   Interpretation of Part IV

(1) In this Part –

'adoption order' has the meaning given by section 72(1) of the Adoption Act 1976;

'associated', in relation to a person, is to be read with section 62(3) to (6);

'child' means a person under the age of eighteen years;

'cohabitant' and 'former cohabitant' have the meaning given by section 62(1);

'the court' is to be read with section 57;

'development' means physical, intellectual, emotional, social or behavioural development;

'dwelling-house' includes (subject to subsection (4)) –

(a) any building or part of a building which is occupied as a dwelling,

(b) any caravan, house-boat or structure which is occupied as a dwelling,

and any yard, garden, garage or outhouse belonging to it and occupied with it;

'family proceedings' means any proceedings –

(a) under the inherent jurisdiction of the High Court in relation to children; or

(b) under the enactments mentioned in subsection (2);

'harm' –

(a) in relation to a person who has reached the age of eighteen years, means ill-treatment or the impairment of health; and

(b) in relation to a child, means ill-treatment or impairment of health or development;

'health' includes physical or mental health;

'ill-treatment' includes forms of ill-treatment which are not physical and, in relation to a child, includes sexual abuse;

'matrimonial home rights' has the meaning given by section 30;

'mortgage', 'mortgagor' and 'mortgagee' have the same meaning as in the Law of Property Act 1925;

'mortgage payments' includes any payments which, under the terms of the mortgage, the mortgagor is required to make to any person;

'non-molestation order' has the meaning given by section 42(1);

'occupation order' has the meaning given by section 39;

'parental responsibility' has the same meaning as in the Children Act 1989;

'relative', in relation to a person, means –

(a) the father, mother, stepfather, stepmother, son, daughter, stepson, stepdaughter, grandmother, grandfather, grandson or granddaughter of that person or of that person's spouse or former spouse, or

(b) the brother, sister, uncle, aunt, niece or nephew (whether of the full blood or of the half blood or by affinity) of that person or of that person's spouse or former spouse,

and includes, in relation to a person who is living or has lived with another person as husband and wife, any person who would fall within paragraph (a) or (b) if the parties were married to each other;

'relevant child', in relation to any proceedings under this Part, has the meaning given by section 62(2);

'the relevant judicial authority', in relation to any order under this Part, means –

(a) where the order was made by the High Court, a judge of that court;

(b) where the order was made by a county court, a judge or district judge of that or any other county court; or

(c) where the order was made by a magistrates' court, any magistrates' court.

(2) The enactments referred to in the definition of 'family proceedings' are –

(a) Part II;

(b) this Part;

(c) the Matrimonial Causes Act 1973;

(d) the Adoption Act 1976;

(e) the Domestic Proceedings and Magistrates' Courts Act 1978;

(f) Part III of the Matrimonial and Family Proceedings Act 1984;

(g) Parts I, II and IV of the Children Act 1989;

(h) section 30 of the Human Fertilisation and Embryology Act 1990.

(3) Where the question of whether harm suffered by a child is significant turns on the child's health or development, his health or development shall be compared with that which could reasonably be expected of a similar child.

(4) For the purposes of sections 31, 32, 53 and 54 and such other provisions of this Part (if any) as may be prescribed, this Part is to have effect as if paragraph (b) of the definition of 'dwelling-house' were omitted.

(5) It is hereby declared that this Part applies as between the parties to a marriage even though either of them is, or has at any time during the marriage been, married to more than one person.

SCHEDULE 4

PROVISIONS SUPPLEMENTARY TO SECTIONS 30 AND 31 ...

Cancellation of registration after termination of marriage, etc.

4. – (1) Where a spouse's matrimonial home rights are a charge on an estate in the dwelling-house and the charge is registered under section 31(10) or under section 2 of the Land Charges Act 1972, the Chief Land Registrar shall, subject to sub-paragraph (2), cancel the registration of the charge if he is satisfied –

(a) by the production of a certificate or other sufficient evidence, that either spouse is dead, or

(b) by the production of an official copy of a decree or order of a court, that the marriage in question has been terminated otherwise than by death, or

(c) by the production of an order of the court, that the spouse's matrimonial home rights constituting the charge have been terminated by the order.

(2) Where –

(a) the marriage in question has been terminated by the death of the spouse entitled to an estate in the dwelling-house or otherwise than by death, and

(b) an order affecting the charge of the spouse not so entitled had been made under section 33(5),

then if, after the making of the order, registration of the charge was renewed or the charge registered in pursuance of sub-paragraph (3), the Chief Land Registrar shall not cancel the registration of the charge in accordance with sub-paragraph (1) unless he is also satisfied that the order has ceased to have effect.

(3) Where such an order has been made, then, for the purposes of sub-paragraph (2), the spouse entitled to the charge affected by the order may –

(a) if before the date of the order the charge was registered under section 31(10) or under section 2 of the Land Charges Act 1972, renew the registration of the charge, and

(b) if before the said date the charge was not so registered, register the charge under section 31(10) or under section 2 of the Land Charges Act 1972.

(4) Renewal of the registration of a charge in pursuance of sub-paragraph (3) shall be effected in such manner as may be prescribed, and an application for such renewal or for registration of a charge in pursuance of that sub-paragraph shall contain such particulars of any order affecting the charge made under section 33(5) as may be prescribed.

(5) The renewal in pursuance of sub-paragraph (3) of the registration of a charge shall not affect the priority of the charge.

(6) In this paragraph"prescribed" means prescribed by rules made under section 16 of the Land Charges Act 1972 or section 144 of the Land Registration Act 1925, as the circumstances of the case require.

Release of matrimonial home rights

5. – (1) A spouse entitled to matrimonial home rights may by a release in writing release those rights or release them as respects part only of the dwelling-house affected by them.

(2) Where a contract is made for the sale of an estate or interest in a dwelling-house, or for the grant of a lease or underlease of a dwelling-house, being (in either case) a dwelling-house affected by a charge registered under section 31(10) or under section 2 of the Land Charges Act 1972, then, without prejudice to sub-paragraph (1), the matrimonial home rights constituting the charge shall be deemed to have been released on the happening of whichever of the following events first occurs –

(a) the delivery to the purchaser or lessee, as the case may be, or his solicitor on completion of the contract of an application by the spouse entitled to the charge for the cancellation of the registration of the charge; or

(b) the lodging of such an application at Her Majesty's Land Registry.

Postponement of priority of charge

6. A spouse entitled by virtue of section 31 to a charge on an estate or interest may agree in writing that any other charge on, or interest in, that

estate or interest shall rank in priority to the charge to which that spouse is so entitled.

SCHEDULE 7

TRANSFER OF CERTAIN TENANCIES ON DIVORCE ETC. OR ON SEPARATION OF COHABITANTS

PART I

GENERAL

Interpretation

1. In this Schedule –

'cohabitant', except in paragraph 3, includes (where the context requires) former cohabitant;

'the court' does not include a magistrates' court,

'landlord' includes –

    (a) any person from time to time deriving title under the original landlord; and

    (b) in relation to any dwelling-house, any person other than the tenant who is, or (but for Part VII of the Rent Act 1977 or Part II of the Rent (Agriculture) Act 1976) would be, entitled to possession of the dwelling-house;

'Part II order' means an order under Part II of this Schedule;

'a relevant tenancy' means –

    (a) a protected tenancy or statutory tenancy within the meaning of the Rent Act 1977;

    (b) a statutory tenancy within the meaning of the Rent (Agriculture) Act 1976;

    (c) a secure tenancy within the meaning of section 79 of the Housing Act 1985; or

    (d) an assured tenancy or assured agricultural occupancy within the meaning of Part I of the Housing Act 1988;

'spouse', except in paragraph 2, includes (where the context requires) former spouse; and 'tenancy' includes sub-tenancy.

Cases in which the court may make an order

2. – (1) This paragraph applies if one spouse is entitled, either in his own right or jointly with the other spouse, to occupy a dwelling-house by virtue of a relevant tenancy.

(2) At any time when it has power to make a property adjustment order under section 23A (divorce or separation) or 24 (nullity) of the Matrimonial Causes Act 1973 with respect to the marriage, the court may make a Part II order.

3. – (1) This paragraph applies if one cohabitant is entitled, either in his own right or jointly with the other cohabitant, to occupy a dwelling-house by virtue of a relevant tenancy.

(2) If the cohabitants cease to live together as husband and wife, the court may make a Part II order.

4. The court shall not make a Part II order unless the dwelling-house is or was –

   (a) in the case of spouses, a matrimonial home; or
   (b) in the case of cohabitants, a home in which they lived together as husband and wife.

Matters to which the court must have regard

5. In determining whether to exercise its powers under Part II of this Schedule and, if so, in what manner, the court shall have regard to all the circumstances of the case including –

   (a) the circumstances in which the tenancy was granted to either or both of the spouses or cohabitants or, as the case requires, the circumstances in which either or both of them became tenant under the tenancy;
   (b) the matters mentioned in section 33(6)(a), (b) and
   (c) and, where the parties are cohabitants and only one of them is entitled to occupy the dwelling-house by virtue of the relevant tenancy, the further matters mentioned in section 36(6)(e), (f), (g) and (h); and
   (c) the suitability of the parties as tenants.

PART II

ORDERS THAT MAY BE MADE

References to entitlement to occupy

6. References in this Part of this Schedule to a spouse or a cohabitant being entitled to occupy a dwelling-house by virtue of a relevant tenancy apply whether that entitlement is in his own right or jointly with the other spouse or cohabitant.

Protected, secure or assured tenancy or assured agricultural occupancy

7. – (1) If a spouse or cohabitant is entitled to occupy the dwelling-house by virtue of a protected tenancy within the meaning of the Rent Act 1977, a secure tenancy within the meaning of the Housing Act 1985 or an assured tenancy or assured agricultural occupancy within the meaning of Part I of the Housing Act 1988, the court may by order direct that, as from such date as may be specified in the order, there shall, by virtue of the order and without further assurance, be transferred to, and vested in, the other spouse or cohabitant –

    (a) the estate or interest which the spouse or cohabitant so entitled had in the dwelling-house immediately before that date by virtue of the lease or agreement creating the tenancy and any assignment of that lease or agreement, with all rights, privileges and appurtenances attaching to that estate or interest but subject to all covenants, obligations, liabilities and incumbrances to which it is subject; and

    (b) where the spouse or cohabitant so entitled is an assignee of such lease or agreement, the liability of that spouse or cohabitant under any covenant of indemnity by the assignee express or implied in the assignment of the lease or agreement to that spouse or cohabitant.

(2) If an order is made under this paragraph, any liability or obligation to which the spouse or cohabitant so entitled is subject under any covenant having reference to the dwelling-house in the lease or agreement, being a liability or obligation falling due to be discharged or performed on or after the date so specified, shall not be enforceable against that spouse or cohabitant.

(3) If the spouse so entitled is a successor within the meaning of Part IV of the Housing Act 1985, his former spouse or former cohabitant (or, if a separation order is in force, his spouse) shall be deemed also to be a successor within the meaning of that Part.

(4) If the spouse or cohabitant so entitled is for the purpose of section 17 of the Housing Act 1988 a successor in relation to the tenancy or occupancy, his former spouse or former cohabitant (or, if a separation order is in force, his spouse) is to be deemed to be a successor in relation to the tenancy or occupancy for the purposes of that section.

(5) If the transfer under sub-paragraph (1) is of an assured agricultural occupancy, then, for the purposes of Chapter III of Part I of the Housing Act 1988 –

(a) the agricultural worker condition is fulfilled with respect to the dwelling-house while the spouse or cohabitant to whom the assured agricultural occupancy is transferred continues to be the occupier under that occupancy, and

(b) that condition is to be treated as so fulfilled by virtue of the same paragraph of Schedule 3 to the Housing Act 1988 as was applicable before the transfer.

(6) In this paragraph, references to a separation order being in force include references to there being a judicial separation in force.

Statutory tenancy within the meaning of the Rent Act 1977

8. – (1) This paragraph applies if the spouse or cohabitant is entitled to occupy the dwelling-house by virtue of a statutory tenancy within the meaning of the Rent Act 1977.

(2) The court may by order direct that, as from the date specified in the order –

(a) that spouse or cohabitant is to cease to be entitled to occupy the dwelling-house; and

(b) the other spouse or cohabitant is to be deemed to be the tenant or, as the case may be, the sole tenant under that statutory tenancy.

(3) The question whether the provisions of paragraphs 1 to 3, or (as the case may be) paragraphs 5 to 7 of Schedule 1 to the Rent Act 1977, as to the succession by the surviving spouse of a deceased tenant, or by a member of the deceased tenant's family, to the right to retain possession are capable of having effect in the event of the death of the person deemed by an order under this paragraph to be the tenant or sole tenant under the statutory tenancy is to be determined according as those provisions have or have not already had effect in relation to the statutory tenancy.

Statutory tenancy within the meaning of the Rent (Agriculture) Act 1976

9. – (1) This paragraph applies if the spouse or cohabitant is entitled to occupy the dwelling-house by virtue of a statutory tenancy within the meaning of the Rent (Agriculture) Act 1976.

(2) The court may by order direct that, as from such date as may be specified in the order –

(a) that spouse or cohabitant is to cease to be entitled to occupy the dwelling-house; and

(b) the other spouse or cohabitant is to be deemed to be the tenant or, as the case may be, the sole tenant under that statutory tenancy.

(3) A spouse or cohabitant who is deemed under this paragraph to be the tenant under a statutory tenancy is (within the meaning of that Act) a statutory tenant in his own right, or a statutory tenant by succession, according as the other spouse or cohabitant was a statutory tenant in his own right or a statutory tenant by succession.

PART III

SUPPLEMENTARY PROVISIONS

Compensation

10. – (1) If the court makes a Part II order, it may by the order direct the making of a payment by the spouse or cohabitant to whom the tenancy is transferred ('the transferee') to the other spouse or cohabitant ('the transferor').

(2) Without prejudice to that, the court may, on making an order by virtue of sub-paragraph (1) for the payment of a sum –

(a) direct that payment of that sum or any part of it is to be deferred until a specified date or until the occurrence of a specified event, or

(b) direct that that sum or any part of it is to be paid by instalments.

(3) Where an order has been made by virtue of sub-paragraph (1), the court may, on the application of the transferee or the transferor –

(a) exercise its powers under sub-paragraph (2), or

(b) vary any direction previously given under that sub-paragraph,

at any time before the sum whose payment is required by the order is paid in full.

(4) In deciding whether to exercise its powers under this paragraph and, if so, in what manner, the court shall have regard to all the circumstances including –

(a) the financial loss that would otherwise be suffered by the transferor as a result of the order;

(b) the financial needs and financial resources of the parties; and

(c) the financial obligations which the parties have, or are likely to have in the foreseeable future, including financial obligations to each other and to any relevant child.

(5) The court shall not give any direction under sub-paragraph (2) unless it appears to it that immediate payment of the sum required by the order would cause the transferee financial hardship which is greater than any financial hardship that would be caused to the transferor if the direction were given.

Liabilities and obligations in respect of the dwelling-house

11. – (1) If the court makes a Part II order, it may by the order direct that both spouses or cohabitants are to be jointly and severally liable to discharge or perform any or all of the liabilities and obligations in respect of the dwelling-house (whether arising under the tenancy or otherwise) which –

(a) have at the date of the order fallen due to be discharged or performed by one only of them; or

(b) but for the direction, would before the date specified as the date on which the order is to take effect fall due to be discharged or performed by one only of them.

(2) If the court gives such a direction, it may further direct that either spouse or cohabitant is to be liable to indemnify the other in whole or in part against any payment made or expenses incurred by the other in discharging or performing any such liability or obligation.

Date when order made between spouses is to take effect

12. – (1) In the case of a decree of nullity of marriage, the date specified in a Part II order as the date on which the order is to take effect must not be earlier than the date on which the decree is made absolute.

(2) In the case of divorce proceedings or separation proceedings, the date specified in a Part II order as the date on which the order is to take effect

is to be determined as if the court were making a property adjustment order under section 23A of the Matrimonial Causes Act 1973 (regard being had to the restrictions imposed by section 23B of that Act).

Remarriage of either spouse

13. – (1) If after the making of a divorce order or the grant of a decree annulling a marriage either spouse remarries, that spouse is not entitled to apply, by reference to the making of that order or the grant of that decree, for a Part II order.

(2) For the avoidance of doubt it is hereby declared that the reference in sub-paragraph (1) to remarriage includes a reference to a marriage which is by law void or voidable.

Rules of court

14. – (1) Rules of court shall be made requiring the court, before it makes an order under this Schedule, to give the landlord of the dwelling-house to which the order will relate an opportunity of being heard.

(2) Rules of court may provide that an application for a Part II order by reference to an order or decree may not, without the leave of the court by which that order was made or decree was granted, be made after the expiration of such period from the order or grant as may be prescribed by the rules.

Saving for other provisions of Act

15. – (1) If a spouse is entitled to occupy a dwelling-house by virtue of a tenancy, this Schedule does not affect the operation of sections 30 and 31 in relation to the other spouse's matrimonial home rights.

(2) If a spouse or cohabitant is entitled to occupy a dwelling-house by virtue of a tenancy, the court's powers to make orders under this Schedule are additional to those conferred by sections 33, 35 and 36.

SCHEDULE 9

MODIFICATIONS, SAVING AND TRASITIONAL ...

Interpretation

7. In paragraphs 8 to 15 'the 1983 Act means the Matrimonial Homes Act 1983. ...

Matrimonial home rights

11. – (1) Any reference (however expressed) in any enactment, instrument or document (whether passed or made before or after the passing of this Act) to rights of occupation under, or within the meaning of, the 1983 Act shall be construed, so far as is required for continuing the effect of the instrument or document, as being or as the case requires including a reference to matrimonial home rights under, or within the meaning of, Part IV.

(2) Any reference (however expressed) in this Act or in any other enactment, instrument or document (including any enactment amended by Schedule 8) to matrimonial home rights under, or within the meaning of, Part IV shall be construed as including, in relation to times, circumstances and purposes before the commencement of sections 30 to 32, a reference to rights of occupation under, or within the meaning of, the 1983 Act.

12. – (1) Any reference (however expressed) in any enactment, instrument or document (whether passed or made before or after the passing of this Act) to registration under section 2(8) of the 1983 Act shall, in relation to any time after the commencement of sections 30 to 32, be construed as being or as the case requires including a reference to registration under section 31(10).

(2) Any reference (however expressed) in this Act or in any other enactment, instrument or document (including any enactment amended by Schedule 8) to registration under section 31(10) shall be construed as including a reference to –

(a) registration under section 2(7) of the Matrimonial Homes Act 1967 or section 2(8) of the 1983 Act, and

(b) registration by caution duly lodged under section 2(7) of the Matrimonial Homes Act 1967 before 14th February 1983 (the date of the commencement of section 4(2) of the Matrimonial Homes and Property Act 1981).

13. In sections 30 and 31 and Schedule 4 –

(a) any reference to an order made under section 33 shall be construed as including a reference to an order made under section 1 of the 1983 Act, and

(b) any reference to an order made under section 33(5) shall be construed as including a reference to an order made under section 1 of the 1983 Act by virtue of section 2(4) of that Act.

14. Neither section 31(11) nor the repeal by the Matrimonial Homes and Property Act 1981 of the words "or caution" in section 2(7) of the Matrimonial Homes Act 1967, affects any caution duly lodged as respects any estate or interest before 14th February 1983.

EDUCATION ACT 1996
(1996 c 56)

PART I

GENERAL

CHAPTER I

THE STATUTORY SYSTEM OF EDUCATION

7 Duty of parents to secure education of children of compulsory school age

The parent of every child of compulsory school age shall cause him to receive efficient full-time education suitable –

(a) to his age, ability and aptitude, and

(b) to any special educational needs he may have,

either by regular attendance at school or otherwise.

PART VI

SCHOOL ADMISSIONS, ATTENDANCE AND CHARGES

CHAPTER II

SCHOOL ATTENDANCE

437 School attendance orders

(1) If it appears to a local education authority that a child of compulsory school age in their area is not receiving suitable education, either by regular attendance at school or otherwise, they shall serve a notice in writing on the parent requiring him to satisfy them within the period specified in the notice that the child is receiving such education.

(2) That period shall not be less than 15 days beginning with the day on which the notice is served.

(3) If –

(a) a parent on whom a notice has been served under subsection (1) fails to satisfy the local education authority, within the period specified in the notice, that the child is receiving suitable education, and

(b) in the opinion of the authority it is expedient t that the child should attend school,

the authority shall serve on the parent an order (referred to in this Act as a 'school attendance order'), in such form as may be prescribed, requiring him to cause the child to become a registered pupil at a school named in the order.

(4) A school attendance order shall (subject to any amendment made by the local education authority) continue in force for so long as the child is of compulsory school age, unless –

(a) it is revoked by the authority, or

(b) a direction is made in respect of it under section 443(2) or 447(5).

(5) Where a maintained or grant-maintained school is named in a school attendance order, the local education authority shall inform the governing body and the head teacher.

(6) Where a maintained or grant-maintained school is named in a school attendance order, the governing body (and, in the case of a maintained school, the local education authority) shall admit the child to the school.

(7) Subsection (6) does not affect any power to exclude from a school a pupil who is already a registered pupil there.

(8) In this Chapter –

'maintained school' means any county or voluntary school or any maintained special school which is not established in a hospital; and

'suitable education', in relation to a child, means efficient full-time education suitable to his age, ability and aptitude and to any special educational needs he may have.

442 Revocation of order at request of parent

(1) This section applies where a school attendance order is in force in respect of a child.

(2) If at any time the parent applies to the local education authority requesting that the order be revoked on the ground that arrangements have been made for the child to receive suitable education otherwise than at school, the authority shall comply with the request, unless they are of the opinion that no satisfactory arrangements have been made for the education of the child otherwise than at school.

(3) If a parent is aggrieved by a refusal of the local education authority to comply with a request under subsection (2), he may refer the question to the Secretary of State.

(4) Where a question is referred to the Secretary of State under subsection (3), he shall give such direction determining the question as he thinks fit.

(5) Where the child in question is one for whom the authority maintain a statement under section 324 [special educational needs] –

(a) subsections (2) to (4) do not apply if the name of a school or other institution is specified in the statement, and

(b) in any other case a direction under subsection (4) may require the authority to make such amendments in the statement as the Secretary of State considers necessary or expedient in consequence of his determination.

443 Offence: failure to comply with school attendance order

(1) If a parent on whom a school attendance order is served fails to comply with the requirements of the order, he is guilty of an offence, unless he proves that he is causing the child to receive suitable education otherwise than at school.

(2) If, in proceedings for an offence under this section, the parent is acquitted, the court may direct that the school attendance order shall cease to be in force.

(3) A direction under subsection (2) does not affect the duty of the local education authority to take further action under section 437 if at any time the authority are of the opinion that, having regard to any change of circumstances, it is expedient to do so.

(4) A person guilty of an offence under this section is liable on summary conviction to a fine not exceeding level 3 on the standard scale.

444 Offence: failure to secure regular attendance at school of registered pupil

(1) If a child of compulsory school age who is a registered pupil at a school fails to attend regularly at the school, his parent is guilty of an offence.

(2) Subsections (3) to (6) below apply in proceedings for an offence under this section in respect of a child who is not a boarder at the school at which he is a registered pupil.

(3) The child shall not be taken to have failed to attend regularly at the school by reason of his absence from the school –

(a) with leave,

(b) at any time when he is prevented from attending by reason of sickness or any unavoidable cause, or

(c) on any day exclusively set apart for religious observance by the religious body to which his parent belongs.

(4) The child shall not be taken to have failed to attend regularly at the school if the parent proves –

(a) that the school at which the child is a registered pupil is not within walking distance of the child's home, and

(b) that no suitable arrangements have been made by the local education authority or the funding authority for any of the following –

(i) his transport to and from the school,

(ii) boarding accommodation for him at or near the school, or

(iii) enabling him to become a registered pupil at a school nearer to his home.

(5) In subsection (4) 'walking distance' –

(a) in relation to a child who is under the age of eight, means 3.218688 kilometres (two miles), and

(b) in relation to a child who has attained the age of eight, means 4.828032 kilometres (three miles),

in each case measured by the nearest available route.

(6) If it is proved that the child has no fixed abode, subsection (4) shall not apply, but the parent shall be acquitted if he proves –

(a) that he is engaged in a trade or business of such a nature as to require him to travel from place to place,

(b) that the child has attended at a school as a registered pupil as regularly as the nature of that trade or business permits, and

(c) if the child has attained the age of six, that he has made at least 200 attendances during the period of 12 months ending with the date on which the proceedings were instituted.

(7) In proceedings for an offence under this section in respect of a child who is a boarder at the school at which he is a registered pupil, the child shall be taken to have failed to attend regularly at the school if he is absent from it without leave during any part of the school term at a time when he was not prevented from being present by reason of sickness or any unavoidable cause.

(8) A person guilty of an offence under this section is liable on summary conviction to a fine not exceeding level 3 on the standard scale.

(9) In this section 'leave', in relation to a school, means leave granted by any person authorised to do so by the governing body or proprietor of the school.

445 Presumption of age

(1) This section applies for the purposes of any proceedings for an offence under section 443 or 444.

(2) In so far as it is material, the child in question shall be presumed to have been of compulsory school age at any time unless the parent proves the contrary.

(3) Where a court is obliged by virtue of subsection (2) to presume a child to have been of compulsory school age, section 565(1) (provisions as to evidence) does not apply.

446 Institution of proceedings

Proceedings for an offence under section 443 and 444 shall not be instituted except by a local education authority.

447 Education supervision orders

(1) Before instituting proceedings for an offence under section 443 or 444, a local education authority shall consider whether it would be appropriate (instead of or as well as instituting the proceedings) to apply for an education supervision order with respect to the child.

(2) The court –

(a) by which a person is convicted of an offence under section 443, or

(b) before which a person is charged with an offence under section 444,

may direct the local education authority instituting the proceedings to apply for an education supervision order with respect to the child unless the authority, having consulted the appropriate local authority, decide that the child's welfare will be satisfactorily safeguarded even though no education supervision order is made.

(3) Where, following such a direction, a local education authority decide not to apply for an education supervision order, they shall inform the court of the reasons for their decision.

(4) Unless the court has directed otherwise, the information required under subsection (3) shall be given to the court before the end of the period of eight weeks beginning with the date on which the direction was given.

(5) Where –

(a) a local education authority apply for an education supervision order with respect to a child who is the subject of a school attendance order, and

(b) the court decides that section 36(3) of the Children Act 1989 (education supervision order) prevents it from making the order,

the court may direct that the school attendance order shall cease to be in force.

(6) In this section –

'the appropriate local authority' has the same meaning as in section 36(9) of the Children Act 1989, and

'education supervision order' means an education supervision order under that Act.

448 Exemption where a child becomes five during term

Where –

(a) a child attains the age of five during the school term of a grant-maintained school, and

(b) arrangements have been made for the admission of the child to that school at the start of the next school term,

then, during the period beginning with his attaining that age and ending with the start of that next school term, section 7 (duty of parents to secure the education of their children) and section 437 shall not apply to the child.

APPENDIX

FAMILY LAW ACT 1996

NB This Act received the Royal Assent on 4 July 1996 but it is not yet fully in force. However, Part I (principles of Parts II and II), s22 (funding for support services), Part III (legal aid for mediation in family matters) and Schedule 8, Part II (amendments connected with Part III) came into force on 21 March 1997 and it is anticipated that Part IV (family homes and domestic violence) will come into force on 1 October 1997. The provisions of Parts I and IV have been included, and connected amendments and repeals covered, in the main body of the text.

FAMILY LAW ACT 1996
(1996 c 27)

PART II

DIVORCE AND SEPARATION

2   Divorce and separation

(1) The court may –

(a) by making an order (to be known as a divorce order), dissolve a marriage; or

(b) by making an order (to be known as a separation order), provide for the separation of the parties to a marriage.

(2) Any such order comes into force on being made.

(3) A separation order remains in force –

(a) while the marriage continues; or

(b) until cancelled by the court on the joint application of the parties.

3   Circumstances in which orders are made

(1) If an application for a divorce order or for a separation order is made to the court under this section by one or both of the parties to a marriage, the court shall make the order applied for if (but only if) –

(a) the marriage has broken down irretrievably;

(b) the requirements of section 8 about information meetings are satisfied;

(c) the requirements of section 9 about the parties' arrangements for the future are satisfied; and

(d) the application has not been withdrawn.

(2) A divorce order may not be made if an order preventing divorce is in force under section 10.

(3) If the court is considering an application for a divorce order and an application for a separation order in respect of the same marriage it shall proceed as if it were considering only the application for a divorce order unless –

(a) an order preventing divorce is in force with respect to the marriage;

(b) the court makes an order preventing divorce; or

(c) section 7(6) or (13) applies.

4   Conversion of separation order into divorce order

(1) A separation order which is made before the second anniversary of the marriage may not be converted into a divorce order under this section until after that anniversary.

(2) A separation order may not be converted into a divorce order under this section at any time while –

(a) an order preventing divorce is in force under section 10; or

(b) subsection (4) applies.

(3) Otherwise, if a separation order is in force and an application for a divorce order –

(a) is made under this section by either or both of the parties to the marriage, and

(b) is not withdrawn,

the court shall grant the application once the requirements of section 11 have been satisfied.

(4) Subject to subsection (5), this subsection applies if –

(a) there is a child of the family who is under the age of sixteen when the application under this section is made; or

(b) the application under this section is made by one party and the other party applies to the court, before the end of such period as may be prescribed by rules of court, for time for further reflection.

(5) Subsection (4) –

(a) does not apply if, at the time when the application under this section is made, there is an occupation order or a non-molestation order in force in favour of the application, or of a child of the family, made against the other party;

(b) does not apply if the court is satisfied that delaying the making of a divorce order would be significantly detrimental to the welfare of any child of the family;

(c) ceases to apply –

(i) at the end of the period of six months beginning with the end of the period for reflection and consideration by reference to which the separation order was made; or

(ii) if earlier, on there ceasing to be any children of the family to whom subsection (4)(a) applied.

5 Marital breakdown

(1) A marriage is to be taken to have broken down irretrievably if (but only if) –

(a) a statement has been made by one (or both) of the parties that the maker of the statement (or each of them) believes that the marriage has broken down;

(b) the statement complies with the requirements of section 6;

(c) the period of reflection and consideration fixed by section 7 has ended; and

(d) the application under section 3 is accompanied by a declaration by the party making the application that –

(i) having reflected on the breakdown, and

(ii) having considered the requirements of this Part as to the parties' arrangements for the future,

the applicant believes that the marriage cannot be saved.

(2) The statement and the application under section 3 do not have to be made by the same party.

(3) An application may not be made under section 3 by reference to a particular statement if –

(a) the parties have jointly given notice (in accordance with rules of court) withdrawing the statement; or

(b) a period of one year ('the specified period') has passed since the end of the period for reflection and consideration.

(4) Any period during which an order preventing divorce is in force is not to count towards the specified period mentioned in subsection (3)(b).

(5) Subsection (6) applies if, before the end of the specified period, the

parties jointly give notice to the court that they are attempting reconciliation but require additional time.

(6) The specified period –

(a) stops running on the day on which the notice is received by the court; but

(b) resumes running on the day on which either of the parties gives notice to the court that the attempted reconciliation has been unsuccessful.

(7) If the specified period is interrupted by a continuous period of more than 18 months, any application by either of the parties for a divorce order or for a separation order must be by reference to a new statement received by the court at any time after the end of the 18 months.

(8) The Lord Chancellor may by order amend subsection (3)(b) by varying the specified period.

6   Statement of marital breakdown

(1) A statement under section 5(1)(a) is to be known as a statement of marital breakdown; but in this Part it is generally referred to as 'a statement'.

(2) If a statement is made by one party it must also state that that party –

(a) is aware of the purpose of the period for reflection and consideration as described in section 7; and

(b) wishes to make arrangements for the future.

(3) If a statement is made by both parties it must also state that each of them –

(a) is aware of the purpose of the period for reflection and consideration as described in section 7; and

(b) wishes to make arrangements for the future.

(4) A statement must be given to the court in accordance with the requirements of rules made under section 12.

(5) A statement must also satisfy any other requirements imposed by rules made under that section.

(6) A statement made at a time when the circumstances of the case include any of those mentioned in subsection (7) is ineffective for the purposes of this Part.

(7) The circumstances are –

(a) that a statement has previously been made with respect to the marriage and it is, or will become, possible –

(i) for an application for a divorce order, or

(ii) for an application for a separation order,

to be made by reference to the previous statement;

(b) that such an application has been made in relation to the marriage and has not been withdrawn;

(c) that a separation order is in force.

7   Period for reflection and consideration

(1) Where a statement has been made, a period for the parties –

(a) to reflect on whether the marriage can be saved and to have an opportunity to effect a reconciliation, and

(b) to consider what arrangements should be made for the future,

must pass before an application for a divorce order or for a separation order may be made by reference to that statement.

(2) That period is to be known as the period for reflection and consideration.

(3) The period for reflection and consideration is nine months beginning with the fourteenth day after the day on which the statement is received by the court.

(4) Where –

(a) the statement has been made by one party,

(b) rules made under section 12 require the court to serve a copy of the statement on the other party, and

(c) failure to comply with the rules causes inordinate delay in service,

the court may, on the application of that other party, extend the period for reflection and consideration.

(5) An extension under subsection (4) may be for any period not exceeding the time between –

(a) the beginning of the period for reflection and consideration; and

(b) the time when service is effected.

(6) A statement which is made before the first anniversary of the marriage

to which it relates is ineffective for the purposes of any application for a divorce order.

(7) Subsection (8) applies if, at any time during the period for reflection and consideration, the parties jointly give notice to the court that they are attempting a reconciliation but require additional time.

(8) The period for reflection and consideration –

(a) stops running on the day on which the notice is received by the court; but

(b) resumes running on the day on which either of the parties gives notice to the court that the attempted reconciliation has been unsuccessful.

(9) If the period for reflection and consideration is interrupted under subsection (8) by a continuous period of more than 18 months, any application by either of the parties for a divorce order or for a separation order must be by reference to a new statement received by the court at any time after the end of the 18 months.

(10) Where an application for a divorce order is made by one party, subsection (13) applies if –

(a) the other party applies to the court, within the prescribed period, for time for further reflection; and

(b) the requirements of section 9 (except any imposed under section 9(3)) are satisfied.

(11) Where any application for a divorce order is made, subsection (13) also applies if there is a child of the family who is under the age of sixteen when the application is made.

(12) Subsection (13) does not apply if –

(a) at the time when the application for a divorce order is made, there is an occupation order or a non-molestation order in force in favour of the applicant, or of a child of the family, made against the other party; or

(b) the court is satisfied that delaying the making of a divorce order would be significantly detrimental to the welfare of any child of the family.

(13) If this subsection applies, the period for reflection and consideration is extended by a period of six months, but –

(a) only in relation to the application for a divorce order in respect of which the application under subsection (10) was made; and

(b) without invalidating that application for a divorce order.

(14) A period for reflection and consideration which is extended under subsection (13), and which has not otherwise come to an end, comes to an end on there ceasing to be any children of the family to whom subsection (11) applied.

8   Attendance at information meetings

(1) The requirements about information meetings are as follows.

(2) A party making a statement must (except in prescribed circumstances) have attended an information meeting not less than three months before making the statement.

(3) Different information meetings must be arranged with respect to different marriages.

(4) In the case of a statement made by both parties, the parties may attend separate meetings or the same meeting.

(5) Where one party has made a statement, the other party must (except in prescribed circumstances) attend an information meeting before –

(a) making any application to the court –

(i) with respect to a child of the family; or
(ii) of a prescribed description relating to property or financial matters; or

(b) contesting any such application.

(6) In this section 'information meeting' means a meeting organised, in accordance with prescribed provisions, for the purpose –

(a) of providing, in accordance with prescribed provisions, relevant information to the party or parties attending about matters which may arise in connection with the provisions of, or made under, this Part or Part III; and

(b) of giving the party or parties attending the information meeting the opportunity of having a meeting with a marriage counsellor and of encouraging that party or those parties to attend that meeting.

(7) An information meeting must be conducted by a person who –

(a) is qualified and appointed in accordance with prescribed provisions; and

(b) will have no financial or other interest in any marital proceedings between the parties.

(8) Regulations made under this section may, in particular, make provision –

(a) about the places and times at which information meetings are to be held;

(b) for written information to be given to persons attending them;

(c) for the giving of information to parties (otherwise than at information meetings) in cases in which the requirement to attend such meetings does not apply;

(d) for information of a prescribed kind to be given only with the approval of the Lord Chancellor or only by a person or by persons approved by him; and

(e) for information to be given, in prescribed circumstances, only with the approval of the Lord Chancellor or only by a person, or by persons, approved by him.

(9) Regulations made under subsection (6) must, in particular, make provision with respect to the giving of information about –

(a) marriage counselling the other marriage support services;

(b) the importance to be attached to the welfare, wishes and feelings of children;

(c) how the parties may acquire a better understanding of the ways in which children can be helped to cope with the breakdown of a marriage;

(d) the nature of the financial questions that may arise on divorce or separation, and services which are available to help the parties;

(e) protection available against violence, and how to obtain support and assistance;

(f) mediation;

(g) the availability to each of the parties of independent legal advice and representation;

(h) the principles of legal aid and where the parties can get advice about obtaining legal aid;

(i) the divorce and separation process.

(10) Before making any regulations under subsection (6), the Lord Chancellor must consult such persons concerned with the provision of relevant information as he considers appropriate.

(11) A meeting with a marriage counsellor arranged under this section –

(a) must be held in accordance with prescribed provisions; and

(b) must be with a person qualified and appointed in accordance with prescribed provisions.

(12) A person who would not be required to make any contribution towards mediation provided for him under Part IIIA of the Legal Aid Act 1988 shall not be required to make any contribution towards the cost of a meeting with a marriage counsellor arranged for him under this section.

(13) In this section 'prescribed' means prescribed by regulations made by the Lord Chancellor.

9   Arrangements for the future

(1) The requirements as to the parties' arrangements for the future are as follows.

(2) One of the following must be produced to the court –

(a) a court order (made by consent or otherwise) dealing with their financial arrangements;

(b) a negotiated agreement as to their financial arrangements;

(c) a declaration by both parties that they have made their financial arrangements;

(d) a declaration by one of the parties (to which no objection has been notified to the court by the other party) that –

(i) he has no significant assets and does not intend to make an application for financial provision;

(ii) he believes that the other party has no significant assets and does not intend to make an application for financial provision; and

(iii) there are therefore no financial arrangements to be made.

(3) If the parties –

(a) were married to each other in accordance with usages of a kind mentioned in section 26(1) of the Marriage Act 1949 (marriages which may be solemnised on authority of superintendent registrar's certificate), and

(b) are required to cooperate if the marriage is to be dissolved in accordance with those usages,

the court may, on the application of either party, direct that there must also be produced to the court a declaration by both parties that they have taken such steps as are required to dissolve the marriage in accordance with those usages.

(4) A direction under subsection (3) –

(a) may be given only if the court is satisfied that in all the circumstances of the case it is just and reasonable to give it; and

(b) may be revoked by the court at any time.

(5) The requirements of section 11 must have been satisfied.

(6) Schedule 1 supplements the provisions of this section.

(7) If the court is satisfied, on an application made by one of the parties after the end of the period for reflection and consideration, that the circumstances of the case are –

(a) those set out in paragraph 1 of Schedule 1,

(b) those set out in paragraph 2 of that Schedule,

(c) those set out in paragraph 3 of that Schedule, or

(d) those set out in paragraph 4 of that Schedule,

it may make a divorce order or a separation order even though the requirements of subsection (2) have not been satisfied.

(8) If the parties' arrangements for the future include a division of pension assets or rights under section 25B of the 1973 Act or section 10 of the Family Law (Scotland) Act 1985, any declaration under subsection (2) must be a statutory declaration.

10 Hardship: orders preventing divorce

(1) If an application for a divorce order has been made by one of the parties to a marriage, the court may, on the application of the other party, order that the marriage is not to be dissolved.

(2) Such an order (an 'order preventing divorce') may be made only if the court is satisfied –

(a) that dissolution of the marriage would result in substantial financial or other hardship to the other party or to a child of the family; and

(b) that it would be wrong, in all the circumstances (including the conduct of the parties and the interests of any child of the family), for the marriage to be dissolved.

(3) If an application for the cancellation of an order preventing divorce is made by one or both of the parties, the court shall cancel the order unless it is still satisfied –

(a) that dissolution of the marriage would result in substantial financial or other hardship to the party in whose favour the order was made or to a child of the family; and

(b) that it would be wrong, in all the circumstances (including the conduct of the parties and the interests of any child of the family), for the marriage to be dissolved.

(4) If an order preventing a divorce is cancelled, the court may make a divorce order in respect of the marriage only if an application is made under section 3 or 4(3) after the cancellation.

(5) An order preventing divorce may include conditions which must be satisfied before an application for cancellation may be made under subsection (3).

(6) In this section 'hardship' includes the loss of a chance to obtain a future benefit (as well as the loss of an existing benefit).

11   Welfare of children

(1) In any proceedings for a divorce order or a separation order, the court shall consider –

(a) whether there are any children of the family to whom this section applies; and

(b) where there are any such children, whether (in the light of the arrangements which have been, or are proposed to be, made for their upbringing and welfare) it should exercise any of its powers under the Children Act 1989 with respect to any of them.

(2) Where, in any case to which this section applies, it appears to the court that –

(a) the circumstances of the case require it, or are likely to require it, to exercise any of its powers under the Children Act 1989 with respect to any such child,

(b) it is not in a position to exercise the power, or (as the case may be) those powers, without giving further consideration to the case, and

(c) there are exceptional circumstances which make it desirable in the interests of the child that the court should give a direction under this section,

it may direct that the divorce order or separation order is not to be made until the court orders otherwise.

(3) In deciding whether the circumstances are as mentioned in subsection

(2)(a), the court shall treat the welfare of the child as paramount.

(4) In making that decision, the court shall also have particular regard, on the evidence before it, to –

(a) the wishes and feelings of the child considered in the light of his age and understanding and the circumstances in which those wishes were expressed;

(b) the conduct of the parties in relation to the upbringing of the child;

(c) the general principle that, in the absence of evidence to the contrary, the welfare of the child will be best served by –

(i) his having regular contact with those who have parental responsibility for him and with other members of his family; and

(ii) the maintenance of as good a continuing relationship with his parents as is possible; and

(d) any risk to the child attributable to –

(i) where the person with whom the child will reside is living or proposes to live;

(ii) any person with whom that person is living or with whom he proposes to live; or

(iii) any other arrangements for his care and upbringing.

(5) This section applies to –

(a) any child of the family who has not reached the age of sixteen at the date when the court considers the case in accordance with the requirements of this section; and

(b) any child of the family who has reached that age at that date and in relation to whom the court directs that this section shall apply.

13 Directions with respect to mediation

(1) After the court has received a statement, it may give a direction requiring each party to attend a meeting arranged in accordance with the direction for the purpose –

(a) of enabling an explanation to be given of the facilities available to the parties for mediation in relation to disputes between them; and

(b) of providing an opportunity for each party to agree to take advantage of those facilities.

(2) A direction may be given at any time, including in the course of

proceedings connected with the breakdown of the marriage (as to which see section 25).

(3) A direction may be given on the application of either of the parties or on the initiative of the court.

(4) The parties are to be required to attend the same meeting unless –

(a) one of them asks, or both of them ask, for separate meetings; or

(b) the court considers separate meetings to be more appropriate.

(5) A direction shall –

(a) specify a person chosen by the court (with that person's agreement) to arrange and conduct the meeting or meetings; and

(b) require such person as may be specified in the direction to produce to the court, at such time as the court may direct, a report stating –

(i) whether the parties have complied with the direction; and

(ii) if they have, whether they have agreed to take part in any mediation.

14 Adjournments

(1) The court's power to adjourn any proceedings connected with the breakdown of a marriage includes power to adjourn –

(a) for the purpose of allowing the parties to comply with a direction under section 13; or

(b) for the purpose of enabling disputes to be resolved amicably.

(2) In determining whether to adjourn for either purpose, the court shall have regard in particular to the need to protect the interests of any child of the family.

(3) If the court adjourns any proceedings connected with the breakdown of a marriage for either purpose, the period of the adjournment must not exceed the maximum period prescribed by rules of court.

(4) Unless the only purpose of the adjournment is to allow the parties to comply with a direction under section 13, the court shall order one or both of them to produce to the court a report as to –

(a) whether they have taken part in mediation during the adjournment;

(b) whether, as a result, any agreement has been reached between them;

(c) the extent to which any dispute between them has been resolved as a result of any such agreement;

(d) the need for further mediation; and

(e) how likely it is that further mediation will be successful.

15 Financial arrangements

(1) Schedule 2 amends the 1973 Act.

(2) The main object of Schedule 2 is –

(a) to provide that, in the case of divorce or separation, an order about financial provision may be made under that Act before a divorce order or separation order is made; but

(b) to retain (with minor changes) the position under that Act where marriages are annulled.

(3) Schedule 2 also makes minor and consequential amendments of the 1973 Act connected with the changes mentioned in subsection (1).

16 Division of pension rights: England and Wales

(1) The Matrimonial Causes Act 1973 is amended as follows.

(2) In section 25B (benefits under a pension scheme on divorce, etc), in subsection (2), after paragraph (b), insert –

'(c) in particular, where the court determines to make such an order, whether the order should provide for the accrued rights of the party with pension rights ("the pension rights") to be divided between that party and the other party in such a way as to reduce the pension rights of the party with those rights and to create pension rights for the other party.'.

(3) After subsection (7) of that section, add –

'(8) If a pensions adjustment order under subsection (2)(c) above is made, the pension rights shall be reduced and pension rights of the other party shall be created in the prescribed manner with benefits payable on prescribed conditions, except that the court shall not have the power –

(a) to require the trustees or managers of the scheme to provide benefits under their own scheme if they are able and willing to create the rights for the other party by making a transfer payment to another scheme and the trustees and managers of that other scheme are able and willing to accept such a payment and to create those rights; or

(b) to require the trustees or managers of the scheme to make a transfer to another scheme –

(i) if the scheme is an unfunded scheme (unless the trustees or managers are able and willing to make such a transfer payment); or

(ii) in prescribed circumstances.

(9) No pensions adjustment order may be made under subsection (2)(c) above –

(a) if the scheme is a scheme of a prescribed type, or

(b) in prescribed circumstances, or

(c) insofar as it would affect benefits of a prescribed type.'

(4) In section 25D (pensions: supplementary), insert –

(a) in subsection (2) –

(i) at the end of paragraph (a), the words 'or prescribe the rights of the other party under the pension scheme,'; and

(ii) after paragraph (a), the following paragraph –

'(aa) make such consequential modifications of any enactment or subordinate legislation as appear to the Lord Chancellor necessary or expedient to give effect to the provisions of section 25B; and an order under this paragraph may make provision applying generally in relation to enactments and subordinate legislation of a description specified in the order,';

(b) in subsection (4), in the appropriate place in alphabetical order, the following entries –

' "funded scheme" means a scheme under which the benefits are provided for by setting aside resources related to the value of the members' rights as they accrue (and "unfunded scheme" shall be construed accordingly);

"subordinate legislation" has the same meaning as in the Interpretation Act 1978;'; and

(c) after subsection (4), the following subsection –

'(4A) Other expressions used in section 25B above shall be construed in accordance with section 124 (interpretation of Part I) of the Pensions Act 1995.'

18 Grounds for financial provision orders in magistrates' courts

(1) In section 1 of the Domestic Proceedings and Magistrates' Courts Act 1978, omit paragraphs (c) and (d) (which provide for behaviour and desertion to be grounds on which an application for a financial provision order may be made).

(2) In section 7(1) of that Act (powers of magistrates' court where spouses are living apart by agreement), omit 'neither party having deserted the other'.

19 Jurisdiction in relation to divorce and separation

(1) In this section 'the court's jurisdiction' means –

(a) the jurisdiction of the court under this Part to entertain marital proceedings; and

(b) any other jurisdiction conferred on the court under this Part, or any other enactment, in consequence of the making of a statement.

(2) The court's jurisdiction is exercisable only if –

(a) at least one of the parties was domiciled in England and Wales on the statement date;

(b) at least one of the parties was habitually resident in England and Wales throughout the period of one year ending with the statement date; or

(c) nullity proceedings are pending in relation to the marriage when the marital proceedings commence.

(3) Subsection (4) applies if –

(a) a separation order is in force; or

(b) an order preventing divorce has been cancelled.

(4) The court –

(a) continues to have jurisdiction to entertain an application made by reference to the order referred to in subsection (3); and

(b) may exercise any other jurisdiction which is conferred on it in consequence of such an application.

(5) Schedule 3 amends Schedule 1 to the Domicile and Matrimonial Proceedings Act 1973 (orders to stay proceedings where there are proceedings in other jurisdictions).

(6) The court's jurisdiction is exercisable subject to any order for a stay under Schedule 1 to that Act.

(7) In this section –

'nullity proceedings' means proceedings in respect of which the court has jurisdiction under section 5(3) of the Domicile and Matrimonial Proceedings Act 1973; and

'statement date' means the date on which the relevant statement was received by the court.

20   Time when proceedings for divorce or separation begin

(1) The receipt by the court of a statement is to be treated as the commencement of proceedings.

(2) The proceedings are to be known as marital proceedings.

(3) Marital proceedings are also –

(a) separation proceedings, if an application for a separation order has been made under section 3 by reference to the statement and not withdrawn;

(b) divorce proceedings, if an application for a divorce order has been made under section 3 by reference to the statement and not withdrawn.

(4) Marital proceedings are to be treated as being both divorce proceedings and separation proceedings at any time when no application by reference to the statement, either for a divorce order or for a separation order, is outstanding.

(5) Proceedings which are commenced by the making of an application under section 4(3) are also marital proceedings and divorce proceedings.

(6) Marital proceedings come to an end –

(a) on the making of a separation order;

(b) on the making of a divorce order;

(c) on the withdrawal of the statement by a notice in accordance with section 5(3)(a);

(d) at the end of the specified period mentioned in section 5(3)(b), if no application under section 3 by reference to the statement is outstanding;

(e) on the withdrawal of all such applications which are outstanding at the end of that period;

(f) on the withdrawal of an application under section 4(3).

21   Intestacy: effect of separation

Where –

(a) a separation order is in force, and

(b) while the parties to the marriage remain separated, one of them dies intestate as respects any real or personal property,

that property devolves as if the other had died before the intestacy occurred.

24   Interpretation of Part II, etc

(1) In this Part –

'the 1973 Act' means the Matrimonial Causes Act 1973;

'child of the family' and 'the court' have the same meaning as in the 1973 Act;

'divorce order' has the meaning given in section 2(1)(a);

'divorce proceedings' is to be read with section 20;

'marital proceedings' has the meaning given in section 20;

'non-molestation order' has the meaning given by section 42(1);

'occupation order' has the meaning given by section 39;

'order preventing divorce' has the meaning given in section 10(2);

'party', in relation to a marriage, means one of the parties to the marriage;

'period for reflection and consideration' has the meaning given in section 7;

'separation order' has the meaning given in section 2(1)(b);

'separation proceedings' is to be read with section 20;

'statement' means a statement of marital breakdown;

'statement of marital breakdown' has the meaning given in section 6(1).

(2) For the purposes of this Part, references to the withdrawal of an application are references, in relation to an application made jointly by both parties, to its withdrawal by a notice given, in accordance with rules of court –

(a) jointly by both parties; or

(b) separately by each of them,

(3) Where only one party gives such a notice of withdrawal, in relation to a joint application, the application shall be treated as if it had been made by the other party alone.

25 Connected proceedings

(1) For the purposes of this Part, proceedings are connected with the breakdown of a marriage if they fall within subsection (2) and, at the time of the proceedings –

(a) a statement has been received by the court with respect to the marriage and it is or may become possible for an application for a divorce order or separation order to be made by reference to that statement;

(b) such an application in relation to the marriage has been made and not withdrawn; or

(c) a divorce order has been made, or a separation order is in force, in relation to the marriage.

(2) The proceedings are any under Parts I to V of the Children Act 1989 with respect to a child of the family or any proceedings resulting from an application –

(a) for, or for the cancellation of, an order preventing divorce in relation to the marriage;

(b) by either party to the marriage for an order under Part IV;

(c) for the exercise, in relation to a party to the marriage or child of the family, of any of the court's powers under Part II of the 1973 Act;

(d) made otherwise to the court with respect to, or in connection with, any proceedings connected with the breakdown of the marriage.

SCHEDULE 1

ARRANGEMENTS FOR THE FUTURE

The first exemption

1. The circumstances referred to in section 9(7)(a) are that –

(a) the requirements of section 11 have been satisfied;

(b) the applicant has, during the period for reflection and consideration, taken such steps as are reasonably practicable to try to reach agreement about the parties' financial arrangements; and

(c) the applicant has made an application to the court for financial relief and has complied with all requirements of the court in relation to proceedings for financial relief but –

(i) the other party has delayed in complying with requirements of the court or has otherwise been obstructive; or

(ii) for reasons which are beyond the control of the applicant, or of the other party, the court has been prevented from obtaining the information which it requires to determine the financial position of the parties.

The second exemption

2. The circumstances referred to in section 9(7)(b) are that –

(a) the requirements of section 11 have been satisfied;

(b) the applicant has, during the period for reflection and consideration, taken such steps as are reasonably practicable to try to reach agreement about the parties' financial arrangements;

(c) because of –

(i) the ill health or disability of the applicant, the other party or a child of the family (whether physical or mental), or

(ii) an injury suffered by the applicant, the other party or a child of the family,

the applicant has not been able to reach agreement with the other party about those arrangements and is unlikely to be able to do so in the foreseeable future; and

(d) a delay in making the order applied for under section 3 –

(i) would be significantly detrimental to the welfare of any child of the family; or

(ii) would be seriously prejudicial to the applicant.

The third exemption

3. The circumstances referred to in section 9(7)(c) are that –

(a) the requirements of section 11 have been satisfied;

(b) the applicant has found it impossible to contact the other party; and

(c) as a result, it has been impossible for the applicant to reach agreement with the other party about their financial arrangements.

The fourth exemption

4. The circumstances referred to in section 9(7)(d) are that –

(a) the requirements of section 11 have been satisfied;

(b) an occupation order or a non-molestation order is in force in favour of the applicant or a child of the family, made against the other party;

(c) the applicant has, during the period for reflection and consideration, taken such steps as are reasonably practicable to try to reach agreement about the parties' financial arrangements;

(d) the applicant has not been able to reach agreement with the other party about those arrangements and is unlikely to be able to do so in the foreseeable future; and

(e) a delay in making the order applied for under section 3 –

(i) would be significantly detrimental to the welfare of any child of the family; or

(ii) would be seriously prejudicial to the applicant.

Court orders and agreements

5. (1) Section 9 is not to be read as requiring any order or agreement to have been carried into effect at the time when the court is considering whether arrangements for the future have been made by the parties.

(2) The fact that an appeal is pending against an order of the kind mentioned in section 9(2)(a) is to be disregarded.

Financial arrangements

6. In section 9 of this Schedule 'financial arrangements' has the same meaning as in section 34(2) of the 1973 Act.

Negotiated agreements

7. In section 9(2)(b) 'negotiated agreement' means a written agreement between the parties as to future arrangements –

(a) which has been reached as the result of mediation or any other form of negotiation involving a third party; and

(b) which satisfies such requirements as may be imposed by rules of court.

Declarations

8. (1) Any declaration of a kind mentioned in section 9 –

(a) must be in a prescribed form;

(b) must, in prescribed cases, be accompanied by such documents as may be prescribed; and

(c) must, in prescribed cases, satisfy such other requirements as may be prescribed.

(2) The validity of a divorce order or separation order made by reference to such a declaration is not to be affected by any inaccuracy in the declaration.

Interpretation

9. In this Schedule –

'financial relief' has such meaning as may be prescribed; and

'prescribed' means prescribed by rules of court.

SCHEDULE 2

FINANCIAL PROVISION

Introductory

1. Part II of the 1973 Act (financial provision and property adjustment orders) is amended as follows.

The orders

2. For section 21 (definitions) substitute –

'21 Financial provision and property adjustment orders

(1) For the purposes of this Act, a financial provision order is –

(a) an order that a party must make in favour of another person such periodical payments, for such term, as may be specified (a "periodical payments order");

(b) an order that a party must, to the satisfaction of the court, secure in favour of another person such periodical payments, for such term, as may be specified (a "secured periodical payments order");

(c) an order that a party must make a payment in favour of another person of such lump sum or sums as may be specified (an "order for the payment of a lump sum").

(2) For the purposes of this Act, a property adjustment order is –

(a) an order that a party must transfer such of his or her property as may be specified in favour of the other party or a child of the family;

(b) an order that a settlement of such property of a party as may be specified must be made, to the satisfaction of the court, for the benefit of the other party and of the children of the family, or either or any of them;

(c) an order varying, for the benefit of the parties and of the children of the family, or either or any of them, any marriage settlement;

(d) an order extinguishing or reducing the interest of either of the parties under any marriage settlement.

(3) Subject to section 40 below, where an order of the court under this Part of this Act requires a party to make or secure a payment in favour of another person or to transfer property in favour of any person, that payment must be made or secured or that property transferred –

(a) if that other person is the other party to the marriage, to that other party; and

(b) if that other person is a child of the family, according to the terms of the order –

(i) to the child; or

(ii) to such other person as may be specified, for the benefit of that child.

(4) References in this section to the property of a party are references to any property to which that party is entitled either in possession or in reversion.

(5) Any power of the court under this Part of this Act to make such an order as is mentioned in subsection (2)(b) to (d) above is exercisable even though there are no children of the family.

(6) In this section –

"marriage settlement" means an ante-nuptial or post-nuptial settlement made on the parties (including one made by will or codicil);

"party" means a party to a marriage; and

"specified" means specified in the order in question.'

Financial provision: divorce and separation

3. Insert, before section 23 –

'22A Financial provision orders: divorce and separation

(1) On an application made under this section, the court may at the appropriate time make one or more financial provision orders in favour of –

    (a) a party to the marriage to which the application relates; or

    (b) any of the children of the family.

(2) The "appropriate time" is any time –

    (a) after a statement of marital breakdown has been received by the court and before any application for a divorce order or for a separation order is made to the court by reference to that statement;

    (b) when an application for a divorce order or separation order has been made under section 3 of the 1996 Act and has not been withdrawn;

    (c) when an application for a divorce order has been made under section 4 of the 1996 Act and has not been withdrawn;

    (d) after a divorce order has been made;

    (e) when a separation order is in force.

(3) The court may make –

    (a) a combined order against the parties on one occasion,

    (b) separate orders on different occasions,

    (c) different orders in favour of different children,

    (d) different orders from time to time in favour of the same child,

but may not make, in favour of the same party, more than one periodical payments order, or more than one order for payment of a lump sum, in relation to any marital proceedings, whether in the course of the proceedings or by reference to a divorce order or separation order made in the proceedings.

(4) If it would not otherwise be in a position to make a financial provision order in favour of a party or child of the family, the court may make an interim periodical payments order, an interim order for the payment of a lump sum or a series of such orders, in favour of that party or child.

(5) Any order for the payment of a lump sum made under this section may –

(a) provide for the payment of the lump sum by instalments of such amounts as may be specified in the order; and

(b) require the payment of the instalments to be secured to the satisfaction of the court.

(6) Nothing in subsection (5) above affects –

(a) the power of the court under this section to make an order for the payment of a lump sum; or

(b) the provisions of this Part of this Act as to the beginning of the term specified in any periodical payments order or secured periodical payments order.

(7) Subsection (8) below applies where the court –

(a) makes an order under this section ("the main order") for the payment of a lump sum; and

(b) directs –

(i) that payment of that sum, or any part of it, is to be deferred; or

(ii) that that sum, or any part of it, is to be paid by instalments.

(8) In such a case, the court may, on or at any time after making the main order, make an order ("the order for interest") for the amount deferred, or the instalments, to carry interest (at such rate as may be specified in the order for interest) –

(a) from such date, not earlier than the date of the main order, as may be so specified;

(b) until the date when the payment is due.

(9) This section is to be read subject to any restrictions imposed by this Act and to section 19 of the 1996 Act.

22B Restrictions affecting section 22A

(1) No financial provision order, other than an interim order, may be made under section 22A above so as to take effect before the making of a divorce order or separation order in relation to the marriage, unless the court is satisfied –

(a) that the circumstances of the case are exceptional; and

(b) that it would be just and reasonable for the order to be so made.

(2) Except in the case of an interim periodical payments order, the court may not make a financial provision order under section 22A above at any time while the period for reflection and consideration is interrupted under section

7(8) of the 1996 Act.

(3) No financial provision order may be made under section 22A above by reference to the making of a statement of marital breakdown if, by virtue of section 5(3) or 7(9) of the 1996 Act (lapse of divorce or separation process), it has ceased to be possible –

(a) for an application to be made by reference to that statement; or

(b) for an order to be made on such an application.

(4) No financial provision order may be made under section 22A after a divorce order has been made, or while a separation order is in force, except –

(a) in response to an application made before the divorce order or separation order was made; or

(b) on a subsequent application made with the leave of the court.'

(5) In this section, "period for reflection and consideration" means the period fixed by section 7 of the 1996 Act.'

Financial provision: nullity of marriage

4. For section 23 substitute –

'23 Financial provision orders: nullity

(1) On or after granting a decree of nullity of marriage (whether before or after the decree is made absolute), the court may, on an application made under this section, make one or more financial provision orders in favour of –

(a) either party to the marriage; or

(b) any child of the family.

(2) Before granting a decree in any proceedings for nullity of marriage, the court may make against either or each of the parties to the marriage –

(a) an interim periodical payments order, an interim order for the payment of a lump sum, or a series of such orders, in favour of the other party;

(b) an interim periodical payments order, an interim order for the payment of a lump sum, a series of such orders or any one or more other financial provision orders in favour of each child of the family.

(3) Where any such proceedings are dismissed, the court may (either immediately or within a reasonable period after the dismissal) make any one or more financial provision orders in favour of each child of the family.

(4) An order under this section that a party to a marriage must pay a lump sum to the other party may be made for the purpose of enabling that other party to meet any liabilities or expenses reasonably incurred by him or her in maintaining himself or herself or any child of the family before making an application for an order under this section in his or her favour.

(5) An order under this section for the payment of a lump sum to or for the benefit of a child of the family may be made for the purpose of enabling any liabilities or expenses reasonably incurred by or for the benefit of that child before the making of an application for an order under this section in his favour to be met.

(6) An order under this section for the payment of a lump sum may –

(a) provide for the payment of that sum by instalments of such amount as may be specified in the order; and

(b) require the payment of the instalments to be secured to the satisfaction of the court.

(7) Nothing in subsections (4) to (6) above affects –

(a) the power under subsection (1) above to make an order for the payment of a lump sum; or

(b) the provisions of this Act as to the beginning of the term specified in any periodical payments order or secured periodical payments order.

(8) The powers of the court under this section to make one or more financial provision orders are exercisable against each party to the marriage by the making of –

(a) a combined order on one occasion, or

(b) separate orders on different occasions,

but the court may not make more than one periodical payments order, or more than one order for payment of a lump sum, in favour of the same party.

(9) The powers of the court under this section so far as they consist in power to make one or more orders in favour of the children of the family –

(a) may be exercised differently in favour of different children; and

(b) except in the case of the power conferred by subsection (3) above, may be exercised from time to time in favour of the same child; and

(c) in the case of the power conferred by that subsection, if it is exercised by the making of a financial provision order of any kind in favour of a child, shall include power to make, from time to time, further financial provision orders of that or any other kind in favour of that child.

(10) Where an order is made under subsection (1) above in favour of a party to the marriage on or after the granting of a decree of nullity of marriage, neither the order nor any settlement made in pursuance of the order takes effect unless the decree has been made absolute.

(11) Subsection (10) above does not affect the power to give a direction under section 30 below for the settlement of an instrument by conveyancing counsel.

(12) Where the court –

    (a) makes an order under this section ('the main order') for the payment of a lump sum; and

    (b) directs –

        (i) that payment of that sum or any part of it is to be deferred; or

        (ii) that that sum or any part of it is to be paid by instalments,

it may, on or at any time after making the main order, make an order ("the order for interest") for the amount deferred or the instalments to carry interest at such rate as may be specified by the order for interest from such date, not earlier than the date of the main order, as may be so specified, until the date when payment of it is due.

(13) This section is to be read subject to any restrictions imposed by this Act.'

Property adjustment orders: divorce and separation

5. Insert, before section 24 –

'23A Property adjustment orders: divorce and separation

(1) On an application made under this section, the court may, at any time mentioned in section 22A(2) above, make one or more property adjustment orders.

(2) If the court makes, in favour of the same party to the marriage, more than one property adjustment order in relation to any marital proceedings, whether in the course of the proceedings or by reference to a divorce order or separation order made in the proceedings, each order must fall within a different paragraph of section 21(2) above.

(3) The court shall exercise its powers under this section, so far as is practicable, by making on one occasion all such provision as can be made by way of one or more property adjustment orders in relation to the marriage as it thinks fit.

(4) Subsection (3) above does not affect section 31 or 31A below.

(5) This section is to be read subject to any restrictions imposed by this Act and to section 19 of the 1996 Act.

23B Restrictions affecting section 23A

(1) No property adjustment order may be made under section 23A above so as to take effect before the making of a divorce order or separation order in relation to the marriage unless the court is satisfied –

   (a) that the circumstances of the case are exceptional; and

   (b) that it would be just and reasonable for the order to be so made.

(2) The court may not make a property adjustment order under section 23A above at any time while the period for reflection and consideration is interrupted under section 7(8) of the 1996 Act.

(3) No property adjustment order may be made under section 23A above by virtue of the making of a statement of marital breakdown if, by virtue of section 5(3) or 7(5) of the 1996 Act (lapse of divorce or separation process), it has ceased to be possible –

   (a) for an application to be made by reference to that statement; or

   (b) for an order to be made on such an application.

(4) No property adjustment order may be made under section 23A above after a divorce order has been made, or while a separation order is in force, except –

   (a) in response to an application made before the divorce order or separation order was made; or

   (b) on a subsequent application made with the leave of the court.

(5) In this section, "period for reflection and consideration" means the period fixed by section 7 of the 1996 Act.'

Property adjustment orders: nullity

6. For section 24, substitute –

'24 Property adjustment orders: nullity of marriage

(1) On or after granting a decree of nullity of marriage (whether before or after the decree is made absolute), the court may, on an application made under this section, make one or more property adjustment orders in relation to the marriage.

(2) The court shall exercise its powers under this section, so far as is practicable, by making on one occasion all such provision as can be made by way of one or more property adjustment orders in relation to the marriage as it thinks fit.

(3) Subsection (2) above does not affect section 31 or 31A below.

(4) Where a property adjustment order is made under this section on or after the granting of a decree of nullity of marriage, neither the order nor any settlement made in pursuance of the order is to take effect unless the decree has been made absolute.

(5) That does not affect the power to give a direction under section 30 below for the settlement of an instrument by conveyancing counsel.

(6) This section is to be read subject to any restrictions imposed by this Act.'

Period of secured and unsecured payments orders

7. (1) In section 28(1) (duration of a continuing financial provision order in favour of a party to a marriage), for paragraphs (a) and (b) substitute –

'(a) a term specified in the order which is to begin before the making of the order shall begin no earlier –

(i) where the order is made by virtue of section 22A(2)(a) or (b) above, unless sub-paragraph (ii) below applies, than the beginning of the day on which the statement of marital breakdown in question was received by the court;

(ii) where the order is made by virtue of section 22A(2)(b) above and the application for the divorce order was made following cancellation of an order preventing divorce under section 10 of the 1996 Act, than the date of the making of that application;

(iii) where the order is made by virtue of section 22A(2)(c) above, than the date of the making of the application for the divorce order; or

(iv) in any other case, than the date of the making of the application on which the order is made;

(b) a term specified in a periodical payments order or secured periodical payments order shall be so defined as not to extend beyond –

(i) in the case of a periodical payments order, the death of the party by whom the payments are to be made; or

(ii) in either case, the death of the party in whose favour the order was made or the remarriage of that party following the making of a divorce order or decree of nullity.'

(2) In section 29 (duration of continuing financial provision order in favour of a child of the family) insert after subsection (1) –

'(1A) The term specified in a periodical payments order or secured periodical payments order made in favour of a child shall be such term as the court thinks fit.

(1B) If that term is to begin before the making of the order, it may do so no earlier than–

(a) in the case of an order made by virtue of section 22A(2)(a) or (b) above, except where paragraph (b) below applies, the beginning of the day on which the statement of marital breakdown in question was received by the court;

(b) in the case of an order made by virtue of section 22A(2)(b) above where the application for the divorce order was made following cancellation of an order preventing divorce under section 10 of the 1996 Act, the date of the making of that application;

(c) in the case of an order made by virtue of section 22A(2)(c) above, the date of the making of the application for the divorce order; or

(d) in any other case, the date of the making of the application on which the order is made.'

Variations etc following reconciliations

8. Insert after section 31

'31A Variation etc following reconciliation

(1) Where, at a time before the making of a divorce order –

(a) an order ("a paragraph (a) order") for the payment of a lump sum has been made under section 22A above in favour of a party,

(b) such an order has been made in favour of a child of the family but the payment has not yet been made, or

(c) a property adjustment order ("a paragraph (c) order") has been made under section 23A above,

the court may, on an application made jointly by the parties to the marriage, vary or discharge the order.

(2) Where the court varies or discharges a paragraph (a) order, it may order

the repayment of an amount equal to the whole or any part of the lump sum.

(3) Where the court varies or discharges a paragraph (c) order, it may (if the order has taken effect) –

(a) order any person to whom property was transferred in pursuance of the paragraph (c) order to transfer –

(i) the whole or any part of that property, or

(ii) the whole or any part of any property appearing to the court to represent that property,

in favour of a party to the marriage or a child of the family; or

(b) vary any settlement to which the order relates in favour of any person or extinguish or reduce any person's interest under that settlement.

(4) Where the court acts under subsection (3) it may make such supplemental provision (including a further property adjustment order or an order for the payment of a lump sum) as it thinks appropriate in consequence of any transfer, variation, extinguishment or reduction to be made under paragraph (a) or (b) of that subsection.

(5) Sections 24A and 30 above apply for the purposes of this section as they apply where the court makes a property adjustment order under section 23A or 24 above.

(6) The court shall not make an order under subsection (2), (3) or (4) above unless it appears to it that there has been a reconciliation between the parties to the marriage.

(7) The court shall also not make an order under subsection (3) or (4) above unless it appears to it that the order will not prejudice the interests of –

(a) any child of the family; or

(b) any person who has acquired any right or interest in consequence of the paragraph (c) order and is not a party to the marriage or a child of the family.'

INDEX

Old Bailey Press

The Old Bailey Press integrated student library is planned and written to help you at every stage of your studies. Each of our range of Textbooks, Casebooks, Revision WorkBooks and Statutes are all designed to work together and are regularly revised and updated.

We are also able to offer you Suggested Solutions which provide you with past examination questions and solutions for most of the subject areas listed below.

You can buy Old Bailey Press books from your University Bookshop or your local Bookshop, or in case of difficulty, order direct using this form.

Here is the selection of modules covered by our series:

Administrative Law; Commercial Law; Company Law; Conflict of Laws (no Suggested Solutions Pack); Constitutional Law: The Machinery of Government; Obligations: Contract Law; Conveyancing (no Revision Workbook); Criminology (no Casebook or Revision WorkBook); Criminal Law; English Legal System; Equity and Trusts; Law of The European Union; Evidence; Family Law; Jurisprudence: The Philosophy of Law (Sourcebook in place of a Casebook); Land: The Law of Real Property; Law of International Trade; Legal Skills and System; Public International Law; Revenue Law (no Casebook); Succession: The Law of Wills and Estates; Obligations: The Law of Tort.

Mail order prices:

Textbook £10

Casebook £10

Revision WorkBook £7

Statutes £8

Suggested Solutions Pack (1991–1995) £7

Single Paper 1996 £3

Single Paper 1997 £3.

To complete your order, please fill in the form below:

Module	Books required	Quantity	Price	Cost
		Postage		
		TOTAL		

For UK, add 10% postage and packing (£10 maximum).
For Europe, add 15% postage and packing (£20 maximum).
For the rest of the world, add 40% for airmail.

ORDERING

By telephone to Mail Order at 0171 385 3377, with your credit card to hand

By fax to 0171 381 3377 (giving your credit card details).

By post to:

Old Bailey Press, 200 Greyhound Road, London W14 9RY.

When ordering by post, please enclose full payment by cheque or banker's draft, or complete the credit card details below.

We aim to despatch your books within 3 working days of receiving your order.

Name

Address

Postcode   Telephone

Total value of order, including postage: £

I enclose a cheque/banker's draft for the above sum, or

charge my   ☐ Access/Mastercard   ☐ Visa   ☐ American Express
Card number

☐☐☐☐ ☐☐☐☐ ☐☐☐☐ ☐☐☐☐

Expiry date   ☐☐☐☐

Signature: ....Date: ....